OFFENSIVE COURT POSITIONS USED IN THIS BOOK

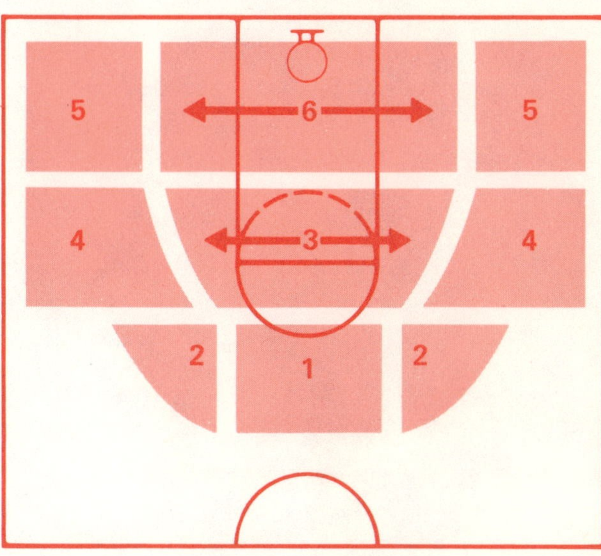

1 Point/Top of the Circle

2 Intermediate Wing Positions

3 High-Post Area

4 Wing Positions

5 Corners

6 Low-Post Areas

Winning Basketball Systems

Frank Hill photo (on jacket and p. ii)/courtesy Boston Herald American.
Chapter opening photos and Figures 8–1, 13–1, 13–2, 13–14, 13–15, 13–16, 13–17, 13–45, 13–49, 13–50, 13–51, 13–55, 13–69, 13–73, 13–74, 13–75, 13–76, 13–79, 13–82, and 13–86 by Greg Cava.
All other photos by Talbot Lovering, Allyn and Bacon staff photographer.

Library of Congress Cataloging in Publication Data

Tarkanian, Jerry, 1930–
Winning basketball systems.

Includes index.
1. Basketball coaching. I. Warren, William E., 1941– joint author. II. Title.
GV885.3.T38 796.32′3′077 80-13522
ISBN 0-205-07099-X

Series Editor: Hiram G. Howard
Design Director: Paula Carroll
Production Editor: Gary L. Schmitt

Printed in the United States of America

Winning Basketball Systems

Jerry Tarkanian
University of Nevada at Las Vegas

William E. Warren
Toombs Central High School
Lyons, Georgia

Allyn and Bacon, Inc.

Boston • London • Sydney • Toronto

for
our wives

Lois and Louise

Contents

Preface

O God, give us serenity to accept what cannot be changed, courage to change what should be changed, and wisdom to distinguish the one from the other.

Reinhold Niebuhr
Prayer (1934)

In broadest terms, modern basketball has become an amalgam of contrasting styles and systems of play. While adopting a particular system may or may not prove advantageous for a coach or team, understanding the philosophy and techniques underlying the various offensive and defensive systems is a prerequisite for continuing success on all levels of play. In writing this book, we have attempted to describe the broadest possible range of basketball ideology, and as a result some parts of the book may have more appeal to certain coaches than others.

Still, this is as it should be. In describing any given system of play, it is necessary to start at the beginning. We have included all of the major styles and systems of play (and a few lesser-used systems as well), taking each from its basic concepts to as far as we deemed necessary to provide a basis for understanding the system. Thus, even if a coach has never used help-and-recover defense or the Wheel offense, to cite two examples, he will still be able to learn what his opponents are trying to accomplish in using such techniques against him, and how they are likely to hurt him in the process.

Although certain parts of this book may be too basic for use at the collegiate or professional levels, or other parts too advanced for youth recreation league or junior high teams, the vast majority of offenses and defenses have been adopted (or adapted) successfully in many high school situations. My first five years in coaching were at the high school level, and Coach Warren has coached girls and boys basketball in junior high and high school for fifteen years, so we can attest that virtually all of the concepts and techniques described in the following pages are well within the limits of most high school players.

We make no claim to completeness in this book, since basketball is not, and never will be, a closed system. Besides, many of the systems are so broad, and can be used in so many ways, that one could literally write forever in one area alone without exhausting the subject or repeating oneself.

Finally, concerning the particular system of play we use at UNLV: we are honored that many coaches across the nation have adopted our system and techniques, but we should stress that the coach's ability to motivate players will be instrumental in making ours or any other system work. *Any* system described in this book can be used to build a winning basketball program if personnel considerations are taken into account and the players understand and believe in the system they are using.

Introduction

The basic premise upon which this book rests is that styles and systems of play are as important as personnel in determining a team's success. Just as every team has a personality that is uniquely its own, it also possesses skills and playing characteristics that make certain styles of play more desirable than others.

We've all seen teams whose players operate so smoothly and efficiently on the court that they appear to be playing on "automatic pilot," independent of coaching or other outside influences. Consider the "Carolina Corners" delay offense popularized by the University of North Carolina's Dean Smith; UCLA's splendid use of full-court zone pressing defenses under John Wooden; the University of Kentucky's 1–3–1 half-court trapping zone defense under Joe B. Hall; and our own Runnin' Rebels' relentless pressure man-to-man defense and transition game at the University of Nevada at Las Vegas. In each case, these teams mastered their particular styles of play to the extent that not only the coaches, but the players and the school as well, became identified with particular styles of play. Instead of stopping to think about what came next at any given moment, the players usually were able to improvise within their systems to meet new and unexpected situations as they arose.

An even more important outcome of mastering a given system of play, however, is that if the system is sound it will lead to a winning basketball program when combined with continuity of capable personnel. Winning consistently requires quality athletes, of course; one does not win a horse race without horses. However, at every level of play from junior high to Division I of the NCAA, successful programs are based on experienced personnel operating within a proven system of play. This combination—quality players using a playing style they understand and believe in—will often provide the winning edge by forcing opponents to play beyond the limitations of their game plan. In the majority of cases, games are won or lost, not by last-second desperation shots, but by teams' gaining or losing control of their opponents offensively or defensively at some stage of the game.

At Long Beach State we controlled opponents with an aggressive 1–2–2 zone defense and inside power game based on high-percentage shot selection. We made our game plan as simple as possible, but played it to the hilt every second of every game. We believed, and our players believed, that *nobody* prepared for games as rigorously as we did, and that we *deserved* to win because of the intensity of our preparations and practices. Our players took pride in our tight 1–2–2 zone coverage and the fact that we weren't going to let our opponents pass the ball inside on us. If they were going to beat us, it was going to have to be with their outside shooting—and we were going to contest their outside shots, as well! We simply were not going to let them beat us inside. Similarly, we geared our offense almost completely toward the low post and inside passes; coaches used to kid me about how we'd start a player at the guard position, and he'd always wind up at the low post. We had trouble recruiting guards when I was at Long Beach State because the kids coming out of high school knew I wasn't going to let them shoot from outside.

Our system of play changed after our first season at the University of Nevada at Las Vegas. We lost a 6′9″ player who transferred to Hawaii and a 7′ redshirt who signed a pro contract, and suddenly our hopes for the next season lay with Ricky Sobers, who would be a senior that year, and several 6′6″ sophomores. We weren't going to have the height to run our power game inside, and our 1–2–2 zone defense wasn't going to keep opponents from getting the ball inside on us. Thus we abandoned the zone defense and decided to go with a half-court pressure man-to-man defense and a fast-breaking offense that could help to nullify our opponents' height advantage. We wanted to keep enough pressure on the ball to force our opponents out of their offensive patterns and cause turnovers, and then keep the pressure on them offensively by fast breaking and going for the quick scores before their big men could get back to stop us. We didn't care whether their center was 8′6″; he wasn't going to reject many of our shots if he was still at *their* end of the court when we took the shot!

A lot of people told us that it couldn't be done, that we'd have to let up somewhere on either offense or defense. Pete Newell, an old friend and an outstanding coach, told me, "You just can't expect kids to go 100 percent at both ends of the court." But we expected it, and they did it. People started calling us the "Hardway Eight" because we used eight players in our system of play, and we were proud of the nickname. Critics said we could not win consistently because of the shots we took, but those shots were a vital and necessary part of our game plan. We had to take those early shots because we didn't want to give the opponents' big men time to get back down court and set up in their position man-to-man or zone defenses, and because we wanted our kids to be confident in their shooting. We didn't want to severely restrict their shooting as we had at Long Beach State. We wanted to make the opponents' big men run as long and as hard as we ran. We wanted to spread them out both offensively and defensively. On offense, we wanted to shoot before the defense was formed; on defense, we wanted to apply such intense pressure that our opponents could not run their offensive patterns. When our opponents were tired, they wouldn't play as tall as when they were fresh. Vince Lombardi used to say that "fatigue makes cowards of us all." If he'd been a basketball coach, he might have changed it to "fatigue makes six-footers of us all."

We didn't just put in a running game or man-to-man defense to complement other areas of our game. We tried to make playing with abandon and intensity a way of life for our kids. We used drills to make the players go on the floor after the ball, we ran them unmercifully until they either got used to it or gave up basketball entirely, and we challenged them constantly to give their best effort 100 percent of the time. Our kids lived with intensity to the extent that suiting up for games was like Roman gladiators preparing to go into the arena.

Not every team can, or will, play with our degree of intensity. We're not advocating that every team *should* try to emulate the Runnin' Rebels; however, every coach should study his personnel to find out what they do best, and incorporate a system of play compatible with his players' talents. The more talent a coach has at his command, the less he'll need to make changes once his players have mastered his system; the less talent he has, the less he'll be able to effectively make changes in his team's style of play. In either case, sudden, drastic changes in a team's basic style of play seldom meet with any great success.

The lowest common denominator in winning basketball games lies in controlling opponents offensively and defensively. Control is achieved through mastering styles and systems of play that are compatible with a team's level of skills and ability. We do not advocate that any system or systems described in this book are better than any others, but that a team is capable of using those systems to develop a winning basketball program. Which system you choose is up to you, of course; however, you should have a blueprint for success in your basketball program which is built around an understanding of the systems of play and how they can be used to get the most out of your personnel.

Winning systems of play include: the transition game and fast breaking; the inside power game; ball control offenses; pressure man-to-man and run-and-jump defenses; basic, matchup, trapping, and help-and-recover zone defenses; and pressing defenses. Even if you do not intend to use a particular system, an understanding of how the various systems work will help you in dealing with other teams that use them.

I

Modes of Offensive and Defensive Control

The controlling intelligence understands its own nature, and what it does, and whereon it works.

Marcus Aurelius

Meditations

1

Concepts of Control Basketball

When I first began coaching, I was aware that there were certain things I wanted my team to do, and other things I wanted to keep our opponents from doing—*scoring and winning* come to mind most easily—but I had no real plan for accomplishing those objectives. Oh, I had some definite ideas about how the game should be played—for example, in five years of high school coaching I played all man-to-man defense, and in six years of junior college coaching I used a 1–2–2 zone defense exclusively—but I'm not sure I could have told you exactly why I didn't like the 2–1–2 zones everyone else was using at that time.

Even in those early days I was opposed to outside shooting. I felt strongly then—and *still* feel strongly, which should surprise those whose knowledge of our attacking philosophy at the University of Nevada at Las Vegas (UNLV) is limited or superficial—that a team will not win games consistently on the basis of outside shooting alone. I'm a firm believer in playing the percentages,* and the percentages seldom favor outside shooting as opposed to passing the ball inside. My high school teams were pattern oriented offensively, and because of this and our emphasis on defense, our games were usually low-scoring affairs.

As a high school coach I liked the idea of fast breaking, but I didn't like the increased turnovers that always accompany fast-breaking and high-speed basketball. My idea of a good fast break was having one, two, or three players down court with no opponents in the defensive half-court to stop them. As might be suspected, our fast break wasn't what you'd call overpowering. Today I'm glad to report that the fast break is alive and well at UNLV.

So I had a few ideas about how the game should be played when I

* Maybe that's why I fit in so well in Las Vegas.

began coaching. Those ideas proved to be surprisingly valid in terms of controlling opponents, although I used them mostly for the wrong reasons. However, I was fortunate to have had some fine players then, and I did not readily perceive what now appears to have been huge gaps and glaring inconsistencies in my basketball knowledge at that time.

As I matured as a coach, I began to see how lucky I'd been in adhering to a style of play through good times and bad. Our style of play might not have been the best for our players, but, looking back as objectively as possible, I can see that most of our opponents didn't have a discernible style of play. They did what their opponents let them do, and didn't do what they weren't allowed to do. When they had better players than their opponents, they won, and when they weren't as good, they lost, often by embarrassingly large margins.

I could give you any number of definitions of a *style of play.* I've considered several possibilities, including: (a) the sum total of a team's offensive and defensive patterns, tactics, and strategy, (b) a team's efforts to organize its preferred movements into an integrated whole, and, more simply, (c) the way a team plays the game. Still, something seems lacking in each of those definitions, so I want to propose a fourth definition of *style of play* to set the tone for all that will follow in this book:

> **A team's style of play consists of everything it does to control opponents offensively or defensively.**

Get used to it. If there's a wave of the future in basketball, it's the concept of *control basketball.* I'm not talking about the old concept of control basketball as deliberate, *ball-control* offenses; I'm talking about the conscious, planned efforts to control your opponents' movements and scoring potential.

Consider the plight of Coach X, a good coach who has never had a losing season. Coach X accepted the head coaching position at a high school where the basketball team won only 12 games in the past three years while losing nearly 60 games. In accepting the job, Coach X was confident that he could turn things around in short order. "It couldn't happen to *me*," he scoffed. "I'm too good a coach for that." Unfortunately, though, it did happen to him. At season's end, Coach X's team had won 7 games and lost 14.

It can't happen, you say? You probably wouldn't know the coach whose sad-but-true story was just described, but the names of the coaches listed in the following table should be familiar.

The coaches listed on page 5 have been among the top college basketball coaches in the nation. That they have undergone losing seasons in their first year of coaching at the schools named indicates in vivid terms that no one is immune to losing, especially when moving into a new situation. When a coach assumes a new coaching position, in which losing

Name	School	First Year at School	Won–Lost Record
C. M. Newton	Alabama	1969	4–20
Richard "Digger" Phelps	Notre Dame	1972	6–20
Frank McGuire	South Carolina	1965	6–17
Norm Sloan	N.C. State	1967	7–19
Al McGuire	Marquette	1965	8–18
C. G. "Lefty" Driesell	Davidson	1961	9–14
Guy Lewis	Houston	1957	10–16
Hugh Durham	Florida State	1967	11–15

Source: *The Modern Encyclopedia of Basketball,* Zander Hollander, ed. (New York: Four Winds Press, 1973).

is more or less taken for granted, his first and most important task may not involve winning, but merely *reducing the opponents' margin of victory.* In Coach X's case, the team's improvement from 4 wins and 19 losses the previous season to 7 wins and 14 losses didn't exactly arouse the home fans to dance in the streets, but he managed to reduce the opponents' margin of victory from more than 23 points per game to a more acceptable deficit of 2.5 points per game. With a weak or extremely unskilled team, one is often forced to find solace in small blessings.

You have to stay in the game before you can win it. If your team consistently falls behind by 15 to 20 points, you can't realistically expect to win many of those games. So how do you keep your team in the game with players who wouldn't know a backdoor cut from a surgical incision? By reverting to a conservative style of play designed to keep the opponents away from the basket when they have the ball, and by working for high-percentage shots when your team has the ball; by dictating the tempo of the game through the use of careful ball-handling and ball-control patterns; and finally, by not taking chances that would allow the opponents to gain offensive and defensive control of the game.

Let us return to the perils of Coach X. After developing his players' skills to the extent of keeping the team in games, the following year he used judicious scheduling to help his team win 25 games while losing only two, but he was proudest of the fact that, in 27 games, his team was never more than *four* points behind at any time.

Thus, after reducing the opponents' margin of victory, the second step in the process is to *win the close games.*

We employ three coaching techniques to increase our team's chances of winning close games. First, we believe in conditioning our players to play with intensity throughout games, particularly in the latter stages when players normally begin to tire. John Wooden used to say that he conditioned his players to play *five* quarters, rather than four quarters or two halves. While every team except UCLA experiences periodic declines in talent, it is inexcusable for any coach to lose games because his players are not in shape to play as hard in the latter stages of games as in the first quarter or half. We like to think that the extra attention we pay to conditioning our players is worth several wins a year.

The second technique we use is to get the players in shape mentally. Because our conditioning and practice regimen is grueling and exhaustive, we don't have much trouble convincing our players that we *deserve* to win every game we play! We remind the players of the blood, sweat, and tears they've expended in practice and ask, "Do you think (our opponent) has worked as hard as you have to win this game? Do you really believe they'll be willing to pay the price you've paid?" If your players believe they deserve to win, they'll fight harder to protect what is rightfully theirs. Hard work makes players tough mentally, and mental toughness wins games.

Finally, and this is particularly true in situations where players are used to losing, we believe in never giving your opponent a chance to come back. Give him enough rope, and he'll hang you.

STYLES OF PLAY

There are two general styles of play, *aggressive* and *passive,* which are distinguishable by the presence (or absence) of movements designed to control the opponents' movements. Aggressive styles of play are characterized by attempts to force the opponents into mistakes or untenable positions on offense and defense, while passive styles usually involve cautious approaches and waiting for the opponents to make a mistake.

Passive Styles of Play

Offensively, playing passively means depending on outside splitting alignments without cutters into or across the lane to set up scoring opportunities, or relying on perimeter ball rotation and outside shooting rather than inside penetration or one-on-one confrontations. Defensively, passive coverage (known as "position" defense), primarily in zone defense, involves staying back to cover the low post and other vulnerable ball-side positions. While never as passive as most basic forms of zone defense, position man-to-man defenses include switching and sinking variations in which emphasis is placed upon stopping penetration rather than forcing errors.

Teams use passive defenses to hide defensive weaknesses, to counteract offensive strengths (particularly inside), to protect players in foul trouble, or, in broader terms, as a kind of position defense in which players maintain their positions, waiting to react and counter offensive moves as they occur. If you are sound defensively, you can win consistently by playing position defense. Offensively, teams play passively in two situations: when they don't want to score or force the action, as in delaying or stalling, and when they aren't willing or able to force the action due to inexperience.

Aggressive Styles of Play

The terms *aggressive* and *passive* do not refer to the amount of movement associated with the execution of a skill by a team or an individual, but to the degree of intensity of those movements. On offense, aggressive movements are identified with attacking styles that lead directly to scoring opportunities; for example, one-on-one confrontations, drives toward the basket, or inside shooting. Outside dribbling or passing around the perimeter of a zone defense are examples of more deliberate offensive movements.

Aggressive defenses are those in which the defenders attempt to force the offensive team into turnovers or ballhandling mistakes, or to take the ball away from the offensive team. Aggressive defenses generally involve considerable risk, since failure to contain the ball or control the ball handler leaves the defense open to attack. Pressing defenses are considered aggressive, for example, because, in addition to creating turnovers and steals, they increase the chances of offensive mistakes. Often, though, it is the *defensive* team rather than the offense that errs. Fast breaking is also considered aggressive: its high-speed movement will improve a team's offensive thrust; however, ball-handling mistakes will occur with greater frequency.

Teams who use aggressive styles of play generally are highly skilled. Unskilled players simply are not able to contain the ball defensively or to minimize ball-handling mistakes on offense when playing aggressively. Where styles of play are concerned, the secret of coaching success lies in knowing when to play aggressively and when to use a safer style of play, and in finding systems your team can master.

MODES OF CONTROL

Height

When a team is blessed with outstanding height, relatively little else is needed to create problems for the opponents. I recall seeing a cover photograph from a sports magazine a few years ago showing four Oregon players collapsed on UCLA's Bill Walton at the low post, with the ball handler wide open in the corner trying to decide whether to shoot or pass to someone else in the clear. That's the kind of enviable situation that arises when you have a dominant big man (or men) inside on offense. Even with tall players of average skill, a team can still exert considerable influence, if not outright control, over its opponents on offense and defense. Height compensates for a multitude of other shortcomings.

Since tall teams are usually (but not always) slower than their shorter opponents, they generally tend to avoid pressing defenses, fast breaking, or pressure man-to-man defense in order to (a) avoid tiring their big men, (b) keep them out of foul trouble, and (c) give them time to set up on offense or defense. Tall teams usually operate from set offenses featuring attempts to work the ball inside to their big men. Defensively, they are likely to use a 1–3–1, 2–3, or 3–2 zone. (The 1–2–2 zone defense permits as many as four players to stay inside to cover the outside ball positions, and tall teams may not need to keep all their big men inside.)

Note: Although lacking speed, a tall team still may fast break or use aggressive defensive coverage, particularly when trapping within their zone alignment.

The more height your team possesses, the greater the likelihood that opponents will be forced outside on offense and that they will not be able to keep the ball away from your big men inside on defense. Rebounding is always difficult against big men regardless of their skill or experience, and *rebounding wins ball games.* Outside shooters, even the very best of them, have bad shooting nights. Rebounders who don't mind crashing the boards seldom have off-nights. The same is true of defensive players. Shooting is a highly refined art form; rebounding involves brute strength, positioning, and a love of physical contact.

Don't get me wrong; there's nothing wrong with outside shooting. We've had our share of net-burners at UNLV. However, it's also nice to have a few guys in the lineup who can spread bodies around as they go after the rebounds when the outside shots don't fall. Besides, the best fast break in history won't get off the ground until somebody on the defensive team gets a rebound and makes the outlet pass to start the break. No team scores consistently on fast breaks after scores.

Speed

Quickness is probably the greatest attribute a team can have. It doesn't matter how tall a player is; if he can't get back on defense to stop the opponents from taking high-percentage shots, his height isn't going to help his team much in those situations. Quick, mobile forwards and centers often can keep the ball away from taller, relatively immobile opponents, and quick guards can make life miserable for ball handlers outside. Speed can tire opponents physically, force them into mental errors when they're not used to playing high-speed basketball, confuse them by taking away vital aspects of their offensive game plan, and wear them down mentally by forcing them to play cautiously in order to avoid turnovers and the resultant, ever-present fast break. Quickness can create spread-court games. Teams may be both fast *and* tall, of course, as were many of UCLA's super-teams of the 1960s and 1970s under John Wooden. Any time you compete against teams who can destroy you with their press, fast break, or set offense, well, when you start trying to find tiny chinks in their armor, you feel like you're using a microscope to observe the craters of the moon! I can't recall ever seeing a tall, fast team that wasn't outstanding.

Speed is deceptive, though. I didn't really begin to understand the function of speed until I came to UNLV and was forced to abandon our zone defense and inside game in favor of a high-speed, aggressive, intensive brand of basketball. In my second year at UNLV, we built a team in which the forwards and center were only 6′5″ to 6′6″ (which is small by college standards). When we decided to junk the 1–2–2 zone defense and the deliberate, control offense I'd lived by in the past, I gained a new sympathy for prison inmates on death row. However, I found out something about the high-speed game that surprised me: *you don't have to be faster than your opponents to fast break against them!*

The success of any given fast break is determined largely in the first 2 to 3 seconds after transition. Training defensive players to anticipate and react to transitions improves the fast break, obviously, but factors other than those most commonly cited also act in favor of the defensive team:

1. In the case of steals, the defenders, facing the ball or their own basket, are in a better position to take advantage of the first second or two after transition. First, the player stealing the ball is either facing his own basket or at least is closer to facing his basket than the player from whom he stole the ball. Many times he will already be in motion toward his own basket and will be moving at top speed when he steals the ball. Second, the players on the offensive team, particularly the ball handler, generally will have to turn around before starting down court to stop the fast break. These factors place the attacking advantage with the fast-breaking team.

2. Offensive teams are generally basket oriented; that is, they are trained to "take the ball to the basket" and attack the defense rather than worrying about the defenders' stealing the ball and fast breaking. When a

shot is taken, for example, certain offensive players will move to the basket to rebound offensively, but in order to rebound effectively they will have to get inside the defenders near the basket. Their momentum, then, will be toward their own basket, and it will involve movement that is necessarily more aggressive than that of the defenders already stationed near the basket. The offensive team's "basket orientation" can work against them in terms of their vulnerability to fast breaking. Only when the defenders can anticipate transition and begin moving down court before the opponents can react will the fast break reach its ultimate effectiveness, however.

3. Most teams aren't used to playing high-speed basketball. I've been told that I couldn't realistically expect my players to give 100 percent effort on defense and then turn around and give the same effort on offense. "They have to rest sometimes," is the argument given. But after working so hard to get the ball, why would they *want* to rest when they have the opponents at a disadvantage? Do they really want to slow down, stop the fast break, and wait for the opponents to get back and set up in their zone defense, and thereby surrender all hope of penetrating on offense, just because they aren't supposed to be able to give 100 percent at both ends of the court? Why work them hard at all on defense if they aren't going to reap the full rewards of their efforts at the other end of the court?

We constantly drilled our players in transition basketball, and as a result we found that even our slower players were becoming involved in the fast break. Fast breaking requires a certain amount of quickness, but the faster a player is able to anticipate, and react to, transition, the less he will have to rely on speed to be a part of the fast break. Even relatively slow players can become involved in the fast break if they are ready to fast break instantly when transition occurs.

The running game depends primarily upon speed and quickness, but it is also habitual; that is, the tendency to run at every opportunity is a voluntary, learned skill. If players do not practice high-speed ball-handling drills and fast breaking, they will not be able to perform the skills involved without committing ball-handling errors and turnovers—but more important, they will be unable to play high-speed basketball effectively against teams who are used to transition basketball and the running game.

Speed can help teams in other ways. Full-court pressing defenses can take advantage of ball-handling weaknesses, and aggressive defenses such as pressure man-to-man or run-and-jump defense can further enhance a team's defensive effectiveness. Individual and team speed never hurt a team's overall chances. You can always slow down a fast team, if necessary, but you'll never speed up a slow team without practicing fast breaking, transition basketball and pressure defense.

Ball Handling and Shot Selection

Some teams simply are not cut out for upbeat, high-tempo basketball. In my own case, I might have had some potentially outstanding fast-breaking teams when I was at Long Beach State, but I'd never have known it because we ran what is known as a *controlled fast break*. In our case, it was a *very* controlled fast break because I was terrified of the idea of ball-handling mistakes. I did *not,* under any circumstances, want to give the ball back to the opponents without a fight, especially after we'd worked so hard to get the ball in the first place. At the first hint of defensive interference with the break, I'd be up on my feet, yelling, "Set up! Set up!" But I've known coaches who were even worse about it than I was. I've seen teams who probably wouldn't fast break if the opposing team packed up its equipment and left the gym.

It's a matter of preference, of course. I doubt that I'll ever go back to our former way of playing now, but there's no denying that ball-control offenses present formidable obstacles. In the 1950s and 1960s, the Shuffle and Wheel continuity offenses were popular precisely because they permitted teams to control the ball for as long as was necessary to set up high-percentage scoring opportunities. Today, perhaps the nation's leading proponent of ball-control offense is Dean Smith of the University of North Carolina (UNC), who uses a three-pronged ball-control attack to devastate opponents. They run a controlled fast break when opportunities arise, falling back into a patient "Passing Game" offense to work for high-percentage shots off a multitude of screens and cuts, then switch to their "Carolina Corners" four-corner delay game when they have the lead in the latter stages of games. With their ball handlers running the delay game, the Tarheels were practically unbeatable when they had the lead and the ball in the last few minutes of games. And whereas most fans react to delay tactics with the enthusiasm of fathers attending PTA meetings when they could be home watching television, Tarheel rooters look forward to the "Carolina Corners" with the frenzied ecstasy of youngsters taking their first roller coaster ride. As one who fell prey to Smith's ball control offenses, I can attest to their inexorable efficiency. Dean Smith is the first to admit that he hasn't exactly been barren of talent at UNC, but his system makes it doubly tough to beat him. His players understand his system to the *n*th degree, and in order to beat them you have to beat their system as well. Everything they do offensively is based on ball control, and you can bet they aren't going to beat themselves.

The Shuffle, Wheel, Passing Game, and delay patterns are not the only ball control or continuity offenses; *any* offense is a ball control offense if it is run with the intent of being repeated until a high-percentage scoring opportunity arises, or of running the clock rather than scoring. Ball-control offenses are not always popular with fans, but they can be terribly effective in keeping teams in contention against superior opponents, and they can also serve to: (a) keep players in foul trouble in the game, (b) slow down the tempo of fast-breaking teams, (c) train young or unskilled players in techniques of proper shot selection, (d) give tired players time to rest, (e) force opponents to switch from zone defense to man-to-man, or (f) have the two or three best shooters taking most of the shots.

Variations of Defensive Control

As has been noted, teams may attempt to control opponents defensively in a variety of ways: by pressing full- or half-court; using a basic zone defense to control the opponents' inside game, or matching up, trapping or using help-and-recover defense from the relative security of a zone alignment; playing pressure man-to-man defense or using run-and-jump techniques with superior defensive personnel; or using sinking or switching man-to-man techniques with slightly less capable personnel. In each case, the amount of defensive control a team is capable of exerting will depend upon the defensive players' skills and the type of defense being used. Position defenses, for example, may entail less risk and provide greater inside coverage than aggressive defenses, but passive coverage never yields the kind of defensive control, or *dominance,* that sometimes results from aggressive coverage.

Not every team should press full- or half-court. If you're going to use a pressing defense, you should expect to pay a price for using it. Even the best pressing teams reasonably expect to regain possession of the ball by stealing or forcing turnovers only a small fraction of the time; obviously, then, these teams will find their opponents beating the presses most of the time, and it is not unreasonable to assume that on many of those occasions the opponents will gain high-percentage scoring opportunities as a result of their beating the press and advancing the ball down court while the defenders are out of position. When the press does not contain the ball or force a turnover, the attacking advantage shifts dramatically to the offensive team.

Tall, quick players are ideal for pressing defenses. (Tall, quick players are ideal for *everything* in basketball.) When players are not both tall and quick, they must at least be *quick* if a team is to succeed with a pressing defense. Beyond quickness, skill and an aggressive attitude are personal traits that help to make a player good at pressing defense. Players who are slow, unskilled players, or players who are not highly motivated are unlikely to be effective in pressing, because it is difficult to hide defensive weaknesses while pressing.

Basic zone defense is generally conservative in nature, ball-side oriented, and designed to keep the ball away from ball-side low post. Although basic zone defense may be effected from any zone defensive alignment, the two most often-used alignments for basic zone coverage are the 1–2–2 and 2–3 alignments. Two kinds of teams use basic zone coverage: teams with players who are too immobile, inactive, or passive defensively to use a more aggressive form of coverage, and teams with weaknesses such as unskilled players or overall lack of height that precludes their playing aggressive defense. Discounting the former from further consideration, using basic zone defense will help to keep teams in games against superior opponents by providing a measure of defensive control, not everywhere on the court, but in those areas of the court where opponents are most likely to beat you. Ideally in basic defense, the ball is forced to one side of the court, where coverage is intensified to the extent that the offensive team will have to rotate the ball to the weak side. Meanwhile, the *defense* will also rotate to the weak side, matching up at first and then providing additional inside coverage as before.

Matchup, trapping, and help-and-recover defenses are no-nonsense zone defenses for teams with superior personnel and no outstanding defensive weaknesses. Many coaches consider matchup zone defense to be among the best defenses in basketball since it combines man-to-man coverage, which can be as aggressive and risky as desired, with the relative security of zone defense. Still, recognizing, and then maintaining, the matchups requires smart, knowledgeable players, and even then the constantly changing matchups may yield matchups and inside confrontations favoring the offensive team.

Trapping is even more hazardous than matchup defense. While matching up is usually done more or less passively by allowing the ball handler and primary pass receivers a certain amount of freedom to operate outside, trapping is always aggressive. At least it had *better* be aggressive: if trapping fails to contain the ball or force a turnover, the offensive team will have a numerical advantage as well as attacking momentum toward its basket. The trapping team will not be able to cut off *all* the passing lanes, so it will attempt to harass the ball handler by double-teaming as the remaining defenders cut off the primary passing lanes.

Trapping may occur anywhere on the court, but the principles involved are the same: with two players trapping the ball handler, two more cutting off the primary passing lanes in that area of the court, and one player back to cover the diagonal passes, at least one offensive player will always be open—if the ball handler can find him. Thus, teams seldom enter lightly into trapping sequences. They will select carefully the location of their trapping movements, and attempt to spring them as quickly as possible, taking advantage of the element of surprise. If the offensive team expects to be trapped, it is unlikely that it will be maneuvered into trapping situations. Without the element of surprise working in its favor, the defensive team will be unable to contain the ball or force a turnover; rather, it will face with almost equal certainty the prospect of giving up a high-percentage shot.

Help-and-recover defense is an aggressive style of zone defense that has the unique goal (among zone defenses) of attempting to deny, or at least hinder, all shots, inside or outside. In order to do this, help-and-recover defense derives its techniques from basic, matchup, and trapping coverages. The primary goal of help-and-recover zone defense is to stop penetration by momentarily switching defensive responsibilities when the offensive team is able to create mismatches in various areas of the court, particularly as a result of rapid ball rotation to the weak side before the defense can recover.

The problem associated with the strict matchup coverage shown in Figure 1–1 is that X_1 *will not move at all with the pass from 05 to 03,* and as a result he will be unable to stop 01 from penetrating after 03 relays the ball to 01. If X_2 covers 01 at the point, X_4 (or somebody else) will have to cover 02. Whoever covers 02, the matchups will be mixed up, perhaps irreparably, when X_2 has to guard 01.

In Figure 1–2, however, the problem is far less imposing. When 03 passes to 01, X_1 still cannot get to 01 in time—but he doesn't have to, since X_2 will move out to stop 01's penetration (and deny the shot) until X_1 arrives. Then, X_2 will either drop back to his original position, or rush to cover 02 if 01 relays the ball to weak side. X_2's job is not easy in the example of help-and-recover defense shown in Figure 1–2, nor will his teammates find *their* roles in help-and-recover any less demanding. Still, the coverage afforded as a result of their efforts is likely to be superior to that of *any* other zone defense if the players know what they are doing and are willing to give the physical effort required to make the defense work.

Pressure man-to-man defense is probably the ultimate defense in basketball. Pressure man-to-man defense involves intense coverage of the

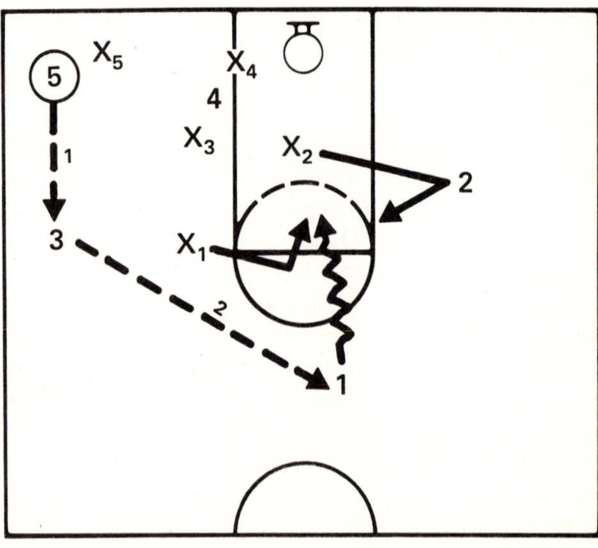

Figure 1–1 Comparing Matchup and Help-and-Recover Defenses in Covering Rotation Passes: *Matchup Defense*

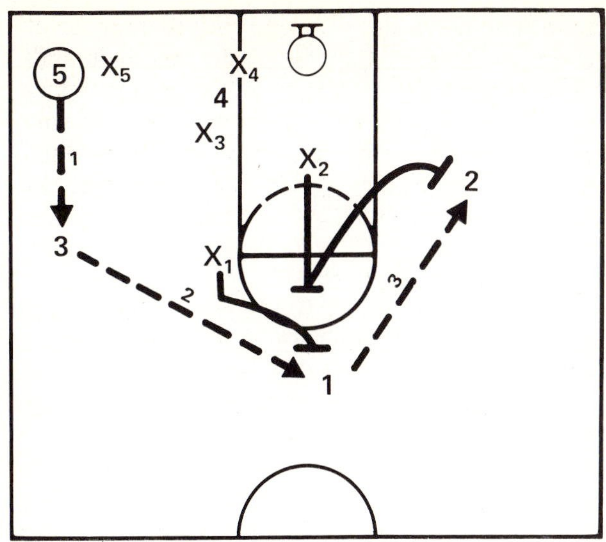

Figure 1–2 Comparing Matchup and Help-and-Recover Defenses in Covering Rotation Passes: *Help-and-Recover Defense*

ball and first pass receivers, but slightly less aggressive coverage of players away from the ball in order to provide added coverage inside if necessary. Players away from the ball will help out inside in the event that the defender on the ball cannot contain his man. In such cases a jump switch will often prove very effective in pressure man-to-man coverage.

Once the ball handler picks up his dribble, the other four defenders will front any players at high or low post and overguard the other players, playing the passing lanes and trying to steal all passes. A University of North Carolina player who had heard about, but not seen, our pressure man-to-man defense was disappointed that we gave up so many backdoor layups. However, in our case at least, it's not bad defense, but part of our game plan. It's a calculated risk we take in our coverage: backdoor cuts are likely to be the *only* passes we give up. We give up more layups from our half-court defense than an inexperienced junior high team—but that's all we're going to give up! We're *not* going to let our opponents play slow, passing the ball around outside until they decide to pick us apart with inside passes. We *won't* let them get the ball to the high or low post. (We front any player at the high or low post.) They can drive on us if they're good enough, and they can throw those backdoor passes from time to time, but they *aren't* going to stand around resting and passing the ball back and forth until they decide to go inside and beat our brains out! (This system has worked extremely well for us: in 1975–76, when we averaged 110.5 points per game, we also averaged just under 27 forced turnovers per game, while committing only 16 turnovers per game ourselves.)

Run-and-jump defense is another aggressive form of pressure man-to-man defense; it contains elements of both the sinking and pressure forms of man-to-man coverage. In run-and-jump defense, players are influenced toward a given court position—the base line, for example—when a second defender coming across from the weak side suddenly appears in the dribbler's path. Instead of trapping, however, the defenders will switch responsibilities, with the man guarding the dribbler switching off to cover the open man—usually an offensive player on the weak side. When the dribbler picks up the ball, as he will likely be forced to do when he sees the second defender blocking his path, he will have no one to pass to; instead of trapping, which always leaves at least one offensive player open, the defenders will still be in pressure man-to-man coverage.

A further advantage of run-and-jump defense is that the second defender will draw an increased number of charging fouls.

Sinking and switching man-to-man defense are generally less aggressive than pressure man-to-man or run-and-jump defense. These forms of man-to-man coverage are similar to zone defense in intent; that is, they increase inside coverage (sinking) and provide alternatives to fighting through screens by making switches automatic (switching). Sinking on the weak side often accompanies pressure man-to-man coverage on the ball side. Most coaches feel that if their players aren't going to fight through screens, they are better off in zone defense.

2

The Four Ps: Program, Philosophy, Personnel, and Patterns

PROGRAM

Program is everything. Your basketball program encompasses everything you do to develop and maintain a winning tradition in basketball at your school. It is the sum total of your efforts, and the efforts of everyone who is even remotely involved in basketball at your school, in developing basketball players and teams under your supervision. Fleeting successes will not hide the deficiencies of a weak program, and momentary setbacks and rebuilding years will not diminish enthusiasm for a strong program. The basketball program under your leadership will accurately reflect the depth of your commitment to basketball, especially in the early years of its formation, and if your commitment is shallow or unstable, you are likely to find coaching an extremely vulnerable profession.

Program reflects commitment. This point cannot be overemphasized. Commitment, or lack of it, may be seen most clearly at the high school level in the coach's efforts to provide a feeder program in basketball in the school and/or community. (The feeder program would include junior varsity and B-teams, junior high teams, intramurals, the encouraging of players to attend summer basketball camps, and a community recreation program for young players.) Without a feeder program, or at least a semblance of one, young players will not begin learning basic individual and team skills and strategies until they try out for the varsity team. In many cases, players will be in the ninth or tenth grade before they start the long, arduous task of becoming basketball players.

Starting a New Program (Or Improving on an Old One)

In starting a new basketball program, or in building upon an existing program, several points must be considered. First, and most important, it is imperative to provide opportunities to play and to *get people involved in your program.* As has been mentioned, a feeder program is vital to your basketball program's success. Junior varsity, junior high teams, elementary teams, intramurals, and community recreation programs can provide youngsters with valuable learning experiences, and if any or all of these outlets for participation are missing from your program, you should explore the possibility of adding them to your program. (Even in a high school situation you should consider these teams to be a part of your program, since your ongoing success will depend to a great extent upon their existence and growth.)

Another way of getting people involved in your program is to provide coaches for the teams in your program. In most cases, the coaches will already be available, especially at the junior varsity or junior high level, but you should consider it your responsibility to provide these coaches with encouragement, materials, and ideas for improving their own performances as well as those of their players. Such encouragement can take the form of informal discussions, staff meetings, compiling and sharing a basketball library, or whatever else may occur to the coach. Dealing with other coaches can be a delicate matter, but if you treat them prudently and within a framework of mutual respect, any resultant problems can be ironed out.

High school athletes can help to administer intramural programs by filling such roles as referees, scorers, timekeepers, and coaches. In recreational programs, parents should be encouraged to coach teams; through their involvement, even at lower levels of play, your varsity program will be strengthened.

Sometimes outside support will not be readily available. Years of disinterest in a weak basketball program may have weakened school and community support to the extent that the coach must take on additional coaching duties to get the basketball program moving at the school.

I consider six concepts to be key factors in developing a successful program at lower levels of play.

1. Youngsters cannot start too early in basketball. Although competitiveness is often overemphasized, children love to practice dribbling and handling the ball. Having squads of young players demonstrate fancy ball-handling skills at half-times of varsity ballgames can help to change public apathy to support a school's basketball program—and, coincidentally, to increase attendance at home games. These skills can be developed in physical education classes and in brief practice sessions on Saturdays or after school.

2. Where no recreation program is available, sixth graders should be permitted to play on junior high teams. The extra year of playing time will produce remarkable results in terms of young players' assimilating the coach's philosophy and style of play.

3. It is more important to win at the junior high or junior varsity level than at the varsity level, especially when the varsity squad has had losing records for several years. A new coach won't change losing attitudes overnight; it is easier to take young players who are not used to losing *or* winning and to make winners out of them than it is to change the attitudes of players who are used to losing.

4. Look for players who display loyalty, a willingness to work hard, and the ability to take instruction. I've been willing to take a chance on kids in my career who came to me with the label of "bad" kids; however, I've always assumed that kids aren't "bad" and have used that as a starting point in working with them. Any kid with loyalty to you and your basketball program can be a good kid.

Competitiveness is more to be desired than natural ability without competitive drive or hustle. I've always believed that, given eight or nine boys of junior high age who listen well, hustle, and sincerely would rather win than lose, my team could hold its own in most leagues regardless of our height, speed, skill, or playing experience.

5. Have a winning formula for coaching strategy at lower levels of play. Although some may argue with my philosophy, I have a winning formula that consists of the following points:

(a) Stress defense in everything you do in practice. Teach your players a basic zone defense, stay in it and play it tight, and make your opponents beat you with outside shooting. Don't use man-to-man defense (except in practice) unless you're clearly superior to your opponent or unless your program is intended to complement that of the high school team.

(b) With unskilled players, double-team the ball-side low-post position.

(c) Offensively, work the ball inside as often as possible, regardless of your opponents' height or your own players' ability to operate one on one in close quarters. There are two reasons for this: outside shots are usually (but not always) low-percentage for inexperienced players, and the opponents will commit more fouls when you get the ball inside. For example, practically all you need to be effective offensively at the junior high level is at least one ball handler, one outside shooting threat—not necessarily a *scoring* threat, since the opponents don't know that your players can't make the shots—and one or two inside players who can work free to get the ball and then shoot it while moving. (This is not to imply that your inside game must be overpowering, of course; it doesn't have to be if your defensive game is more or less solid.)

The higher the level of play, the less chance this basic, conservative style of play will have of succeeding. Yet with small or inexperienced teams it is often the best available alternative, even on the varsity level. It involves a minimum of risk and a maximum of potential for allowing (but not forcing) the opponents to make mistakes. Chapter 12 explores these concepts in greater detail.

6. Whenever possible, schedule opponents you can beat or at least play even with. While such a statement may be distasteful to some, we're talking about creating winning attitudes, and, to quote an old maxim, "Nothing Succeeds Like Success."

As a team gains confidence and experience and increases in skill, the schedule should be made progressively more difficult. Championship contenders need high-level competition to sharpen their skills and prepare them for the pressures of tournament play. Still, unskilled players need to win to gain confidence in their growing abilities, and the coach who unnecessarily loads his schedule with opponents he cannot beat is defeating his own purposes. True, there are lessons to be learned from playing superior opponents, but teams used to losing do not need an overabundance of losses to teach them how to lose.

PHILOSOPHY

Every basketball coach has, or should have, a philosophy of how he feels basketball should be played. That philosophy can be reflected in many ways. A coach may, for any of several reasons, prefer controlled offenses to freelance patterns; zone defense to man-to-man defense; a running game to more conservative approaches; full-court scrimmaging to drills in practice; or he may even prefer defense to offense (or vice versa). A team has only x number of hours of practice time available to learn the offensive and defensive patterns, strategies, and skills it will use in the upcoming season, and without a cohesive and coherent basketball philosophy the coach's efforts are likely to be disorganized and confused, and his players' preparation will be lacking in several areas.

Note: One of the quickest and most effective, yet least desirable, ways to develop a sound personal philosophy of basketball is to undergo a losing streak or a rebuilding season. It's not the most enjoyable method, of course, but it certainly is effective. Experience is usually a fine teacher, and learning to stretch a little talent a long way can prove invaluable to a coach. If a coach's foundations in basketball are tenuous, a losing streak can teach him about the game very quickly. Losing consis-

> tently will either force him to shore up his areas of weakness or it will drive him from the coaching ranks. Darrell Royal, former head football coach at the University of Texas, said of his sport: "Football doesn't build character. It gets rid of weak ones." The same holds true for basketball.

Awareness of one's personal philosophy brings order and understanding to the coaching process. If you were to start on a long trip by car, you would find a road map beneficial for planning the best route to your destination. In like manner, organizing your thoughts concerning how you feel basketball should be played will help you to determine the best way to prepare your players for the season. While you can and should learn from others at every opportunity, you should develop your coaching philosophy to complement your own personality. You may emulate another coach you admire, but not to the extent of losing your own identity. You cannot be somebody else.

When we speak of a personal philosophy of basketball, we are not talking about comparisons between styles or systems of play; rather, we are describing coaches' attitudes toward those styles and systems. Although much of a coach's emerging philosophy involves decisions between contrasting or contradictory styles of play, certain concepts are basic to all coaches and philosophies: you either believe them or you don't, but you ignore them at your peril.

1. Hard Work Yields Success. There are no shortcuts to success. All of us know that. If Team A's players and coach work harder to achieve success than Team B's over a given period of time, Team A's program eventually will surpass Team B's. Unless you're Mandrake The Magician, you're not going to pull blue-chip 6′8″ 240-pounders out of a hat. Good players come and go, but dedicated, hard-working coaches and winning systems of play endure.

Material is important. Problems can arise when abundant talents are performing elsewhere and you have to play against them, or when your players are deficient in such vital areas as height, speed, rebounding, ball handling, shooting, or defense. In such cases, coaching takes on added significance in terms of a team's chances for success.

At a recent coaching clinic, a coach from a perennially powerful basketball school was scheduled to speak. "I'll be frank with you," the coach began. "We have 2,200 students at my high school, and an abnormally large number of them are fine athletes. I'm supposed to be talking to you about zone offenses today, but we have so many good athletes at our school that practically anything I want to run works for us. We don't do anything in our zone offenses that most of you don't do; we just have the talent to do it better."

Coaches coming into a new situation, or coaches trying to establish a basketball program, seldom have such a wealth of talent to draw from. For every team that goes through the regular season undefeated, hundreds of other teams must scratch, claw, and struggle for every win—and even then they may fall by the wayside. If you're going to keep up with the coaches who have an endless supply of talent at their disposal, you'd better set as your goal to work harder than they do.

A good rule-of-thumb for every coach is: *Work harder than your players.* The work you do as a coach may not be the same as that expected of your players, but if you're going to expect them to give countless hours of blood, sweat, and tears to become basketball players, you should be prepared to set an example for them by your own dedication and willingness to work. You don't have to get out on the court and scrimmage with your players to prove your dedication. You do, however, owe your team your best efforts in terms of preparing yourself for the upcoming season. Plan your practices beforehand. Know what you want to accomplish. Study the styles and systems of other coaches and other teams, with an eye toward incorporating appropriate styles into your own program. Above all, don't expect to get by with shortcuts to success. If the path to success were easy, everyone would be a winner.

2. Believe in Yourself, Your Players and Your System of Play. Three aspects of the coaching situation exist: the coach, the players, and the system of play. When at least two of these aspects reach the point of entering into what Austrian theologian-philosopher Martin Buber called *dialogue,* or "opening oneself unto the possibility of the other," learning and understanding are likely to result.

a. The Coach and His System. If you have strong doubts about the soundness of your system of play, you can hardly expect your players to embrace it eagerly, although they may win on talent or ability alone despite their misgivings about the system of play itself. Far more likely, however, your players' on-court performances will be inconsistent and sporadic, reflecting your own confusion. You won't convince your players that any given style of play is best for them until you're sure of it in your own mind.

Study the game. Attend coaching clinics and read what other coaches have written. Find out what the best coaches are doing now. Everything you read and hear may not be immediately applicable to your present situation, but you won't improve your situation if your mind is closed to new ideas.

b. The Players and the System. It's always preferable, but certainly not mandatory, for the coach to get along with his players. If, however, the players thoroughly accept and understand the coach's system, their play may not be affected by their attitude toward the coach, even if it happens to be negative. Regardless of whether the players like the coach, they should respect him and his system of play. If the players do not like or believe in the style or system of play they are using, their dissatisfaction will show up in their on-court performance.

c. The Players and the Coach. One of the most difficult aspects of coaching is that of motivating players, whether individually or as a group. Every coach has his own methods of motivation, guided by his temperament, personality, and closeness to his players. No ideal way of dealing with players has yet been identified, nor is any universal method expected to be unearthed in the near future. Players must be treated as individuals, but they should also be expected to subordinate themselves to the needs of the team.

To return to an earlier point, *program is everything.* No player, coach, or system of play should be placed above the team in importance. Often, players or coaches incorrectly assume that their value to the team entitles them to make arbitrary decisions based on their personal preferences, feelings, or emotions as opposed to what is actually best for *the team.* It is even more important for the coach to control himself than it is for the players, since only the coach can make decisions on behalf of the team. Spelling out behavior expected of team members, for example, falls within the coach's duties, yet the coach who makes rules solely on the basis of personal preferences or whims is asking for trouble. If you as coach simply cannot abide shoulder-length hair, or facial hair, or what you consider to be slovenly dress or personal appearance, you have the right as coach to make and enforce rules governing them; however, you also have the obligation to the team to provide coherent reasons for making those rules.

When a player knowingly flaunts team rules or expects special considerations because of his status on the team, he should be convinced by whatever means necessary that he is no more than a single link in the chain that ties a team together. The coach is a single link, too, even though he is the link that determines how everyone else performs. Unfortunately, coaches often forget that they, too, are part of the system. If the coach's behavior or demands are contrary to the common goals of the team, it is the behavior or demands that should be changed, not the goals.

The relationship between a coach and his players is not subject to rules or guidelines beyond the suggestion that the greatest virtues a coach can have in his dealings with players are fairness, honesty, and consistency. Some coaches prefer to remain aloof from their players, while others prefer being close to their players away from the court. The coach can be equally effective either way if he is fair, honest, and consistent.

3. Set Specific, Realistic Goals for Yourself and for Your Team. Such a statement may appear self-evident, but in many cases a team's primary goal—winning—may not be a viable possibility, especially for new coaches in undeveloped basketball programs. In such cases, making winning your only criterion for success will inevitably lead to disappointment. Winning is always a desirable goal, although it may not always be a realistic one. Pride can be built even in the midst of a losing season when team goals are such that they can be achieved. For instance, building a strong defense is a cornerstone for all basketball programs that are worth their salt. A realistic goal in situations in which winning is not even a remote possibility might be to stay within ten points of the opponents, or, even better, to keep the opponents from scoring more than, say, fifty points. These goals are concrete, and thus are easier for players to comprehend than nebulous game plans pursuing overoptimistic notions of victory. Players can be proud, even in defeat, if they have pursued and accomplished goals which, although short of victory, further their development and allow them a measure of self-respect.

Above all else, this book is concerned with the possibility of controlling opponents; thus, you should not be surprised to find that we advocate controlling superior opponents by controlling their ability to run up the score on you. This is the first step in teaching young players what the concept of controlling opponents is all about. First, you try to find ways to prevent the opponents from beating you badly; then, as your players' skills increase, you search for ways to win the close games; finally, you try to use your players' skills within a system of play that will allow you to dominate play and control the flow of action for long periods of time, and perhaps for entire games.

Coaches should set both short- and long-range goals for their teams. Where weaker teams are concerned, the short-range goal is often merely to survive from game to game. In all cases, the long-range goal is to win through program continuity.

4. Make Your Players Play Your Way. If you can't control your players and their on-court performance, you won't be able to control your opponents' performance either. Regardless of your relationship with your players, *you're* the one who is being paid to make the decisions. With *your* head on the chopping block when things go wrong, you owe it to yourself to run the team, make the rules, set the goals, install the system of play, and see to it that things go as smoothly as possible.

One of the best pieces of advice a new coach could ever receive is: *Surround yourself with players who believe in or at least accept your philosophy of the way the game should be played.* You may not win all the time, but losing will be a lot easier to take.

There's an old saying among coaches that "you graduate your problems." What problems? Are they players who don't like you, their teammates, the school, your style of play, or that they're getting too little playing time to suit them? Or are they parents who verbally draw and quarter you from the stands because their son, who plays defense with the finesse of a wooly mammoth and the mobility of a large rock, is "riding the pine"—sitting on the bench—when he should be out on the court giving his impression of a tree. It's nothing personal to you, of course—all you're trying to do is win a few games here and there—but to Problem Player or Problem Parent it's intensely personal: you're the greatest scourge of mankind since Attilla the Hun! Winning isn't really important to them. It's nice, of course, but winning or losing pales in comparison to the thrill of seeing Problem Player out there on the court doing his thing, even when his "thing" consists of dribbling the ball as if it were still in the box it came in, or shooting from 40 feet out with a form similar to that of soldiers lobbing hand grenades. If you tried to understand the player in question, you'd see that he's just "going through a phase," although it's difficult to imagine *any* athlete (or nonathlete) who is not going through some kind of phase in life! It doesn't matter that other players and other parents have the same rights; it's *you,* the coach, who's keeping Problem Player from reaching the pinnacles of success. So what if he can't even score against players on the freshman team in practice? So what if he's so slow that you time him in wind sprints with a calendar? If you were any kind of coach at all, you'd see that he's better than the collection of Neanderthals you have out there now!

This is why I prefer to have no more than eight accomplished players on my team. If you have more than eight quality athletes on your team, they're going to expect (or worse, *demand*) more playing time than you're giving them, and the resultant friction, backbiting, grumbling, complaining, and decay of team morale may erode your team's potential like a spreading cancer.

5. Find Players You Can Teach and Patterns They Can Run. This statement also deserves special mention. When I'm recruiting, I don't look for tall guys, or quick guys, or great shooters, although those attributes are undeniably important; instead, I try to get the best *athletes* I can find. I don't care whether they're 5′8″ or 7′4″; if they're the best athletes available, I want them! I'll fit our playing style to their talents, whether we play the inside power game offensively with big men, or the racehorse brand of basketball that has become associated with us at UNLV. However, so many coaches do it the other way around: they go after *any* prospect who's 6′11″ or taller, even if he's still learning how to climb stairs, feed himself, and hold a basketball in two hands. I've seen teams recruit boys 6′10″ who couldn't even dunk a basketball, and once I heard about a coach recruiting a 6′9″ kid with a long neck, whose shoulders were level with the shoulders of two of his 6′4″ teammates!

I like to have tall guys around, but they have to be good athletes. Announcers discussing Arkansas in their pregame comments during the 1978 NCAA tournament kept talking about how much trouble Arkansas' 6′4″ trio of Sidney Moncrief, Ron Brewer, and Marvin Delph were going to have stopping their taller opponents, but by halftime the commentators always seemed to be saying how much trouble the opponents were having in stopping Moncrief, Brewer, and Delph. There's not a coach in the universe who wouldn't have given his eye teeth, an arm, leg, kidney, and lung to have had those three in his starting lineup. I know I certainly would have. Describing them as "good jumpers" is like calling Muhammad Ali a "good boxer." All three of them could have jumped up and changed the light bulbs in the gym!

I go for the athletes every time. If they have athletic ability and athletic sense, you can teach them anything. Good athletes literally play over their heads consistently, not just because they're coachable, but also because they're undermatched against equal or taller opponents who *aren't* good athletes.

One thing that never ceases to amaze me is how some kids who play the game don't really love it. I've known of situations where a coach didn't dare leave practice even for a minute to answer the phone, because he knew that when he got back his kids would be in the bleachers talking or sleeping. Nobody needs players like that.

Our kids at UNLV really love the game. I'll bet if you were to take a poll of our players right now, you'd find that every one of them has played basketball somewhere today. It's not my influence on them; they just love to play basketball. If a kid really loves the game, he's not going to be hard to coach. It's also a lot of fun, to have the kind of kids that, when you take them aside and tell them that they need to work on a certain phase of the game, you know they're going to do it on their own, without your having to read them the riot act.

Archimedes declared, "Give me a lever, and I shall move the world!" If you would move the world with your basketball team, your fulcrum must be grounded in pride and determination, and your lever is the willingness of your players to pay the price of victory. Every winning basketball program is based on the acquisition and retention of players who are willing to take risks and work beyond the comfort zone. If you can surround yourself with such players, winning will be inevitable.

Many coaches purposely make their basketball tryouts rigorous and demanding, not only to get their veterans in shape, but also to find out who is willing to pay the price and who will give up when the going gets rough. Physical skills are important, but the importance of a positive, aggressive attitude toward the game cannot be overemphasized.

If you can teach your players, you'll see a lot of progress in your program. Having coachable players means that you're not going to have to spend your time trying to convince them that what you're doing is sound. You can waste an incredible amount of time trying to teach players who think they know it all already.

Once you have players you can teach, your next step is to find offensive patterns and defenses they can run. The simpler your patterns, the better off you'll be in the long run. Not every team has to run intricate patterns that look good. You can be just as effective running one pattern, and running it right, with no variations or changes whatsoever.

When I was at Long Beach State, we took pride in our 1–2–2 zone defense. I told our kids, "We're not going to make any changes in our game plan. I *want* them (our opponents) to know we'll be in a 1–2–2 zone defense, but we're going to play it so tight all night that they'll think they're wearing girdles!" And at UNLV, when we were playing San Francisco in the NCAA Tournament, our two big guys got in foul trouble early in the second half playing pressure man-to-man defense, and the announcers kept saying we'd have to go to a zone defense to protect our big men, but we never did. We stayed in our man-to-man defense all night and won the game. Afterwards, the reporters asked why we didn't go to a zone. Well, we didn't even have a zone defense to go to. We hadn't practiced zone defense, and we weren't going to go to it because *we couldn't* and because I don't like to make changes. The more changes you make, the farther you get from your original game plan. Also, every time you change defenses, you lose a little intensity, and intensity is our game. We believe in coming at you the same way every time, but doing it so aggressively and tenaciously that you never attain the momentum necessary to disrupt our game. It doesn't always work, of course, but I think we've proved that it works for us. Besides, I have all I can handle in teaching my players to master *one* defense in the course of a year. If I had to find forty more ways to play defense, my players and I would be basket cases within a week!

A simple pattern is one your players understand and can run successfully. You may have the deepest insights into offensive and defensive theories of play since Dr. Naismith first tacked a peach basket onto a wall, but if your players can't translate your theories into effective defensive coverage or points on the board, you're no better off than if you were coaching in Sanskrit or hieroglyphics. Find what your players can do best, and let them (or make them) do it. Don't worry about how it looks. Don't let a macho image of how you should be playing stand in the way of your winning. You don't have to be fancy or clever to win games; all you have to be is *effective*.

Offensive Philosophy

Early in his career, a coach should establish in his mind a general system of play that he feels is best, and then he should develop that particular system to its maximum strength. There are many systems of play, and all of them are good if they are based upon certain basic rules such as having motion and continuity within the offense, and providing floor balance and positioning for rebounds. The system of play should be simple, easy to teach, and easy for the players to understand.

The coach should make every effort to make his offensive system work before he considers making changes. It is perilous for a coach to watch another team play and to decide that its offense is better than the one he is running, and then make changes prematurely. He should investigate another offense thoroughly before switching styles or systems of play. Often, a slight omission, a small detail, or just a slight mistake by one of the players can make an offense function improperly. The coach should have a thorough knowledge of his system and should attempt to correct such mistakes before he considers changing his style of play. If he feels that he must make a change in his style of play in order to improve his team's performance, he should make sure he understands completely the new offense he is going into. Merely watching another team play or talking to another coach isn't enough. He should borrow and study game films. He should sit down and talk personally with the other coach. He should go over everything by himself and make sure he understands all the details involved in building the offense.

A team's offense should correspond to its defense. If it is playing an aggressive style of defense, it should play an aggressive style of offense. If it is playing a control game, it should play a cautious defense. Defense and offense are, or should be, interrelated. The coach should decide whether he wants his team to use a fast break, and if so, to what degree he intends to use it. He should take into consideration the kind of players he generally gets from the community he lives in and the school in which he coaches. In certain areas, and in certain schools, you tend to find a certain kind of player whose style of play identifies and is consistent with the way the game is played in that particular area. For instance, in the Ivy League, known for its high academic requirements, the players tend to possess less individual skills than some of the other major leagues throughout the nation. Most Ivy League offenses are based on team concepts involving the players' helping each other to get free, and their team patterns are generally complicated.

I think the same holds true to a certain extent in high schools. Kids usually learn to play the game the way they've seen it played, and as a result high schools generally get certain kinds of individuals. The coach should take such factors into account in selecting his offense, particularly if he has just moved into a new coaching position.

The coach can use the same basic offense year after year, making adjustments within the offense through better use of personnel. If he had an outstanding center, for example, he would want to build an offense in which the ball was directed toward the center position. If he had a tall center who was not very active, he would want to play him primarily in the low post area. If he had no big man and his front line was small, the coach might run his regular offense, but move his center to the high post or out to the side slightly, leaving the middle open for his driving and cutting game. If he had large guards, he might use the same offense, running his guards in to the low posts and using variations of this type of play.

I've always believed in getting the ball in to the post position. With the exception of our *early game* offense at UNLV, I've always stressed the importance of getting the ball inside to the post position. We've posted our forwards, and posted guards as well. This is, I feel, an often overlooked part of the game in which coaches sometimes fail to press their advantage. If you have a large guard being covered by a small man, your guard may be extremely effective operating from the post areas.

There are two schools of thought concerning the building of an offense in basketball. Some coaches operate their set offense with a large series of set plays involving all five men. Much of their practice time is spent learning the different plays and developing timing in execution. Other coaches, myself included, prefer an offense that revolves around plays involving one, two, three, four, *or* five men. The merit of this style of offense is that it lends itself well to the part method of instruction. Each part of the offense is broken down into individual drills, starting with one-on-one and progressing to two-on-two, three-on-three, four-on-four, and finally to five-on-five situations. The offense is built through the use of progressive drills, and as each small part is mastered, the coach may move on to the next part.

Defensive Philosophy

I have always believed that defense is the foundation and heart of the game of basketball. It is primarily through the medium of defense that a team manifests hustle and aggressiveness. We try to promote a positive defensive attitude among our players. We want them to feel that our kind of defense will win games for us. We want our players to take pride in their ability to accomplish our defensive objectives. Therefore, we strive to develop each player to become fundamentally sound, aggressive, challenging, and daring in his defense. I believe that, with modern day basketball, pressure man-to-man defense, if properly employed, can be the most effective defense used. It can force a pattern team out of its set style of play, and it can force individual players to shoot from beyond their normal shooting ranges.

Our defensive objectives are: (1) to prevent our opponents from playing the kind of game they want to play and (2) to maintain constant pressure on the opponents to force them into committing turnovers. The second objective helps us to obtain the first. In a sense, it implements the first objective, because by exerting pressure on our opponents, we force them to play a different kind of game than they had planned. Beyond this factor is, of course, the desire to capitalize on our opponents' mistakes. Pressure defense may be applied over the full court, three-quarter court, or half-court. It may even originate at the conventional defensive position at the top of the circle. However, we feel that pressure must be kept on the ball at all times, as well as on the man who is ready to receive the next pass.

We like to have our offense grow out of our defense. A good pressing defense can create quick transitions from defense to offense. Your defense can score many points for you. Because of the increasing use (as well as the potential) of pressing defenses, I feel it is important for a team to be a fast-breaking team. A fast-breaking team can handle pressing defenses far better than a ball-control team that does not fast break. A pressing defense will force you to play a running game, and you must be able to handle the ball while moving quickly to beat a pressing defense.

Fast-break basketball is also a favorite among the spectators. It is important to sell basketball in your community and among your students, and I think you can do this best by playing an exciting brand of basketball. A pressing defense and a running, fast-breaking team will be exciting and stimulating for the fans.

A strong defense builds confidence in a team. The team that takes pride in its defense and plays good, solid defense knows that on off-nights, or nights in which their shooting is not adequate, they will still be in the ballgame and have an excellent chance of winning. Psychologically, a strong defense places an immediate burden upon opponents, who may feel called upon for a special effort to combat the defense's solidarity. They will be cautious in their offensive attack, constantly on the alert for some kind of unexpected defensive strategy. All of this will limit their usual freedom in attacking—which is, of course, an advantage to the defensive team.

In addition to pressing defenses, zone defenses have grown in popularity across the nation in the last few years. The old theory that a zone defense can be beaten by a good outside-shooting team doesn't necessarily hold true. If a team is playing a zone defense aggressively and is following sound fundamental rules, it can eliminate the outside shot through hustle and hard work.

Important Coaching Methods

To be a successful coach, you must be a good teacher. You should follow the laws of learning and understand the learning process derived from, and involved with, explanation, demonstration, imitation, criticism, and repetition. Learning is a matter of forming habits, and the successful coach will attempt at every opportunity to instill good playing habits, as well as to correct bad habits, in his players. The outstanding player possesses more good playing habits (skills) than the average player, but the coach should be aware that, even without superstars, his team can be highly successful if his style of play minimizes his players' weaknesses and/or maximizes his opponents' weaknesses. The coach's goal, then, should be to help his players to master a given offensive and defensive system: the better his players are fundamentally, the better his system will operate. The system can maximize your strengths and minimize the effects of your weaknesses, for example, by not pressing full-court with tall, slow players while at the same time working the inside power game at your end of the court. When your system complements your players' strengths and minimizes their weaknesses, you will find that you have more practice time available for instilling good playing habits, and less practice time required for trying to teach the players your system of play.

If your system is right for the team, your players will learn it quickly. If they don't learn it quickly, well, as the sheriff says, "You're in a heap o' trouble, boy!" You want your players to learn the system quickly so they can concentrate on the game's action as it unfolds rather than stand around and wonder what they're supposed to do next. Also, if your players understand their system of play, you can increase skills development and practice your system at the same time. For example, in our moving game offense we start with one-on-one movements and options and work our way up from two-on-two play to five-on-five. We stress at each stage such important aspects of the system as court balance, clearing movements, cuts, screens, and the like, but at the same time we're working on individual and team skills, which takes us back to square one: we're trying to instill and improve good playing habits. If you choose your system carefully and then study the system from every conceivable angle, you can find a way to simplify it for your players and then break it down into a series of smaller (or shorter) segments that will improve basic skills as well as repeat the movements contained in the system of play.

I really think this is the best way to coach. I'm sold on it. Everything we do in our practices is related to basic skills, yet we've arranged them sequentially according to how they relate to our system of play. That's why our kids understand our system of play so well. Virtually all our practice time is spent working on individual and team skills that directly relate to our system of play. The following guidelines will help you to develop your players' understanding of your system of play.

1. Use lectures, photographs, movies, diagrams, mimeographed materials, charts, bulletin boards, rules discussions, team meetings, and the like, to supplement your daily practices. You never know what's going to reach a player until you try it. The broader your approach, the greater your chances of success.

2. Insist on punctuality and proper attire (whatever you consider it to be) for all team functions. The coach sets the example himself.

3. Do not permit any horseplay in practice. I believe that, other things being equal, players tend to do in games what they do in practice. One of the hardest things to teach players is to concentrate on what they're doing and on what's going on around them on the court at all times. Horseplay is definitely *not* conducive to concentration.

4. Insist on strict attention. Some coaches don't want their players, or even their assistant coaches, to talk during practice. Granted, it is

difficult to coach without talking, but anything that detracts from a player's concentration during practice should be eliminated.

5. Show patience. The formation of good playing habits takes time. Try not to expect too much too soon from unskilled players; however, two things you should always expect from your players are hustle and the willingness to learn.

6. Teach new skills and concepts early in your practice periods, then repeat them daily until they're learned.

7. Be careful to avoid harsh public criticism of your players. Use praise as well as censoring. Try to build your players' confidence.

8. Encourage teamwork and unselfishness at every opportunity. Many players have begun using a raised hand or waved fist to acknowledge a teammate's assist that led to an easy score. (We don't use this technique; even as the ball is going through the hoop, our players are already moving into position to full-court press, so we don't have time for such acknowledgment. Still, the idea is a good one for teams less involved in pressing immediately after scores.)

9. Do a lot of individual coaching.

10. Develop pride in your team. A team with pride is a tough team to beat. An individual or a team with pride will go beyond its normal limitations.

PERSONNEL

For purposes of discussion, let us describe a *tall* player as one who is capable, by virtue of his height alone (other things being equal), of covering the low-post position by himself on defense. (Admittedly, this makeshift categorization does not do justice to the medium-sized super leaper, but one cannot always have everything in neat receptacles. Coaches are advised to place such players into whatever categories their ability to deny the inside pass to the low post describes them.)

Using these tenuous guidelines we can construct six possible lineups: five tall players, four tall players and one small player, three tall players and two small players, two tall players and three small players, one tall player and four small players, and five small players.

Before analyzing the potential within each lineup, however, we should stress that each lineup has its particular strengths and weaknesses, depending to a great extent upon the athletic ability and basketball skills of the players involved. For example, although a starting lineup of five seven-footers would appear to give a team unbeatable advantages, such would not be the case unless at least one of the players was proficient enough at ball handling to beat the opponents' presses.

Five Tall Players

Although many teams have had five or more tall players on their squad at one time, few have ever dared to play a super-tall lineup for more than a few moments at a time. There are several reasons for this. First, tall players are likely to outweigh their smaller counterparts, since the phases of the game in which they excel—rebounding, blocking out under the boards, and so on—require great outlays of physical strength. Tall players are therefore unlikely to possess the added stamina to play a full-court running game as well. (One or two tall players on a given team might be able to in isolated cases, but finding five such players on one team is unheard of.)

Second, tall players are not as likely to possess the ball-handling skills or speed of smaller guards: being tall, their dribble will be higher unless they exaggerate their stance or lean forward, and either of these acts may tire them out. It is true that tall players are faster and quicker than they used to be, but, as in the previous case, tall players who guard smaller ball handlers usually will expend more energy moving around the perimeters of the court than will their diminutive counterparts. Exceptions exist, of course. No one in his right mind would insist that an Earvin Johnson, Julius Erving, or Rick Barry could not play guard as well as the position demands; however, we're talking about a regular team, *one* team, blessed with such height that both an Erving and a Barry could man the guard spots. It's possible, yes, but extremely unlikely. Shorter players generally are quicker and more agile than taller players.

Finally, tall players usually operate near the basket in junior high and high school since most schools at those levels of play cannot afford to waste their limited supply of height at the guard positions. As a result, the potentially outstanding 6′6″ player is often deprived of the chance to develop ball-handling skills during his formative years. (He may learn those skills on his own, of course, through playground ball, recreation leagues, and the like, but he is unlikely to develop them on his junior high or high school team.)

Thus we can see that the greatest hindrance to success in a lineup of five tall players usually involves ball handling and beating the presses. If your big men can handle the ball well enough to beat full-court pressure defense, you're a good bet to be highly successful. But if smaller teams attack your five tall players' ball-handling weaknesses like an onslaught of army ants, you might be better served by reducing the height of your lineup slightly to improve your ball handling. And if your big guards aren't as mobile and fundamentally sound as your opponents' guards, you might consider playing a zone defense, possibly a 1–3–1 half-court trapping defense, rather than wearing out your big guards in a man-to-man defense. The trapping alignment will force lob passes over or around the zone, and it will give your big men enough time to cover the pass receivers with each pass.

As a final thought, we suggest that, if your tall lineup is not extremely active and durable, you should forego playing a full-court pressing defense and drop back into the relative security of your half-court defense. A 94-foot game will sap your players' strength like water squeezed from a sponge, and besides, you don't need to harass the opponents into ball-handling mistakes at your end of the court if you're going to deny them good shots at their end of the court. Playing the percentages with big men means keeping them fresh and out of foul trouble on defense, and working the ball inside on offense where your height can wear the opponents down.

If your players are taller than their opponents, you don't have to run the opponents into the floor to beat them; all you have to do is wear them down with your inside game, stop their fast break and running game, and wait for them to beat themselves. It's not that easy, of course—there are no guarantees in this life except higher prices, raised taxes, and the fact that coaching is more difficult than you thought it was going to be when you started—but it's also true that the game of basketball belongs to the big men.

Four Tall Players and One Small Player

The key to the success of four-tall, one-small lineups is usually the small player's ball-handling ability. Depending on your big players' ability, of course, you *know* that your half-court defense won't hurt you because it will force opponents to shoot from the perimeters and thereby will increase the likelihood of your tall players' dominating the boards. Offensively, you can count on dominating your opponents inside most of the time, since few teams will have the personnel to match up with *four* big men. Thus, your success with such a lineup will often rely heavily upon the skills of the small ball-handling guard, who will key your team's efforts to beat the presses and control the ball on offense.

Few four-tall, one-small lineups fast break well consistently, and when they do, it's usually the result of court-length passes to the small guard breaking down court or running a fly pattern after steals on defensive rebounds. However, this maneuver has a drawback for the offensive team: if the long pass cannot be made, the team must get the ball down court without the services of the best ball handler. Inside screens, post interchanges—practically *any* offensive pattern based on working the ball inside and forcing one-on-one defensive matchups—will work with a four-tall, one-small lineup. A double-stack offense, for example, will permit your ball-handling guard to control the ball while the tall players maneuver into position for inside passes. More likely, however, opponents will play a zone defense against such lineups in order to force you to shoot from outside and to keep as many of their own players inside as possible. If your outside shooting is weak, you still may dominate the offensive boards, but you'll want to find zone offensive patterns to give you the best inside shot available. You may prefer having your point guard shoot from outside in order to allow the other four players to play volleyball with the rebounds until someone scores; however, when you have four tall players in the lineup, you should be aware that you can accomplish the same objective by working the ball inside for a high-percentage shot.

Defensively, you may or may not want to use a full-, three-quarter, or half-court press, depending on the speed and stamina of at least two of your tall players. (It usually takes at least three quick players to press effectively.) At any rate, your half-court defense should be effective enough with the presence of four tall players to allow you to take chances on defense. If you can play effective man-to-man defense for long periods of time without worrying about your players' tripping over their tongues in fatigue, then that's the defense you should teach them. If your players aren't fundamentally sound or experienced enough to play man-to-man defense, you still should be able to match up from a 1–3–1, 1–2–2, or 3–2 zone to cause your opponents no end of grief in working for an open shot. (You don't want to play an even-front zone with only one mobile outside defender.) You can trap from your zone alignment without unduly fatiguing your big men in the press. In certain cases you can even use a combination (diamond-and-one or box-and-one) zone defense, with your small guard harassing the opponents' best outside shooter.

Three Tall Players and Two Small Players

At this point, we reach the kinds of lineups a coach is more likely to have or to see on other teams. The three-tall, two-small lineup is considered ideal by many coaches, because it provides versatility in attacking opponents. With three tall players a team can be assured of having at least two rebounders near the basket when shots are taken, and the presence of two small players doubles the number of players involved initially in fast breaking over teams with one guard.

Most coaches prefer two-guard attacks. Opponents can trap one ball handler easily enough in pressing defenses, but the presence of a second guard who is capable of leading the fast break will force most opponents into more cautious tactics. The second guard usually provides greater overall team speed and defensive mobility, too, and he increases a team's ability to play a full-court press or a man-to-man defense.

With three tall players, a team can and should go inside offensively from their half-court offense. If even one of the big men can get down court quickly in transition, the team's fast break will assume awesome proportions. Such teams can be extremely versatile on offense and defense.

A three-tall, two-small lineup might play man-to-man defense, of course; however, it could also be expected to use a 2–3, 2–2–1, or 1–1–3 zone defense. A team may use a 1–3–1 or 1–2–2 zone defense with three tall players, too, but the 2–3, 2–2–1, and 1–1–3 zone alignments all keep the three big men inside with the ball at the point.

Two Tall Players and Three Small Players

In dissecting and analyzing lineups, it quickly becomes apparent that the less height a team possesses, the more difficulty it will encounter in controlling opponents. If you have two tall players in your lineup to the opponents' three, four, or five big men, it doesn't take a great deal of insight to realize that one or more of your small players will have to defend someone who is taller than he is. Quickness and playing aggressively help to reduce the disparity, of course, but equally important is your own—the coach's—role in preparing your players for such close encounters. In scouting an opponent, you will note their strengths and weaknesses both individually and as a team. Using your analysis of the opponents' skills, you will decide who each of your players will guard and how best to defend them. Assuming that you match up your two big men with the opponents' two best tall men, you will still have to decide which of your players will assume responsibility for the third big man and how that player can best be neutralized. Can he be kept away from the boards? Does he fight for inside position, or can he be pushed around at will? Can your small man keep the ball away from him inside? When he gets the ball, does he go to the basket, or does he maneuver for the short jumper or hook shot? Can he go either way with the ball equally well? Knowing the answers to questions such as these, an aggressive guard can often do a creditable defensive job on a taller opponent.

Two-tall, three-small lineups are often perfectly suited for a full-court pressing defense, fast breaking, and the transition game. The players' speed, quickness, and defensive ability, not their height or lack of it, will determine the success of the various pressing defenses. In like manner, transition basketball is nothing more than switching from defense to offense and getting the ball down court before your opponents can switch from offense to defense and get back down court to stop you. Although height often makes might in basketball, teams with only two tall players have three candidates for fast breaking. If the defense fails to get at least three of its players back to stop the fast break, the offensive team will have numerical superiority in its favor at the end of the break.

This is, in fact, the basis of all fast breaking: to set up easy, high-percentage shots before the defenders can get back to organize their defense and force the ball farther from the basket. (Other advantages of fast breaking were discussed in Chapter 1; more advantages are provided in Chapter 4.)

Describing offensive styles used by such teams is impossible because of the great variety of styles available. For example, a team may use a tandem post alignment inside, continuity patterns, or outside shooting—practically any pattern known. Offenses involving two or three small players can be extremely versatile in their approach to offensive basketball.

Defensively, many teams with two-tall, three-small lineups play man-to-man defense. As was explained previously, the chief difficulty encountered with man-to-man defense from three-guard lineups is that of covering the opponents' third (and possibly *fourth*) tall player. In zone defenses, the most obvious alignments with two tall players are the 1–2–2, 2–1–2 and 1–3–1 alignments, all of which keep the big men inside when the ball is at the point.

One Tall Player and Four Small Players

The natural tendency is to stress the importance of the small player when considering a lineup consisting of one small player and four tall players. In the case of the lineup with only one tall player, the importance is in no way diminished; in fact, it may well be heightened, since many coaches—and I put myself in this category—tend to panic when considering their chances of winning without at least one dominant big man in the post area. The key word is, of course, not *big man,* but *dominant:* if your big man controls opponents inside, you can run a one-man zone defense inside, with your four other players covering opponents outside man-to-man.

Unless the big man is a skilled defender and dominant rebounder, however, he and his teammates are facing a more than literal uphill struggle: in man-to-man coverage, he may be drawn outside to cover his man, or else the opponents may attack from the high post; in zone defense, the opponents' ball and player movement may accomplish the same objectives, and also reduce the big man's rebounding effectiveness. (The small weak-side players in zone defense will also have considerable difficulty rebounding against their taller opponents.)

The presence of one tall player in the lineup provides a team with an inside scoring threat; however, opponents with two or three tall players may limit the big man's effectiveness by constantly overguarding, fronting or siding him to deny him the ball, keeping the ball outside and forcing the team to shoot from the perimeters of the court.

Another problem associated with a one-tall, four-small lineup is the possibility of the tall player's getting into foul trouble. When the opponents have a decided height advantage, it is imperative that the advantage not be increased by your tall player's picking up fouls early in the contest. Thus, many coaches will use a 1–3–1, 2–3, or 2–1–2 zone defense to keep their big man inside, and drop teammates back to help out if necessary. (Zone defenses are often used to protect players in foul trouble, but they can keep players out of foul trouble as well.) Man-to-man defense will be most effective when the opponents have no more than one effective big man, but even then it is likely to fail if their big man (or men) can draw your tall player out from the basket by hitting perimeter shots from 10 to 15 feet out.

On the other hand, a one-tall, four-small lineup is conducive to the use of pressing defenses, especially when the opponents are tall and/or slow. An aggressive pressing defense and fast breaking can reduce opponents' height advantages and force them into playing a 94-foot racehorse game. When opponents are able to control your inside game defensively, you may find it imperative to play the transition game in order to mount any kind of offensive attack. At any rate, you want to avoid getting yourself into a situation in which you have to rely upon outside shooting to win games. You may have fine outside shooters on your team, but you will not win consistently with small players on the strength of outside shooting alone.

Offensive patterns featuring constant ball and player movement can also help to free your tall player or his teammates for high-percentage shots or one-on-one confrontations.

Five Small Players

I feel a special kinship for teams with no tall players. Partly because UCLA and a few other schools always seem to sign the nation's tallest high school players, and partly because of my particular recruiting philosophy, I don't seem to get as many big men as other coaches and schools. I try to get the best athletes I can find, regardless of their height, and most top-notch athletes, like the general nonathletic population, aren't 6′11″ or taller!

Having five small players in the lineup is a situation that invariably greets coaches who move into new positions; after all, the coach who was at the school previously didn't leave because he was embarrassed to coach a team with that much talent! And if your five dwarves aren't quick, aggressive, and highly skilled, you may be in for the longest siege since Hitler decided to let his troops enjoy a winter vacation in Russia in 1942. (If your players are short, slow, and/or unskilled, but aggressive enough to at least scratch when they itch, you are referred to Chapter 12, "A Basic Winning System for Young or Unskilled Players." It was written especially for you.)

If your players are experienced, fairly quick, and range in size somewhere between 5′10″ and 6′6″ you don't have to roll over and play dead for your opponents. You should be aware that you have options available which, although they may not be as desirable as those available to teams with three or four tall players, can help your team to control larger opponents. Reconcile yourself to this fact, though: if your team is small, you're going to have to do a better coaching job than your rivals in order to give your team a fighting chance against taller opponents. You may have to adapt or discard many of your previous notions about how the game should be played, but by working hard to blend your players' skills into a workable system of play, you'll become a better coach. Coaching small players will teach you the meaning of "extracting a quart from a pint jar." In some ways it's a humbling process, but it can also be eminently satisfying, particularly when you can acknowledge that your own role in the team's success was considerable. We've all seen teams that were so top-heavy with talent that the coach's main decisions involved which five players to play on the court at one time. With small players, however, you know that you'd better be ready to do the coaching job of your life!

With five small players, you'll have to use a pressing defense of some kind. You probably won't be able to stop the opponents' inside game, and if you let them bring the ball down court without opposition, they'll beat your brains out with lob passes to the low post or cutters into the lane. And because you aren't likely to get many offensive rebounds, your offensive strategy must be based on constant ball and player movement and on high-percentage shots. (For present purposes, we're discussing the traditional approaches to styles of play involving small players.)

Defensively, man-to-man coverage with five small players is likely to work only when it is played aggressively, as described in Chapter 8. Forms of man-to-man defense other than pressure man-to-man—for example, sinking or switching—simply will not work with five small players. Trapping from a man-to-man or zone defense is extremely risky, too, since small players cannot readily deny passes after the ball handler picks up his dribble.

Using zone defense may be the only alternative left for some teams with extremely small personnel. If you can't keep the ball away from the low post by matching up or single-guarding, double-team at the low post. If you have to double-team, decide which outside shot you'd prefer to give up, or which player you'd rather give the shot to. If you match up, make sure you have your players in position to take advantage of the matchups, and not the reverse. You don't want to defend one on one against taller opponents unless the matchups favor *your* players. Finally, keep the ball away from the high post. You may have to double-team when the high post man has the ball, and thus make your defense vulnerable to backdoor cuts and layups. It's easier to deny the pass entirely than to guard the big man after he's received the ball at the high post.

The two most dangerous zone defenses for small teams are the 1–3–1 and 2–2–1. Both are considered high-risk defenses for small players because it is easy for opponents to work the ball to the baseline or low post against such alignments. Other defenses, such as the 1–2–2, may keep as many as four defensive players inside at all times. The reader is referred to Chapters 3, 9, 10, 12, and 14 for deeper insights into the workings of the various zone defensive alignments and strategies.

PATTERNS

The best that can be said about patterns at this point is that the best patterns are those your players can run. No matter how clever or good-looking your patterns seem on paper, they are as useless as 4′6″ pivotmen if your players can't make them work on the court. Patterns derive their value from the way teams are able to use them. Some coaches would have you believe that universal offenses exist, but don't count on it. The "passing game," for example, is basically an all-purpose, freelance offense featuring minimal dribbling and a maximum of passing opportunities, particularly off inside screens and post interchanges. However, if your players aren't highly skilled, you're going to find them doing a lot of standing around instead of making the smooth, coordinated cuts that some teams do so well.

Not every team has to look smooth to be effective, though. Your best bet is to find out what your players can do, and let them do it as much as possible. If it works for your team, it's a good pattern for you to run. If it doesn't work, forget it, no matter how dear to your heart it may be.

Patterns should provide opportunities for the offensive team to work the ball inside. Working for outside shots alone without attempting to go inside is almost always low-percentage basketball. (We may *take* the outside shot at UNLV, but we're always looking for the opportunity to go inside. There's a world of difference between that and working exclusively for the inside shot the way we did when I was at Long Beach State.) Even when a team has no authentic inside attack, outside shooting by itself is hardly the answer. The threat of an inside attack is necessary, especially against zone defenses, if for no other reason than to deter the opponents from moving outside and taking the perimeters away as well, leaving the offense with nowhere to go, and nothing to do when they get there.

CONCLUSION

A coach should select an offensive and a defensive system early in his career, and stay with them until a time for changes is clearly indicated. Before he installs his systems he should have studied their theory and application as thoroughly as possible. He should be prepared to make adjustments and add variations as needed, but he should be very careful about making radical changes. If he feels that his system is not accomplishing the goals he has set, he should study new offenses and/or defenses from every angle before adopting them. One of the greatest mistakes a coach can make is to have a middle-of-the-road philosophy, or a philosophy in which the coach does not have complete confidence in his system and is constantly changing his team's style of play, thinking that a new formation will provide the solution to his problems. There are no secrets in basketball. It is not *what* you do, but *how* you do it that determines its effectiveness. Many times the mastery of small details determines the success or failure of a given offense.

The offenses and defenses should be kept as simple as possible. Many times a team will never reach the peaks it is capable of reaching because it uses too complicated a system of play. It is far better to have an offense with only a few plays or variations than one that players fail to learn properly. An offense with just a few options, or a few things to be done properly, can be very successful. It is important that every player understands his assignments and does them instinctively. This can be done better with an offense that is kept simple, rather than one that is practiced through repetitive drills.

NLV
NLV

3

Zone vs. Man-to-Man Defense

Defensive basketball is divided into two broad, general categories: *man-to-man defense* and *zone defense*. The distinctions between the two are not as sharply defined as they once were, due to the emergence in recent years of combination defenses, zone defenses played like man-to-man defenses, and man-to-man defenses played like zone defenses.

The lines separating zone and man-to-man defense are not always clear, but they exist. In man-to-man defense, each defensive player guards a particular offensive player wherever he goes. Defenders may have to switch responsibilities periodically, but after switching they maintain one-on-one coverage as before. In zone defense, on the other hand, defensive players set up in specific positions and defend areas of the court rather than covering specific players. The defensive player will cover a certain area of the court, or *zone,* guarding any offensive player who enters his zone of responsibility, but he will not leave his zone to cover a player's cut to another area of the court.

MISCONCEPTIONS CONCERNING ZONE AND MAN-TO-MAN DEFENSE

Countless variations of the original concept of zone and man-to-man defense have arisen over the years. As a result, many of the notions concerning zone defense have become confused.

1. **Zone defense is easier to teach (or to play) than man-to-man defense.** The basic movements of zone defense with different ball positions are quickly and easily learned. As will be shown, each player learns where to play with the ball at five to seven different outside court posi-

tions.* Still, the defensive techniques used to cover the ball handler and other offensive players are the same in zone and man-to-man defense. Ultimately, every zone defense eventually involves man-to-man coverage.

2. Man-to-man defense is better than zone defense. All good teams use man-to-man defense. Zone defense is lazy defense. There are seeds of truth in all of the previous statements. Man-to-man defense can be better than zone defense; *most* good teams use man-to-man defense at least occasionally; and zone defense *can* be used to play lazy defense.

The deciding factors, though, are the players' defensive ability, team needs, and the attitude of the players toward their defensive responsibilities. Man-to-man defense is unquestionably the best defense in basketball—if your players are defensively sound and aggressive and if your team plays man-to-man defense better than zone defense. For one reason or another, many teams are better defensively when they're playing zone defense. If your team stays with man-to-man defense when its use is clearly contraindicated, you're liable to get your brains beaten out of you—but you'll retain the *macho* image, for what it's worth, that goes along with playing man-to-man defense.

Not all good teams use man-to-man defense. It might be true, though, to say that all good teams use man-to-man defense at least occasionally, if for no other reason than to give the opponents something new to think about, or as a change of pace from zone coverage.

Any defense can be played lazily. True, zone defense provides more opportunities for lax coverage without losing defensive control completely, but zone defenses do not have to be played that way. Aggressive forms of zone defense such as trapping or help-and-recover defense require at least as much effort as man-to-man defense. Even basic zone defense should not be played lazily.

3. There's only one way to play man-to-man defense. I've known coaches who, when scouting an opponent, would write down in their notes that "they played man-to-man defense" and leave it at that, as if there were nothing more to be considered. Actually there are at least *five* different styles of man-to-man defense, and countless variations of these five styles. The five styles are: pressure man-to-man, switching man-to-man, sinking man-to-man, trapping man-to-man, and run-and-jump defense.

Pressure Man-to-Man Defense. At UNLV, we play an extremely aggressive brand of pressure man-to-man defense, with sinking, switch-

* These positions are: the two baseline corners, the two *wings* (near the sidelines, approximately even with the free-throw line extended), and the *point* (the area around the top of the circle). Some coaches consider the two *intermediate wing* positions (located between the wings and the point) to be part of the point area.

ing (especially jump switching), and trapping used as necessary to keep constant, intense, defensive pressure on the opponents. We harass the ball handler, front inside, and overplay all passing lanes to receivers who are one pass away from the ball. Our goal is to force the ball toward the sideline, contain the ball handler, and leave him with no one to pass to. We go after the passing lanes so fiercely that practically the only pass we give up is the backdoor cut and pass that gives the opponents a layup. We must give up more layups than any team in the nation, but we *don't* give up the outside passes that let our opponents stand around on offense. They may get more than their share of layups against us, but not without working for them.

Many teams using pressure man-to-man defense will employ semizone coverage inside when they're cutting off the passing lanes or harassing the ball handler outside.

Sinking Man-to-Man Defense. In sinking, or *sagging,* man-to-man defense, one or more defenders away from the ball drop off their men to provide added coverage inside. Sinking defense, then, employs many of the concepts of zone defense. While the ball handler and primary pass receivers may be covered as in pressure defense, one or more defenders who are two or three passes away from the ball will drop off to help cover any inside cuts or movements.

Switching Man-to-Man Defense. In pressure defense, defensive players generally attempt to "fight through" screens and picks set by the offensive team, rather than sliding behind the screens or switching defensive assignments. (We are not saying, however, that switching is necessarily less aggressive than going over the top of screens. In at least one type of switching—jump switching—the switches can be extremely aggressive.) In switching man-to-man defense, all switches are made automatically when screens are set, as in zone defensive coverage. Whereas other forms of man-to-man defense require that either the player being screened or the player making the switch call the maneuver aloud, no verbal command or signal is necessary in switching man-to-man defense. The players involved will switch regardless of whether it's called or not.

Trapping Man-to-Man Defense. Zone coverage is generally more conducive to leading players into trapping situations than man-to-man coverage; thus, trapping is rarely seen from man-to-man defense. When it is used, trapping from man-to-man coverage usually occurs in conjunction with screens set by the offense: instead of fighting through the screens or switching, both defenders involved in covering the screen leap out and trap the ball handler, relying on the element of surprise to stun the ball handler into fumbling the ball away, making a bad pass, or otherwise turning the ball over to the defensive team.

Run-and-Jump Defense. Run-and-jump defense is the newest and most popular style of man-to-man defense in use today. It is so radically different that one is tempted at first to dismiss run-and-jump as a fad like

Hula Hoops and Mohawk haircuts. Yet its underlying theory is both innovative and imaginative. Run-and-jump defense is as valid a form of man-to-man defense as pressure, sinking, switching, or trapping.

Basically, run-and-jump defense is a form of man-to-man coverage similar to that seen in trapping zone defense, but instead of trapping the ball handler, the defenders switch at the last second. A ball handler is overplayed toward the sideline and apparently permitted to drive the baseline, for example. Away from the ball, a defender sags away from his man and moves quickly into position to trap the dribbler (or draw a charging foul if he is driving). The player originally guarding the ball handler will continue on and away from the dribbler to pick up the open player on weak side.

Run-and-jump defense is an advanced, aggressive form of defense requiring alert, intelligent personnel. When a team is superior defensively, however, run-and-jump coverage can be as effective as any form of man-to-man defense, especially since the techniques involved in its execution are so alien to most other forms of man-to-man coverage.

4. All zone defenses are alike. On the most basic level, that of merely putting five players out on the court in a zone defensive alignment with no thought of their controlling the offensive team or influencing ball or player movement, it is probably true that all zone defenses are more or less identical. However, when one digs slightly deeper into the theory underlying zone defenses and their usage, one finds a broad array of defensive goals to suit practically every situation that can arise in basketball.

One point that will be repeated constantly in this book concerning zone defenses is that, when the ball is clearly established on one side of the court or the other, all zone defenses are alike—at least, they are identical in the areas to be covered. Even then, however, a team may select any of several different methods of covering the ball, ball-side corner, ball-side low post, ball-side high post, point, weak-side high post and weak-side low post.

When the ball is established on one side of the court, the basic zone alignment is of little or no consequence. Many years ago zone defenses retained their basic shape regardless of the position of the ball. Nowadays, though, advanced maneuvers such as trapping, matching up, and help-and-recover and combination defenses have put an end to such simplistic notions as the one that *all zone defenses are alike.*

5. If you know what defense your opponents use, you don't have to scout them. The patent absurdity of this contention apparently is not as obvious as it ought to be. Some coaches profess not to believe in scouting at all, while others confine their efforts to telephone calls to coaches whose teams have played a certain opponent:

"What kind of defense do they run, Coach?"

"They ran a 1–2–2 zone against us."

"Okay, what do they do on offense?"

A more logical sequence of questions might be, "How do they run their 1–2–2? Do they match up? Do they trap? If so, where do the traps occur? How many people do they keep back on the weak side? Do they double-team the low post on the ball side? Do they cover the high post, too?"

STRENGTHS OF ZONE DEFENSE

1. The defensive players' court positions with various ball and player movements are easily learned. It takes much less time to teach the basic movements of a given zone defense than man-to-man. Where a team may devote 50 percent of its practice time to learning man-to-man coverage, zone coverage will take only about 30 percent. This is not to say that the skills required to cover players from various court positions are easily mastered—they aren't—but the movements to those positions are easily memorized, even by less advanced players.

2. Zone defense may be used with players at any level of skill and experience. Zone defense is likely to be the *only* effective form of defensive coverage with grossly unskilled players and teams.

3. Most forms of zone coverage tend to keep tall defensive players inside or near the basket. This in turn tends to limit the effectiveness of opponents' tall players, as well as forcing (or keeping) the ball outside and improving defensive rebounding. The continuing presence of a tall man inside on defense provides added protection for the low post position.

4. Players can be aggressive in their outside coverage in certain forms of zone defense. If, for example, the outside defenders play the passing lanes or double-team the ball handler, they will have help inside if their men beat them. If an offensive player gets by his defender, he still must deal with the rest of the zone defense. Zone coverage tends to reduce driving and penetrating off the dribble, although exceptions to this rule may be found in isolated cases.

5. Zone defense is strong against weak outside shooting.

6. Zone defense can be used to keep players out of foul trouble or to protect players in foul trouble. While fouls are always possible when one player guards another, much of the time a team spends in zone defense involves players' defending positions on the court, not guarding specific players. Zone defense may be used to hide a player who is weak defensively. Certain positions in zone defense require little or no skill on the part of the participant to provide adequate coverage. An example of such coverage is the point guard in a 1–2–2 or 1–3–1 basic zone coverage who guards the ball handler in the vicinity of the top of the circle and then slides to the ball-side high post with the pass to the wing.

At any rate, zone defense allows a coach to play his personnel where he wants them and not where offensive movement dictates, as is the case with man-to-man defense. Adjustments are easier to make from zone defense than from man-to-man.

8. Zone defense can slow down the tempo of a fast-breaking team. By keeping the ball outside and giving up only low-percentage shots from the court's perimeters, teams using zone defense can force fast-breaking opponents into a ball-control-oriented offense when they would prefer to use a "run-and-gun" style of attack. It takes longer to get a shot against a zone defense than it does against a man-to-man.

Still, the zone coverage will be ineffectual if the opponents' fast break moves the ball down court and into shooting position before the defenders can get back and set up in their zone defense.

9. Zone defense tends to keep players in position to fast break when transition occurs, whether by steals, turnovers, or defensive rebounds.

10. Zone defense is excellent for use against offenses that feature screening or cutting patterns. In one sense, zone defense is a kind of man-to-man defense in which switching is automatic. Any time offensive players screen or cut, defenders in zone coverage will alter or switch their defensive assignments automatically. The prevalence of continuity or freelance motion offenses in basketball today has brought about an increase in the use of zone defenses.

WEAKNESSES OF ZONE DEFENSE

1. Openings always exist somewhere in zone defense. Whether the offensive team possesses the necessary skills to attack and exploit the weaknesses of a given style of zone coverage is another question, but the openings always exist. Most zone defenses are particularly weak along the *seams* of the zones, or the gaps between defenders where their responsibilities overlap. Thus, the offensive team is likely to set its players along, or cut them into, those seams as a means of attacking the zone coverage.

If the defensive team has no weaknesses, or if its opponents have no offensive strengths capable of controlling the defense, it probably would be in man-to-man rather than zone coverage.

2. Zone defense can be used to allow players to rest. Although many fundamentally sound, hustling players may prefer zone defense for one reason or another, *all* unaggressive players like zone defense. Players who would rather stand up on defense than assume a wide-base, low defensive stance, or walk as opposed to sliding, will always find security in zone coverage. Zone defense is most effective when played aggressively.

Even with players who work hard on defense, constant ball rotation from one side of the court to the other around the outside perimeter of the defense can lull the hardiest of defenders into relaxed, automatic movements and responses which may catch one or more defensive players out of position when the offensive team attempts to penetrate the zone.

3. Tall, slow players may find openings in zone coverage with relatively little work on their part. If the offensive team has big players who are too unskilled or too passive to work themselves free against an aggressive man-to-man defense, these players may find it easier to get open against the zone, especially when cutters and/or ball rotation temporarily confuse the defenders.

4. Zone defenses generally are weak against good outside shooting. Most zone defenses are designed to bolster a team's inside coverage, not to protect against outside shooting proficiency.

It is difficult to defend from zone coverage against a team with a strong inside and outside game.

5. The "automatic switching" aspect of zone defenses can create mismatches that favor the offense. Overloads can also provide mismatches favoring the offensive team.

6. Zone defense is impractical when a team is behind in the latter stages of a game. In such cases, the only kinds of zone defense that are likely to have any effect on the offensive team's ability to hold the ball are the most aggressive zone coverages, especially trapping.

Most coaches prefer man-to-man defense in such situations. Zone defense generally is not conducive to catch-up tactics and strategy.

7. Generally it is easier for a team to switch from man-to-man to zone defense than the reverse. If forced out of a zone defense, it is difficult to play good man-to-man defense.

II

Controlling Opponents Offensively

It is vain to look for a defense against lightning.

Publilius Syrus

Maxim 835

4

Runnin' Like the Rebels

1975–76 Runnin' Rebels (29–2)

UNLV 96	Oregon State 85
UNLV 118	Colorado 88
UNLV 105	Syracuse 83
UNLV 86	Duquesne 83
UNLV 98	Arizona 94
UNLV 122	South Alabama 82
UNLV 129	California (Irvine) 57
UNLV 116	Old Dominion 90
UNLV 101	Santa Barbara 83
UNLV 107	Utah 90
UNLV 116	Houston 92
UNLV 108	Michigan 94
UNLV 100	Pan American 95
UNLV 111	Cal State Northridge 72
UNLV 90	Seattle 89
UNLV 88	Iowa State 82
UNLV 129	Portland State 114
UNLV 80	New Mexico 73
UNLV 120	Nevada-Reno 98
UNLV 125	Nevada-Reno 91
UNLV 139	Northern Arizona 101
UNLV 107	Seattle 77
UNLV 118	Pepperdine 101
UNLV 91	Pepperdine 93
UNLV 122	Centenary 92
UNLV 164	Hawaii (Hilo) 111
UNLV 114	Hawaii 99
UNLV 124	St. Mary's 86
UNLV 90	Loyola Marymount 69
UNLV 103	Boise State 78
UNLV 109	Arizona 114 (Overtime)

UNLV PPG: 110.5
Opp. PPG: 88.9

EXCERPTS FROM A SCOUTING REPORT ON UNLV

• UNLV is a very good, talented team. It will take a good effort to beat them. They are big, strong, and very quick. They have balanced scoring and work very hard defensively. They play best in a *run-and-shoot* game.

• Their defense is very aggressive and physical. They overplay, hold, body check, take the charge, and are constantly gambling and diving for the ball.

• Nevada is a great perimeter shooting team.

• Transition from defense to offense is super. You must get back quickly.

• Their offensive rebounding is excellent—they send four men to the board.

• They use full-court man-to-man pressure defense. They leave the man taking the ball out of bounds alone, attempting to double-team the player receiving the in-bounds pass.

• They are very quick and physical on defense. Always looking to steal the dribble.

• I would suggest you prepare for UNLV's defense by permitting your players to hold, tag, body check, overplay, and dive for the ball in your practice sessions.

• You must control the tempo of the game against them. Be selective with your choice of shots. You are likely to get only one shot, and then they're running down your throat again.

THE FAST BREAK

I have for many years believed very strongly in fast breaking, although my attitude toward its execution has changed in recent years. I think it is, or should be, an important part of every team's offensive attack. Teams that do not fast break are giving up the chance of getting easy baskets. The fast break can give you a balanced attack.

Teams that do not fast break also can be easily pressed. A good pressing team will eventually force its opponents into running, and if the opponents are not accustomed to running—if the fast break is not part of their game—they will likely be forced to play a style of ball which they are unaccustomed to playing, with a resulting reduction in their offense's overall effectiveness on those nights.

Thus, I feel that the fast break is a very important part of your offensive arsenal. A very good fast-breaking team will create a lot of problems for pressing defenses, and the way pressing defenses have spread throughout the country in recent years, teams need every advantage they can get in combatting the effectiveness of the presses.

Advantages of Fast Breaking

1. Many teams are unable to stop it.

2. Failure to fast break could give the opponents an edge in rebounding. We rebound four men offensively against ball-control teams because we don't have to retreat so quickly. When I was at Pasadena City College, there was one club in our league that refused to fast break under any circumstances, so when we played them we would send all five men to the offensive boards for rebounds.

Additionally, teams that do not fast break give your team a chance to tie up the rebound. When they get a rebound, you can immediately clamp the rebounder with two men, since you don't have to worry about their getting the ball out fast and gaining an advantage on you at the other end of the court.

3. The fast break can be a team's knockout punch. Close games can be broken open in a matter of seconds. Fast breaking is both a vitalizing agent for the fast-breaking team and a demoralizing agent for opponents. The fast break is a team's best weapon against a pressing defense, and it is also extremely effective against zone defenses. No matter how tightly an opponent plays its zone defense, fast breaking can confuse the defensive coverage as well as spread it out over the entire length of the court.

4. Fast breaking provides a means of catching up quickly when behind. A ball-control team must be content to whittle away at opponents' leads, and sometimes the offensive team can play the clock in such situations. The fast-breaking team can make up big deficits in a hurry. It is an excellent method for getting cheap baskets.

5. Fast breaking is a spectator's game. It provides action, speed, and daring plays, and the increased scoring certainly lends added thrills to games.

6. Fast breaking is a player's game. It gives opportunists a chance to operate. Some players are just too good to hold back, and a fast-breaking style of play gives them the opportunity to move quickly, handle the ball, and exploit individual skills that they might not get to use in a ball-control offense. Fast-breaking offenses permit more freedom and use of individual initiative and natural talents.

Fast breaking is fun to play. It certainly helps your recruiting. The first thing many high school prospects want to know is, "Will the team run with the ball, or will they hold the ball and work for good shots?" Players prefer the running, fast-breaking game, and I think that teams that basically play control basketball have a harder time recruiting than those that fast break.

Disadvantages of Fast Breaking

1. The high-speed ball handling involved in fast breaking may increase turnovers, floor mistakes, and the likelihood of committing charging fouls. (Although the last point normally is a minor concern, the coach will weigh the advantages of fast breaking against this kind of disadvantage in deciding whether, and to what extent, he wants his team to fast break.)

2. Fast breaking can sometimes upset the tempo of pattern-oriented teams, particularly when playing against opponents with superior fast-breaking attacks. Generally, coaches prefer to avoid getting into running games when the opponents are better at it than they are.

3. You need at least one competent ball handler to fast break effectively. On the other hand, you'll need at least one good ball handler to do *anything* effectively on offense, so this argument is specious at best.

4. Players have to *want* to fast break for the technique to be effective more often than occasionally. If a team is basing a high percentage of its offensive attack on the transition game, the players will have to be willing to play hard-nosed, aggressive defense to create the turnovers, and then work hard to fill the passing lanes before the opponents can adjust to the transition. In this sense, at least, fast breaking is a state of mind as well as a style of play.

It is important to know when to fast break. The fast break can be a tremendously effective way of getting cheap baskets, but it must be an organized, planned break. Players must recognize when the fast break exists and when to call it off.

> **Note:** As will be shown, at UNLV we don't "call off" our fast break when the defense adjusts quickly and we no longer have the advantage; instead, we go into our early game offense designed to set up a scoring opportunity quickly regardless of the opponents' court positions. Still, teams that use controlled fast breaking* will insist that, when the opponents are able to get back and stop the initial thrust of the fast break, the offensive team should call off the break, set up, and move into its half-court offensive pattern as smoothly and quickly as possible. Without becoming embroiled in controversy over differing styles of fast breaking, the best I can say is that our system works best for us.

If you have a good, sound offensive system and your team is able to capitalize on the advantages that the fast break provides, you will have

*Controlled fast breaking refers to fast-breaking systems in which teams attempt to fast break without unduly risking loss of the ball, particularly when no offensive numerical superiority exists at the end of the break. The term *controlled fast breaking* does not imply that other systems of fast breaking are uncontrolled.

an advantage over your opponent. With today's intricate defenses and presses staring you in the face every time your players take the court, you probably need every advantage you can get!

Our kids are proud of the reputation they've earned as a running, high-scoring team. Everywhere I go, coaches want to know all about our fast break and half-court offense. I tell them, "Our offense is our defense. Our offense is our transition/fast-breaking game." Many of them don't seem to hear me. They seem to think that we run our fast break different from other teams, or that I've found a way to manipulate the Os and Xs to produce 100+ point games.

Actually, though, we spend very little time working on half-court offense. Out of a two-and-a-half-hour daily practice, we spend no more than ten to fifteen minutes working on offense, with that time spent working on our bring-in plays and inbounding the ball after scores. Our offense is our transition game. We spend the bulk of our practice time working on defense, transition, fast breaking, and conditioning.

Our offense starts with the inbounds pass after an opponent scores. We want to get the ball down court within four seconds after the ball goes through the net. We aren't afraid to throw the court-length pass if the opponents are slow getting back on defense; we'll throw it either from out of bounds or after the first pass is caught.

We like to designate one person to recover the ball and make the inbounds pass every time after an opponent scores. It's a difficult, thankless task requiring a special kind of person. He must be able to make the court-length pass quickly and accurately, but he must also be an unselfish player: in our scheme of play, we may shoot at the other end of the court before the inbounds passer even reaches our half-court. We have trouble finding a kid who is really enthusiastic about being our inbounds passer, but he's the most important link in our fast-breaking attack. Whenever we've had trouble finding a good inbounds passer (or keeping him healthy), we've had trouble with that entire aspect of our offense. I had a player named Jackie Robinson who inbounded the ball for us a few years ago, and he broke his ankle a week before our first game. I spent the whole time he was out of the lineup making changes, trying to find a combination that didn't slow our attack in one way or another. One player would be too slow getting out of bounds with the ball, another couldn't make the long pass, and every time I'd make another change it would slow us down.

We lane our fast break (that is, we assign specific lanes to specific players) and designate our ball handlers. We expect our players to fill their lanes (and nobody else's) regardless of where they are when transition occurs. This slows us down slightly in some instances, but we feel that the constant repetition of the pattern pays dividends in the long run because our players become familiar with the fast-break pattern. Laning the fast break eliminates confusion in the players' minds concerning their responsibilities after transition has occurred. We want our fast breaks to be strictly patterned, at least during the formative stage. After opponents'

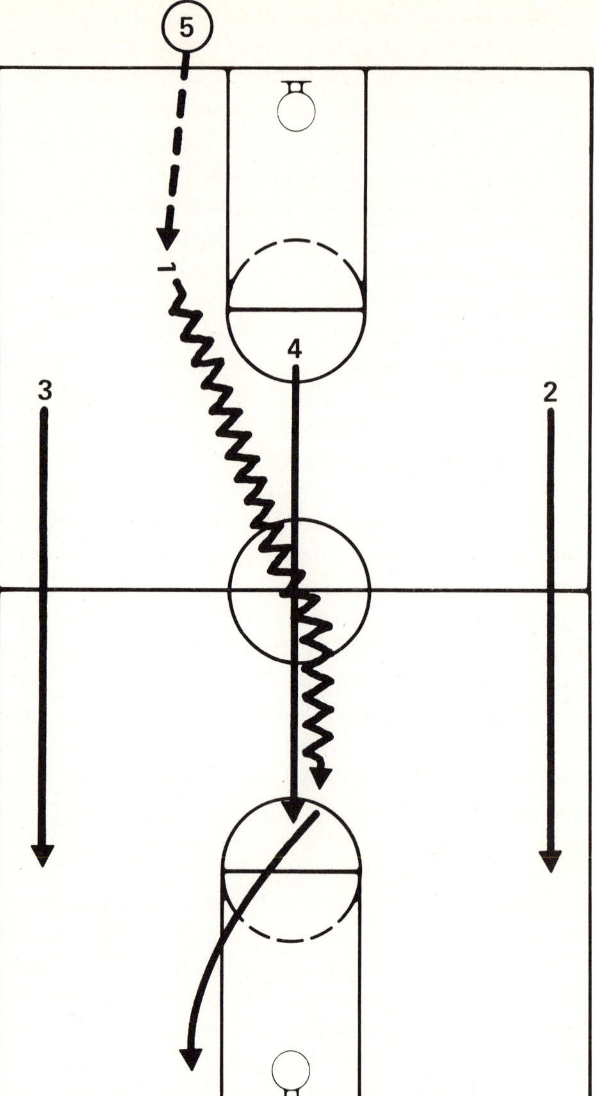

Figure 4–1 UNLV Fast Break After Scores

scores, for example, we want the *same* player (05 in Figure 4–1) stepping out of bounds with the ball to make the inbounds pass every time, the *same* player (04) streaking down the middle anticipating the breakaway pass, the *same* two players (02 and 03) filling the same sideline passing lanes, and the same player (01) acting as primary ball handler nearest the basket.

We aren't so inflexible in our attack as to expect 05 to pass to 01 every time; in fact, we'd prefer that he throw the court-length pass whenever 04 is open. 05 will pass inbounds to either 04 or 01, but not to 02 or 03 along the sidelines. We don't want 05 to throw the ball out of bounds while trying to hit 02 or 03 breaking down the sidelines.

This, then, is our fast break after scores: as soon as 01 catches 05's pass, he will turn and look for 02 or 03 along the sidelines. (04 usually will be covered by this time, since most opponents retreat down court in the middle of the court rather than along the sideline passing lanes.) If either 02 or 03 is open, 01 may throw a lead pass to him. If neither man is open, 01 will take the ball down as fast and as far as he can. In the early season, 02 and 03 will be open most of the time, particularly when the opponents try to press us by putting pressure on 01; however, as the season progresses, we'll find opponents covering 02 and 03 to slow down our attack. In this case, 01 will race down court with the ball, taking advantage of the wide coverage to attack the middle.

If 01 passes to 02 or 03 along the sideline, we do not have that player bring the ball back to the middle. Instead, the player (#50 in Figure 4–2) continues down the sideline, looking for an open shot from the wing or for a pass inside. The point guard will cut through the middle, looking for a return pass from the wing. If he doesn't get it, he continues through the lane to the weak-side low post. If the wing still hasn't taken a shot or passed the ball away, he looks for the trailer coming; however, we want the wing to shoot whenever he's open.

In like manner, when the wings are covered, the ball handler will take the ball down as fast as he can, looking for the opportunity to penetrate or take the shot from the top of the circle. If the ball handler is covered, he will pass to the wings and continue to the weak-side low post.

Figure 4–2 Fast Breaking After the Pass to the Wing

The wing will shoot if he is open or pass back to the ball handler cutting into the lane if the defense fails to cover his cut. If the low post is open, the wing will pass inside.

If the wing passes inside, the trailer will cut to the weak-side low post to rebound, and the point guard and weak-side wing will rotate as shown in Figure 4–3.

If, as is more likely, the wing does not pass inside, we'll reverse the ball by passing back to the trailer out front. (See Figure 4–4.)

Figure 4–3 Passing to the Low Post Inside

Figure 4–4 Passing to the Trailer

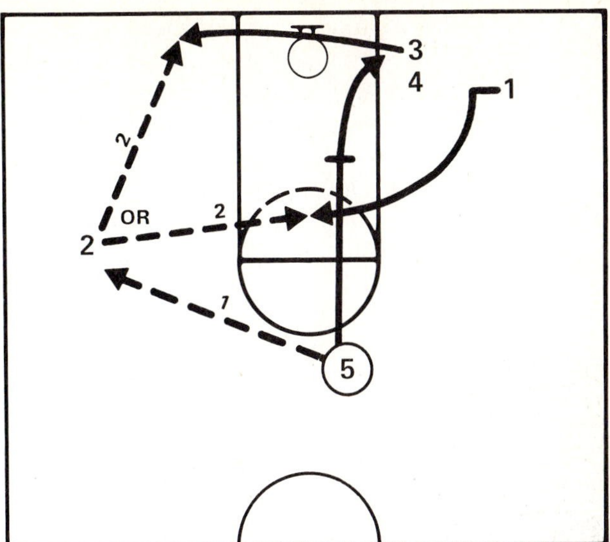

Figure 4–5 Rotation Continued, 05 Passing to 02

When the wing passes to the trailer, the point guard will start a shuffle cut around an inside double screen (Figure 4–5). The wing can set his screen low, as shown in the figure, or high. His screen is only momentary. If he sets the high screen, he should look for a pass from the trailer as he cuts into and across the lane.

> **Note:** When the wing passes to the trailer, the point guard will cut as shown in Figure 4–5, but not necessarily behind a *double* screen: instead of setting the double screen inside with the low post, the wing may cut around the low post into the lane and continue to the weak-side low post.

We tell the trailer that when he receives the pass at the top of the circle he will have no more than half a second to start his drive, or the wing will bring his man into the lane. We don't want the trailer (or anybody else, for that matter) holding the ball.

If the trailer does not shoot or pass to the point guard cutting around the screen, he will relay the ball to the weak side (Figure 4–5). The wing will continue across the lane, and the trailer will set a double screen inside with the low post for the point guard to cut into the lane in the vicinity of the high post. In almost every case, we would have taken the shot by now, since we've already had three passes and at least eight options.

At the conclusion of the movements shown in Figure 4–5, 02 had the ball at the wing with the option of passing to 03 at the low post or 01 at the free-throw line. Pattern continuity arises when 02 passes to 01. (See Figure 4–6.)

As the wing attempts to penetrate the middle one on one, the inside players move to the corners to give him more room to maneuver in. If he is stopped, he will pass outside and circle outside away from the ball. The receiver will then try to drive the middle. If he is also unsuccessful in penetrating, he'll pass and cut away from the ball, with the pattern continuing until someone takes a shot. However, we never reach this point; somebody always shoots before we get this far.

If, instead of passing to the right wing initially, the point guard passes to the left wing, he will cut to the weak side as before, but the low post will reverse to the top of the circle and the trailer will fill the ball-side low post. (See Figure 4–7.)

The movements following the inside interchange and the trailer's cut to the low post are identical to the early game pattern previously described: the wing passes to the top of the circle and screens inside for the point guard cutting across the lane and behind their double screen. If he passes to the wing, he will move inside to double-screen for the point guard cutting into the lane in the high-post area, with the original left wing player continuing across the lane to the ball-side low post.

Note: This pattern could also be set up by instructing the low post player to play the ball-side low post on whichever side the point guard passes to, cutting across the lane to the low post if he passes to the left wing. The trailer would then always play the outside position shown in Figure 4–2.

When we steal the ball, we want our best ball handler to take the ball down court in the ensuing fast break if we aren't going to have a

Figure 4–6 Setting Up One-on-One

Figure 4–7 Setting Up the Early Game from the Point Guard's Weak-Side Pass

breakaway open layup. If, for example, a forward steals the ball, we'd rather have a ball-handling guard bringing the ball down, even if the break is slowed down slightly as a result. Our reasoning is that if we aren't going to get the layup we want at least four of our players involved in the initial stages of the fast break. Designating our ball handler slows down the break slightly at times, but not as much as you'd think. Also, this tactic ensures good ball handling, and following the same route down court every time eliminates confusion on the part of the players involved in the fast break.

As an example of our laning technique, assume that defender X_4 has just stolen the ball from 04 in the corner, as shown in Figure 4–8. X_4 will either throw the long pass down court to X_2 or X_3 filling the sideline passing lanes, or relay the ball to X_1 to start the break. X_4 may even begin advancing the ball down court himself as he looks for 01, but he will not take the ball all the way. He will pass to 01 as soon as 01 can free himself to receive the pass.

An important point in the fast-breaking pattern after transition is that X_2 and X_3 will follow the same lanes regardless of their court position when transition occurs. The only exceptions to this rule arise when the player who steals the ball is in position to score on a breakaway layup without resorting to the regular fast-breaking sequence.

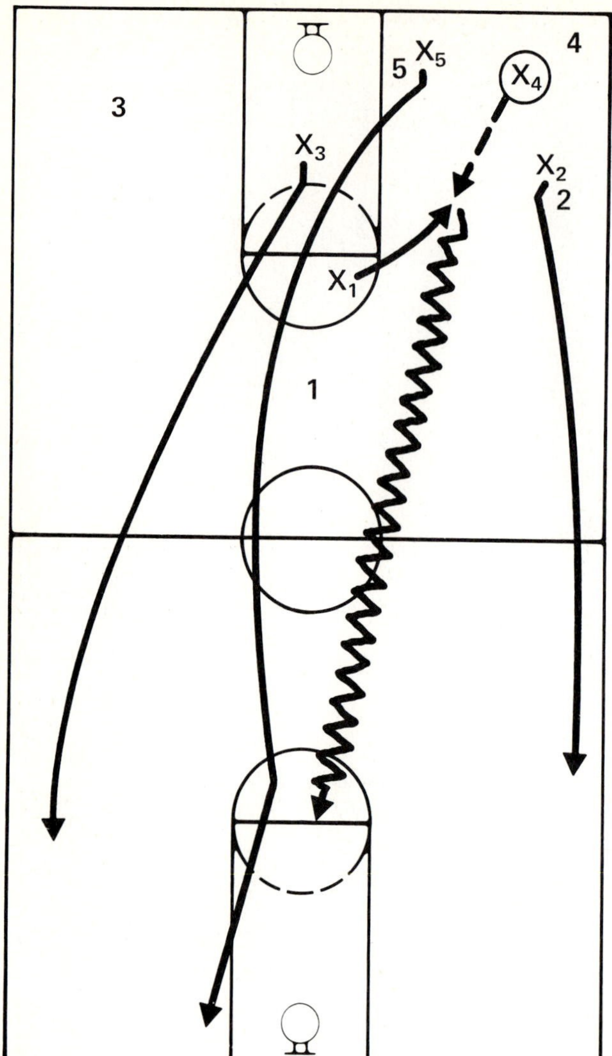

Figure 4–8 Fast Breaking After Transition

When we described the fast-breaking pattern after scores (Figure 4–1), X_5 inbounded the ball and X_4 moved down the middle of the court and set up at the low post. In our transition pattern after steals or turnovers, this arrangement—X_4 fast breaking, X_5 acting as trailer—is not always feasible. In Figure 4–8, for example, X_4 has stolen the ball and will serve as trailer in the fast break. X_5 will move down court as quickly as possible, whether in front of or behind 01, and fill the low-post position. Regardless of whether X_4 or X_5 makes the outlet pass and trails the play, X_1, X_2, and X_3 will follow their lanes down court.

Our first priority in fast breaking is to get the ball down court

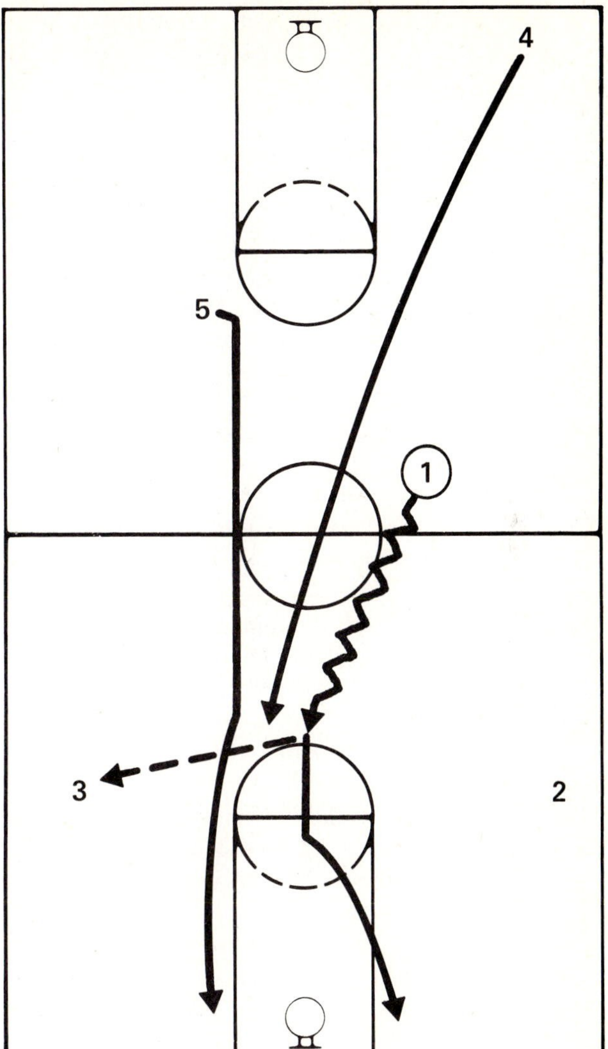

Figure 4–9 Organizing the Early Game Pattern After Transition

quickly. Our second priority is to get as many of our players as possible involved in the break. We want to score directly off the break, but if we can't, we want to go into our early offense as quickly as possible. Figure 4–9 shows how we set up our fast break pattern when the big men are not involved in the early stages of the fast break beyond making the outlet pass.

If X_4 or X_5 steals or recovers the ball, he will make the outlet pass and serve as trailer in the fast break. In Figure 4–9, however, 05 is trailing the play with 04, but 05 will fill the ball-side low-post position after 01 passes and cuts to the weak-side low post. After 01 passes and cuts and 05 cuts through the lane to the low post, the pattern is set. 03 will shoot, pass to 05 at the low post, or pass to 04 trailing the play, and then move inside to set a double screen low for 01.

And that's our set offense. We're always looking for the open shot, which isn't necessarily a high-percentage shot in conventional terms. With the fine outside shooters we've had at UNLV, we consider practically *any* open shot to be a high-percentage shot for us. (We used to tell our players, "Take the first shot you can get." After watching them throw bricks halfway up the bleachers for a while, though, we changed it to, "Take the first *decent* shot you can get." Before we changed, some of our early practices looked more like an army launching mortar rounds than a basketball practice!) We don't want our opponents to relax or stand around as we pass the ball back and forth around the perimeter. We feel—and I think this makes us unique in our approach to the game—that if we have to slow the game down with a series of passes that do not lead to a quick shot, we'd rather be on defense and wear our opponents down that way. Everything we do, including taking shots that many people consider low-percentage, is designed to keep the tempo of the game as fast as possible. Because we do everything at full speed, we play the high-speed game extremely well. It's the one advantage we always have, and we want to exploit it as fully as we can. We're not as tall as many of our opponents, and sometimes we don't have as many blue-chip athletes, but when those all-Americans take the court against us, they'd better be ready to run full speed for forty minutes. When we played the University of San Francisco in the NCAA Tournament a few years ago, they had those marvelous athletes James Hardy, Bill Cartwright, and Winfred Boynes, and we knew if we didn't take it to them with everything we had for forty minutes over the entire 94 feet of floor space, they'd blow us out of the game. Their players simply were better than ours. Therefore we ran sprints the whole week before that game, after six months of playing basketball, because we knew they wouldn't be doing it. We were afraid they'd beat the daylights out of us, so we really worked hard on our conditioning. They were taller than we were, and we had to front their forwards as well as Cartwright, but we believed we could wear them down.

Because we shoot so quickly, we commit fewer turnovers than we might with a different offensive attack. However, although we shoot quickly, our goal is to work for the *good* shot. To exemplify this, let's return to the fast-breaking pattern we described earlier. When 01 brings the ball down, we want him to look for the shot from the top of the circle if 04 is covered and the defense stops his penetration. If 01 passes to 03, 01 will cut to the weak-side low-post position, and 03 will shoot if he's open. If 03 passes to 05 trailing the play, 05 will shoot if he's open. If 05 passes to 02, 02 will shoot if he's open. We want to take the first good shot we have. Each player cuts after passing the ball. (See Figure 4–10.)

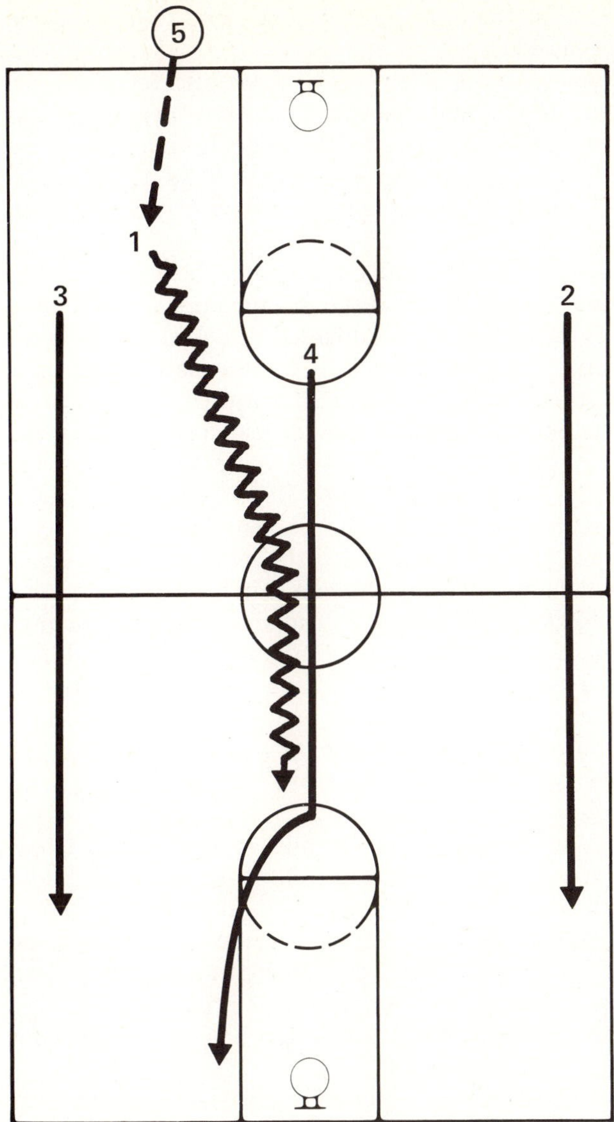

Figure 4–10 Laning the UNLV Fast Break

Our definition of a *good shot* is "a shot within a player's shooting range." We try to restrict our players' shooting habits as little as possible. If a player can go up and shoot with a man in his face and still have a decent chance of making the shot without changing his rhythm or the arch of the shot, we think it's a good shot for him to take. We take some bad shots, but I'd rather have our players take a few bad shots than spend their time worrying about whether it's the right shot for them to take.

Coaches used to believe that the only good shot was one that was wide open, but it just isn't true today.

Our offense is simple. We don't run a lot of complicated patterns; we'd rather have our kids think about shooting than what they're going to do next and who they're supposed to pass to. We come down and pass the ball to the wing; he either shoots, or passes and cuts. This doesn't overburden the players' minds, and it keeps them focused where we want—on shooting.

This offensive system is diametrically opposed to the way I used to coach. When I was at Long Beach State, I used to churn inside every time a player of mine shot from farther than 10 feet. We looked for the wide open shot, or, preferably, for opportunities to get the ball inside. Our whole offense was built around the inside game, and we'd wait forever if necessary to take just the shots we wanted. But it seemed that I never had any good shooters. Glen McDonald played two years for me at Long Beach, but he never shot well. After I left Long Beach, Glen had a fabulous senior year and went on to play for the Boston Celtics. He hit 62 percent of his shots in his senior year, and led the league in shooting.

Later, I asked Glen about the dramatic change in his shooting after I left. He told me, "Coach, I've always been a good shooter. I just couldn't shoot for you." He explained that every time he missed a shot he'd look over to the bench and see me going into convulsions, and it would mess up his confidence. As I thought about what Glen had told me, I realized I'd had other kids come to me with reputations as outstanding shooters, and most of them hadn't shot well either. Still, I wasn't about to change my philosophy. Old ways die hard.

When I moved to the University of Nevada at Las Vegas, I had another hot-shooting prospect, a freshman from Texas named Eddie Owens. Everybody I talked to said Eddie was the most fantastic shooter they'd ever seen. Still, he had only an average freshman year for me; he didn't score well at all. High school and college coaches who had seen Eddie play in high school couldn't believe the change that had come over him in college. They didn't say it, but I think they shared my growing suspicion that I'd messed up his shooting.

It all came together when a series of disasters forced us to change our entire game plan. We lost our two biggest players, both of whom were instrumental to our inside game, and suddenly we had no attack at all. To compensate for this loss of height we decided to run with the ball. We wanted to get the ball down court before the opponents' big man (or men) could set up on defense, and in order to do this we'd have to take the outside shots. Our kids would have to be in great shape, but with proper conditioning, a high-speed offense, and relaxed, confident shooters we thought we could improve our offense considerably.

We also felt that, since we'd probably play a lot of close games, we could increase our chances in those games by hitting our free throws. We spent thirty minutes a day shooting free throws. Any player who made less than 80 percent of his free throws in practice had to shoot an extra one hundred foul shots. Once the season started, we used game stats, and anybody who made less than 70 percent in games had to come in and shoot one hundred extra free throws the next day.

If your team is weak on offense, you aren't going to alter things appreciably by conventional means. Anybody can play tough, hard-nosed defense, but no amount of hustle is going to make an errant shot drop in the basket. Shooting a basketball accurately is a complex skill involving timing, delicate fingertip "touch" in gripping and releasing the ball, and a wide range of coordinated hand-eye movements and adjustments. If your kids don't pay their dues by spending hours practicing and improving their shooting form on their own, no amount of coaching is going to help them. Still, we've found that, in our style of play, even mediocre or poor shooters can increase their scoring potential appreciably by being a part of the fast break. If you can get your players to work hard on defense and anticipate transitions, they can improve their scoring by filling the lanes and shooting layups. The more players score, the more they'll want to score. And if they really want to score, they'll work harder on defense as well as work on their own time to improve their shot. The main reason we can get our kids to work so hard on defense is that they know their efforts will lead to their scoring more points. Some people have said that kids won't give 100 percent at both ends of the court, but ours do. It doesn't take much incentive to work hard on defense if there's a good chance that it's going to be *you* putting the ball in the basket at the other end of the court. And when transitions occur, we have absolutely *no* problem motivating our kids to join in the fast break. They know that if they don't fill their lanes, *they* won't be the ones taking the shots.

I'm not saying that our players hog the ball; they don't. They're expected to pass the ball any time a teammate is in a better position to advance the ball down court or score. However, they also know that, when the shot is theirs to take, they're expected to shoot the ball. This frees their minds to concentrate on the shot.

I wouldn't advise every team to adopt this playing style and emulate the Runnin' Rebels, but I *would* advise coaches to practice high-speed basketball. Any team can play a slow-tempo game, but if your kids aren't used to playing an upbeat, high-speed game, they won't be able to deal with teams that are used to that playing style. Other teams may beat us occasionally, but they won't do it by playing a slow game. We won't let them do that.

Finally, if you're going to adopt this playing style, don't expect it to pay dividends immediately in every game. It takes time to wear opponents down. Small strokes fell great oaks. Your kids have to believe that, no matter how the game goes in its early stages, the latter part of the game is theirs.

An example was described to us by a friend who adopted this style of play. His high school team jumped to an early 15–6 lead in a game against a vastly superior opponent with two outstanding big men, then saw the lead evaporate as the opponents began fast breaking against them. At halftime, the opponents had taken a two-point lead, but they were beginning to tire visibly. In the second half, his players outscored their exhausted rivals, 48–6. This same coach said that, in the 23 games they played that year (they were 17–6 for the season), they were behind as late as the fourth quarter in *13* games.

5

The Inside Power Game

The more traditionally oriented reader will note with relief that we're back to high-percentage basketball in this chapter. We take leave of the frenetic, reckless scrambling and breathless frenzy of the fast-breaking, UNLV style. In this chapter we'll examine at our leisure a more familiar style of offensive attack—the inside power game.

It would not be a great exaggeration to say that "all coaches would like to be able to play the inside power game." The power game is as basic to offensive basketball as man-to-man defense is to defensive basketball. It is based on the premise that the closer to the basket a shot is taken from, the greater the likelihood of a player's making the shot. In power-game offenses, a team does not merely work for high-percentage shots, as is the case with continuity patterns and ball-control offenses; rather, the offense is geared almost completely toward working the ball inside to a team's big man (or men) for one-on-one confrontations near the basket.

Obviously the offensive player who sets up in, or cuts to, the low-post position or flashes into the lane for a quick pass must be durable physically, since his proximity to the basket will draw opponents in swarms. However, he must also be aggressive mentally, if the power game is to succeed. If the inside player approaches one-on-one confrontations timidly, the power game simply will not work. When a player has the necessary strength or possesses enough offensive moves and finesse to operate well in one-on-one confrontations inside, the power game can be used to devastate opponents. As will be shown, power offenses are incredibly simple to operate, since all that is needed is the opportunity to isolate the big man one-on-one. The big man usually stays inside; he moves outside only when it is absolutely necessary to continue the offense.

Not every team can or should run a power-game offense. I'd used the power game for fourteen years at four different colleges when we decided to abandon it in favor of our present tactics at UNLV; in giving up the power game, we felt like we'd suffered a death in the family. However, you need at least one, and preferably two, big men who can operate effectively inside on offense, or else the power game will bog down into a series of meaningless outside passes. The power game must be played aggressively to succeed, and if your players are either too small or too passive to work the inside game, you'll probably be better off in some kind of continuity pattern that involves movement by all of the players.

THE LONG BEACH STATE POWER GAME

While I was at Riverside City College from 1960 to 1965, we developed two basic man-to-man offenses: one we called our *moving game,* and the other we called our *power game.* We felt that these offenses complemented each other beautifully. Our moving game was built around having four or five men in continuous motion at all times, trying to make the defensive players turn their backs to the ball and thus be unable to get help from their teammates.

Our power game had different goals; the primary goal was to work the ball inside to the low post. We didn't want a lot of movement of personnel in our power game; instead, we tried to create mismatches with the defensive team, posting our biggest players low, passing inside to them, and then letting them operate one-on-one from that position. When we were running our moving game and (a) we didn't get the type of shot we wanted, (b) we couldn't work the ball in close, or (c) the defense was able to stop our driving game, we switched to our power game. If we played a team we felt we were superior to, we used our power game exclusively.

I used the power game at Riverside City College, and later at Pasadena City College and Long Beach State. I believed in it then, and I still do. The power game doesn't require a great deal of movement, and it can be used to gain an offensive advantage from mismatched positions.

In our basic power-game set, shown in Figure 5–1, 01 was our point guard; 02 was the high post; 03 the weak-side wing, or wing away from the inside stack (03 set up at the weak-side low post and cut outside to the wing position); 04 the ball-side (or power-side) low post; and 05 the power wing.

We often had the player who was being guarded by the opponents' best rebounder bring the ball up-court in order to take him away from the defensive boards. (This technique is not shown in the diagrams.) Any two of the four players could step out to receive the ball, depending on who we wanted to leave in the low-post position. The player who brought the ball up-court passed to either of the two players who stepped out to a forward (wing) position. The player receiving the pass immediately looked inside,

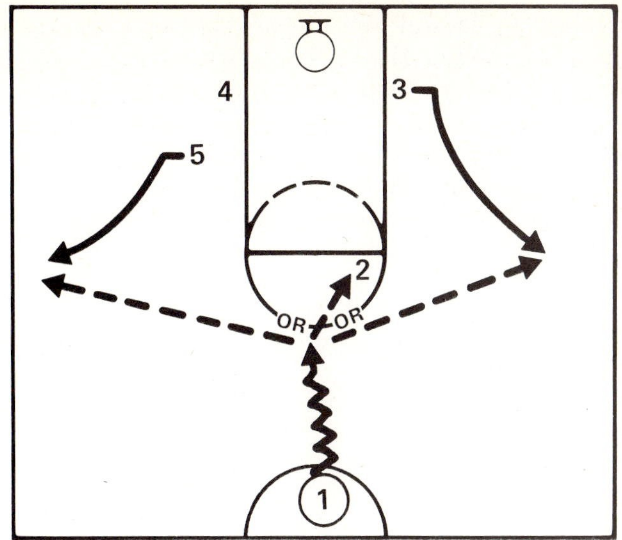

Figure 5–1 Basic Power-Game Movement

trying to get the ball to the man at the low post. If he was able to pass inside, as shown in Figure 5–2, he flared to the corner to prevent the defense from double-teaming the low-post player.

If the ball handler (05 in Figure 5–2) couldn't pass inside to the low post, he would pass the ball back to the point guard, who relayed the ball to the forward on the other side of the court to repeat the process. At this point we were in a double post (high-low) alignment.

If the defense fronted our low-post player and dropped the high-post

Figure 5–2 Power Game with Pass to Power Wing

defender (X_4 in Figure 5–3) in back of him to deny the inside pass, we broke our weak-side post man (02) to the ball-side high-post position.

When power wing 05 passed to high post 02, 05 would cut to the basket behind a rear screen set by 04. 02 would pivot at the high post, looking for 05 cutting low. Then, on *eye contact*, 04 would flash into the post area, also looking for 02's pass. (See Figure 5–4.)

We used the same kind of inside movement when 01 passed to 02 at the high post initially (Figure 5–5), and when we reversed the ball to 03 at

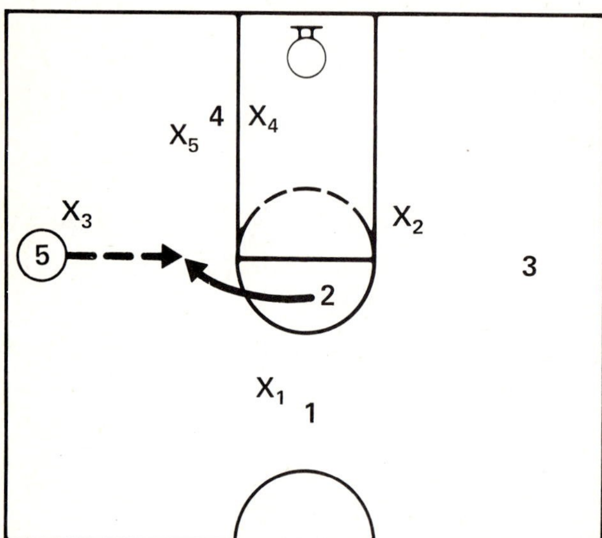

Figure 5–3 02's Cut to Ball-Side High Post with Low Post Double-Teamed

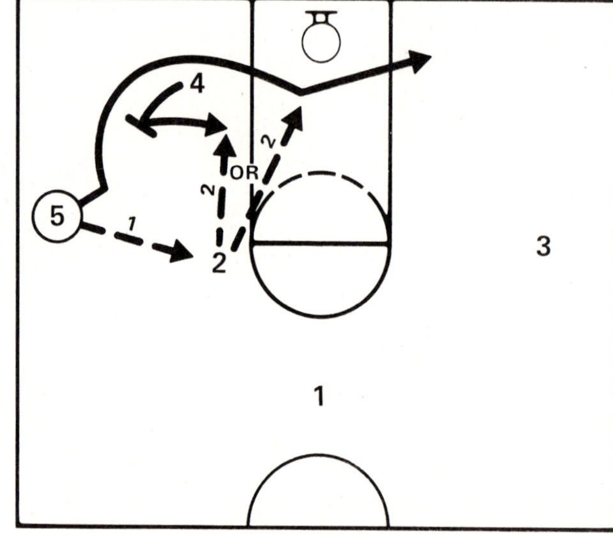

Figure 5–4 Power Movement with Pass from Wing to High Post

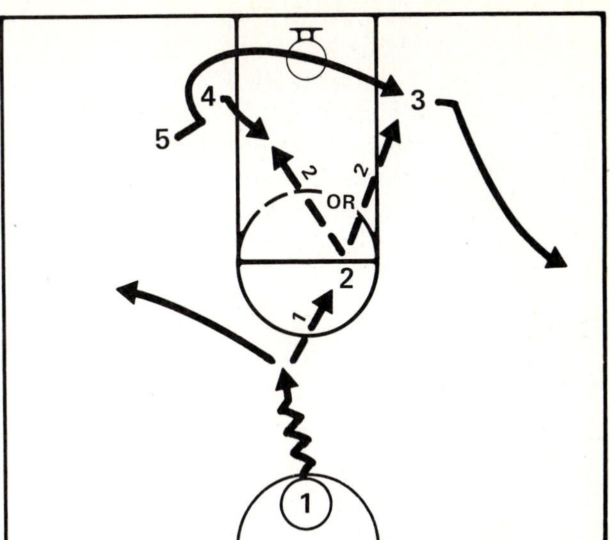

Figure 5–5 Power Movement with Initial Pass to High Post

the weak-side wing as well (Figure 5–6). (Note in Figure 5–5 that 01 clears *away* from 02 at the high post in order to provide another passing option and eliminate the possibility of double-teaming the high post.)

When the ball handler's initial pass was to the weak-side wing, 02 had the option of either sliding to the low post if the defense let him, or holding his position at the high post. 05, reacting to 02's movement (or lack of it), would cut to either the low or high post. 03 always looked for

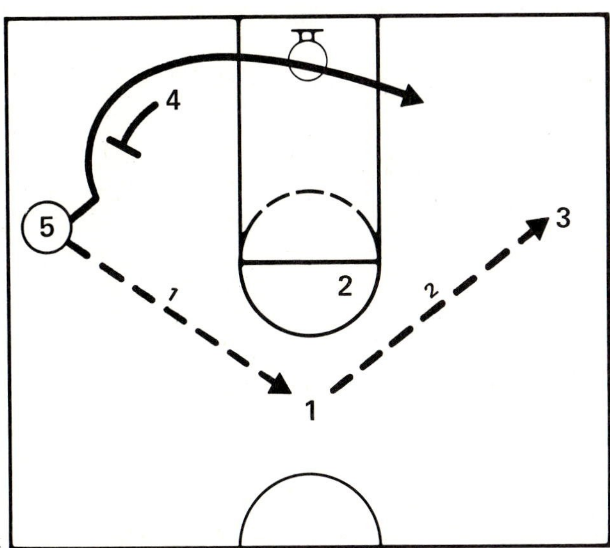

Figure 5–6 Power Movement with Ball Reversal

the low post first. After passing inside, 03 would flare to the corner. (See Figure 5–7.)

In Figure 5–5 we described 02's passing options to 04 and 05 when the initial pass was made to the high post. Figures 5–8 and 5–9 illustrate two additional options off that pass, the return pass to the point guard (Figure 5–8) and the pass to the weak-side wing (Figure 5–9). In Figure 5–8, after 05 cut around 04's rear screen and into the lane, 02 would sometimes choose to return the ball to 01, who had flared to the power side

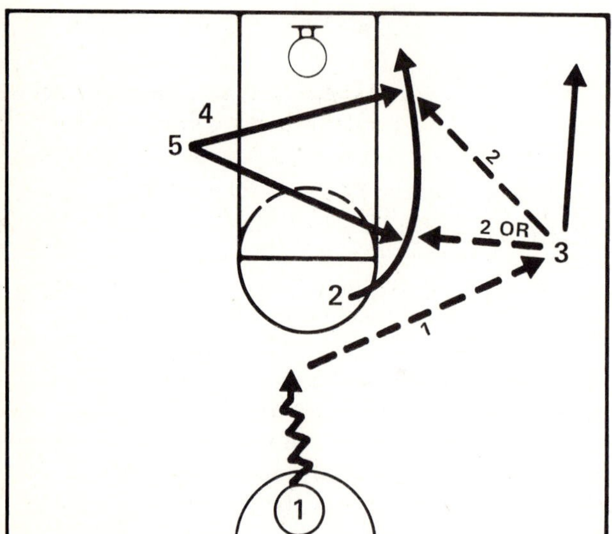

Figure 5–7 Power Movement with Initial Pass to Weak-Side Wing

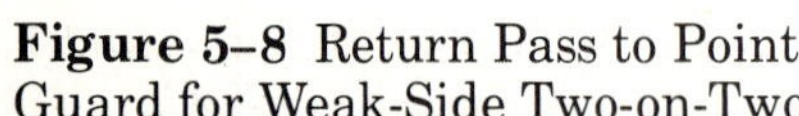
Figure 5–8 Return Pass to Point Guard for Weak-Side Two-on-Two

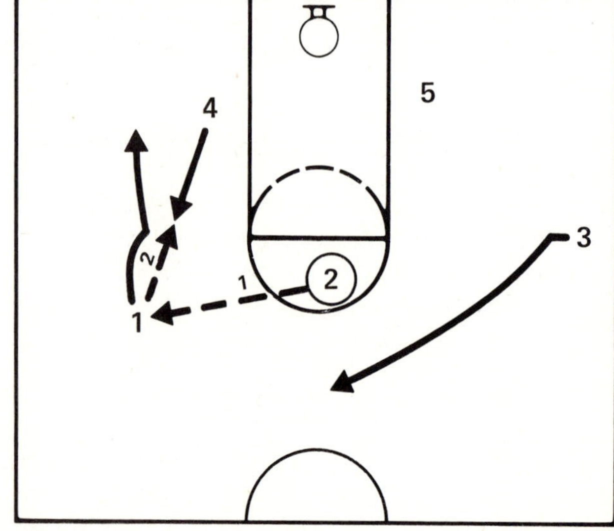

of the court. 01 and 04 then went two-on-two from the weak side; for example, by 04's breaking into the weak-side high post for give-and-go action.

In Figure 5–9, 02 passed to the weak-side wing 03. 03 dumped the ball low to 05, who had crossed the lane off the rear screen by 04 and posted low. 03 flared to the corner, with 01 filling the point for court balance.

Following the movements shown in Figure 5–9, 03 sometimes was

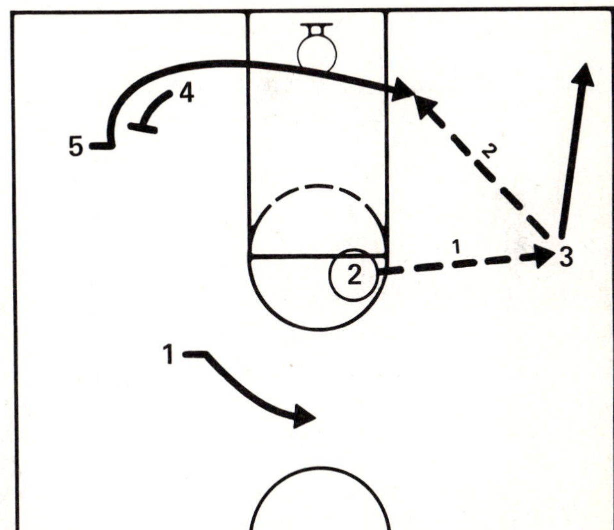

Figure 5–9 High Post's Pass to Power Wing

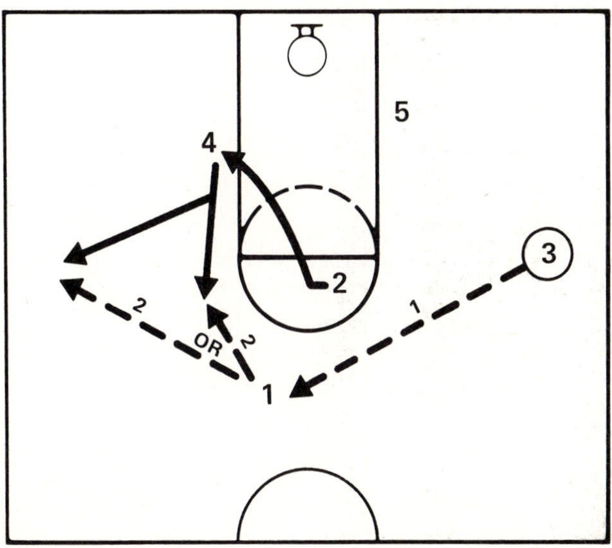

Figure 5–10 Continuing the Power Movement Reversals

unable to work the ball inside to 05. In this case, 03 reversed the ball to 01 at the point. (See Figure 5–10.)

04 had the option of cutting to the high post or breaking to the wing for a pass from 01. If 04 broke to the wing to receive 01's pass, he either worked his man one-on-one from the weak side or looked for 02 cutting into and across the lane from the high post.

When the wings were pressured before the initial pass, 03 emptied through the lane and filled the point for balance, and 01 dribble-chased 03

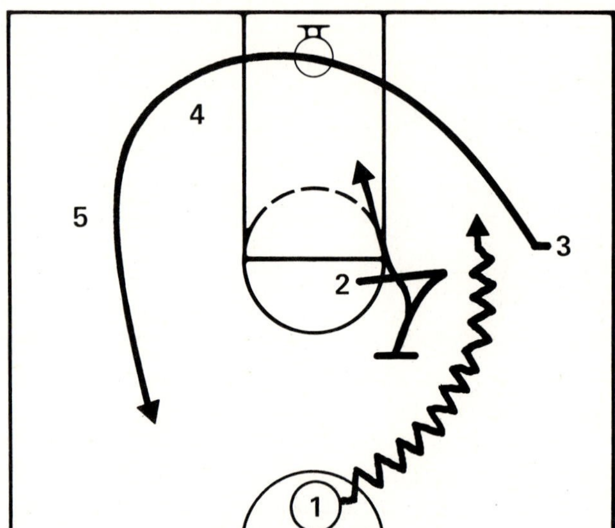

Figure 5–11 Clearing Pattern for Point Guard's Dribble-Chase

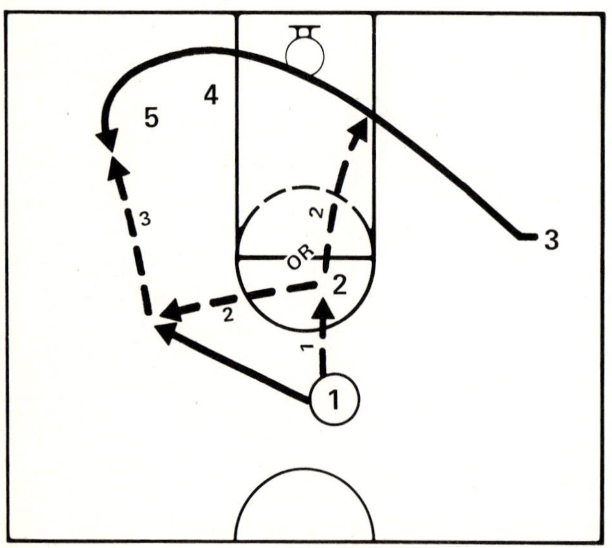

Figure 5–12 03's Backdoor Cut with Pass to High Post

on the weak side (Figure 5–11). 02 stepped out from the high post to create a pick-and-roll, with 01 dribbling hard off the screen and looking for 02's roll to the basket.

We had three or four other options off our basic power game series. In Figure 5–12, 01 passed to 02 at the high post, and 03 cut hard through the lane looking for a bounce pass from 02. 01 could either follow 03 as the secondary cutter (not shown in Figure 5–12) or slide away from the ball in a clearing movement. If 03 wasn't open for 02's pass, 03 continued into and through the lane and, as 02 passed to 01, 03 cut behind the power-side double screen set by 04 and 05 to receive 01's pass for the jump shot.

Figure 5–13 shows another option we sometimes used to work a pick-and-roll with 02 and 03. 01 passed to 03 at the weak-side wing and cut to the corner off high post 02. 02 and 03 would then have a pick-and-roll from the wing area. 05 screened down for 04, who filled the top for balance.

Sometimes, when opponents overplayed the high-post and wing passes, we had 03 screen for 05 cutting across the lane and into the wing area for 01's pass from the top of the circle (Figure 5–14). 02 cleared to the other side of the free-throw line. 03 continued through the lane and set a second screen, this time for 04 breaking across the lane to the low post. 03 continued out to the wing position, and the sides of the floor had been exchanged easily and quickly. The motion was the same once the ball was entered to either wing or the high post.

This offense was very easy for our players to learn. It isn't complicated at all, but it does require proper timing in making the pass to the post man. The post man must maintain his position on the man guarding

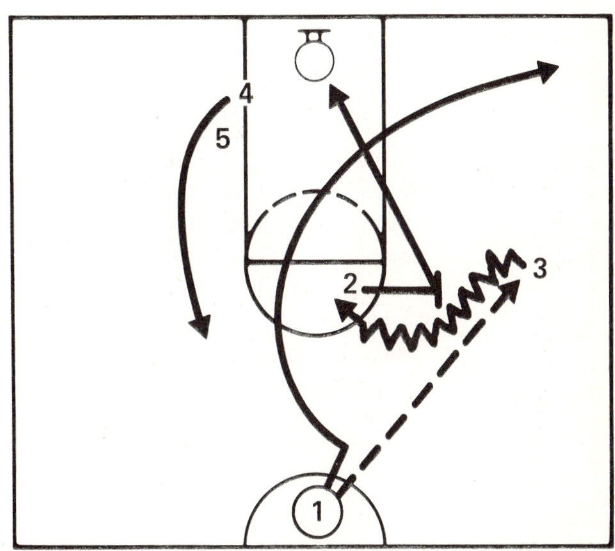

Figure 5–13 Point Guard's Cut Creating Pick-and-Roll with 02 and 03

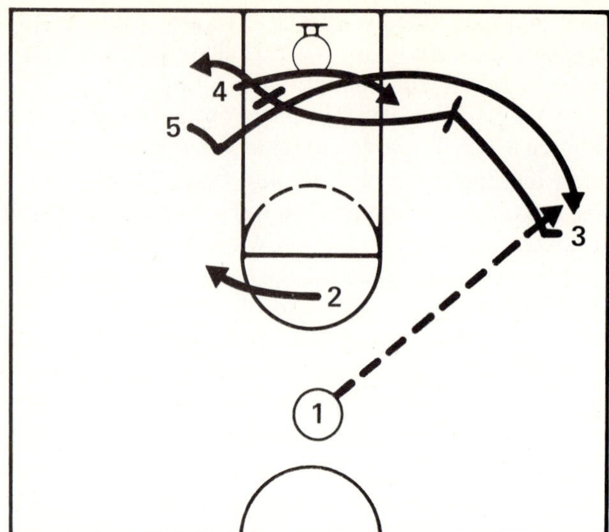

Figure 5–14 Baseline Exchange

him when he sets up in the post area. The forward who has stepped out must become an active passer. We encouraged—*insisted* is a better word—that every effort be made to get the ball inside to the low-post position. If, as happened to us many times, the defense collapsed everybody around the low-post position, we worked the ball around outside, hoping to get a good, high-percentage perimeter shot. Many opponents gave us the outside shot because of the constant threat of our post play inside.

Our three outside men were allowed to do anything they wanted on offense. They could cut to the weak-side or ball-side corner, maintain their positions, or exchange positions. The post men were also free to exchange positions. Both sets of movements, inside and outside, are similar to those described in Chapter 7.

We used this offense effectively at Riverside City College, Pasadena City College, Long Beach State, and in our first year at Nevada–Las Vegas. The power game as we played it can also be used effectively against zone defenses, particularly if you have two big men inside. It keeps the big men inside, which is useful if your big men lack the mobility to move outside. It is also effective when you play a team that has a couple of good rebounders, because you can always draw the rebounders outside. Many times you can force a zone defense into playing what actually amounts to a sinking 1–2–2 zone or sinking man-to-man defense by employing the power game properly. We were successful in using our power game against a zone defense or against combination defenses. When we played teams that switched from man-to-man to zone defenses, we went to the power game and concentrated on getting the ball inside to the low post, regardless of what kind of defense they were in.

Our zone offense used to contain many of the elements of our power game. It was a 1–2–2 double-post offense from which we either played the power game or moved the ball-side post man to the corner and cut the weak-side post man to the high post to set up a 1–3–1 alignment. (See Figure 5–15.)

I realize that this is very basic, but that's just the point I'm emphasizing. It doesn't have to be complicated in order to be successful. We were trying to work the ball in to the low post, not to confuse the defenders. We wanted to work on them one-on-one 4 to 6 feet from the basket. I think too often we as coaches try to make things too complicated, maybe so we can look like we're doing more coaching than we actually are. I feel I'd rather have the kids do the work and get the credit for our wins. If we could get the ball inside with one or two passes and a minimum of cuts, we didn't need a lot of movement. If teams switched defenses on us, we could adjust easily to rotate our personnel and the ball to the other side of the court.

Referring to Figure 5–15, I feel that it's important to come into the seam from *behind* the zone instead of trying to cut through the zone. Cutting from behind the zone means that the defenders will not see the cutter until he is cutting front of them, whereas cuts through or across the zone are usually picked up early by the defenders' peripheral vision.

Many man-to-man principles can be applied to zone offenses. We liked to drive against zones and then pass the ball off quickly, just as we did in our moving game. We also liked to post against zones. We would cut a man through the middle of the zone whenever possible. We liked to cut a

Figure 5–15 Power Game Used as a Zone Offense

man along the baseline zone. Sometimes we'd rebound a guard or outside player by running him directly to the basket in anticipation of a shot and getting good rebound position.

We usually played three men outside in zone offenses. We told them to adjust into the defensive seams in freelance fashion. We passed and adjusted. Each time we passed we went into the seams of the zone defense. While the three outside men were holding their positions in the seams, the two post men played into open areas, and when openings appeared in the middle of the zone, the weak-side post man cut across rapidly into the open area. If the cutter wasn't open, he rotated back into the basic alignment. Any time the players manning the outside positions adjusted all the way to the baseline, they moved to the opposite side of the court, cutting directly inside the basket and continuing in the same manner.

By cutting men into open areas and adjusting into the seams, teams can get high-percentage shots against zones without resorting to outside shooting exclusively. Too many times a team runs up against a zone defense, and the players think that they have to beat the zone by shooting from outside. I don't think it's necessarily true. If a team exercises good judgment, patience, and poise, the players can get inside the zone by adjusting into the seams. You have to get inside the zone a majority of the time to beat it. It's difficult to beat a good ball club when most of your shots are from outside.

From this section we can see that the goals of power offenses are, first, to work the ball inside to the low post; second, to provide enough movement by the other players to deny the opponents the opportunity to double-team the man at the low post; and third, to force one-on-one confrontations that will increase the likelihood of making the inside pass. Any offensive alignment or pattern that draws or forces the defensive players into one-on-one coverage may be used as a power-game offense.

In our discussion of the inside power game so far, we kept the players' movements to a minimum as we attacked the seams in a series of freelance movements. We continue our discussion with post interchanges and inside screens and stack patterns, where the movements are more patterned but are no more difficult to teach or to learn.

POST INTERCHANGES

The movement shown in Figure 5–16 is known as a *post interchange*. It is likely to be more successful against a zone defense than a man-to-man defense, since the simple cuts will not force the defenders to switch. The only important point to be made concerning such cuts is that the player cutting away from the ball will always go baseline, while the cutter toward the ball will cut into the lane.

The movements in Figure 5–17 are identical to those shown in Figure 5–16 except that 05 sets a screen to brush off 04's man as he crosses the lane. (The screen shown in Figure 5–17 will work against a 1–3–1 zone defense, since only one deep defender is in the lane when the movements occur, but it will not work against a 1–2–2 zone defense. The two inside defenders will switch defensive assignments automatically, regardless of whether the post men interchange or screen.)

Figure 5–18 depicts a variation of the low-post interchange in which the weak-side low post man 04 cuts into the lane and continues to the

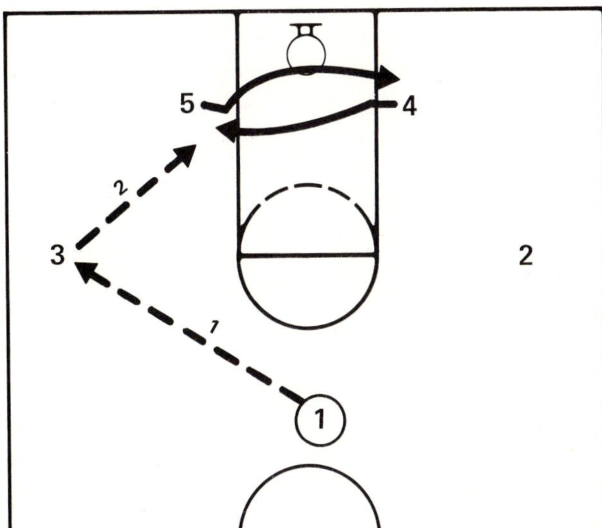

Figure 5–16 Low-Post Interchange

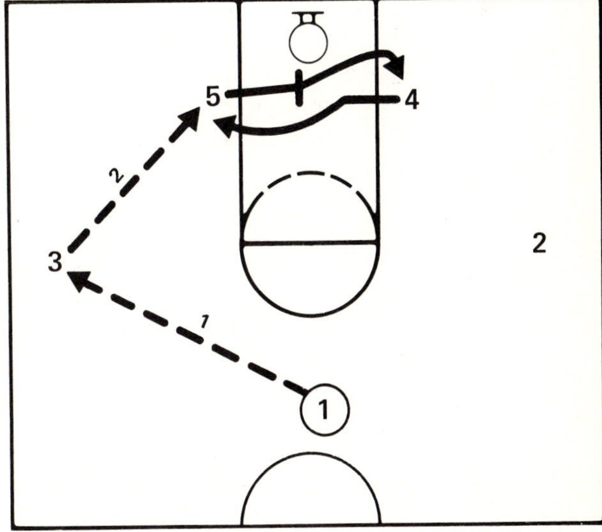

Figure 5–17 Low-Post Screen

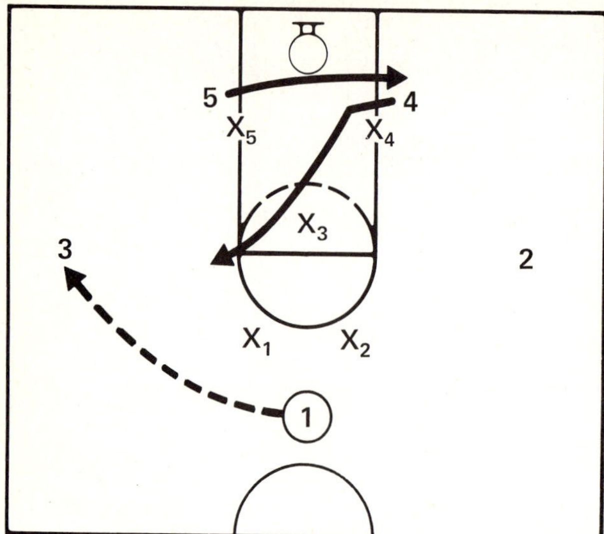

Figure 5–18 Variation of Low-Post Interchange

high post. This movement, used primarily against zone defenses, may serve to draw X_5 to the high post, in which case 05 can move back across the lane to the ball-side low post; or it may spring 04 open in the middle of the lane or at the high post. In either case, however, it will force the defenders into one-on-one coverage of 04 and 05.

The movement in Figure 5–19 is common to the so-called "passing game" patterns. It is ideal as a power-game movement against a man-

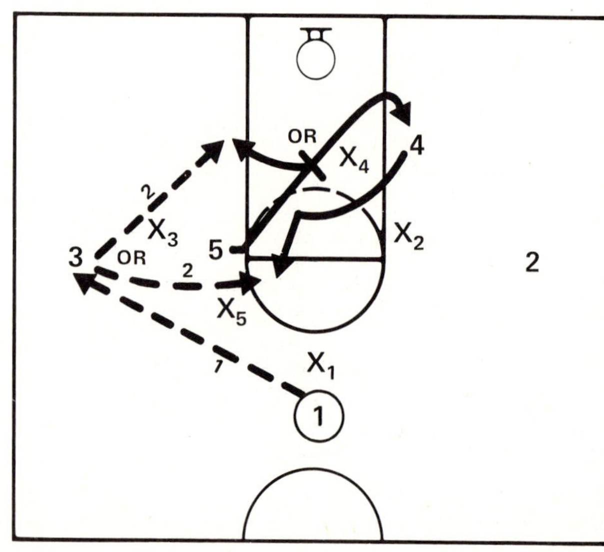

Figure 5–19 High-Low Post Interchange (Screen)

to-man defense, since the screen not only keeps both players inside but also alters the matchups. (Note that 04's movement to the high post may also serve as a decoy for 05 pivoting and cutting to the ball-side low post instead of clearing to the weak side.)

INSIDE SCREENS AND STACK PATTERNS

The objective of the inside screens shown in Figure 5–20 is to pass to 04 or 05 without their having to go outside to get the ball. When the pass is made, the player setting the screen will usually empty to the weak side, or to the ball-side corner, to permit the ball handler to work more effectively one-on-one.

Incidentally, movements similar to those shown in Figure 5–20 can provide an excellent way of working the ball inside to a guard who operates well at the low post. Instead of cutting toward the high post, around the screens set by 02 and/or 03, 04 and 05 will cut toward the wing positions, with 02 and 03 maintaining inside position on the players they screened at the low post.

We used two variations of this movement, without the screen, to win an important game once. Late in the game, our opponents' foul difficulties created a height advantage for us at the guard position. In order to take full advantage of the situation, we put our taller guard at the 03 (wing) position, passed to 05 cutting outside, and had 05 relay the ball quickly to 03 before the defense could adjust to help 03's man cover him. (See Figure 5–21.) Then, when the opponents caught on to what we were doing, we switched to a 2–1–2 alignment with our tall guard at the weak-side guard

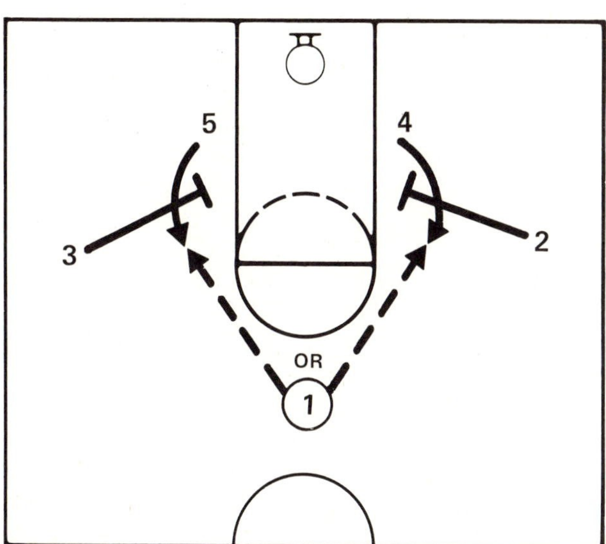

Figure 5–20 Inside Screens

slot (02 in Figure 5–22), then split the post after passing to the wing. This gave our offense a different look, although our big guard ended up getting the ball at the low post in both cases.

If you have a player who operates well near the basket, you might consider devising patterns to get him the ball at the low post. You don't have to use your center at the low post if another player is more effective at that position. We made a career out of cutting our outstanding 6′6″ guard, Ed Ratleff, to the low post when I was at Long Beach State. Ed was

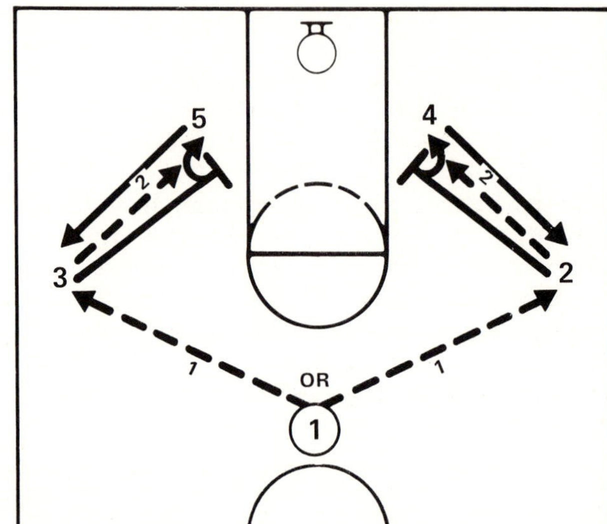

Figure 5–21 Double Inside Screen

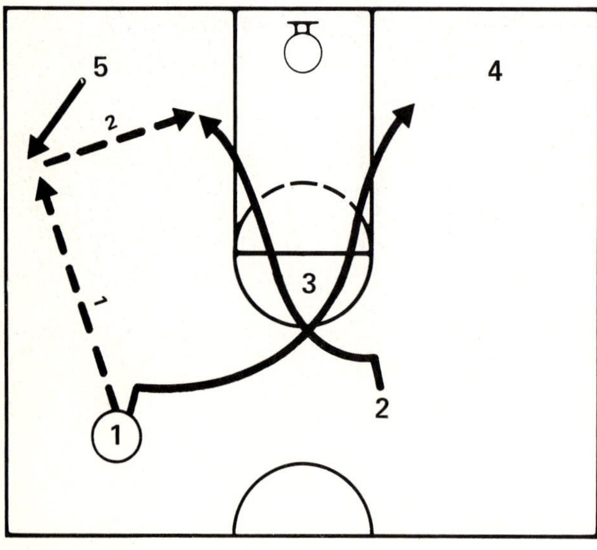

Figure 5–22 Splitting the Post for Guard's Inside Power Game

strong inside and outside, but we liked to isolate him inside as often as possible. He ate up those small guards whenever we posted him low against a man-to-man defense. (Come to think of it, he usually wore out forwards guarding him at the low post, too.)

To me, the real value of the inside power game is that it's based on pitting strength against strength at the low-post position, and if you have *anybody* in your lineup who operates effectively at the low post, all you have to do is devise a way to get the ball to him inside in one-on-one coverage, and let things go from there.

THE STACK OFFENSE

Stack offenses have been around for years, but they probably gained their greatest popularity with Fred Jucker's two-time NCAA Champion Cincinnati Bearcats in 1961–62 and 1962–63, and Bob Cousy's Boston College teams of the late 1960s. Stack patterns feature limited ball handling, with one player handling the ball almost exclusively, and an increased potential for inside offensive play.

Stack offenses are not continuity patterns; rather, they are a group of set plays from the alignments shown in Figures 5–23 and 5–24. Bob Cousy asserted that the nature of the stack alignment and cuts tends to force zone defenses into man-to-man coverage.*

Figure 5–23 Stack Offense, Basic Alignment and Moves

* Bob Cousy and Frank G. Power, Jr., *Basketball: Concepts and Techniques* (Boston: Allyn and Bacon, 1970).

Figure 5–24 Stack Offense, Pass to Weak Side

In the basic stack movements shown in Figures 5–23 and 5–24, the point guard (#14) controls the offense with his dribble. The key to using the stack is the point guard's penetrating dribble to freeze at least one of the defenders. His dribble is generally lateral rather than directly into the defense, with the direction of other players' movements dictated by the defensive alignment.

In using the stack offense, 01 is, of course, the team's best ball handler. The cutter on the right side should be the team's best outside shooter. The inside post men should be the best offensive rebounders and inside players. The cutter on the left side should be an effective outside shooter or ball handler; however, in the absence of these skills, he still maintains defensive balance when 01 moves out of his basic position.

Although the stack formation can be used in much the same way as an outside splitting alignment, it has two attributes that can make it potentially superior in terms of its effect upon the defense:

1. The variety of inside and outside cutting and screening angles is such that, unless the offensive team runs the same options every time, the defensive players never really know in advance where the cutters are going. Therefore, the defenders are unlikely to overplay the passing lanes to stop the pattern.

2. Cuts from the stack alignment are performed from closer to the basket than in conventional splitting patterns, which tends to strengthen a team's offensive inside game. As a result, outside shots will be achieved with greater difficulty than before, but most coaches would hardly consider this to be a weakness of the pattern.

CONCLUSION

In terms of strategy, at least, power-game offensive patterns are incredibly simple. In some cases the only player moving on offense will be the center at low post, who will cut back and forth across and around the lane, trying to work himself free to receive a pass inside. However, if such a situation will get the ball inside without resorting to more complicated patterns of movement, nothing more would be necessary. I used power-game offenses at Riverside City College, Pasadena City College, and Long Beach State, and from those experiences I gained a lot of respect for the philosophy behind the power game.

In using any kind of power-game offense, your first concern is always to get the ball inside to the post. The less movement, ball or player, used in working the ball in to the post, the better off you're going to be. In working the power game, you may have to take the outside shot, but your players should be attuned to the idea of looking inside every time they get the ball. If it takes only one pass to set up the inside confrontation, you're in good shape. You can add movement to the pattern, if necessary, but your players should never be so involved in cutting and screening that they forget to look for the inside pass.

Finally, before installing a power-game offense you would be well advised to evaluate your inside scoring potential. If a guard or forward is your only player who operates well from the low post, then the only way your power game is going to be effective is to isolate that guard or forward at the low post. If no one on your team can fill the low post adequately, your players will probably be more effective in some kind of continuity pattern.

6

Man-to-Man Continuity Patterns

Continuity patterns are not the same as power-game offenses, although the objectives of the two are similar: both are used to produce high-percentage shots, preferably inside. They differ in the kinds of inside shots to be taken, the players designated to take the shots, and the fact that the big men stay inside exclusively in most power-game variations, whereas they may be expected to move outside periodically in the course of running continuity patterns. Continuity patterns usually use screens and cuts away from the ball to spring a cutter free, whereas power-game screens are used almost solely by and for the big men inside, as in post interchanges.

The nature of the shots that are attempted in power-game and continuity patterns is likely to differ from the general conception. In continuity patterns, the cuts are longer and players rely more upon quickness and speed in getting to the basket after cutting around the screen than is the case in power-game screening patterns. In shooting power layups, the player goes up powerfully with the ball, protecting it with his body if necessary, and should expect defensive pressure because his screen was designed to free him to receive an inside pass, not to provide him with an easy layup.

Figures 6–1 and 6–2 illustrate the difference in the kind of inside shots that teams are likely to achieve from pattern-oriented offenses and continuity patterns. (We are assuming that in both cases the pass receiver inside will take no more than *one dribble* before going up for the layup.) Figure 6–1 shows one variation of the beginning movements in the Wheel pattern. 01 will have an open layup if the defense does not drastically alter its coverage by switching. However, 05's cut in Figure 6–2 is far more likely to receive intense defensive pressure since defenders X_4 and

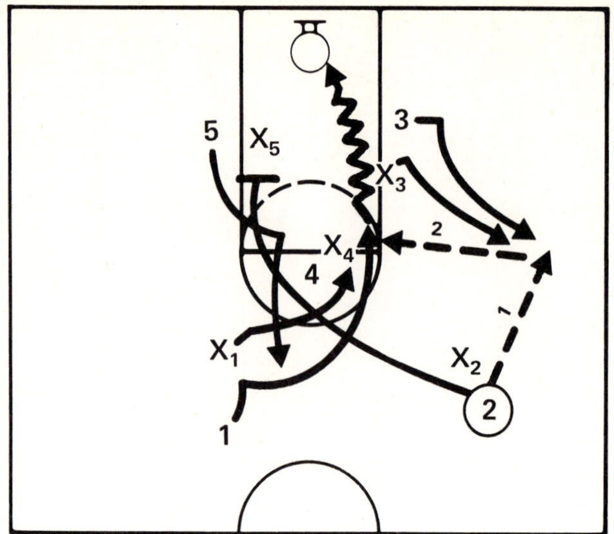

Figure 6–1 Comparing Continuity-Type Screens with Power Game Post Interchanges: *Continuity-Type Screen*

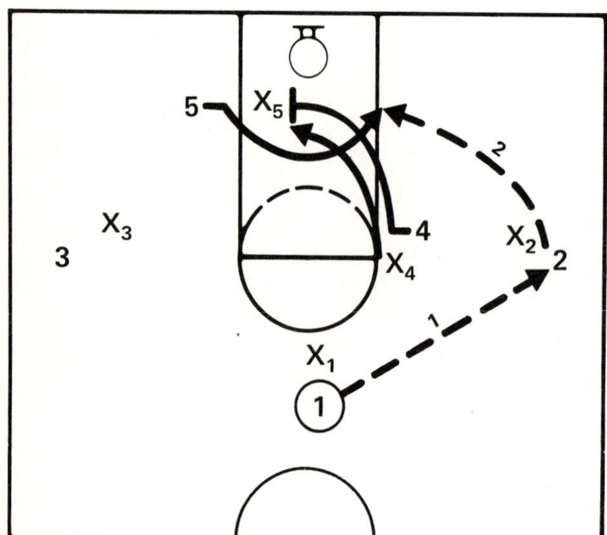

Figure 6–2 Comparing Continuity-Type Screens with Power Game Post Interchanges: *Power Game Post Interchange*

X_5 will not have to move as far from their basic positions to effect the switch and stop the layup.

We do not claim that one cut is superior to the other, or that either cut will result in an unguarded layup; rather, we're saying that 01, who is scissoring around 04's high screen in Figure 6–1, is hoping for an open layup, while 05 in Figure 6–2 would like an open layup, but is expecting to be covered shortly after receiving 02's pass. The difference is slight but important—a matter of *intent* rather than execution. Many teams that run a continuity pattern will avoid the inside pass to 01 in Diagram 6–1 if the defense switches; for example, if X_5 drops off 05 to cover 01's cut and X_1 picks up 05 at the free-throw line. However, if that same team runs an inside power-game offense, it will make the pass to 05 in Figure 6–2 *every time,* regardless of whether X_4 and X_5 switch to stop the layup.

Generally, then, we can say that success in running continuity patterns is based to a great extent on execution, timing, and finesse, whereas power-game offenses rely upon size, strength, or effective one-on-one play inside. In a continuity pattern, a guard coming around an outside screen might try to outrun a switching forward to the basket or fake him out of position for a short jumper; in a power-game offense, the forward or center receiving the inside pass will take the ball to the basket whether the defense switches or not. He'll take anything given to him, but he's also prepared to jam it home anyway.

When the Shuffle offense first appeared in the early 1950s, it was hailed as the first all-purpose offense in basketball, equally effective against zone and man-to-man defenses. Later, Garland Pinholster of Oglethorpe University popularized the Wheel offense, and proponents of the two systems argued incessantly over the relative merits and shortcomings of each.

However, time and extensive experimentation have revealed that, like practically everything else in life, there are few absolutes in basketball. The Shuffle, Wheel, and other continuity patterns have limitations that underscore the necessity of fitting offensive patterns to the available personnel. For example, it is generally accepted that, in most cases, man-to-man patterns are less effective than zone offenses in attacking zone defenses. The single exception to this can be found in the styles of attack employed against a matchup zone defense, where man-to-man continuity patterns may provide more ways of attacking the matchups than regular zone offenses.

A set play is a series of specific movements designed to yield an open shot from a high-percentage scoring area; whereas a continuity offense is a pattern in which the basic sequence of movements may be repeated without stopping to return the players to their original positions when scoring opportunities do not arise.

THE SHUFFLE OFFENSE

The Shuffle offense was developed by Bruce Drake at the University of Oklahoma in the early 1950s, and was popularized by Joel Eaves at Auburn University shortly thereafter. The Shuffle concept features constant movement by all players, screens away from the ball that yield inside or high-percentage outside shots, and player rotation that gives all five players shooting options and scoring opportunities. The basic Shuffle movements require five good ball handlers who are capable of executing such fundamentals as screening, cutting around screens, and recognizing situations that require automatics (for example, backdoor cuts). However, it is more important that the players be thoroughly indoctrinated in the Shuffle philosophy of patience and waiting for high-percentage scoring situations to develop.

Although it is no longer in vogue, the Shuffle offense can still provide a potent offensive scoring thrust for teams that are patient enough to wait for the defense to make a mistake.

In Figure 6–3, 03 passes to 02. 02 will turn toward the basket immediately and determine without hesitating whether he can shoot, drive, or pass to 03 cutting around 05. If he decides against these alternatives, he will pass to 01 cutting outside and move to the high post to screen for 05 cutting to the top of the circle. 02 continues to the weak-side low post. 04 brushes his man off on 02 and cuts across the lane to the high post. Meanwhile, 01 will have considered: (a) shooting or driving the baseline, (b) passing to 03 cutting into the lane toward the basket, and (c) passing to 04 cutting into the lane and continuing to the high post. If none of these alternatives seems particularly appealing, 01 will pass to 05 at the top of the circle to begin the continuity rotation to the other side of the court.

The key to the success of these movements, and to those involved in the continuity rotation and automatics as well, lies in the players' ability to take advantage of deficiencies in the coverage whenever opportunities arise. No pattern, whether continuity or set play, will work consistently if the players are not prepared to break the pattern and go one-on-one when

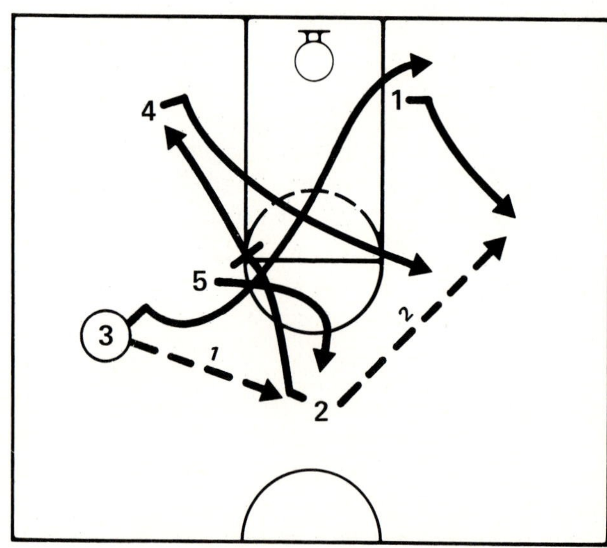

Figure 6–3 Basic Shuffle Movements

the defense adjusts its coverage to stop the basic movements of the pattern.

Shuffle continuity consists of 01 passing to 05 at the top of the circle and cutting through the lane to the low post. 02 cuts outside to receive 05's pass. 03 cuts to the high post behind 01's pick. 05 screens for 04 who cuts to the top of the circle. 05 continues to the weak-side low post, as shown in Figure 6–4. The basic movements are now ready to be repeated.

However, the defense often will attempt to thwart the rotation by overplaying 05 and cutting off 01's outlet pass shown in Figure 6–4. When this happens, 03 will step out to the ball-side corner and 01 will pass to 03 and cut hard to the basket, looking for a return pass and layup. (See Figure 6–5.) (Movements of this sort, which are made when the defenders overplay the passing lanes to block the pattern's continuity, are known as offensive *automatics.*)

If the return pass to 01 is not made, 01 will continue through the lane and empty, 04 will cut outside to fill 01's position, and 05 will attempt to step in front of (or cut behind) his man and break toward the basket for a pass and layup. 02 will fill 05's position. If 05 does not receive a pass from 03, he will move to the high post.

This pattern may be repeated as often as necessary to draw the defense into more conventional, sagging coverage at the top of the circle and elsewhere. The spread alignment should provide the offensive team with ample opportunities for one-on-one play, backdoor cuts, and the like, especially when the defensive players overplay the passing lanes.

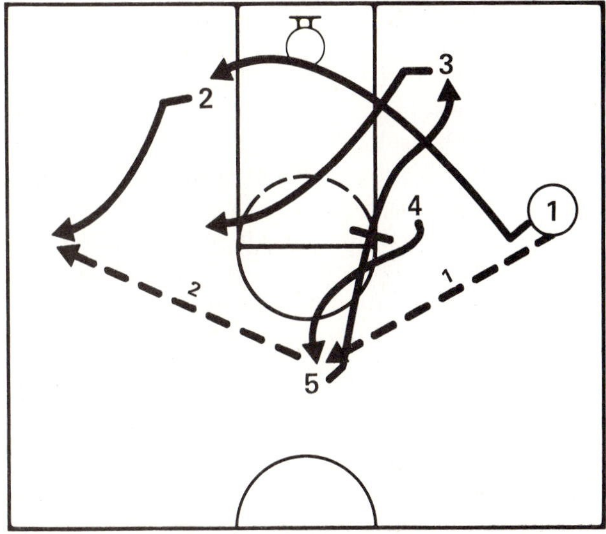

Figure 6–4 Shuffle Continuity

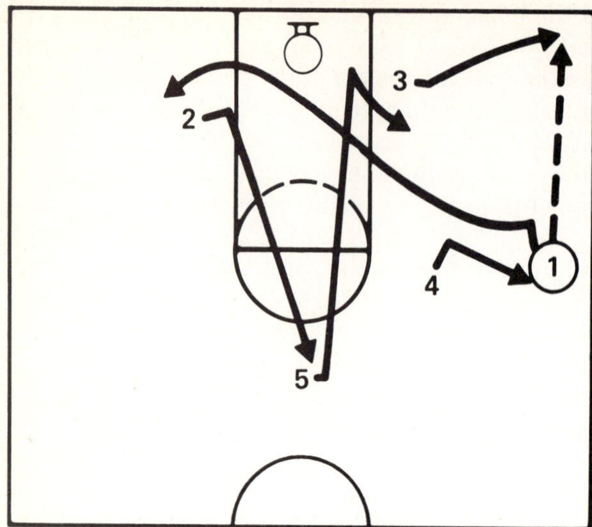

Figure 6–5 Pass-and-Cut Automatic When the Defense Overplays the Rotation to the Point

We reiterate at this point that the descriptions of the Shuffle and other man-to-man offenses are extremely rudimentary, and they in no way describe the broad range of offensive potential of any or all of the patterns. The options, automatics, and variations of the basic pattern are practically limitless, as are those of other man-to-man continuity patterns. Entire books have been devoted to some of these patterns and their variations, and the coach desiring to learn more about continuity offenses is advised to consult any of the fine books that are available on the subject.

Three-Man Shuffle Variation

Although the Shuffle offense possesses many strong points, it has one distinct disadvantage that renders it useless to many teams with limited personnel: it requires five good ball handlers who are capable of playing all five positions in the Shuffle rotation. For teams that have only a few capable ball handlers, or players who are not used to such sophisticated approaches to man-to-man offense, the "Three-Man" variation of the original Shuffle offense can provide the same kind of offensive thrust without entrusting the ball-handling chores to all five players.

In the Three-Man Shuffle Variation, most of the ball handling is done by the post players, 04 and 05 in Figures 6–6 and 6–7. As 01 passes to 05 cutting to the high post and clears to the side, 02 and 03 scissor around the weak-side high post 04. 02 continues through the lane to the ball-side corner, and 03 cuts to the top of the circle. 04 then returns to his weak-side low-post position. (This is not shown in Figure 6–6.)

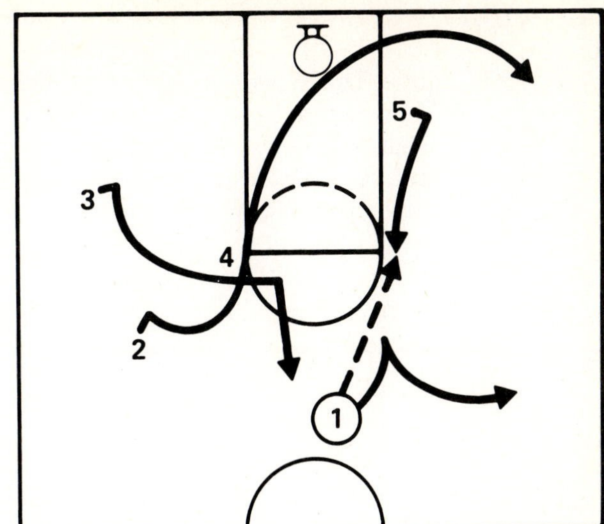

Figure 6–6 Three-Man Shuffle Offense, Basic Movements

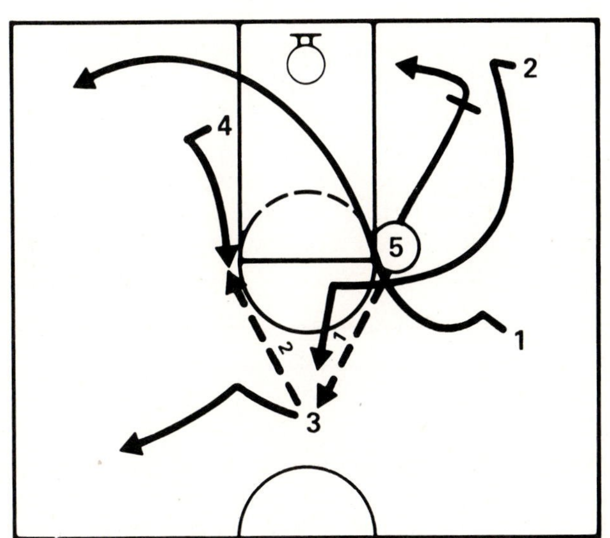

Figure 6–7 Three-Man Shuffle Rotation

Rotation in the Three-Man Shuffle begins with 05 passing to 03. 04 cuts to the high post to receive 03's pass, and 03 clears to the side after passing. 01 cuts around 05 and continues across the lane to the corner. 05 screens for 02 and returns to the low post. 02 cuts around 05 and, if he is not clear for the shot, slides outside to the top of the circle. The pattern is now ready to be run again, although only 04 and 05 occupy their original positions.

THE WHEEL OFFENSE

The Wheel offense is similar to the Shuffle in that both systems feature single and double screens away from the ball, high-percentage shot selection, and patient ball handling. Although many variations of the basic pattern exist, the one shown in Figures 6–8 and 6–9 is as good as any continuity offense currently in use in its potential for exploiting a wide range of defensive errors.

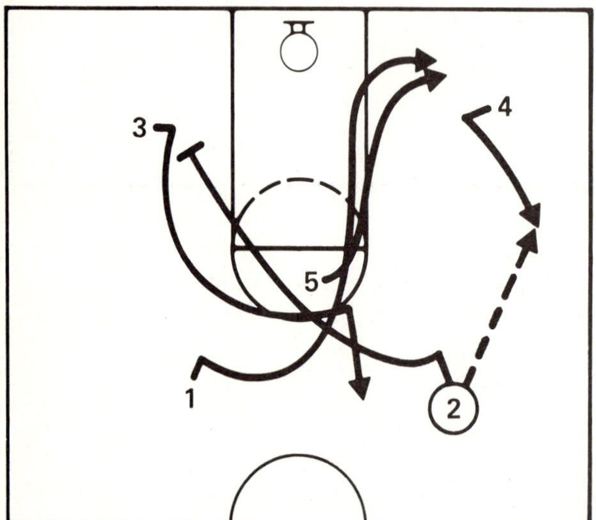

Figure 6–8 Wheel Offense, Basic Movements

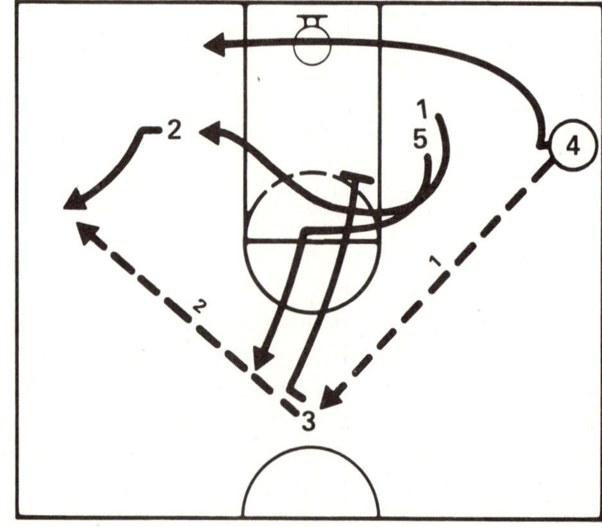

Figure 6–9 Wheel Continuity

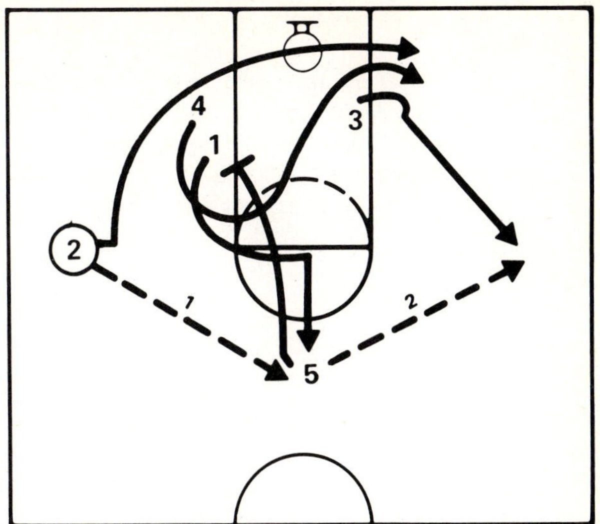

Figure 6–10 Wheel Continuity, Rotation

Unlike the Shuffle, the Wheel offense can be run from many offensive alignments. In the 2–1–2 alignment shown in Figure 6–8, 04 cuts outside to receive 02's pass. 02 and 01 split the post around 05. 02 continues low to screen for 03, and 01 continues to the ball-side low post. 05 follows 01 to set a double screen for 04. 03 cuts around 02 and, if he doesn't receive 04's pass, 03 continues to the top of the circle.

04 passes to 03 and cuts around the double screen set by 01 and 05. He then slides to the ball-side low post. 02 cuts outside to receive 03's pass. 03 moves low to screen for 05, and 01 cuts across the lane behind 05 and 03 to set a double screen with 04. 05 cuts around 03's screen and, if he doesn't receive 02's pass, continues to the top of the circle. (See Figure 6–9.)

Figure 6–10 shows the same continuity from the other side of the court.

Four-Man Wheel Variation

Coaches often find themselves in the uncomfortable position of wanting to "hide" one or more players, or to keep those players out of the general flow of the offense because of poor ball-handling skills, weak shooting, or any of countless other reasons. Whatever the case, continuity offenses, such as the basic Shuffle or Wheel, that require each player to handle the ball are likely to fail regardless of other players' skills when one or more players are unable to perform the necessary skills. Even a perfect screen avails nothing if the passer is unable to get the ball to the open player.

It would be nice to merely teach the players in question those skills required to execute the pattern. However, time limitations dictate that, for many coaches and teams, the answer lies in adapting continuity patterns such as the Shuffle or Wheel to the limitations of their personnel.

One such adaptation is the Four-Man Wheel variation. The Four-Man Wheel "hides" one player by using him to form the inside double screen on either side of the court (Figure 6–11).

The Four-Man Wheel variation has an added bonus: the weak-side

Figure 6–11 Four-Man Wheel Variation, Basic Movements

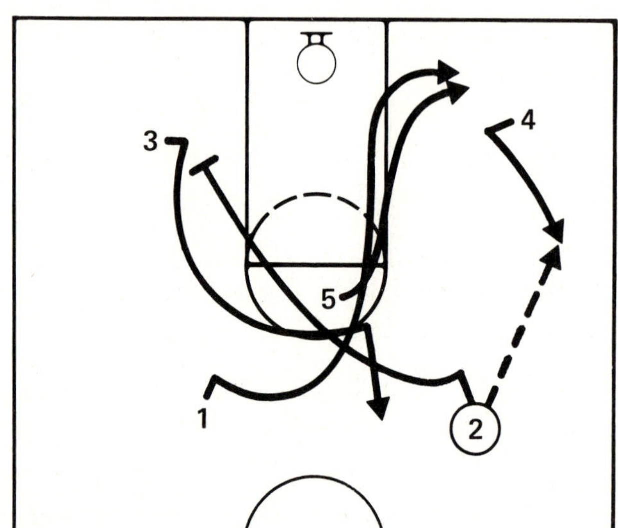

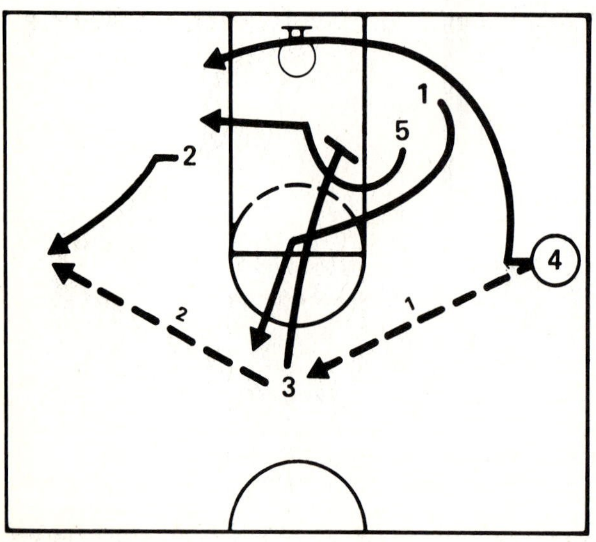

Figure 6–12 Four-Man Wheel Variation, Rotation

outside cut (01 from the low post to the top of the circle in Figure 6–12) may come off a double screen instead of a single screen if 05 delays his cut to the ball side.

WEAK-SIDE SCREENING OFFENSE

This continuity pattern is easy to learn, it uses cutters toward and away from the ball side of the court (including a screen on the weak side), and it provides outside rotation to change both the matchups and the areas in which openings arise in the defense. The screening position also can be used to hide a fundamentally weak offensive player, or to attack the defense when the players relax their coverage of 03's weak-side cuts to overplay the rest of the pattern.

01 passes to wing 05 and moves to the top of the circle. 03 moves to the weak-side high post and screens for 02, who cuts to the ball-side corner behind 03. (See Figure 6–13.) Ball rotation consists of 05 passing to 01, who relays the ball to 04 as 03 goes to the weak side again to screen for 05. 05 cuts into and across the lane to the ball-side corner. 02 moves out to 05's wing position, and the offense is ready to be run to the other side of the court again. (See Figure 6–14.)

Whenever the ball is passed to the corner, the passer cuts through the lane and the outside players rotate toward the ball in the familiar single-cutter-through pattern (Figure 6–15). The screening pattern is then ready to be repeated.

The weakness of the Weak-Side Screening Offense is the difficulty

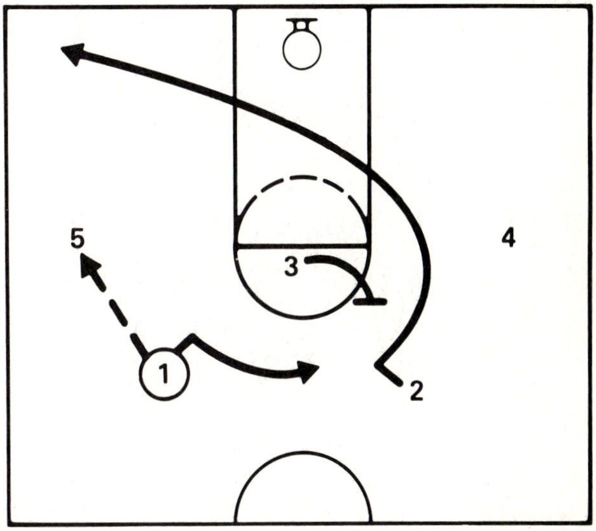

Figure 6–13 Weak-Side Screening Offense, First Movements

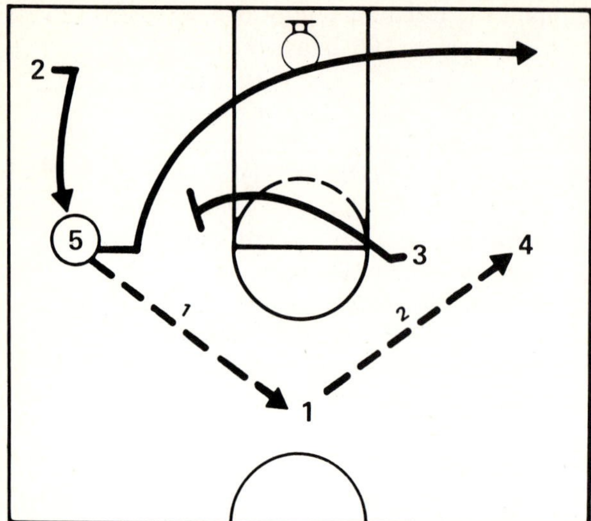

Figure 6–14 Weak-Side Screening Offense, Rotation

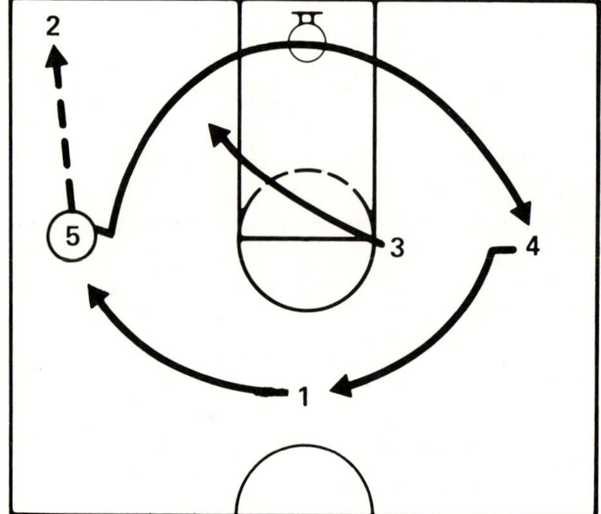

Figure 6–15 Single-Cutter Movement in Weak-Side Screening Offense

that is sometimes encountered in passing the ball from the wing to the point when 01 is overguarded. In such cases, the offense must resort to automatics such as 01's cutting backdoor to the basket for the pass, going one-on-one or two-on-two, or 03's cutting to the ball side to receive a pass or to set up to split the post.

OFFENSIVE AUTOMATICS

One of the greatest problems facing many coaches, especially those with teams of limited skills or playing experience, is when their players follow their basic offensive pattern too closely and for too long a time, and ignore scoring possibilities that arise out of their basic pattern.

For example, a wing player receives a pass from the top of the circle, passes to the corner, and cuts inside and across the lane in an outside cutter pattern without ever having looked inside to see if the weak-side low-post player was open cutting toward the ball. No harm was done in this particular case, except that a potential scoring opportunity was overlooked. However, the situation changes if his teammate in the corner is covered. If he passes to the corner without looking, the pass will be intercepted, and if neither he nor the player in the corner is prepared to deal with the situation by reverting to what is known as *automatics,* the entire offensive pattern is jeopardized.

When a team adheres too closely to its basic offensive pattern over a long period of time, the defenders are likely to attempt to interrupt the pattern by overplaying the passing lanes. If a team has no modifications or contingency movements that are designed to keep the defense honest, the offense is likely to become bogged down on one side of the court, or the ball will become locked in one player's possession until a turnover or held ball results.

Every continuity pattern should contain automatics that are designed to free the ball or create new scoring opportunities. Since even experienced players sometimes have trouble recognizing the automatics required in a pattern's continuity, these situations and the measures necessary to restore offensive continuity must be drilled into the players at great length.

It is beyond the scope of this book to deal in depth with the broad array of automatics in the various man-to-man offenses presented. However, we can exemplify the goals of teaching automatics by studying two aspects of one offense, the Wheel, which requires automatics when the defense overplays.

In Figure 6–16, 02 has passed to 04 and split the post with 01. 05 has dropped to the ball-side low post to form a double screen with 01. (Compare with Figures 6–8 and 6–9.) 02 has screened for 03, but the defense has switched and the player guarding 03 is overplaying and denying the rotation pass.

When 04 sees that he cannot pass to 03 to continue the pattern, he looks to 01 inside and signals the automatic. 01 steps out to receive 04's pass—the defense can hardly overplay *that*!—and 04 passes and cuts through the lane to the weak-side low post. 02 moves out to an intermediate wing position and 05 moves to the high post to screen for 03 cutting

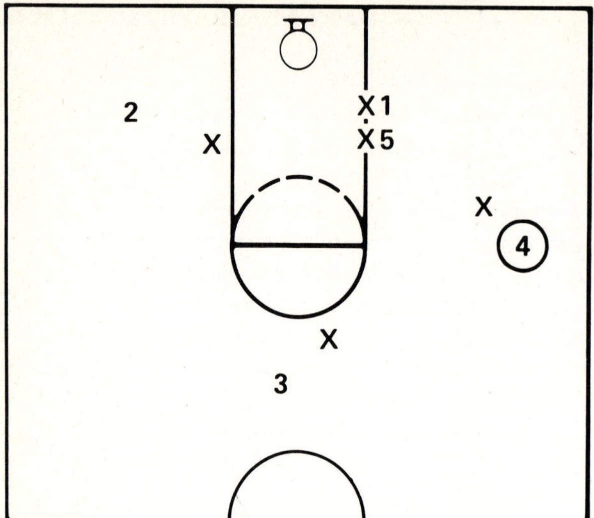

Figure 6–16 Defensive Overguarding to Set Up Automatic "Step Out" to Corner in Wheel Offense

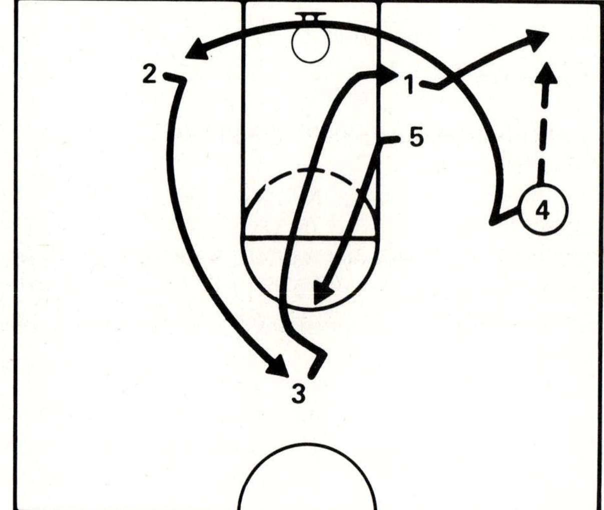

Figure 6–17 Automatic "Step Out" Movement in Wheel Offense

low. (See Figure 6–17.) If 03 does not receive 01's pass, he will set up at the low post and 01 will dribble outside to reset the offense. (See Figure 6–18.)

In Figure 6–19, the wing passes back to the point and cuts around the double screen, but the man who guards the receiver cutting outside is overplaying and denying the pass.

Figure 6–18 Resetting the Offense from "Step Out" Automatic

Figure 6–19 Defensive Overguarding to Set Up "Step Out" to Wing Position in Wheel Offense

When 03 sees that he cannot pass to 02, he signals the automatic and 01 steps out toward the wing for 03's pass. 02 and 03 move inside on the weak side. 04 cuts around the double screen and slides to the low post to set the ball-side double screen with 05. 02 cuts around 03 and moves to the top of the circle for 01's pass. 03 cuts outside to receive 01's pass, and the pattern is ready to be run again. (See Figure 6–20.)

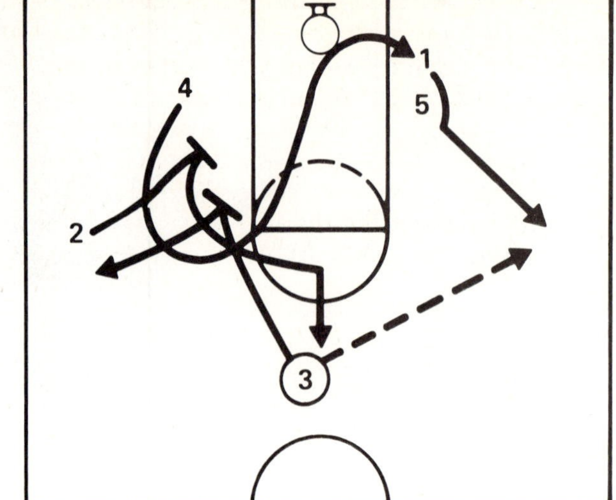

Figure 6–20 "Step Out" Wheel Automatic from Point

THE PASSING GAME

When a team runs a Shuffle or Wheel offense, it runs either the basic, repetitive pattern or automatics designed to provide other avenues of attack or to re-establish the pattern. With "passing game" offenses, however, there is no similar pattern for a team to follow or re-establish, and therein lies much of the passing game's ultimate effectiveness: if the offensive team is never sure of its movements in advance, the defensive team certainly is not going to anticipate the pattern and adopt automatic responses such as overplaying the passing lanes or switching automatically.

"Passing game" offenses basically involve one or more screens set away from the ball that are designed to free a player away from the ball. Passing game offenses therefore work best with players who are willing and able to play without the ball. Dribbling within the passing game is purposeful; that is, it is held to a minimum except when a player has received the ball in a position that is favorable for driving or one-on-one play. Detractors who are unfamiliar with the specifics of passing game philosophy sometimes feel that the lack of dribbling constitutes over-regimentation and detracts from individual initiative, and thus is a weakness of passing game offenses. Such reactions probably reflect a reluctance to change as much as a mistrust of the supposedly unnatural lack of dribbling in passing-game offenses. After all, most teams keep dribbling to a minimum in their zone offenses, too. More importantly, the Shuffle and Wheel offenses are not designed to promote dribbling either; few continuity offenses except weave patterns feature more than token dribbling in their execution.

Rather than use patterns, players select their movements, cuts, and screens from a series of predetermined court positions and the location of the ball. For example, one elementary movement seen in many passing game offenses is the high-low post interchange. (See Figures 6–21 and 6–22.)

In the movements shown in Figures 6–21 and 6–22, 04 and 05 are performing a function known as *balancing the posts.* This can be accomplished in a variety of ways, but the two examples shown in Figures 6–21 and 6–22 illustrate a particular kind of balancing movement used when

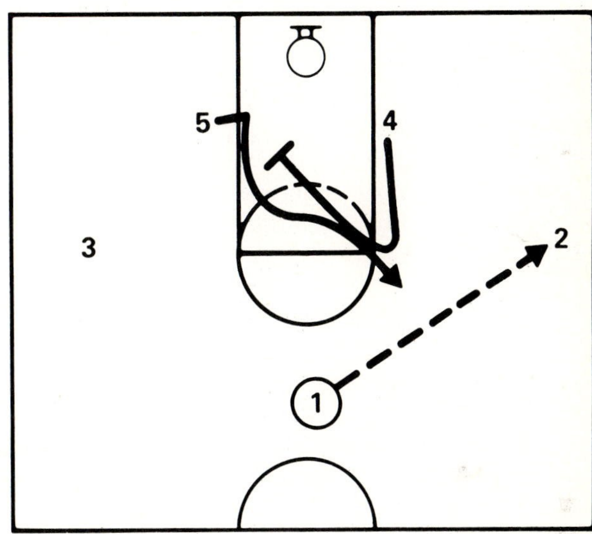

Figure 6–21 Balancing the Offense for Post Interchange from Double Low Post Alignment

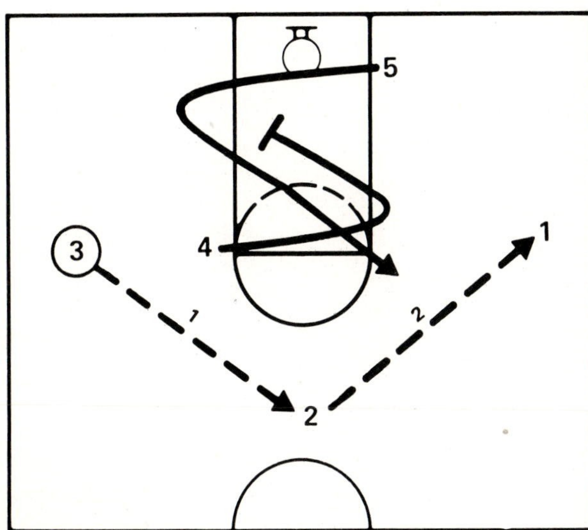

Figure 6–22 Balancing the Offense for Post Interchange from High-Low Post Alignment

one post player (04) does not operate particularly well with the ball one-on-one. This kind of balancing can hide a passive or inexperienced player.

If a team was not interested in hiding a particular player, 04 would still cut to the high post with 01's pass to 02 in Figure 6–21; however, in Figure 6–22, 05 would cut to the ball-side high post with 04's slide to the weak-side low post, and 05 would screen for 04 cutting to the ball-side high post.

The reason the cuts to the high post precede the screen in the lane is to provide a maximal screening angle. It would be nice to merely move across the lane to screen from a double low-post alignment like that shown in Figure 6–21, but the passing and screening angles are of such disparity that the screen often fails to contain the cutter's man. (To be most effective, the passing and screening angles should be as identical as possible.)

Angles are important in passing game offenses. Perimeter passing angles should be diagonal (for example, wing-to-point-to-wing), rather than parallel to the baseline or sideline, in order to reduce the likelihood of stolen passes. Examples of these diagonal passing and screening angles often encountered in passing game offenses are shown in Figures 6–23 and 6–24.

The most important aspect of the passing game offenses is reading the defense and making whatever cuts the defense gives you. Players must be able to set legal screens, and their movement to and from various court positions should be constant. Passing game offenses will seldom succeed when players stand around watching the ball. (The same could be said of other continuity offenses, of course, but in other types of continuity

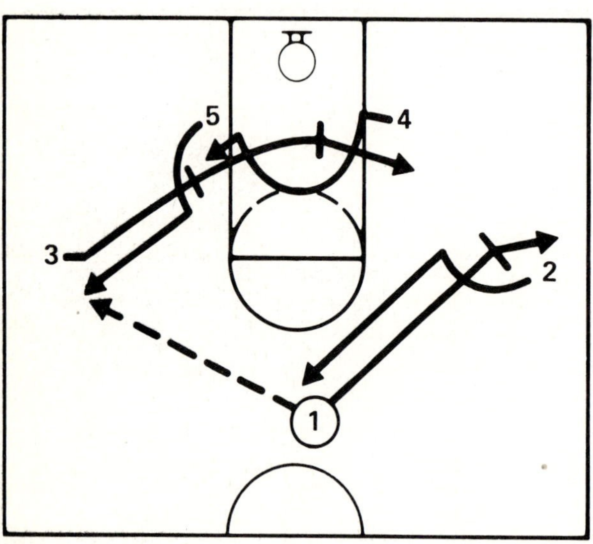

Figure 6–23 Typical Diagonal Passing, Screening, and Cutting Angles in Passing Game Offenses (*Example #1*)

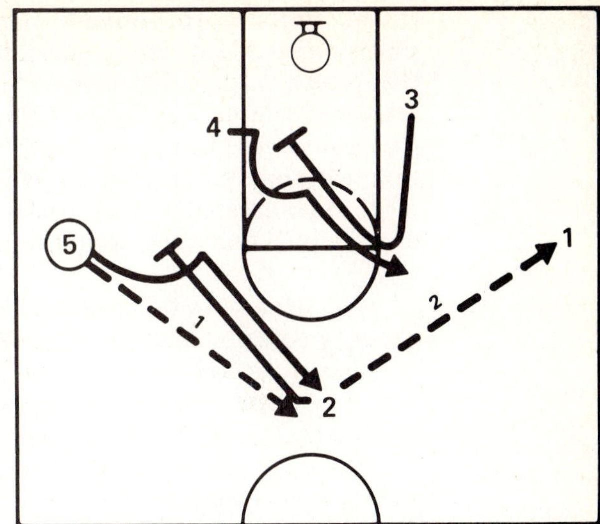

Figure 6–24 Typical Diagonal Passing, Screening, and Cutting Angles in Passing Game Offenses (*Example #2*)

offenses, such as the Shuffle or Wheel, the players follow predetermined routes in their patterns.) Because passing games are freelanced rather than patterned, there is a need for continuous movement to keep the defensive players occupied.

Players involved in passing games follow *rules* rather than patterns. These rules are both general and specific. General rules include:

1. Always move after passing the ball. The direction of the movement may vary—for example, away from the ball to screen or clear, toward the ball to screen for the pass receiver or set up a give-and-go, toward the basket in a backdoor cut, and so on—but the need for movement is always present. We know that movement is vital to continuity offenses; in the passing game, it is mandatory. A good rule to follow is, *If you don't know what to do at any given moment in the passing game, don't do it standing still. Keep moving!*

2. Always move to meet passes. This does not necessarily mean moving toward the ball; it means at least moving away from the defender.

3. When in doubt, set a screen. Looking for opportunities to set or receive a screen can exert a positive influence on a team's overall offensive performance. It is purposeful, directed, and keeps the players moving as well as concentrating on what they're doing. The worst imaginable situation in the passing game is to have one player with the ball and four teammates standing around watching him as he tries to set up his shot.

4. Balance the offense before setting or receiving screens. Players must thoroughly understand the court positions from which they plan to attack the defense if they are to properly set up attacks by screening. The multiple screens seen in passing game offenses are seldom the result of random movements. While no predetermined pattern exists to guide players' movements away from the ball, they will constantly move to fill vacated positions, set screens, cut into openings, go backdoor, and the like, from predetermined areas of the court.

5. Attempt to take the ball into scoring areas. Penetration will always create problems for the defense beyond those encountered in running basic patterns.

Specific rules will govern player options after passing the ball (cut to the basket, screen away from the ball); after receiving a pass (shoot, drive, pass-and-cut); after setting a screen (roll to the basket, flare to spread the defensive coverage, cut back toward the ball); after receiving a screen (going over the top or behind the screen as dictated by defensive coverage to establish a passing angle away from the defender, or even sliding away from the screen when the defender tries to go around the screen); and maintaining court balance (setting up high-low alignments as shown in Figures 6–21, 6–22, and 6–24, or realigning the players in desired court positions after freelance movements such as backdoor cuts or flashing into the middle).

Examples of typical passing game movements and options are shown in Figures 6–25 through 6–27.

In Figure 6–25, 01 passes to 02 and screens on the weak side for 03

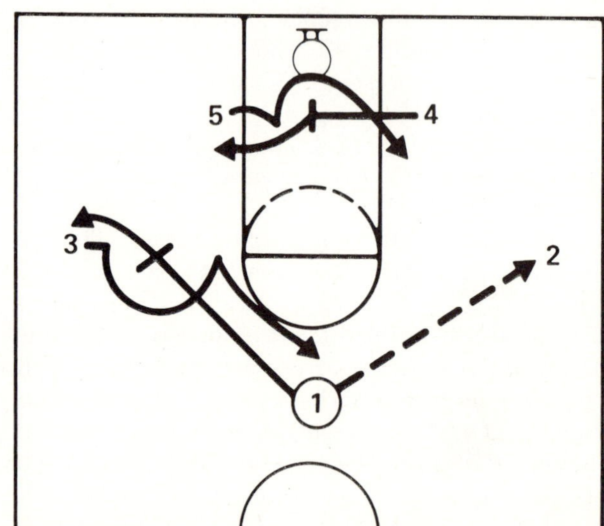

Figure 6–25 Setting Up the Passing Game

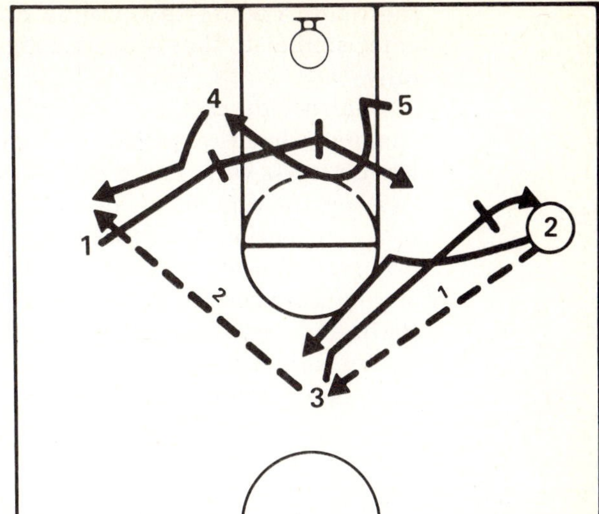

Figure 6–26 Ball Rotation, Passing Game

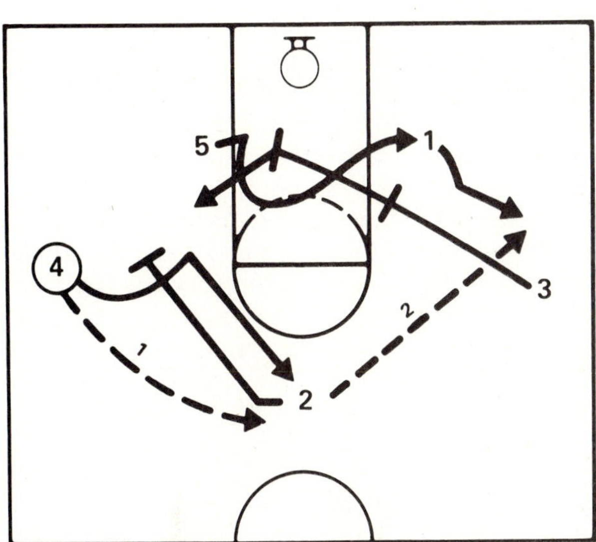

Figure 6–27 Continuing the Passing Game Movements

cutting into the high-post area. 04 screens for 05 cutting across the lane toward the ball. 03 fills the point position.

The movement is continued in Figure 6–26 with 02's pass to 03. 01 moves inside to screen for 04 cutting outside, then continues into the lane to screen for 05 cutting across the lane. 03 passes to 04, who looks inside to pass to 05 if possible. 03 moves to the weak side to screen for 02, who cuts to the free-throw line and then to the point.

Figure 6–27 shows the same rotation back to the original side of the court. The North Carolina State Wolfpack ran a splendid passing game similar to that shown in Figures 6–25 through 6–27 very successfully.

Although passing-game offenses possess certain weaknesses—for example, they are sometimes vulnerable to pressure defense when the offense starts with all the cutters initiating motion from scoring areas—I consider the concept underlying passing-game offenses to be among the best in offensive basketball. The passing game is basically a freelance offense, and when it is used for its one-on-one potential as well as for its screening and cutting possibilities, it can be a formidable offensive attack. Successful coaches such as Dean Smith, Eddie Sutton, Norm Sloan, and Bobby Knight have used passing-game offenses, which adds credence to the passing game's validity as a style of offensive attack.

THE MOVING GAME

We felt that our moving game complemented our inside power game at Long Beach State, giving us additional options with which to attack the defense. The moving game provided a great deal of motion in our offense—it was a driving, aggressive style of play in which we were able to exploit our opponents' defensive weaknesses. When it was executed properly, the moving game caused our opponents to lose sight of the ball while defending against the cuts, which in turn denied them the chance to double-team as our players' individual freedom expanded to take advantage of one-on-one situations. We also felt that team morale was given a boost because the four players (excluding the center) played all the positions. While the moving game provided ideal opportunities to showcase the talents of an outstanding individual player, all the players were given the opportunity to go one-on-one during the offense's freelance continuity.

Moving Game Drills

We began our moving-game drill sequences with a one-on-one that had the guards and small forwards working together in one area, and the centers and big forwards going against each other in another area. As offensive players finished their turn they became the next defensive players, with the previous defenders moving to the end of the offensive line. The defensive men had to secure possession of the ball before they could move to the offensive line.

One-on-One Play (Creating a Lead). The first step of this drill is to create a lead against tight defensive coverage (Figure 6–28). The offensive man must throw fakes to the basket and free himself to receive the

Figure 6–28 Creating a Lead and Subsequent One-on-One

ball in a normal operating position, using either a stride or a jump stop. After pivoting to face the basket, he can incorporate an offensive move such as a rocker step, crossover step, or hesitation step to gain an offensive advantage, particularly in his first two dribbles. (Emphasizing aggressive movements in the first two dribbles underscores the importance of using attacking techniques in one-on-one confrontations; therefore, this drill is especially effective in weaning players away from dependence on long dribbling sequences. If a player consistently needs ten to twelve dribbles to set up his shot, this kind of drill may be exactly what he needs to break that habit.)

Although this drill is designed to improve offensive habits, it also can be an effective defensive drill. After each player has become proficient in creating the leads, using proper footwork, and maneuvering offensively, the next step is to move on to two-on-two situations.

Two-on-Two Play. We used all of the possible two-man play situations included in our offensive system: guard-and-guard, guard-and-forward, guard-and-center, and forward-and-center. Two-man play demands timing and coordination of thinking as well as execution.

In the moving game we liked to pass and move away from the ball, specifically with a *give-and-go* (Figures 6–29 and 6–30) or a *jab-and-go* (Figures 6–31 and 6–32).

In the give-and-go, the guard who makes the pass cuts in front of his man and continues to the basket, clearing to the weak side if he doesn't get the ball. In the jab-and-go, the guard fake-steps in one direction and cuts to the basket the other way. As another option, the guard can pass,

Figure 6–29 Give-and-Go Cut, Two-Man Drill (*a*)

Figure 6–30 Give-and-Go Cut, Two-Man Drill (*b*)

Figure 6–31 Jab-and-Go Cut,
Two-Man Drill (*a*)

Figure 6–32 Jab-and-Go Cut,
Two-Man Drill (*b*)

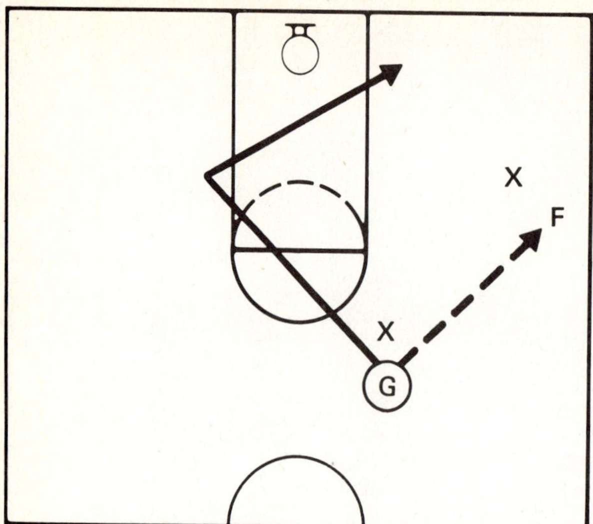

Figure 6–33 Weak-Side Cut, Reverse and Post Up

cut away from the ball, cut across diagonally, and reverse and post up. (See Figure 6–33.)

Timing and coordination are of the utmost importance in these situations. Upon receiving the ball, the forward must be able to make the pass at the right moment.

Timing and coordination should be emphasized in two-on-two drills, but the players should also be encouraged to use their one-on-one skills. If a player can beat his man after receiving the pass, he should disregard the two-on-two and without hesitation take advantage of his one-on-one superiority. Failure to take advantage of one-on-one opportunities can stifle the effectiveness of any pass-oriented offense.

Incidentally, the same kinds of guard-to-forward passes and movements shown in Figures 6–29 through 6–32 can be used with a forward at the wing and a center in the post, or with a guard and a center.

Three-on-Three Play. Much of the time spent in our moving-game practice dealt with three-on-three situations. We felt that the three-on-three, with its almost endless variations, was the heart of our moving-game offense. We'd have the guard bringing the ball down court pass to a forward who was creating a proper lead, and cut away from the ball and screen for the other guard. (See Figure 6–34.)

In the movements shown in Figure 6–34 it is important that the screening guard be stationary before the cutting guard makes his move around the screen. The cutting guard who is going to free himself to receive the ball must carry his man into the screen and use proper timing in coming off the screen.

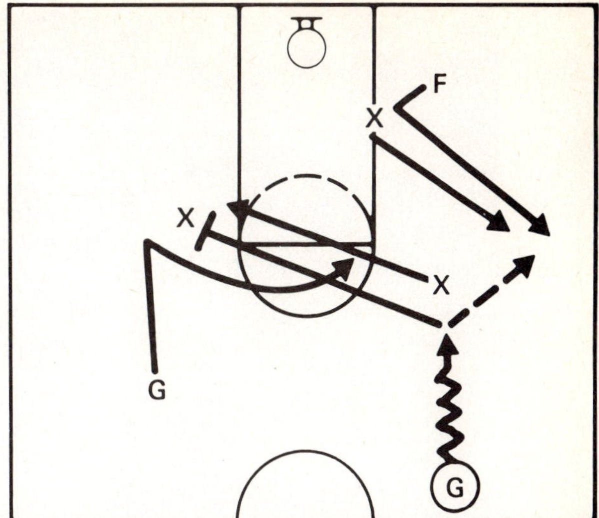

Figure 6–34 Basic Three-on-Three Movement

If the defense is able to execute a successful switch, the screening guard can use a false screen, or "fake screen-and-roll" (Figure 6–35), or else he can cut back toward the ball—a move called, appropriately enough, a *cutback* (Figures 6–36 and 6–37).

If the defenders overplay the screening movement, the screening guard may not screen at all; instead, he may fake the screen and roll suddenly to the basket (Figure 6–35), or he may cut back outside, either to the free-throw line as shown in Figures 6–36 and 6–37, or as high as the

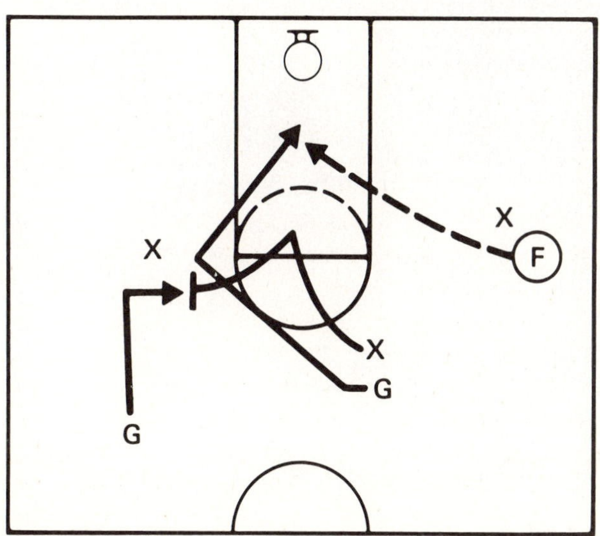

Figure 6–35 Fake Screen and Roll

Figure 6–36 Cutback Movement (*a*)

Figure 6–37 Cutback Movement (*b*)

top of the circle. Players should understand, and be able to use, the movements that can combat defensive overplaying and switching in the moving game. In Figure 6–35, instead of actually setting the screen, the guard moving down to set the screen suddenly pivots and cuts into the lane as the defensive guards switch.

Sometimes the defensive forward overplays the forward who creates the lead, attempting to either deny or intercept the pass. In such cases, our rule was that, whenever a defender overplayed the passing lane, the potential pass receiver must immediately reverse direction and cut to the basket. We didn't want our forward to stand around at the wing and watch the action, so if he couldn't shake his man by the time he reached the wing, he would cut back to the baseline.

The ball handler would pass to the other guard creating *his* lead, and then cut inside to screen for the forward cutting around the screen toward the ball. (Of course, the ball handler could also have passed to the forward going backdoor to the basket.) In setting the screen shown in Figure 6–38, the guard must find the defensive forward, and the forward who is freeing himself must steer his man directly into the screen that is being set. He must not come too soon, but should wait until the screen is set and then break off the screen quickly. Again, he should be made aware that, if he is overplayed, he should cut immediately for the basket. If the switch occurs, he should roll back. The guard who set the screen should roll toward the basket.

To return to Figure 6–34, when the ball handler passed to the forward and screened away from the ball, the forward passed to the other guard coming off the screen in the vicinity of the high post. Ideally, the

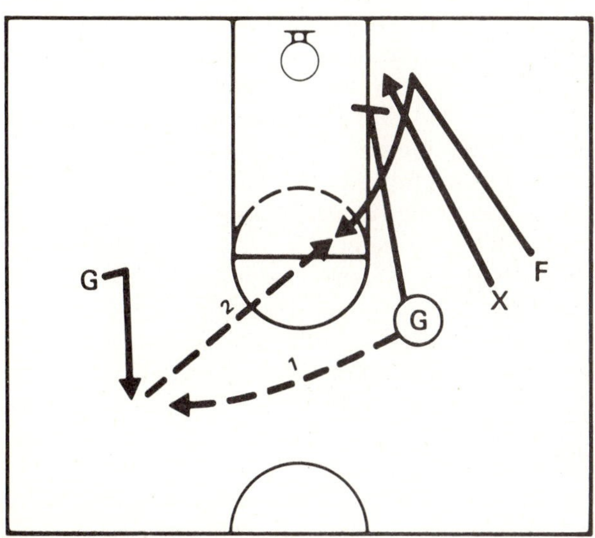

Figure 6–38 Inside Screen Off Guard-to-Guard Pass

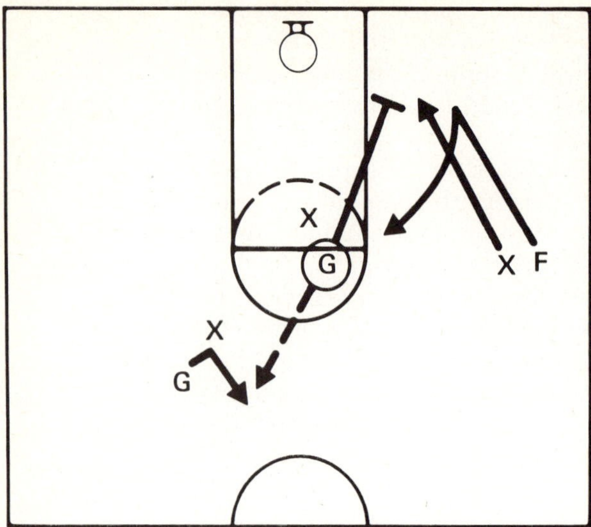

Figure 6–39 Inside Screen from Continuity

guard would work his man for a high-percentage one-on-one shot, but sometimes other opportunities arose. (See Figure 6–39.)

After passing to the guard coming around the screen, the forward cut to the baseline. The ball handler passed to the other guard creating a lead, and moved inside to screen the forward's defender. The forward cut around the screen to receive the ball. The screening and cutting principles are identical to those described previously.

In teaching this offense, we started by making the defense play it straight, without switching. Once the players mastered the use of screens and the ability to get off them, we let the defenders switch.

Occasionally we used a center in our three-man game. When the ball was passed to the center, we didn't use splitting cuts (for example, splitting the post) as many other teams did; instead, we insisted on our players' running *straight cuts*. (See Figures 6–40 and 6–41.)

Most teams will split the post after passing to the center. We went away from the splitting motion to straight cuts. In all parts of our moving game, our main goals were to keep the defense spread, make the defenders turn their backs on the ball, and deny them the opportunity to double-team the ball. Splitting cuts would have made the latter goal more difficult to achieve, which is why we used straight cuts instead. The quick diagonal cuts also create floor space, and in creating floor space the player who has received the ball is isolated to work one-on-one. As before, we encouraged our players to take advantage of one-on-one or two-on-two situations. (See Figures 6–42 and 6–43.)

Cuts that are designed to create floor space for the ball handler provide additional room in which he can try to beat his defensive man.

Figure 6–40 Straight Cuts, Three-on-Three (*a*)

Figure 6–41 Straight Cuts, Three-on-Three (*b*)

Figure 6–42 Creating Floor Space, Guard-to-Forward Pass (*a*)

Figure 6–43 Creating Floor Space, Guard-to-Forward Pass (*b*)

During this and all of our drills, we encouraged the player driving for the basket to go all the way to the basket unless the defensive center switched off. As soon as the defensive center started to make the switch, the ball handler immediately dumped the ball off to our offensive center or post man. The driver obviously had to exercise great judgment in making the pass: he had to know when he should go all the way to the basket and when he should release the ball to the center.

The driver also should know that, if the defense is providing help from a forward or guard, he must immediately release the ball to the open man. Because this movement and its options require split-second timing, it must be drilled constantly. It is of paramount importance that players learn to use proper judgment in driving and making the pass, and in the use of screens.

Four-on-Four Play. In our four-on-four, we used two guards and two forwards. We ran four-on-four every day of the season. Actually, the way we ran our moving game, our forwards and guards were constantly interchanging, so we often had our forwards operating from the guard slots, and vice versa. For this explanation, however, we'll use the basic guard-forward alignment. (See Figure 6–44.)

The first thing we taught in our four-on-four was balancing the

Figure 6–44 Basic Four-on-Four Alignment

court. If we had a guard passing to a forward and cutting diagonally to the basket, the other players had to balance the court or fill the vacated court positions. Each player was expected to recognize the areas where court vacancies could occur, and he had to know whose responsibility it was to balance the court if the shot could not be made from one part of the offense.

At this point, we liked to point out to our players that, with the continuous, fluid motion prevailing throughout the offense, and going directly from one phase to another without pausing or stopping, we could not afford to stop to reorganize the pattern. To do this, our guards and forwards had to learn all four positions on the court.

After balancing the court, our players learned our double-screen offense. As with the three-on-three, it was initiated by the ball-handling guard coming down court and passing to either a guard or a forward, and then cutting away from the ball. If he passed to the forward on his side, he moved across to screen for the other guard. (See Figure 6–45.)

More frequently, however, when 01 passed to 03 and turned to screen for 02, he would find 02 already moving over to screen for 04. When 01 saw this, he would change his direction and continue across to set a double screen for 04. (See Figure 6–46.)

While the double screen was being set, the forward with the ball had the side of the court open to him to work one-on-one against his man. If he didn't gain an early advantage, he would pass to the forward coming off the double screen. The forward had to use proper footwork in coming off the screens, of course, and he would steer his man into the picks. He was open to receive the pass a surprisingly large percentage of the time if he

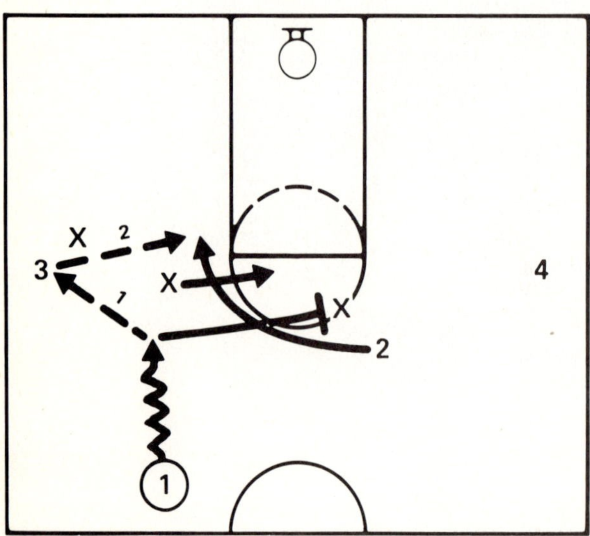

Figure 6–45 Four-on-Four, Basic Movements

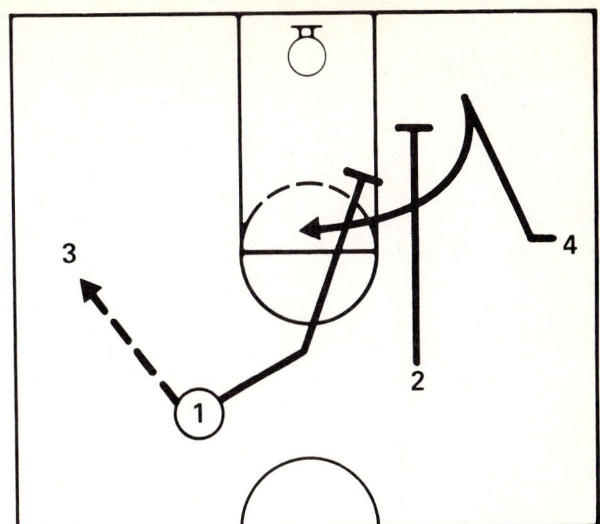

Figure 6–46 Weak-Side Double Screen, Four-on-Four Play

had cut off the picks closely. (If he came off the screens and felt pressure being applied to him, he reversed and cut to the basket immediately. Then, if 03 had neither passed to 04 nor worked his man one-on-one, 04 and the two guards would balance the court or reset themselves in their original court positions, possibly as shown in Figure 6–47.)

If the guard coming down court with the ball passed to the other guard, he would set a screen for the forward on his side. (See Figure 6–48.)

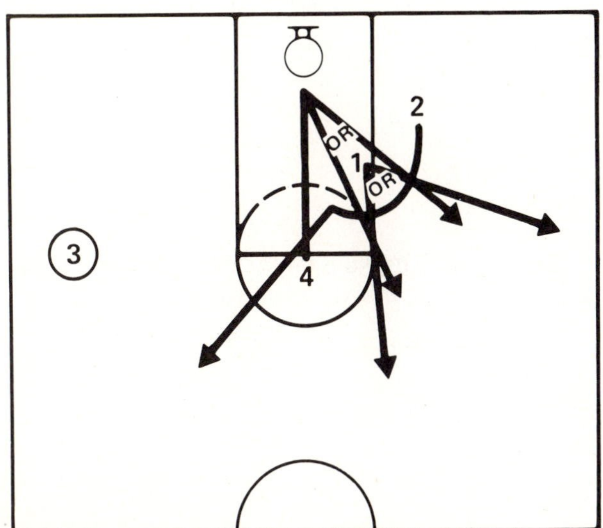

Figure 6–47 Balancing the Court

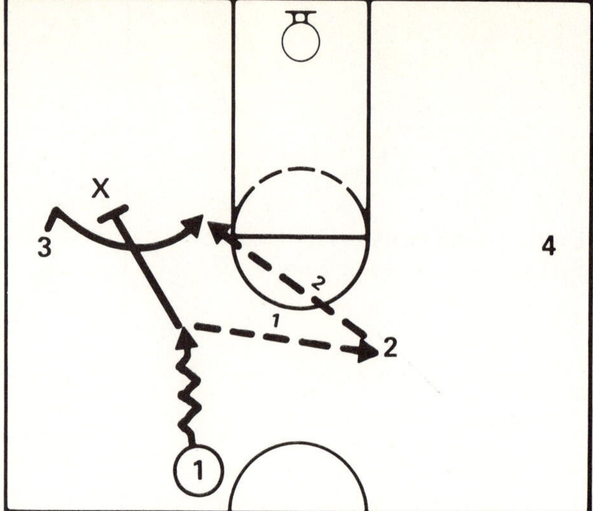

Figure 6–48 Guard-to-Guard Pass, Four-on-Four Play

02 had the option of working his man one-on-one instead of passing to 03, or of passing to 04 and setting a double screen for 03. (See Figure 6–49.)

As was the case with all our screening movements, we started out by making the defense play it straight, without switching. Once the offensive players were able to set and use the screens properly, we allowed the defenders to switch and taught the offensive players to use false screens and cutbacks.

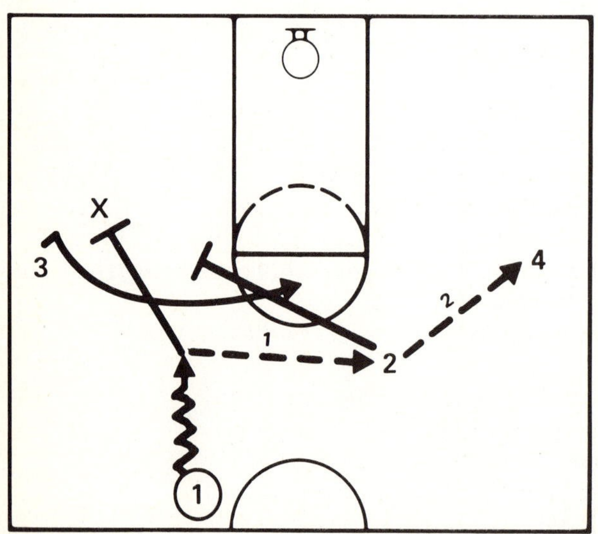

Figure 6–49 Double Screen After Guard-to-Guard Pass

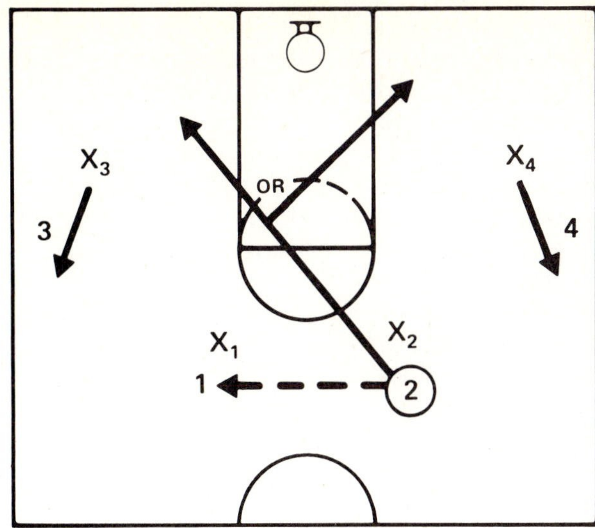

Figure 6–50 Guard-to-Guard Pass and Diagonal Cut

Another movement we used in practicing four-on-four was a guard-to-guard pass and diagonal cut (Figure 6–50). After 02 passed to 01, he made a quick diagonal cut. This emptying movement created floor space for 01 to drive, especially if 02 reversed to the weak side. If 01 went to his left, defensive forward X_3 could move into position to help out, and 01 had to find 03 immediately and pass to him. (03 could either clear to the baseline or cut to the basket.) If X_3 did not drop off 03, 01 took the ball all the way to the basket. This sequence of movements provides excellent drill in one-on-one play, and in recognition of when to pass off and when to take the ball all the way to the basket. We encouraged our forwards and guards to drive as hard as they could toward the basket.

Five-on-Five Play. While we practiced four-on-four at one end of the court, an assistant coach worked individually with our centers at the other end of the court. We spent a great deal of time working with our centers because a good post man is very difficult to defend and it is difficult to keep the ball away from him. If we were running our four-man guard-forward game properly, all our center had to do was beat his man one-on-one, since the other four players' movements eliminated most of the normal defensive help inside. This was exactly what we were after in our moving-game offense.

Perhaps we should state at this point that both our power game and our moving game were designed to yield high-percentage shots, especially inside, and one-on-one confrontations that were free of defensive double-teaming. The power game and moving game differed in the movement by all five players. In the power game, player movement was severely restricted; it was secondary to such concerns as posting movements, inside cuts, and keeping the big man near the basket for one-on-one confrontations and rebounding. In the moving game, continuous movement by the guards and forwards was designed to free not only the center but also the guards and forwards for one-on-one confrontations, lay-ups, inside passes, and the like, without double-teaming.

Our center always started away from the ball. (As the guard brought the ball down court, the center set up at a post position away from the ball.) He could break to the ball any time he wanted to; however, we encouraged him not to come to the ball too often. If the ball was moved around rapidly and brought to the side of the court the center was on, we wanted him to work hard to maintain position on the man guarding him. If we had a good post man, we instructed our players that, whenever they got the ball on the same side of the court the center was on, they should make every effort to pass the ball inside to him.

We expected our center to anticipate passes from his driving teammates. Lined up away from the ball originally, the center was often open when the guards or forwards drove to the basket and the defensive center switched off to stop them. He maintained his position so no one could cut in front of him to deflect the pass. Ideally, the center should be an excellent offensive rebounder, since he is generally lined up on the weak side in a good position to rebound missed shots.

Our centers used any or all of three post positions as opportunities arose: high post, low post, or the area between them known as medium, or intermediate, post. Whenever the center saw a situation such as a reverse or give-and-go developing, he immediately cleared across the lane to the weak side away from the ball, to open up the court for the play to develop. When the center received a pass at the medium or high post from a guard or forward, he waited for cutters to make their moves before working for his own shot. If he received the pass at the low post, he began his one-on-one moves immediately.

Moving Game Rules

Rule No. 1 You must move every time you make a pass. This is the most important rule. Pass and move.

Rule No. 2 You may go one-on-one any time you can beat your man for a good percentage shot. You must take your man *immediately*. If you wait too long, the defense will have help, and teammates cutting to the basket may inhibit your own one-on-one play. Do not force the one-on-one movement; you'll have other opportunities.

Rule No. 3 Any time your defensive man doesn't maintain vision (that is, if he loses sight of you while watching the ball), cut for the basket. The guards will cut directly down the lane and the forwards will cut underneath for whichever post position is open.

Rule No. 4 The tougher the defense plays you, the more you must be prepared to play without the ball.

Rule No. 5 You must maintain floor balance as much as possible.

Rule No. 6 Preliminary offensive movements are made at one-half to three-quarter speed. Only the final cut to the basket is at full (yet controlled) speed. You should try to lull your defender into relaxing with a smooth, easy motion, then make a hard cut which will be more difficult for him to anticipate and control.

Rule No. 7 The nearest man to the ball must always be prepared to receive the next pass. He must go to meet the ball. If he is overplayed, he should make a hard cut to the basket. Never allow a teammate to be bottled up; this will stagnate the offense.

Rule No. 8 There must be motion on the weak side. The weak-side forward should work for a good percentage shot. He should exchange with the guard on his side of the court, if action is being developed on the other side of the court, to keep the weak-side defenders occupied.

Rule No. 9 In the course of running our offense, guards may wind up as forwards, and then they will have rebounding responsibilities depending on the position they are in when the shot is taken.

Rule No. 10 Any time there is an overbalance in size because of a defensive switch, if the person with the size advantage goes immediately to the low-post position, every effort must be made to work the ball inside to him while the advantage exists; that is, before he can be double-teamed.

Rule No. 11 Upon receiving the ball you must make your play immediately. Pass the ball to the first open teammate and keep the ball in motion. Do not wait for a play to develop. Within two seconds after receiving the ball you should either make your play or pass the ball.

Rule No. 12 Make sure that you are occupying your defensive man at all times. Always be a threat to cut for the basket, to receive the ball, and to drive. Keep the defensive man occupied. Don't let him stand still and watch the ball.

The power game is most effective with tall players or strong, bulky players who can take advantage of offensive mismatches or one-on-one confrontations originating from the low post. During my five years at Long Beach State we had players like 6′8″ 240-lb. Roscoe Pondexter and 6′6″ Ed Ratleff, a guard, and we didn't need a lot of movement in our offense to get the ball to them at the low post. In many cases, a simple cut to the post and an inside pass were all that was necessary to give us an offensive advantage.

Through our moving game, we hoped to provide our players with a high degree of individual freedom. The moving game presented us with many opportunities to drive, and we felt that through the moving game, when we got the ball inside to our center, the guards' and forwards' movements made it difficult for the defense to sink back on our center. We also liked to post our guards and forwards out of our moving game.

We like what we've been able to do offensively at Nevada–Las Vegas, but from time to time I've wished that I'd kept our moving game, or at least altered it to meet the needs of our newer playing style at UNLV. I really believe in the moving game; it's a solid offensive attack that has many advantages for teams with players who are capable of refining the timing and coordination of the screens, cuts, and passes involved in its execution.

Don't be surprised if you see our Runnin' Rebels using an adapted moving game sometime in the future. It's too effective a style of attack to merely gather dust or provide an anchor for cobwebs in my basketball file.

7

Attacking the Zone Defenses

As was explained in Chapter 3, teams use zone defenses for a variety of reasons. One basic reason common to all teams that use zone defenses, though, is the desire to provide added protection near the basket. As a result, attacking the zone defenses usually involves moving offensive players into, through, or along the seams between defenders' zones of responsibility in order to confuse the coverage, move inside defenders out of position to cover the cutters, and/or create additional scoring opportunities.

PRINCIPLES OF ZONE OFFENSES

1. The easiest way to beat a zone defense is to move the ball down court and into scoring position before the opponents are able to get back and set up. Fast breaking provides high-percentage shots without undue defensive pressure, and it forces the opponents to think in terms of retreating instead of attacking on defense.

2. Outside alignments or patterns will not seriously challenge the defense unless the threat of inside penetration also exists. Zone defenses generally provide strong inside coverage, but if no inside penetration is attempted, the defenders will have little trouble maintaining defensive control inside and outside.

In Figure 7–1, the defensive team is already matched up with the offense's 1–2–2 alignment. For example, the left wing may be open, but unless some kind of movement beyond what is shown in the figure occurs, no offensive player is likely to become a serious scoring threat. For example, the ball-side corner is open when the wing has the ball, but the corner

Figure 7–1 Defending Against an Outside Alignment from Matchup

defender is only 8 to 10 feet from him; if the pass is made, the defender will move into a close guarding position, and other defenders will sag toward the ball accordingly. Offensive players probably will still be more or less open, but the ball handler in the corner will have to throw a lob pass to reach any of them, and the defenders will thus be able to cover them without switching defensive assignments or responsibilities.

Inside penetration can confuse the matchups or coverage, or force the inside defenders to stay inside. Even if the penetration doesn't work, it will force the defenders to think about what they're doing and who they're covering, rather than moving and responding automatically because they know the matchups will not change.

Few teams are so naive in their approach to zone offense as not to present some kind of inside movement, even if it is no more sophisticated than having the low-post player follow the ball from side to side. However, even this simple movement can produce scoring opportunities, as shown in Figure 7–2. 03 has the ball. As 03 passes to 01, 04 cuts into the lane, keeping inside position on X_4. 01 fakes a pass to 02, drawing X_2 outside and away from 04, and lobs the ball over X_4 to 04 for an easy

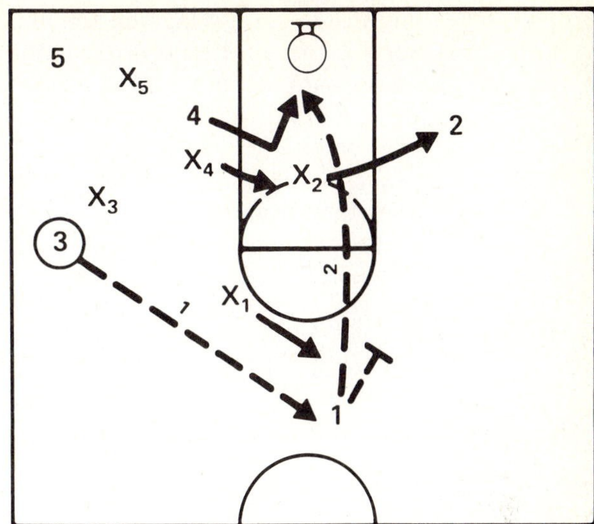

Figure 7–2 Making the Inside Pass

inside shot. This is, of course, only one of many possible opportunities that the offensive team can try to create by working the ball inside.

> **Note:** If X_1 is unable to cover 01, X_2 will have to cover 01 and X_4 will have to move across the lane to cover 02. In this case, X_5 will have to cover 04.

Every zone offense should provide at least a semblance of an inside scoring threat. A given offensive player may be incapable of scoring even if he is left alone on the court for five minutes, but the opponents must treat him as a legitimate scoring threat whenever he sets up at the low post or cuts into or across the lane. They must respect him, if for no other reason than the importance of covering the court positions he occupies or passes through. As far as the defense is concerned, *any* offensive player with the ball at or around the low post is considered a scoring threat.

3. Ball and player movement are prerequisites for success in zone offenses. Whether player movement takes the form of cutter patterns, inside or perimeter screens, or sliding movements along the seams of the zones, it keeps the defense honest and, when combined with a series of quick passes, exploits any weaknesses in the coverage.

4. You will not beat good zone defenses consistently if you don't have at least one shooter who is capable of making an occasional outside shot. If nobody on your team is even remotely capable of rattling the rims from the outside, you can expect to find opponents staying inside and giving you the outside shot that your players can't make (or won't take). This was one of the problems I encountered at Long Beach State, back when I cringed every time my players shot from farther than 10 feet from the basket. I was the victim of a vicious circle of outside-shooting ineptitude which I had helped to create: by transmitting to my players my lack of confidence in their outside shooting ability, I ensured that they weren't going to make the shots, and in not making the shots their confidence was further undermined. The opponents, sensing our indecision and reluctance to take the outside shots, tended to lay back and give us the outside shots that I didn't want my kids to take.

SPLITTING THE DEFENSE

The term *splitting the defense* refers to the offensive tactic of setting, or moving, players into the gaps between defenders. At the top of the circle, for example, an even-front zone is split by placing a player between the two outside guards (Figure 7–3), while an odd-front zone is split by setting *two* players between the defensive point guard and the wings (X_2 and X_3 in Figure 7–4).

As shown in Figures 7–3 and 7–4, splitting the defense can force two players to guard the ball handler, or it can at least prevent them from covering any other player until the pass is made. In Figure 7–4, 01's attempted penetration between X_1 and X_3 cannot go unchallenged. 01's movement between X_1 and X_3 will force both defenders to cover him be-

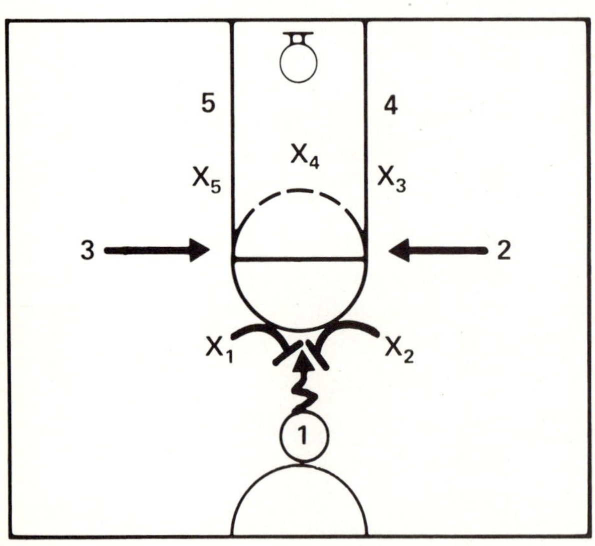

Figure 7–3 Splitting the 2–3 Zone and Forcing the Outside Double-Team

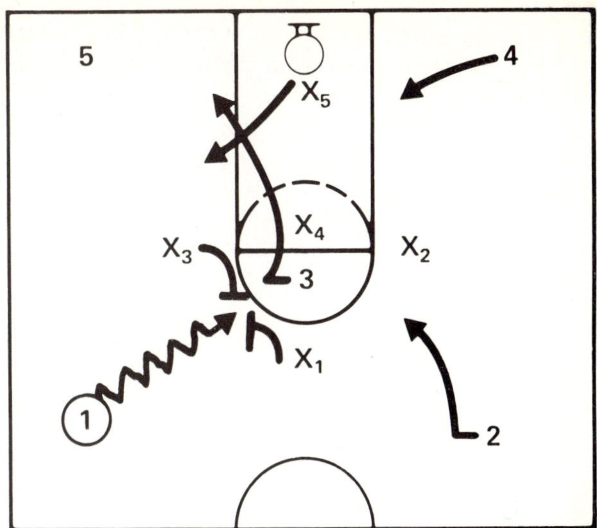

Figure 7–4 Splitting the 1–3–1 Zone and Forcing the Outside Double-Team

cause, if either man drops back, 01 will merely continue to dribble toward him until he has to pick him up.

Continuing our analysis of the movement in Figure 7–4, 03's cut and 02's slide add new dimensions to the problems besetting the defense when X_1 and X_3 double-team ball handler 01. Even if X_4 covers 03's movement to the low post and X_5 covers 05 in the corner, X_2 will be hard pressed to cover both 02 and 04 on the weak side.

01's penetrating dribble into X_1 and X_3 in Figure 7–4 is known as *freezing the defense*, since 01's movements tend to "freeze" one or more defenders in their tracks. Once two defenders are frozen in their coverage, the offensive team has numerical superiority elsewhere if the ball handler is capable of getting the ball to the open man.

Meanwhile, 02 and 05 are spreading the defensive coverage. Their apparently random positioning suddenly takes on new significance, especially in light of 03's sliding movement into the lane and on to the low post: situated along the perimeters of the defense in primary passing lanes, 02 and 05 must be covered by X_2 and X_5, but X_2 cannot guard 02 and still cover the diagonal pass to 04 at the weak-side low post.

Another dimension has been added to the splitting and spreading technique in Figure 7–5. The movements of ball handler 01 and his teammate 02 are identical to those shown in Figure 7–4. The positions occupied by 03, 04, and 05 are approximately the same as before, but the players occupying these positions are different: 03 has cut inside the lane as before, but if he doesn't receive 01's pass immediately, he cuts outside to 05's baseline position. 05 cuts behind the defense to the weak-side low post, and 04 cuts into the lane and continues to the high post.

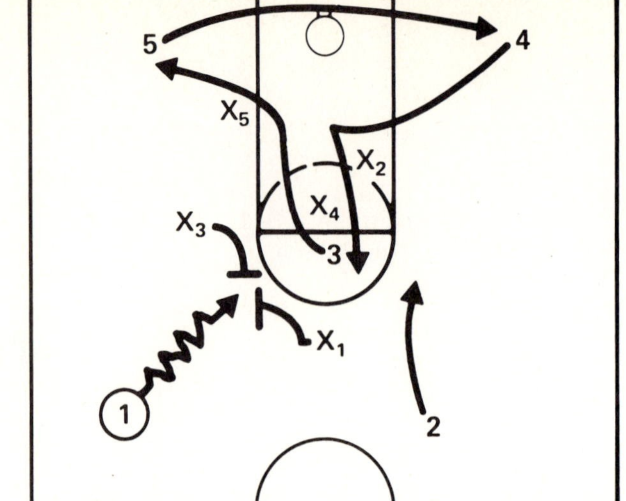

Figure 7–5 Offensive Splitting and Spreading with Inside Rotation

The net effect of these movements is to confuse the defensive coverage to a far greater extent than either the basic alignment by itself or 03's cut to the low post as 01 penetrates between X_3 and X_1. When 03 cuts low, will X_4 cover his cut, or will X_5 pick up X_3?

The answer to the previous question will depend on the type of coverage, of course, but regardless of whether X_4 or X_5 covers 03's cut, the result will merely be changing the offensive team's area of vulnerability. If X_4 drops low with 03's cut as shown in Figure 7–6, X_5 (or possibly X_2)

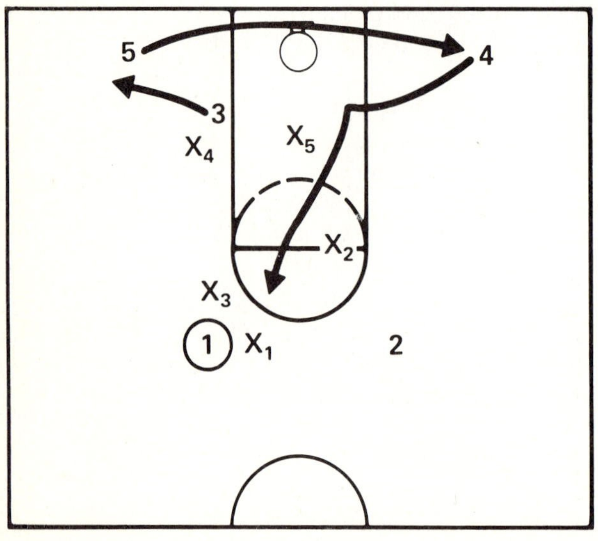

Figure 7–6 X_4 Covering 03's Cut

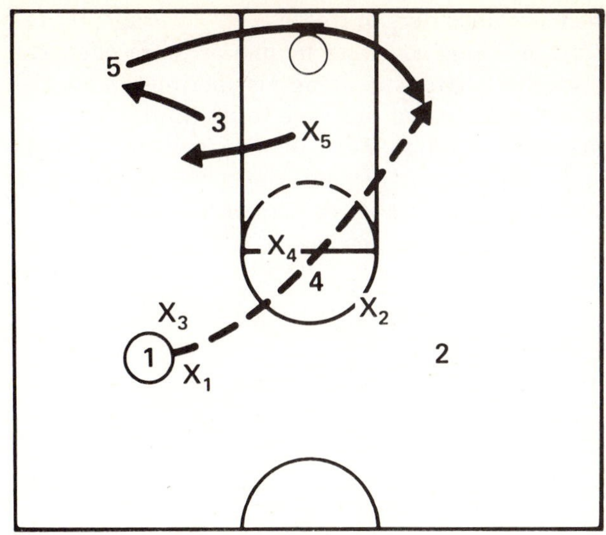

Figure 7–7 X_5 Covering 03's Cut

will have to cover 04's cut to the high post. If either X_2 or X_5 covers 04's cut, 02 and 05 will be guarded by only one man, which reduces the defensive team to the same dilemma they started out with in the first place!

If X_4 remains at the high post (Figure 7–7), X_5 will have to cover 03's cut, in which case 05 may not even have to cut at all to take full advantage of flaws in the defensive coverage.

Thus, we find three components of the splitting-spreading concept that may reduce the effectiveness of zone defense: the ball handler's pene-

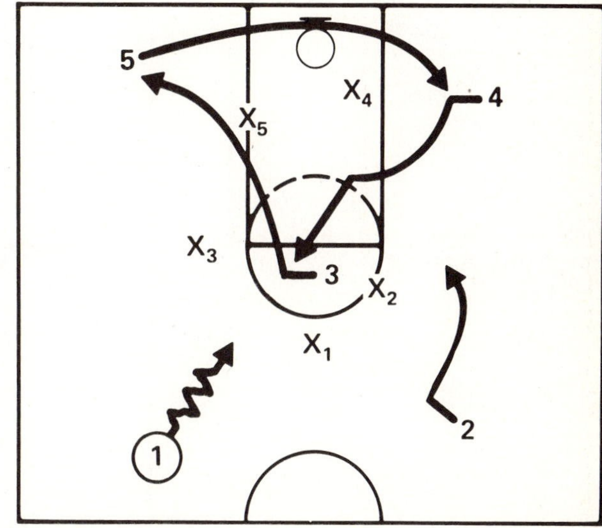

Figure 7–8 Splitting and Spreading Against 1–2–2 Zone Defense

trating movement between two defenders to freeze their coverage, movements along the seams of the inside coverage by one or more offensive players, and use of the spread alignment along the perimeters of the outside coverage to stretch the defensive coverage to its limits.

In examining Figures 7–8 through 7–10, it may appear that the 2–1–2 alignment presents difficulties beyond those found in other alignments—as indeed it does *if* X_1 is able to retreat and cover 03 in Figures 7–9 through 7–10. (In a 2–3 zone defense, X_5 will cover 03, but in

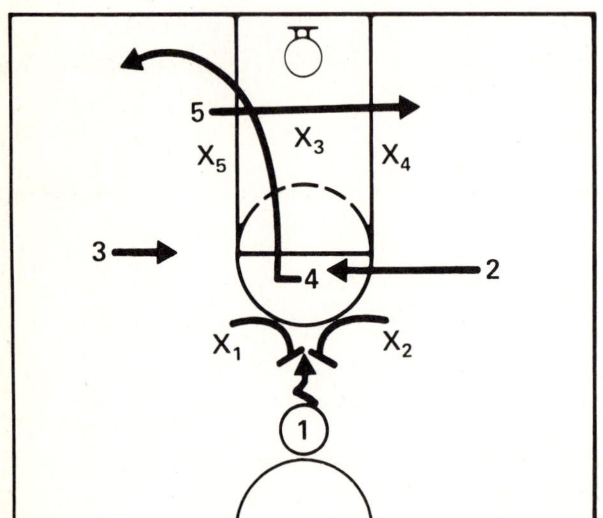

Figure 7–9 Splitting and Spreading Against 2–3 Zone Defense

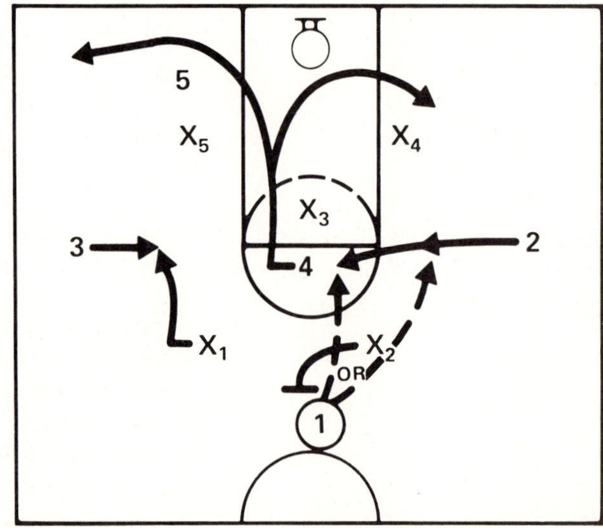

Figure 7–10 Splitting and Spreading Against 2–1–2 Zone Defense

2–1–2 coverage X_1 is responsible for wing man 03.) However, X_1 hardly has a desirable angle on 03 to stop his penetration.

If X_3 covers 03 as shown in Figure 7–11, 02 and 05 will have the same two-on-one advantage with X_4 as they had in the previous situations. This situation differs in that X_1 and X_2 will be retreating quickly after 01 passes the ball away, and the offensive team will need quick, accurate passes by both 01 and 03 if they are to take advantage of the defenders' difficulties in covering the remaining offensive players.

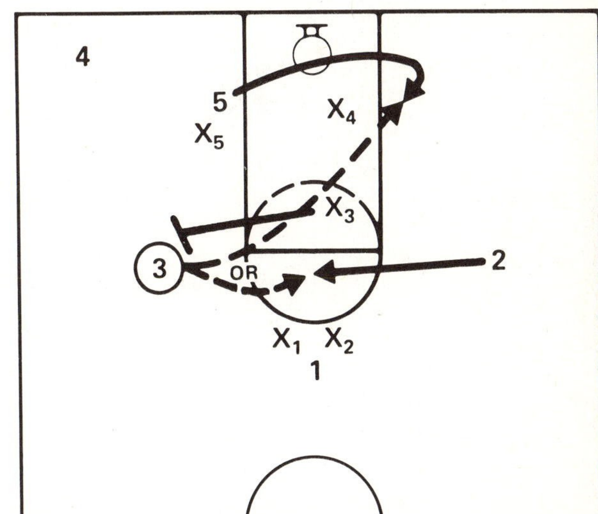

Figure 7–11 X_3 Covering the Wing Pass, 2–1–2 Zone Defense.

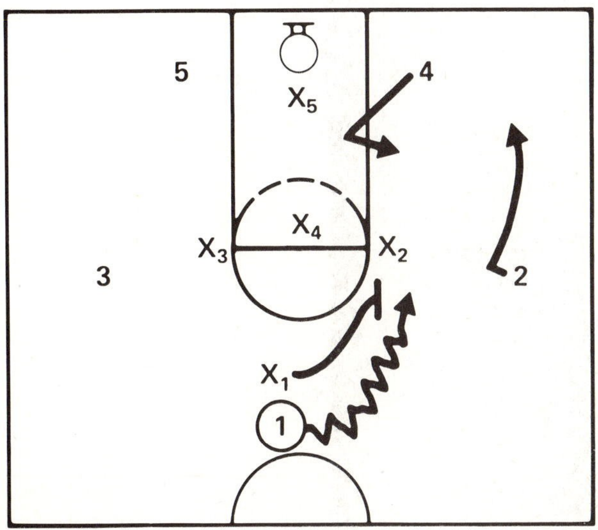

Figure 7–12 01 Forcing an Outside Double-Team Against 1–3–1 Zone Defense

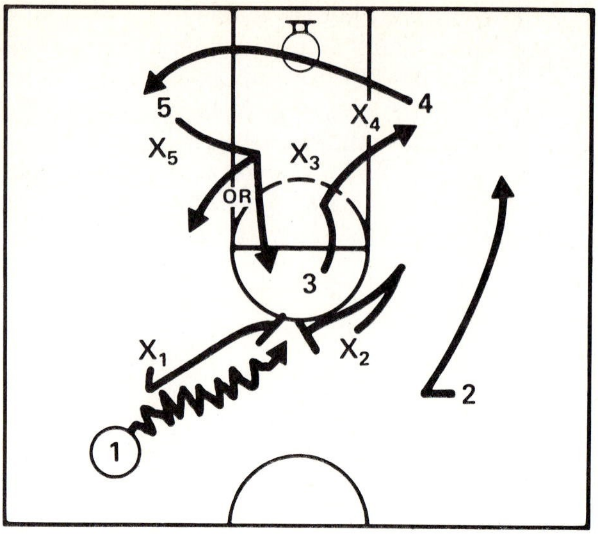

Figure 7–13 01 Forcing an Outside Double-Team Against Even-Front Defense

It also is possible to force double coverage from outside match-ups, although the defenders sometimes must be coaxed to alter their intentions. (See Figure 7–12.)

01 is covered by X_1 in Figure 7–12. X_2 and X_3 are matched up with 02 and 03, although X_4 and X_5 are not matched up inside. (As will be shown in Chapter 10, however, X_4 and X_5 can match up easily in such situations.) 01 dribbles toward X_2, who may retreat a short distance but eventually will have to stop 01's advance. If X_1 begins to retreat, 01 can slide toward X_1 to keep the defenders confused. The objective of the entire movement is to free 02 along the perimeter, or at least to force X_4 or X_5 to cover 02. If this happens, X_4 or X_5 will have to cover 04 at the low post, and X_3 will have to cover 05 at the weak-side low post and 03 at the weak-side high post.

The "sliding dribble" to force outside double-teaming against an even-front zone defense is shown in Figure 7–13.

CUTTER PATTERNS

As was explained previously, the objective of inside rotation against zone defenses is to confuse the defensive coverage in the lane or near the basket. Similarly, outside players may cut through the lane to confuse or disrupt *all* defensive coverage, inside or outside. Also, cutter patterns can alter the matchups to favor the defense, provide weak-side overloads to take advantage of strong ball-side defensive coverage, or draw the defenders inside and pave the way for open perimeter shots via outside rotation toward the ball.

Cutters to the Ball Side

Examples of ball-side cutter patterns are shown in Figures 7–14 through 7–16. We should note that these examples by no means exhaust the possibilities for sending cutters to the ball side of the court.

Each of the cuts shown in Figures 7–14 through 7–16 establishes an offensive ball-side overload. As will be the case with other sections of this chapter, the movements shown in these figures are usually seen as part of a larger series of movements designed to probe the defense for weaknesses.

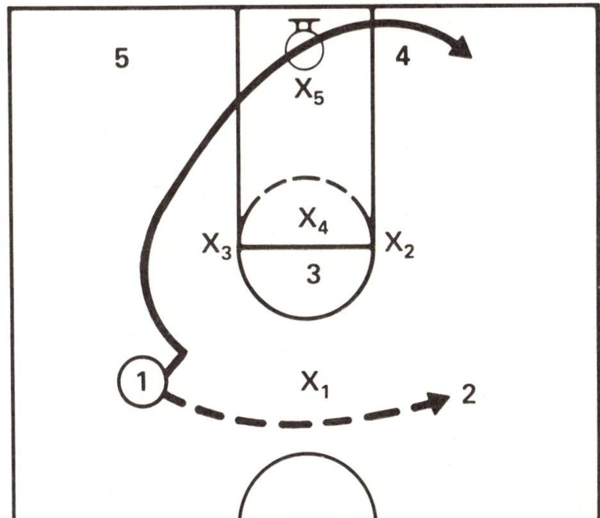

Figure 7–14 01's Cut to Ball-Side Corner

Figure 7–15 02's Cut to Ball-Side Corner

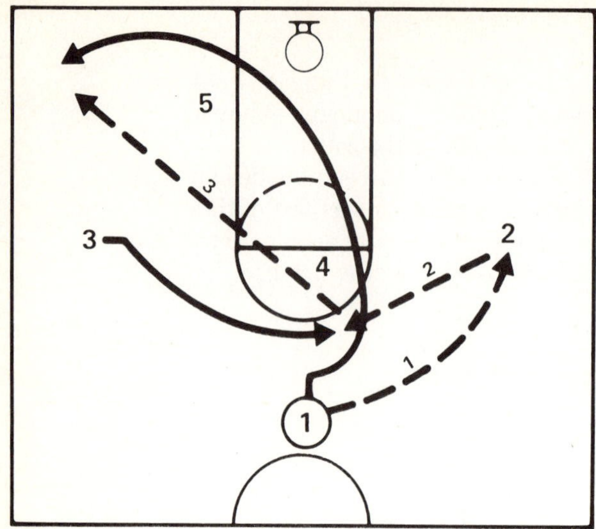

Figure 7–16 Point Guard's Cut to Ball-Side Corner

Cutters to the Weak Side

While cutters to the ball side attempt to find immediate opportunities to attack the defense, cutters to the weak side generally must wait for ball rotation to provide their scoring opportunities (Figures 7–17 through 7–20). These movements to the weak side are just one facet of a team's overall zone offensive strategy, and they are often accompanied by other movements such as inside crisscrossing or inside rotation.

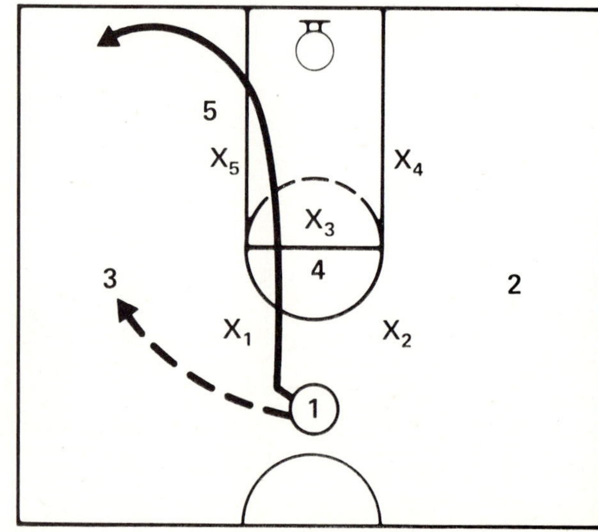

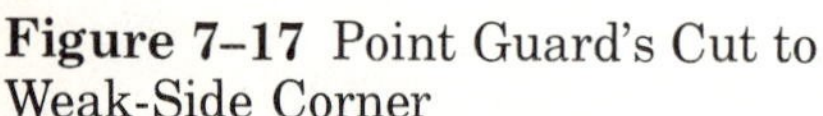
Figure 7–17 Point Guard's Cut to Weak-Side Corner

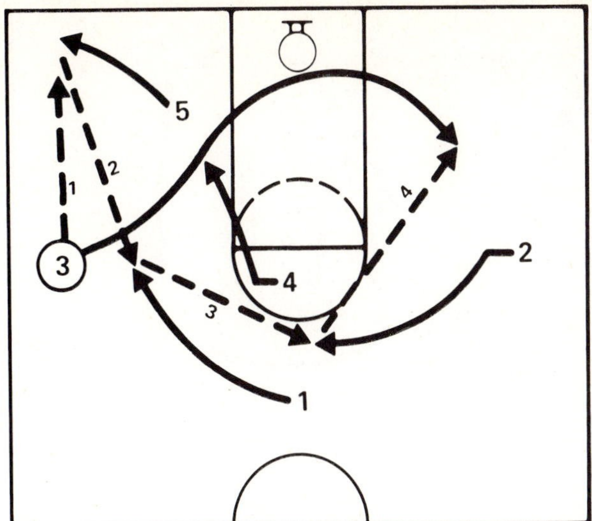

Figure 7–18 Wing's Cut to Weak-Side Corner

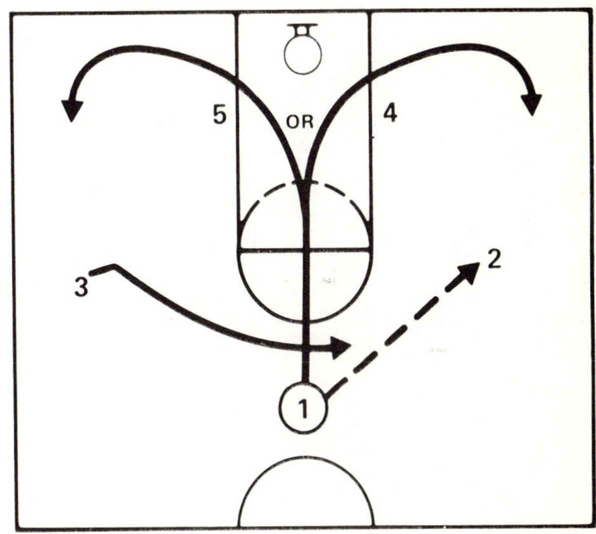

Figure 7–19 Single-Cutter Patterns with Outside Rotation Toward the Ball (*Example #1*)

Figures 7–19 and 7–20 are largely self-explanatory. We should mention, however, that other techniques may accompany the cutter patterns. For example, in Figure 7–19, 05 may cut into and across the lane to the high post, or in Figure 7–20, 04 may cut into the lane and continue to the ball-side high post instead of cutting to the vicinity of the weak-side high post. Also in Figure 7–20, note that 02 and 04 do not cut outside to 01 and 02's original positions; instead, they will attempt to take advantage of the defenders' dropping back to cover 01's cut by making their own cuts to

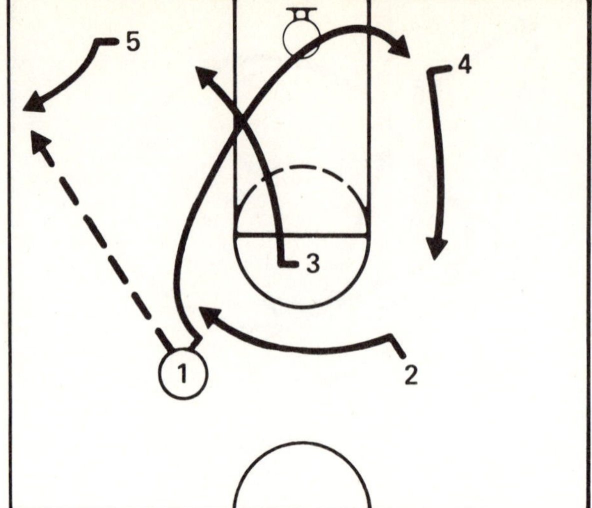

Figure 7–20 Single-Cutter Patterns with Outside Rotation Toward the Ball (*Example #2*)

positions closer to the basket than they would have taken otherwise.

When the cutter does not receive the ball during his cut, or afterward as a result of ball rotation, the offensive team can either rotate the ball and the players toward the weak side, as has been described previously, or they can reverse the process and run it from the other side of the court. (See Figures 7–21 and 7–22.)

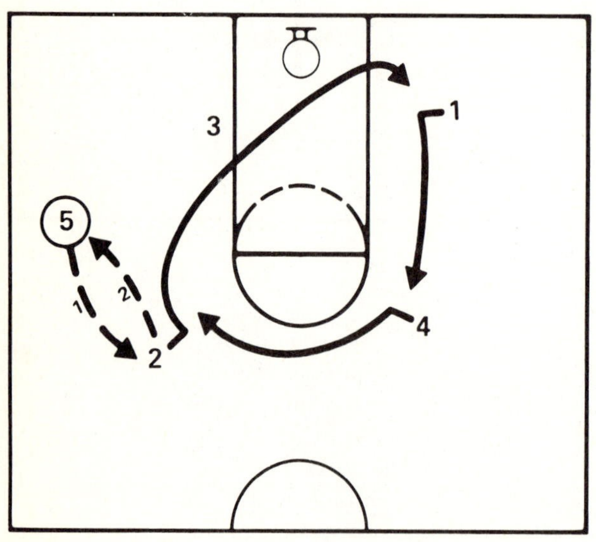

Figure 7–21 Repeating and Rotating the Single-Cutter Pattern (*Example #1*)

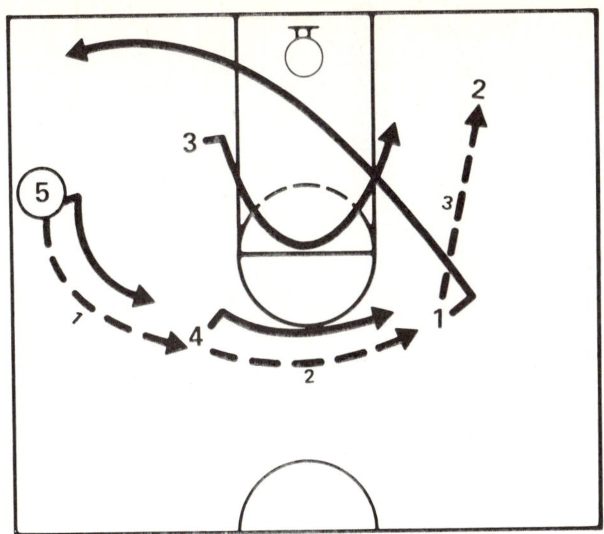

Figure 7–22 Repeating and Rotating the Single-Cutter Pattern (*Example #2*)

OVERLOADING

The term *overloading* refers to the offensive strategy of setting or cutting more than one player into the zone of responsibility of a single defender, or having a majority of players on one side of the court. In a true overload, one defender is not only responsible for two players, but the two players are far enough apart that he cannot guard both of them adequately at the same time. Thus the stack alignment depicted in Figure 7–23 is not a true overload, although it may shift into an overload, for example, if 05 cuts to the corner. As the alignment stands, X_5 can guard both 04 and 05 simultaneously.

In Figure 7–24, though, the distance between 05 in the corner and 04 at the low post is such that X_5 cannot guard both players. He can, and will, guard *one* of them, but he cannot guard both.

Thus we can see that having a majority of one's players aligned on one side of the court does not necessarily constitute an overload. (If it did, we would consider any 1–3–1 offensive alignment an overload.)

The overload alignment forces defenders farther toward the limits of their zones of responsibility than do the balanced alignments. In Figure 7–24, X_5 will have to cover 05 if 03 passes to the corner, which means that X_3 or X_4 will have to move quickly into position to guard 04. However, if X_3 drops to the low post, X_1 will have to drop back to cover the high-post position, leaving 03 open at the wing. And if X_4 moves across the lane to cover 04, X_2 will have to drop back slightly to deny the crosscourt pass from 05 to 02. Neither of these problems is insurmountable for the

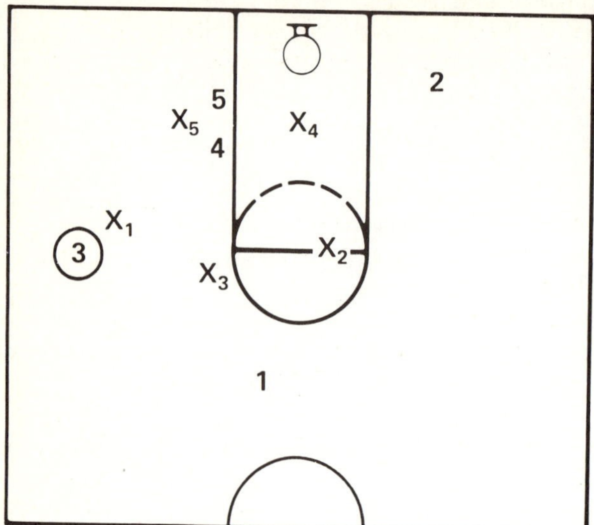

Figure 7–23 Ineffective Overloading

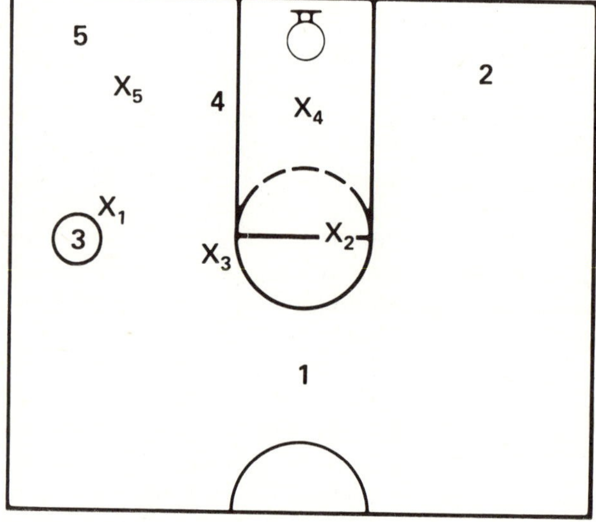

Figure 7–24 Using Overloading to Spread the Defensive Coverage

defense—they may merely match up X_5 on 05, X_1 on 03, X_4 on 04, X_3 on 01, and X_2 on 02, for example—but they will have to come to terms with the problems created by the overloading.

Teams generally use overloading for any of three purposes: to force the defenders to match up when the matchups favor the offensive team, to spread the coverage on the ball side, weak side, or the entire half-court, or to set four offensive players against three defenders in a confined area. As a result, overload alignments are often used as power game zone offenses.

The major weakness of overload alignments and patterns is that they allow the defense to match up without difficulty when the matchups favor the *defensive* team. Overloads may be set up in any number of ways, including those shown in Figures 7–14 and 7–16.

Overload Alignments

There are five basic overload alignments: three of them feature three players on the ball side, and the other two feature four players on the ball side.

Of the three-man overloads shown in Figures 7–25 through 7–27, the first is by far the most frequently encountered. Its strength is that it tends to force single coverage of the low-post position; its weakness is the distance of the rotation passes from wing to point to weak side, which may give the defenders time to move to the weak side and cover the pass receivers.

The three-man alignment shown in Figure 7–26 is seen less frequently, primarily because 03 and 05's positions are closer to the basket than in Figure 7–25, and the passing lanes are easier to cover. The strength of the alignment is the increased mobility and versatility afforded the post man by the change in his positioning. 04 can slide high or low toward openings in the defense.

The third alignment (Figure 7–27) is useful against defensive alignments that stress corner coverage but neglect the ball-side high-post position. The alignment adapts well to the kind of crisscrossing inside movements that will be shown in Figures 7–34 and 7–35.

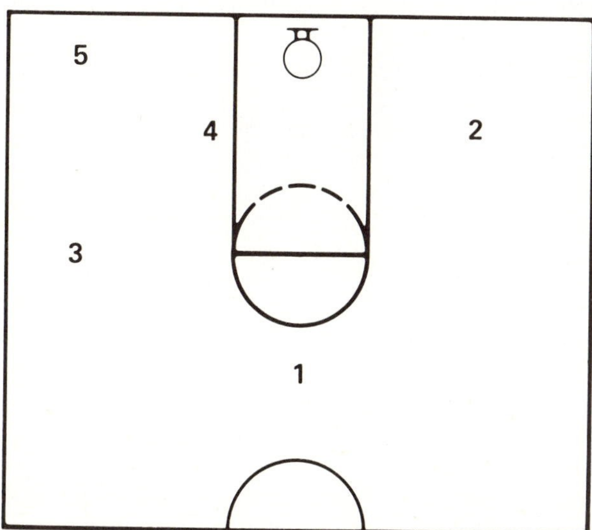

Figure 7–25 Three-Man Overload Variations (*Example #1*)

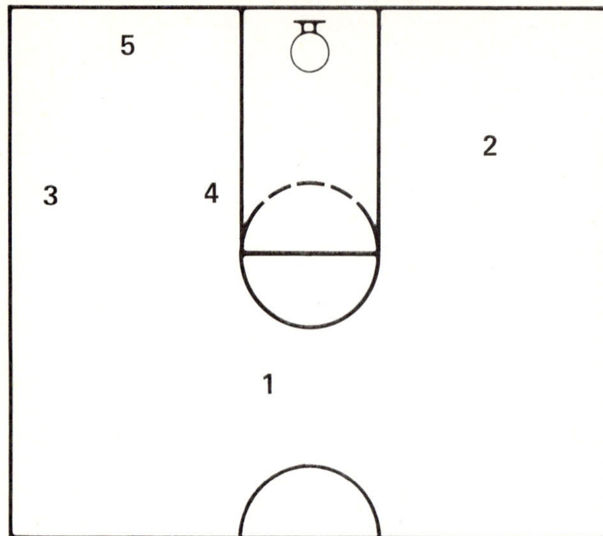

Figure 7–26 Three-Man Overload Variations (*Example #2*)

Figure 7–27 Three-Man Overload Variations (*Example #3*)

Whereas three-man overloads are strongest against zone defenses featuring four players on the ball side and only one player back to cover the weak-side rotation passes, four-man overloads are strongest against zone defenses that have two players back to cover the weak side in ball rotation and only three men on the ball side. Also, four-man overloads generally are slow in rotating the ball and players from one side of the court to the other, and having eight players on one side of the court tends to reduce the effectiveness of one-on-one confrontations.

Of the two alignments shown in Figures 7–28 and 7–29, the first is by far the more prevalent. In Diamond overloads, the wing and intermediate wing players usually are out of effective shooting range, and the corner man is too near the basket to spread the coverage. However, neither alignment is likely to attack the defense effectively if four defenders are also on the ball side. In summary, then, four-man overloads generally are less effective in attacking zone coverage than three-man overloads.

Overload Rotation

Many methods exist for rotating the ball and players from the ball side to the weak side. The considerations for selecting a method of rotating the overload from one side of the court to the other include: Do you want to keep your big man (or men) inside? Are you trying to hide a weak offensive player or players? Do you have only one good outside shooter? How many passes will it take to rotate the ball from the wing or corner to the weak-side area you plan to attack?

If your team has only one big man, you'll probably want to keep him inside, following the ball from the low post across the lane to the other

Figure 7–28 2–2 (Box) Overload Alignment

Figure 7–29 1–2–2 (Diamond) Overload Alignment

Figure 7–30 Setting Up an Overload from 1–3–1 Alignment

low-post position. With only one post player the offense will operate best from a 1–3–1 alignment, as shown in Figure 7–30.

In order to keep the post man (04 in Figure 7–31) inside with the ball on either side of the court as shown in Figures 7–30 and 7–31, 05 probably will have to play both corners. (As an alternative, the wing could cut to the weak-side corner after passing, but there is no evidence that his cut is

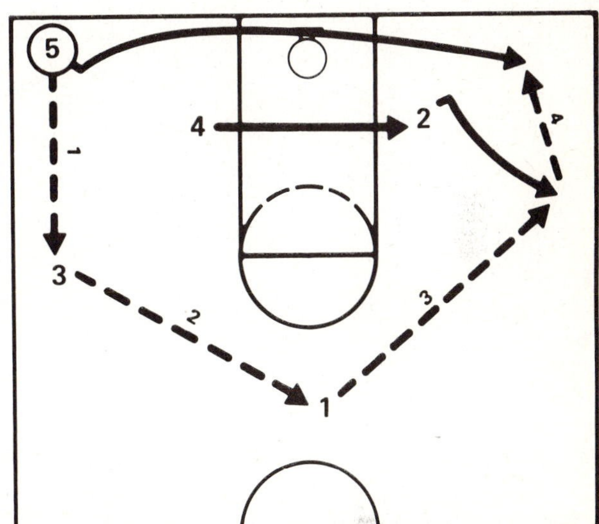

Figure 7–31 Overload Rotation, Keeping the Big Man Inside

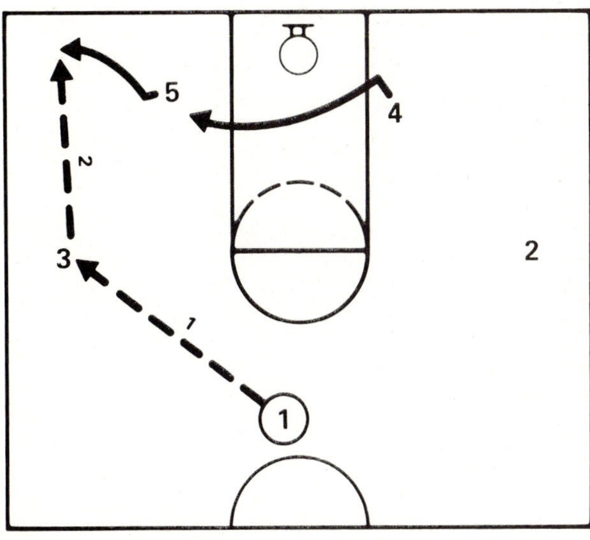

Figure 7–32 Post Men Alternating Between Low Post and Corner (*a*)

faster or more effective than 05's cut. 05's cuts, on the other hand, are easily learned by players on any level.)

With two post players the variety of movements is broadened considerably. The post men may alternate between the corner and the low post (Figures 7–32 and 7–33), criss-cross between the high post and low post (Figures 7–34 and 7–35), and rotate through and around the lane from the weak-side low post to the ball-side high post to the ball-side low post to the weak-side low post, and so on (Figures 7–36 and 7–37).

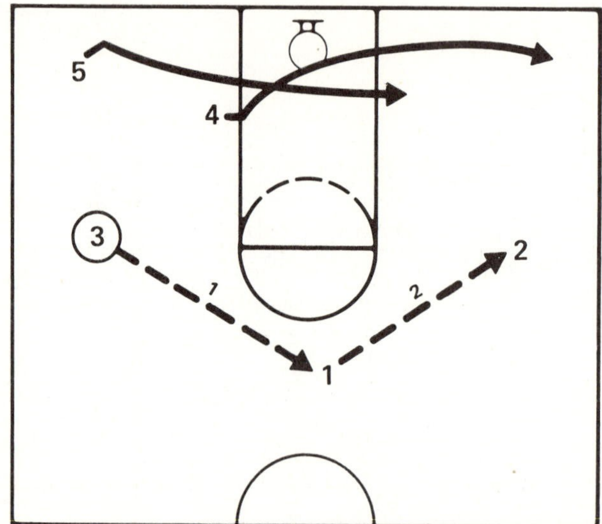

Figure 7–33 Post Men Alternating Between Low Post and Corner (*b*)

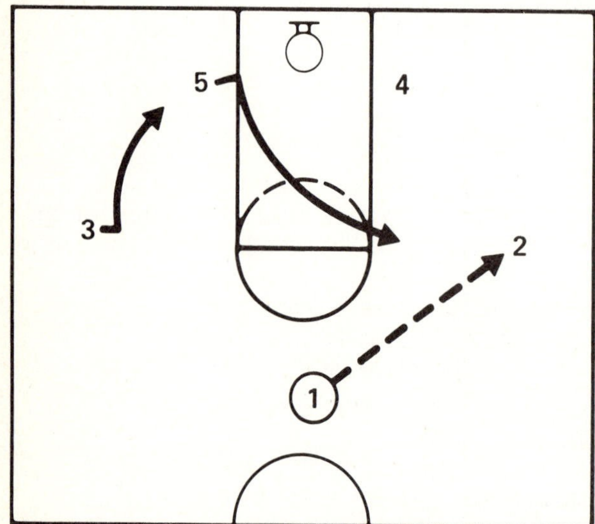

Figure 7–34 Post Men Crisscrossing Inside (*a*)

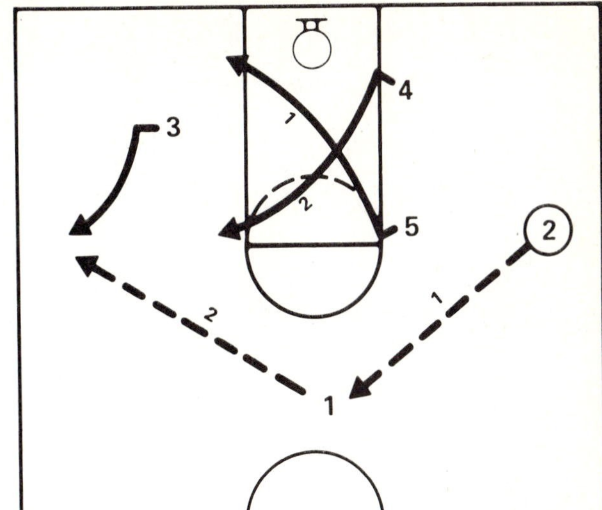

Figure 7–35 Post Men Crisscrossing Inside (*b*)

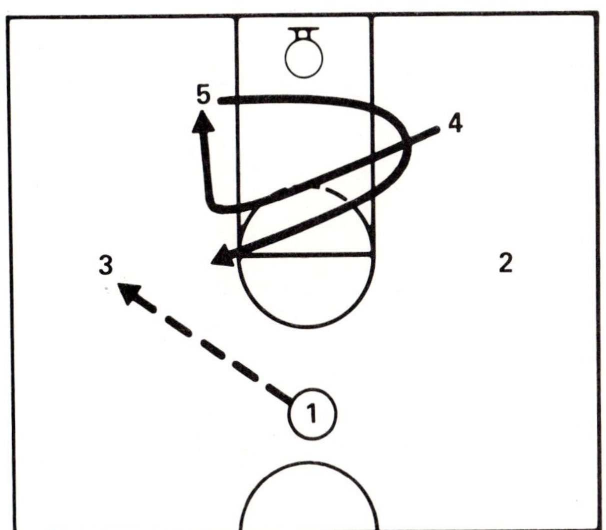

Figure 7–36 Post Men Rotating Through and Around the Lane (*a*)

Concerning movements such as those shown in Figure 7–35, 05's cut to the low post is far less likely to be open than 04's cut into the lane and then to the high post after 05 has cut. 05's cut is intended to draw the defenders deep so 04 can be clear when cutting into the gap in the defensive coverage.

All the cuts into and across the lane to the ball-side high post in Figures 7–34 through 7–37 involve "cutting to the opening." This means the players do not necessarily make their cuts as shown in the figures;

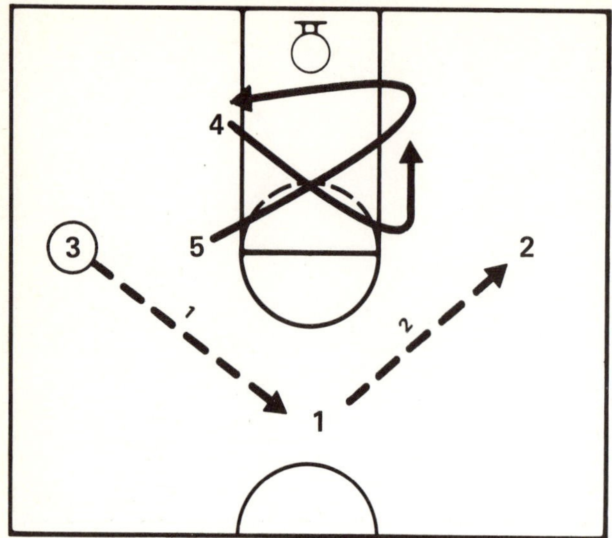

Figure 7–37 Post Men Rotating Through and Around the Lane (*b*)

rather, they cut to whatever area of the court is left open by defensive reaction to the previous cut. In all cases, the cut to the ball side should not be made automatically.

SCREENING PATTERNS

Screens inside the lane generally are considered to be unproductive against a zone defense, because zone defensive techniques feature automatic switching when the offense sends cutters into the lane, sets screens, or otherwise attempts to confuse the defensive coverage. The only form of screening that is likely to be effective against a zone defense is to screen along the perimeters of the defense, particularly the baseline, the corners of the free-throw line, and the top of the circle. Screening patterns are so many and varied as to be practically limitless.

Screening from Splitting Alignments

Sometimes teams are able to attack zone defenses by splitting the defense and then setting screens at the point or either corner of the free-throw line, as shown in Figures 7–38 and 7–39.

Note: The splitting alignment in Figure 7–39 occurs at the high post, not at the point.

Figures 7–38 and 7–39 illustrate the kind of point screens that are available from splitting patterns. In Figure 7–38, 02's screen of X_2 will

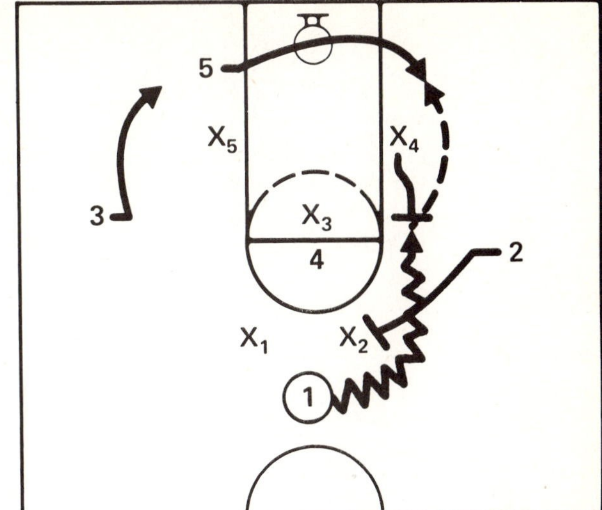

Figure 7–38 Splitting and Screening Against 2–1–2 Zone Defense

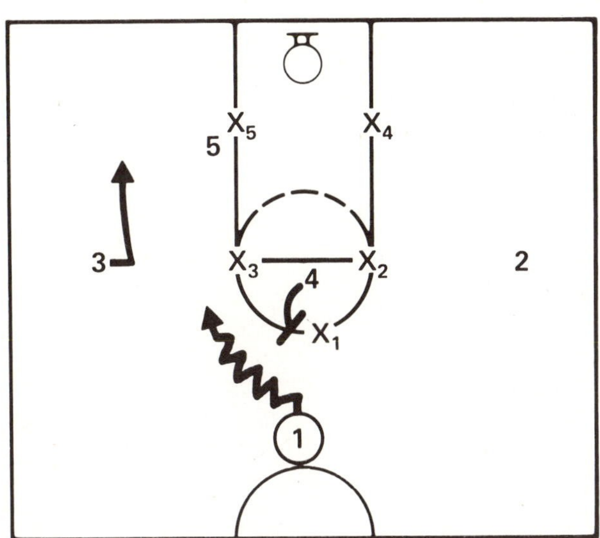

Figure 7–39 Splitting and Screening Against 1–2–2 Zone Defense

allow 01 to dribble outside the screen, but the zone concept will prevent 01 from driving all the way to the basket. Either X_3 or X_4 (probably X_4, since X_3 will not want to release from covering 04 at the high post) will pick up 01, in which case 01 will have to pass to 05. In Figure 7–39, high post 04 sets the screen, this time on X_1 as 03 slides away from X_3 toward the corner. If X_3 comes up to cover 01, 03 will be open. (Additionally, 04 may roll into the lane toward the basket after screening for 01, since in many cases defenders will neglect the player who sets the screen.)

Baseline Screens

As a rule, baseline screens are more effective than screens at or beyond the free-throw line. Since zone defenses concentrate their coverage inside, screens that limit coverage along the baseline will reduce the effectiveness of the rest of the inside coverage as well. The illustrations of the patterns and plays should be considered a representative sample of baseline screening techniques; they are in no way a compilation of *all* the possible techniques a team might use.

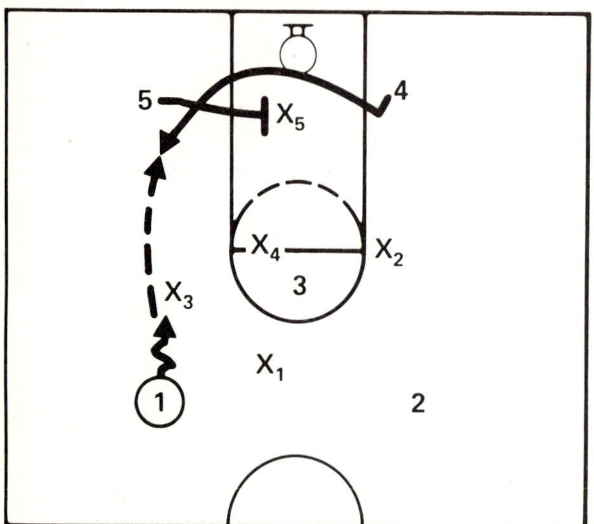

Figure 7–40 Baseline Screen Against 1–3–1 Zone Defense

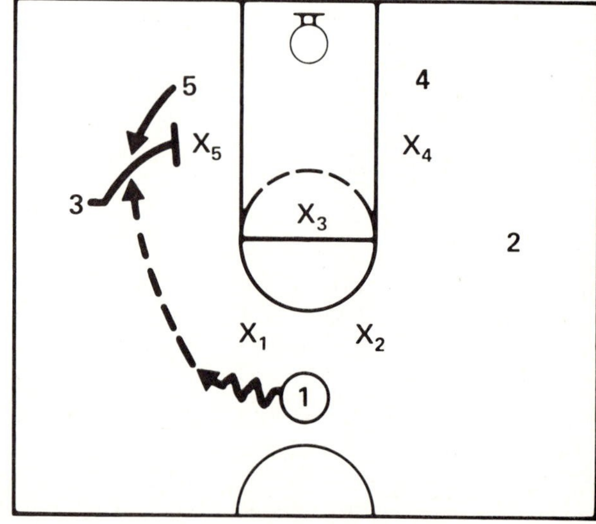

Figure 7–41 Baseline Screen Against 2–1–2 Zone Defense

In Figures 7–40 and 7–41, inside defender X_5 is screened away from the baseline in order to free an offensive player cutting behind the screen for a short jump shot. The defense may elect to fight through the screen, but the real beauty of the concept of baseline screening is that the defenders cannot stop the pattern by switching, since no defenders occupy the outside area where switching would occur.

The same kind of screen as that shown in Figures 7–40 and 7–41 can be effected from a stack alignment. (See Figures 7–42 and 7–43.)

In Figures 7–42 and 7–43, X_4 and X_5 will have to cover cutters 02

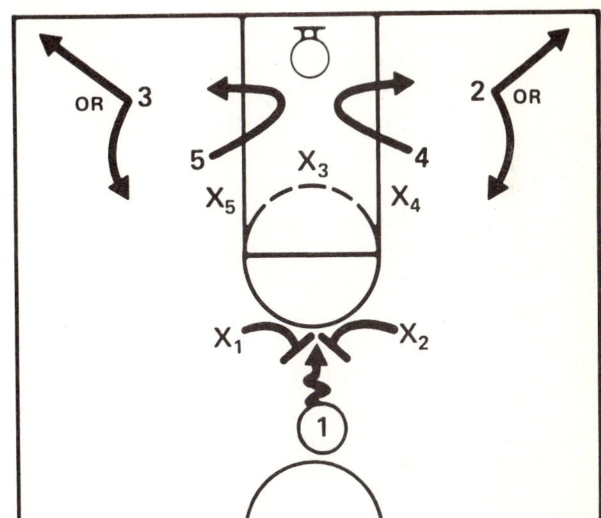

Figure 7–42 Variations of Screen and Cut from Stack Alignments (*Example #1*)

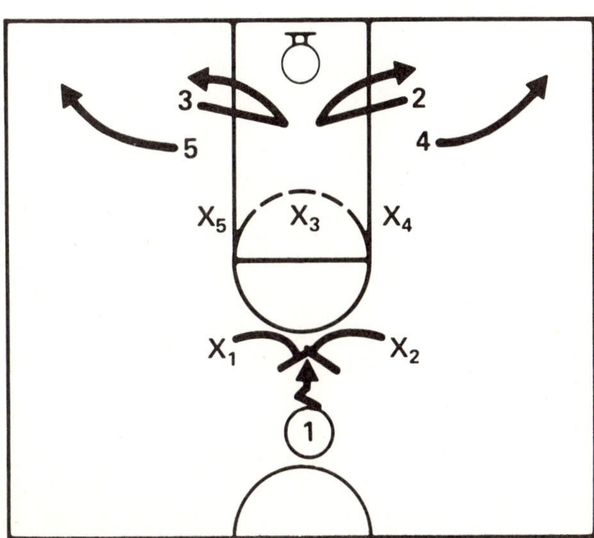

Figure 7–43 Variations of Screen and Cut from Stack Alignments (*Example #2*)

and 03, because X_3 is frozen in position in the middle of the lane. (X_3 can hardly be expected to cover either of the cutters since he has no way of knowing the direction of the pass before it is made.) The defense's most likely course of action is to have X_4 or X_5 fight through, or go around, the screen to cover the cutter, with X_3 moving across to pick up the player who sets the screen. Still, this action forces the defenders to match up, regardless of whether they want to or not or whether the matchups favor the offense or defense.

A 2–3 offensive alignment can be a dependable zone offense when it is based on screening along the baseline. (See Figures 7–44 and 7–45.)

01 passes to 02 to draw the defense slightly toward 02's side of the court. 02 passes back to 01, and 04 cuts across the lane and behind 05's screen (Figure 7–44). 05 will of course screen out the nearest inside defender. 01 passes to 04. In rotation, 04 passes to 01, 01 relays the ball to 02, and 05 cuts across the lane and behind 03's screen to receive 02's pass (Figure 7–45). 04 moves inside before screening for 03 cutting across the lane.

This pattern can be run as shown or it can be used to set up an overload, as will be shown in Figure 7–46. The player cutting behind the screen, 04 in Figure 7–44, may cut to the corner or go around the screen for the closer shot (Figure 7–46).

In Figure 7–46, 04's cut will be determined by the direction of X_5's movement to cover 04: if X_5 goes to the baseline side of 05, 04 will cut toward the middle; however, if X_5 goes over the top of the screen, 04 will continue toward the corner. In either case, 04's cut around the screen will force the defense into matchup coverage even if X_5 covers 04 in the corner.

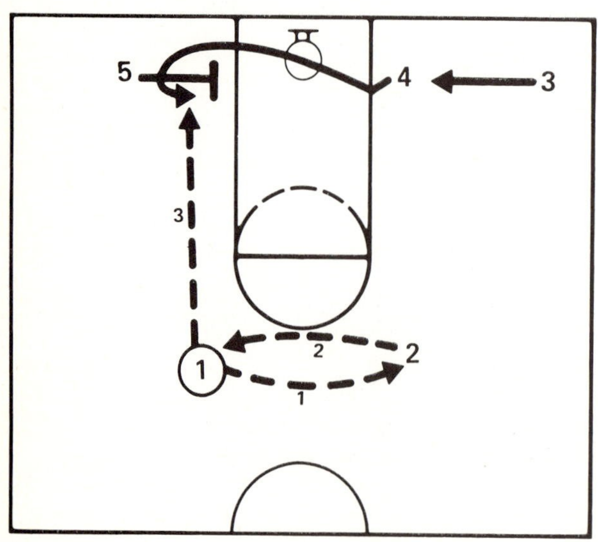

Figure 7–44 2–3 (Baseline) Screening Pattern

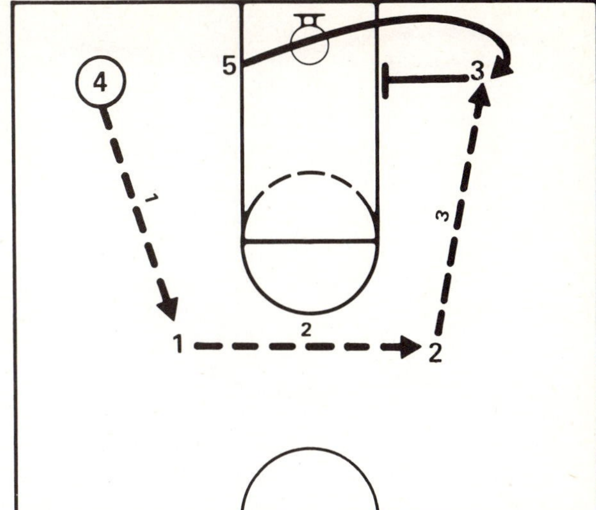

Figure 7–45 2–3 (Baseline) Screening Pattern, Rotation

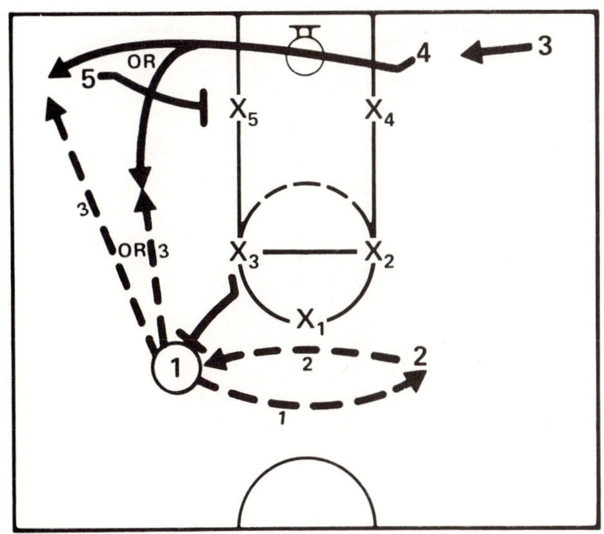

Figure 7–46 Optional Cuts Off the Inside (Baseline) Screen

01's sideline move in Figure 7–47 will further spread the defensive coverage, and thus will facilitate the pass inside to 05 from the corner or the wing.

Some teams prefer to set up the baseline screens from a 2–1–2 alignment, as shown in Figure 7–48. A slight advantage to be gained from this alignment is that 03 can cut either way with an equal chance of success. The weakness of 03's cut is that it telegraphs the direction of the cut, since 03 is positioned in front of X_3 initially.

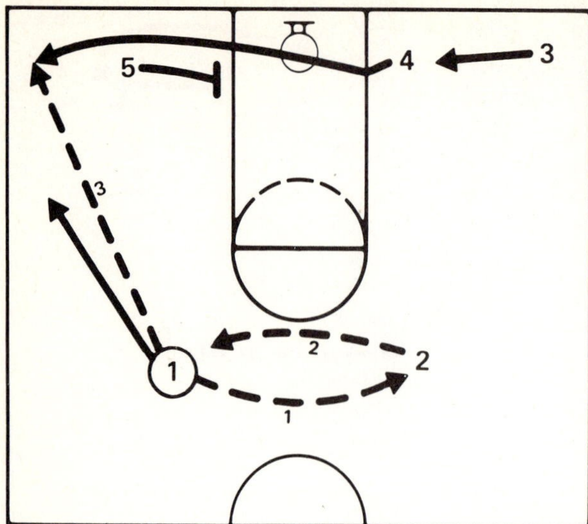

Figure 7–47 Setting Up an Overload from the Baseline Screening Movement

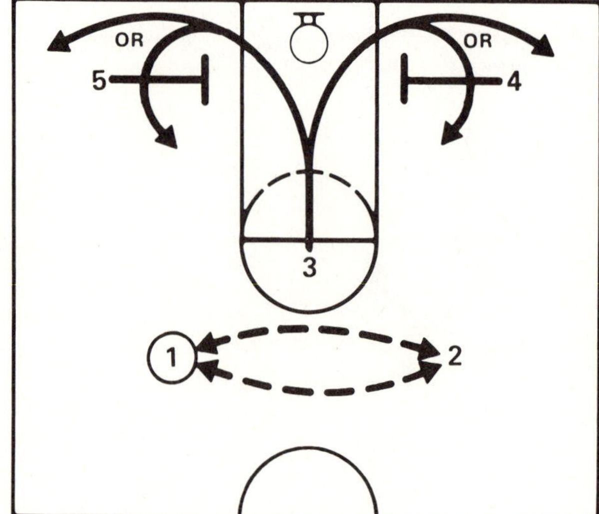

Figure 7–48 Setting Up the Baseline Screen from a 2–1–2 Offensive Alignment

CONCLUSION

We have not attempted to describe a single system of zone offense in this chapter because no single zone offense is intrinsically superior to any other. Instead, we've tried to show how a coach can use various movements associated with a zone offense to construct a system (or systems) to attack zone defenses.

I've probably wasted as much paper as any human being on this planet, manipulating 0s and Xs and trying to find that elusive set of movements that constitutes the ideal zone offense. As a result of my investigations, I can state categorically that: (a) there is no such beast as a universal zone offense, and (b) if there were such a beast, it would probably take the form of a system of movements similar to those shown in this chapter, only in freelance form or keyed by ball or player movements or other signals. The ideal zone offense would require skilled, experienced players, and it would be difficult enough to require constant movement and defensive adjustment yet simple enough to be mastered by all the offensive players involved. It would have to work against *all* zone defensive styles and alignments, and in an almost infinite variety of situations.

III

Controlling Opponents Defensively

Those that I fight I do not hate,
Those that I guard I do not love.

William Butler Yeats

8

Man-to-Man Defensive Techniques and Strategy

INTRODUCTION

The decision to use man-to-man defense is but the first step in defining a team's defensive intentions. Decisions must also be made concerning the following:

a. Will coverage of the ball handler be tight or loose?

b. Will coverage of primary pass receivers (those who are one pass away from the ball) be tight or loose?

c. Will coverage of players two or more pases away from the ball be tight or loose?

d. In combatting screens, will defenders switch automatically, will they switch when they are unable to go over the top of the screen, or will they fight through all screens without switching?

e. Will the ball handler be influenced toward the sideline (by overplaying), or will he be played "straight up" (that is, in a direct line between the ball handler and the basket)?

As might be expected, the answers to these questions depend on the style of man-to-man coverage being used.

PRESSURE MAN-TO-MAN DEFENSE

Defensive Philosophy

Simply stated, our man-to-man pressure defense stresses the disruption of the opposition's offensive flow. We concentrate on applying forty minutes of intense defensive pressure to the other team, with offensive impatience and errors being the desired results.

Our defense intends to:

1. Apply extreme perimeter pressure and force everything to the outside (sideline and baseline).
2. Overplay all passing lanes.
3. Never allow the ball into the high or low post.
4. Keep the ball on one side of the court by denying the reversal (dribble or pass).
5. Have five players in position at all times to apply defensive pressure, or to help a teammate if the pressure breaks down.

Playing with Intensity

I've always been a firm believer in aggressive basketball. I just don't like the idea of laying back and waiting for the opponents to take the game to you. Our golden rule of basketball is: *Do unto others—first!* We believe that, if you intend to control your opponents, you're going to have to convince your players that hard work is the key to success. We've convinced our kids that no one in basketball works as hard as we do, and that nobody is as tough physically or mentally as we are. We believe that, if we play as hard as we can for forty minutes, we will beat anyone we play.

To me, at least, the biggest waste in the world is a very talented kid who won't play hard. I cringe inside whenever I see a big guy who has a world of potential yet takes advantage of every shortcut he can find, loafs on defense, stands around on offense, and walks or jogs down court when he should be running. I hate to see kids like that. It's natural to avoid pain and to look for shortcuts, but players can be conditioned physically and mentally to play hard. The real players—the athletes—are the ones who can play hard. I don't care if a guy is so tall he can step over Volkswagens; he should be trying to put out the same 100 percent effort expected of everyone else. If he isn't willing to give that kind of effort, you and he would both be better off in the long run if he quit your team, joined the band, and tootled his flute elsewhere.

You can't accept half-hearted practices. If you let a player get away with loafing for one day in practice, you'll probably never get him back to any kind of sustained 100 percent effort again. The tempo for the season's practices is set on the first day of practice. Motivation doesn't come from your pregame talk; by then it's too late. Motivation is developed over every practice session. Every kid will loaf or slack off if you let him. On the first day of practice everyone will go 100 percent; however, as the newness wears off and the drudgery of endless repetition sets in, some players will let up and try to coast. If you let them go without being hard on them one day, they will not try any harder the next day—and even worse, a habit of lackadaisical effort will have been established. Soon they'll be giving you a half-effort every day while thinking they're giving 100 percent. That's why I don't believe in easy practices. We never have easy practices at UNLV. We have shorter practices sometimes, but never easy ones. Practices have to be difficult.

I've known coaches who believed that practice should be fun. You can have fun and work hard, but you must establish on the practice floor the same degree of intensity of effort that you intend to bring to actual games. If players don't practice hard, they won't play with intensity in games. If they won't take a charge in practice, they won't do it in games. If they establish lazy habits in practice, you can expect them to repeat those habits in games. If they think it isn't important to play hard in practice, they'll also take it upon themselves to decide when they will and will not go 100 percent in games. And they'll blame *you* for the team's failures if you haven't worked them hard enough. We've found that the best way to keep players from grumbling is to tire them out.

Nowhere within our system of play is the need for hard-working players more clearly indicated than in pressuring the ball handler, both before and after he picks up his dribble. If players fail in this respect, no other aspect of our half-court coverage is likely to work as planned: we may not be able to keep the ball away from the low post *or* high post, which will permit the opponents to attack us from inside, and our overplaying the primary passing lanes outside will likely result in an endless procession of backdoor cuts and layups or offensive advantages inside.

If the defender on the ball fails to do his job, his teammates will be severely handicapped in the execution of their own responsibilities. In the NCAA Tournament game that we played against the University of San Francisco, we had our 6′7″ Larry Moffitt fronting USF's 7′1″ Bill Cartwright, and our guard on the ball wasn't pressuring their ball handler, so he kept lobbing passes over Moffitt which Cartwright stuffed into the basket on the way down. I watched a videotaped broadcast of the game later, and the television announcer kept saying "Moffitt is going to have to learn that he can't front a man like Cartwright like that!" But it wasn't Larry's fault at all; Larry was doing exactly what we wanted him to, and he would have been successful if the defensive guard hadn't backed off his man and given the ball handler room to make the passes!

We make covering the ball handler closely and aggressively our main concern in every practice. If a kid slacks off his man, we'll get all over him, telling him that he's selling out his teammates, and we'll stay on top of him until he starts doing his job. We'll go to great lengths to make him understand that he *can't* slack off when his man has the ball. If he isn't pressuring the passer, he's a traitor to his teammates who are trying to do *their* job to the best of their ability.

I believe you have to let the players know when you're upset with their performance. You can't let sloppy play, loafing, or players losing their concentration continue for extended periods of time unless you're willing to lose the players completely in terms of effort and morale. I watched a friend's team practice once, and his players were really dogging it; they were standing up on defense, turning their backs on their men in backdoor cuts, and letting their men drive on them time after time. Finally, one player just walked off the court in the middle of a play. An assistant coach walked over to the kid, put his arm around the boy's shoulders, and talked to him quietly for a few minutes. Then, the boy walked into the dressing room and didn't return for the rest of practice.

My friend the head coach must have realized how strongly I was opposed to such goings-on. "He's got problems," the coach explained quickly, indicating the player, "and we're trying to go easy on him while he works them out."

I just don't feel that the basketball court is the place for a player or coach to work out *any* problems except those dealing with basketball. I'm not saying that kids don't bring their problems to practice with them—they do, constantly—but I want my players to understand that I'll work with them 24 hours a day, if necessary, to help them solve their problems with girl friends, family, and the like. But I expect *them* to help *me* solve *my* basketball problems on the court for three hours a day. I've patched up so many marital squabbles and problems with girl friends and parents that I sometimes feel more like Dear Abby than a basketball coach. However, I'd rather do it after practice, away from the basketball court. I love my players, and they know it. I couldn't get the kind of prolonged, intensive effort they've given me and *not* love them. Still, they understand that, whenever they're out on the court, we all have a job to do, and *my* job is to see to it that they do *their* jobs to the best of their ability.

I play favorites, I'll admit. My favorites are the guys who bust a gut to do their job to the best of their ability every second they're on the court, not only when it's easy, at the beginning of practice or when we're 35 points ahead in games, but also when they're tired, hurting, or we're hopelessly behind in games and they have every reason in the world to slack off and take it easy, but they don't. If it is humanly possible, I'll give that kind of kid as much playing time as I can. To have a *good* team —depending on what you consider *good* to be—you must have average athletes who put out a super effort, good athletes who put out a good effort, or outstanding athletes. To have a *championship* team, though, your good-to-outstanding athletes must give an outstanding effort. I prefer the latter, of course—I could hardly expect to succeed by recruiting inferior athletes—but when all the superstars are on the other team, the only way we're going to play them as equals is to outhustle them. *This* goal, at least—outhustling the opponents and working harder than the opposing coach—is within reach of every team and every coach.

When victories are on the line, the kids you can count on will be the ones who are used to hard work. In a lot of cases—and I don't think this point gets the kind of recognition it deserves—playing well in pressure situations means playing with intensity when you're scared, or working so hard that you don't have time to stop and think about being nervous. We've found that the easiest way to deal with this problem is to decide what a total effort consists of for them, and to demand that they play at that level for *every second of every practice.* It's hard to do that, but the end result is that our kids learn what a total effort feels like, and they get used to it after awhile. We don't give them the chance to establish a pattern of half-speed practicing that will carry over into games. Whenever anybody slacks off at practice, we jump on his case immediately. We pull him out and ask him what his problem is. We ask him why he isn't giving 100 percent when everybody else on the court is, or if he expects to continue playing at half-speed. We make a big issue out of it because it *is* a big issue, and by the time we're finished with him, he's surprised that we haven't frisked him for concealed weapons, read him his rights, and booked him for impersonating a basketball player. If we let it go, though, we'd lose him in terms of attitude. Once a degree of effort has been established in a player's mind, you won't change it. We try to make everything as intense as possible in our practices. Habits are easier to make than to break.

You don't just tell your players to play hard; you drill it into them from the first day of practice. The players don't particularly like it, but they're aware of the alternatives. Concerning games, we tell our players, "You're going to be in a street fight for forty minutes." We expect them to play with total abandon and total intensity throughout every inch of the 94′ × 50′ court every second they're in the game. It's only a game, or so they say, but to our kids it's also *survival,* and pride. We like to think that we work harder than anybody this side of the Siberian salt mines, and we're not about to roll over and play dead just because our opponents are supposed to have a better team than ours. We believe in our system of play, and our kids are mentally disciplined to defend every inch of the 94-foot floor like the Texans at the Alamo.

We expect our kids to play hard. To play hard, they have to concentrate completely on what they're doing. We don't want them to relax, mentally or physically. Our kids aren't really as quick as everybody thinks they are, but by concentrating and being alert on defense they gain an extra second or two when transition occurs. Making your kids play hard, whether you're using our system or somebody else's, can add several wins per year to your total over what you'd accomplish without playing hard. Playing hard will make your kids quicker in every phase of the game.

Pressure Man-to-Man Theory

Although much of this chapter deals with the theory and practice of pressure man-to-man defense, in our case it also includes the offense. As will be explained in greater detail later, our pressure man-to-man defense, transition game, and fast break *is* our offense. We don't want to separate them; in fact, we try to tie them together in everything we do.

The dimensions of a basketball court are 94′ × 50′. That's *4,700* square feet of playing area. Our objective is to play as hard as we can over every foot of floor space. In so doing, we spread out the opponents and reduce the factor of player size on the court. We usually aren't as tall as our opponents, and if we let them play the way they want to, their big men would demolish us in the relatively small areas near the baskets at both ends of the court. By playing pressure man-to-man defense, we make their big men work harder to get the ball on offense, and we force them farther outside in order to get the ball. By playing a nonstop transition/running game, we make their big men play a high-speed full-court game which most big men don't like to play. They'd prefer to trot down court and set up in a slow zone defense or patient offensive pattern that gives them time to catch their breath, but we aren't about to let them do that. We will *not,* under any circumstances, let our opponents play a slow game.

We believe that, in order to exert the greatest defensive pressure, we cannot use a zone defense. I felt like I was losing an old friend when we junked our 1–2–2 zone in favor of a pressure man-to-man defense, but you can't really play the running, transition game from a zone defense. You also can't pressure your opponents defensively to control the tempo of the game. When you use a zone defense you can't cut off the passing lanes as well, since the zone defense is used above all else to protect the post areas. You can keep the ball away from the big man if you try hard enough—we proved that with our 1–2–2 zone at Long Beach State—but you aren't as likely to take the ball away from the opponents as you can with a pressure man-to-man defense. You won't force them out of their basic patterns. Zone defense is basically negative; that is, it is used to stop opponents from doing something. The bigger your opponents, the less you'll stop them from doing. If you use a zone defense, the least you can expect is to see their big man set up inside and rest, even if you're successful in keeping the ball away from him. Then, at the other end of the court, he'll block every inside shot your players take.

That's why the zone defense is not good enough for us. We don't want big men to hurt us at *either* end of the court, and to reduce their effectiveness we have to tire them out, or, if they're not going to run with us, they can take it easy getting back on defense and watch us score before they get back to reject our shots. It's all the same to us. If they loaf on offense, they won't score. We'll front them any time they're in the post areas.

I hated to scrap the 1–2–2 zone. It kept the meat and potatoes on our table for eleven years. But I don't think I'll ever go back to it. (At least, I hope not.) It just doesn't provide the kind of *total* defensive control that we can get from the pressure man-to-man.

I've always believed in making the game as simple as possible. We vary our full-court pressing coverage to a certain extent, but I like the idea of freeing our kids' minds. When they're constantly trying to remember which variation of which defense they're running, or where they're supposed to cut in their offensive patterns, I think they lose some of their intensity. For every change you make, your kids will lose a little more intensity. Soon they'll be spending more time thinking about what they're doing than doing it.

I also think that if you can teach your kids to play hard and to execute properly, they'll make less mistakes and at the same time they'll force the opponents into committing more mistakes. If your players are used to playing hard and running hard, they'll beat opponents who aren't used to playing that way. I'm convinced that our fast break is effective, not so much because we're quicker than our opponents, but because (a) we've been able to cut down our transition time from defense to offense, and (b) our opponents make more mistakes in their coverage than we do in our execution. We practice transition and high-speed execution in everything we do. Our fast break depends on beating opponents in the first three to four steps after transition. Games are often won by a single step.

Most teams fast break occasionally. We fast break relentlessly. We fast break after steals, defensive rebounds, successful field goals and free throws—in short, every time we regain possession of the ball. In 1975–76, when we were 29–2, we averaged 124 ball possessions per game to our opponents' 116. That's *240* total ball possessions in a forty-minute game, with the ball changing hands an average of once every *ten seconds,* over a 31-game schedule. (We averaged 94 shots per game that year.) If we don't get the layup, we go into our early game offense, taking the first open shot we get. Most teams will take the ball out and run their set offense, but our set offense isn't effective. Our transition game is where we're strongest, so we'd just as soon be on defense if we can't get the quick score. I know we've been accused of playing back-yard basketball, but there's method in our madness. We don't want our opponents to relax on defense, which they will if we set up and run our patterns patiently, and we *know* that they're not going to relax on offense, because we aren't going to let them.

Incidentally, lest we be accused of using a style of play beyond the skills of junior high or high school players, numerous high school coaches of both boys' and girls' teams have reported favorable results from using our high-intensity techniques and philosophy.

Note: Coach Warren, the co-author of this book, went 17–6 with a small, relatively inexperienced, but extremely quick, high school girls' team in the first year he used these methods, averaging 57 points per game to his opponents' 35. The following year, his girls won 20 games and lost 3, scoring 73 points per game to the opponents' 38. His starting lineup in those years measured 5′1″, 5′2½″, 5′3″, 5′4″, and 5′5″!)

The only limiting factor in using this system is *speed*: a team full of extremely slow players probably would not be effective in full-court pressure man-to-man defense, and possibly in half-court pressure man-to-man as well. However, we still maintain that *every* player should learn to play at his own full speed, if for no other reason than to protect himself when confronting opponents who will force him into a high-speed game.

And you'd better believe a quick team can force a slower team to increase the tempo of its game: I mentioned earlier that our 1975–76 squad caused an average of 29 turnovers per game, with ball possessions averaging only *ten seconds* each for an entire 31-game season. Well, Coach Warren's girls averaged *21* steals and *34* forced turnovers per game in 1978–79. In a 32-minute high school game, they averaged *1.7* steals or forced turnovers per minute! We've found that many otherwise splendid opposing players simply cannot adjust to a high-speed pressure game because they're not used to playing that way themselves. They're used to walking the ball up the court, setting up leisurely, and working the ball around the perimeters and inside until they get the shot they want, then trotting back down court on defense. They may *want* to employ all those tactics, but we're not going to *let* them: we're going to try to take the ball away from them the first second they gain possession, by pressing them all over the court, by trying to steal the ball, by taking charging fouls, by overplaying the passing lanes—by doing everything we can to disrupt the rhythm of *their* game and to establish our own tempo.

I honestly believe that our system of play makes our players look and play better than they really are. We've had weaknesses on all of our teams in the past—usually a lack of height was the major weakness—but because of the extreme pressure we keep on our opponents, (a) they are usually unable to fully exploit our weaknesses, and (b) we pinpoint, and are able to use, their own weaknesses when we attack them. We play our system so well that even superior opponents are often unable to establish their own system of play. We like to say, "When you play the Runnin' Rebels, you play the game *our* way. We won't let you play it *your* way."

A third aspect of our "play hard, play fast, and execute properly" philosophy is that it builds pride in performance. When Vince Lombardi was coaching the Green Bay Packers, rival coaches and players knew that the Pack was going to come at them with the "Green Bay Sweep" practically every other play. The only things they didn't know were: (a) the direction in which the sweep was going to be run, and (b) how to stop it. The Packers executed so well that, even when the opponents guessed correctly, they usually couldn't stop the Packers' backs from grinding out large chunks of yardage whenever they ran the sweep.

We used the same kind of tactic at Long Beach State with our 1–2–2 zone defense, and we're doing it now with our pressure man-to-man defense. Our kids are proud of the fact that, regardless of who we're playing, we can take the opponents out of their regular offense and make them play our way. We give up a lot of points, but that's due as much to our high scoring as it is to any of our supposed defensive shortcomings. Teams always make more mistakes when they're playing an aggressive, high-risk defense. Also, when a team averages 110.5 points and 94 shots per game as we did in 1975–76, the opponents are obviously going to have more opportunities to score. It comes with the territory, as they say.

Whereas zone defenses are designed to provide added protection in selected areas of the court, our pressure man-to-man coverage is designed to get us the ball, preferably without the opponents' taking a shot. We're not trying to force the opponents to take bad shots; we're trying to recover the ball before they're able to shoot at all. We try to force the other team to turn the ball over as often as possible. The year we set the record of 110.5 points per game, our opponents averaged 29 turnovers per game to our 14.

The high-intensity pressure defense we use creates turnovers, which in turn create scoring opportunities that wouldn't have occurred otherwise. If the players know that their defensive efforts are going to lead to scores, they'll work harder on defense, and they'll also become involved in the ensuing fast break. I doubt if I could get the same kind of prolonged effort out of our kids if they knew that they were going to have to slow down and set up when they got to our end of the court. They love the idea of easy scores, even if the defensive efforts that are required to create and set up the fast-breaking layups are anything but easy.

We have a simple game plan. We play the tightest possible brand of pressure man-to-man defense. We're not going to drop back into zone defense part of the time or back off in our man-to-man coverage, not even if our players get in foul trouble or if our opponents are threatening to blow us out of games. We don't make changes; we're going to come at you the same way every time, without surprises or "gimmicks." About a third of our opponents try to hold the ball on us, in styles ranging from cautious ball-control offenses to four-corner delay patterns, but it doesn't really matter to us. We're going after the ball no matter what they do. They can't shut down our offense because our offense springs from our defense and transition game. They can't keep players back to stop our fast break, because we fast break from transition, and few teams practice their offensive patterns in order to drill their players in stopping fast breaks.

We don't practice zone defense, nor do we try to familiarize our players with other variations of man-to-man coverage. It's hard enough for our kids to master *one* style of defensive coverage without our packing their minds with a different defense for every situation. When we played the University of San Francisco in the NCAA Tournament, our only two big men picked up their fourth fouls late in the game. The TV announcer said we'd have to go to a zone defense. After the game we were asked why we hadn't shifted to the zone. It was because we didn't have a zone defense to change to, and we still don't have one.

Pressure Defensive Techniques

In teaching defensive coverage of the ball handler, we want our players to assume a nose-to-belly-button low defensive stance, as close as they can get to the ball handler. We stress keeping the feet as far apart as possible, especially when moving (gliding) with the dribbler. We'll have players assume a defensive stance and then hold it for thirty seconds. We have a drill called "Run, Glide, Run" in which the players alternate the sliding *glide* movement with full-speed running on coaches' signals to permit them to practice the footwork involved in changing directions and speeds from a defensive stance to running, and vice versa.

The defender on the ball uses a stance with his inside foot forward to influence the dribbler toward the sideline (Figure 8–1). We'll drill players in covering the ball handler from this position on either side of the court. We'll tell the dribbler to try to turn the corner and drive, or spin-dribble back to the middle if the defender cuts him off. The defender, on the other hand, will try to force the dribbler toward the corner. If he is successful and the dribbler reverses toward the middle, the defender will try to draw a charging foul.

Figure 8–1 Guarding the Ball Handler, Sideline Influence

Once the ball comes across the half-court line, we try to force the dribbler toward one sideline or the other. When I was at Long Beach State, we used the same kind of tactic with a zone defense, and I love the idea. It's so simple that a lot of people overlook it. With the ball established on one side of the court, the offense's attacking advantage is cut in half.

When the ball is established at the sideline, the only primary scoring areas are the ball-side corner, the low post, and the high post (Figure 8–2). This is true whether the defense is in man-to-man or zone coverage and regardless of the type of offense being used. Even continuity or free-lance patterns that feature screens away from the ball are designed to get the ball to players cutting toward the ball.

The first step in our pressure man-to-man coverage, then, is to *force the ball handler to dribble to one side* of the court. We don't particularly care which side he goes to, but we do *not* want him to attack the middle of the court or pass to the high post. We don't want him to reverse or spin-dribble to the middle. If the defensive player allows his man to reverse to the middle, he is either loafing or not concentrating—probably the latter. We'd prefer that the ball handler not be allowed to pass to a teammate along the sideline. We want him to dribble to the sideline.

The second step in the process is to *deny the pass to the high post.* We always front the high-post player. We don't care how small the player guarding the high post is, or how tall his man is; we expect him to front his man. We do not want the opponents to attack us from the high post. Everything we do on defense depends on our keeping the ball away from the high post. We haven't had a practice in five years in which we didn't

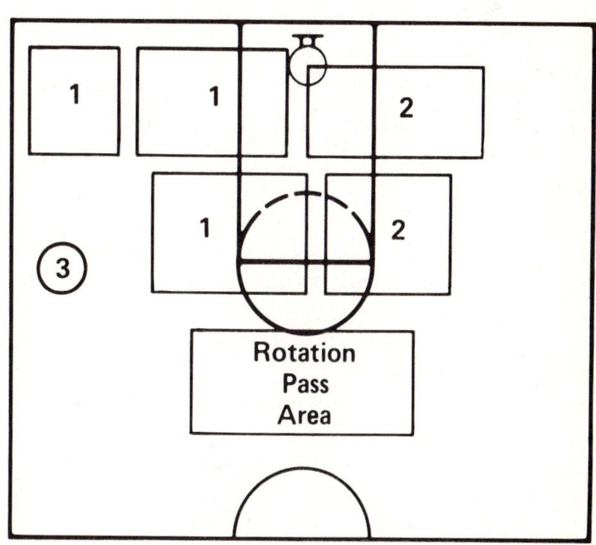

Figure 8–2 Primary (1) and Secondary (2) Scoring Areas with the Ball Established on One Side of the Court

work on denying passes to the post. We never play behind the post man.

We feel that, if we're going to front the posts, we're going to have to put a lot of pressure on the ball. Our centers generally have been small at Nevada–Las Vegas, and without pressure on the ball handler, the opponents' big men would wear us out at the high post. When an opposing player at the wing has the ball and is not dribbling, we want our man to smother him, playing right up in his face and making him lean over backwards to protect the ball. We want to cover him so closely that he can't make a good pass. The defender will keep his hands moving at the level of the ball, trying to deflect the pass or to force a bad pass that we can pick off. We practice this kind of coverage daily. It's extremely important to our overall defense. *We do not want our opponents to make the pass to the high post;* we'll do practically anything short of declaring war to deny those passes!

When the post man is playing high, our center will front him on the ball side. When the ball is rotated from one side of the court to the other, we don't specify whether our center will slide in front of, or behind, the opponents' post man in order to front him on the other side. We just tell him to front the high post on both sides of the court. If the post man steps out high, the center will find it easier to go behind him to his other side, but if the center backs up or moves along the side of the lane toward the basket, it will be easier for our center to slide across in front of him. However, we're going to front him even if he goes up and sits in the stands.

Along with this, we try to overguard any wing men along the sidelines to deny them the ball. We hope that, as the ball handler is forced to dribble toward the sideline, the wing occupying that position will vacate it to give him operating room. When a dribbler at the sideline picks up his dribble, he is limited in what else he can do: shoot (unlikely), or pass the ball away. (We overplay *all* passing lanes when the dribbler picks up the ball.) If the ball handler is able to pass to the wing, however, the wing man may dribble, pass, or shoot. We prefer to limit the available alternatives at the sideline to as few as possible, which means that we'll overplay any offensive players at the wing positions to deny them the ball. You can't play good pressure defense and allow passes.

In covering the wing, we want the defender positioned at the wing with his inside foot forward and a hand in the passing lane to deny the pass. After the pass is made, say, from the point to the wing, we want the defender covering the passer to move approximately two steps toward the ball and one step behind the line of the ball, or the imaginary line between the ball handler and the receiver. (See Figures 8–3 and 8–4.)

There are two reasons for the one-step-back, two-steps-to-the-side movement after the ball handler passes the ball away. First, the movement backward helps to neutralize 01's possible backdoor movement, and it helps X_1 to maintain vision on both the ball and his man. Second, the

Figure 8–3 Covering the Point Guard Before Pass to the Wing

Figure 8–4 Covering the Point Guard After Pass to the Wing

two steps toward the ball permit the defender to step into the passing lane and to intercept the return pass without running into 01, who probably will be stepping forward and reaching for the ball.

We work with our players (particularly the forwards) every day in denying the lead pass to the wing. We overplay him high (toward mid-court) so he can't get his body in front of the defender. If he steps out and comes toward the ball, the defender will step out and slide toward the ball, maintaining the same close, overplaying stance.

When the wing manages to catch the ball despite our tight coverage, we want the defensive man to play him so he can't drive to the middle or pass to the high post. This means covering him like an extra layer of skin, which in turn means that the ball handler will probably drive the baseline. (We're taking away his other options.) Once he begins driving, the defender will try to beat him to our established cutoff point 3 feet outside the free-throw lane along the baseline. Then we'll have a weak-side defender come over to draw the charging foul. (See Figures 8–5 and 8–6.)

Figure 8–5 02 Emptying with 01's Dribble to the Sideline (*a*)

Figure 8–6 02 Emptying with 01's Dribble to the Sideline (*b*)

As the dribbler moves toward the sideline, we want to deny the reversal, or reverse pivot and dribble back toward the middle. We don't do this as well as we should, but the theory is great. Also, because we put so much defensive pressure on the ball handler, he's usually willing to take whatever we give him—in this case, access to the sideline.

When we drill our guards in covering the dribbler outside, we'll use two balls and divide the court in half, with an offensive player and a defensive player playing one-on-one on either side of the court. We'll have the defensive players force the dribblers toward the sideline corners, and if either of the dribblers turns the corner, his defender will do his best to beat him to the cutoff spot. Then we'll bring the four players together and add a coach to the drill. One of the offensive players will dribble once and pass to the coach near the sideline. The guards will take two steps inside their men in order to force them to cut behind the defenders if they are to get the ball. We're denying the pass and forcing the backdoor cut. When the offensive men go backdoor, the defenders will snap their heads around and sprint with them to the basket, doing their best to deny the pass.

Once the ball reaches the sideline, the third step in our coverage takes shape: we want to force the ball handler toward the baseline—specifically toward the baseline corner—rather than the middle of the court. Putting this concept into practice without giving up baseline drives is easier said than done. In effect, what we're asking our kids to do is to deny the reversal to the middle without giving up the baseline drive. In terms of priorities, our first concern is to deny the reversal. If they have a player at the high post, we front him, and if a teammate has filled the vacant position at the point, we play his passing lane as well. We over-guard the ball handler toward the sidelines, since we want him to go to the baseline rather than the middle. (See Figure 8–7.)

If the dribbler tries to drive the baseline, we have a cutoff point where we want our defender to try to beat him to. Our cutoff point is 3 feet outside the free-throw lane. We expect our man to do his best to stop the drive, but it's not the easiest thing in the world to do. We work on it constantly, and every year we get a little better at it, but during the first year that we tried to do it, our opponents literally wore us out with layups. However, even if we can't stop the dribbler, we *don't* want him to come to the middle.

Low-Post Coverage

Our goals in covering the low post are slightly different—actually they are *expanded*—from the low-post coverage I used in our 1–2–2 zone defense at Long Beach State. In our zone coverage we attempted to bait passes inside to the low post. In our pressure man-to-man defense, our goal is not only to deny the inside pass but to make the low-post player

Figure 8–7 Forcing the Baseline Movement from the Sideline

vacate that area. In order to do this, we guard the low post from the outside in, in a technique we call "V-fronting" (Figures 8–8 and 8–9).

In V-fronting (we also call it *bottom fronting*), our ball-side inside defender will play outside the man at the low post, rather than between the offensive player and the basket or the ball. His position at the low post's side rather than in front of him should still tend to discourage passes inside, and a weak-side defender will double-team the low post man with him if the wing lobs the ball inside. Our primary reason for siding rather than fronting is to force him to move into (and across) the lane to the weak side rather than cutting to the ball-side corner. We want to isolate the ball handler at the sideline and force him to drive the baseline. If we allowed the low-post man to cut to the corner, (a) the wing would be unable to drive, and (b) he probably would pass to the corner instead. We don't want him to select either of those alternatives; we want him to drive. To do this, we have to guard the low-post man toward the basket rather than the corner, influencing him toward the weak side in the hope that the ball handler will drive. (If the low-post man cuts to the high post, the defender will maintain his V-front coverage as he adjusts high.)

Figure 8–8 Covering the Low Post, V-Fronting

Figure 8–9 V-Fronting

We also work hard at training our players to take the charge. When you play our kind of pressure man-to-man defense, you're encouraging players to drive on you. Your players have to be willing to draw the charging foul. I don't believe you can be effective in a pressure defense if your kids won't take the charge. When the defender beats the ball handler to the cutoff point, he must square himself to the basket, face the dribbler, and remain stationary to draw the charging foul.

I really believe that players, even kids who used to be nonaggressive, can be taught to love to take the charge. You'll have to sell them on the idea, though; most kids won't do it naturally. The ones who don't do it either haven't been taught to or are afraid of getting hurt. We've never had anyone get hurt from taking a charge. Kids get hurt when they take half a charge, trying to avoid part of the contact.

Reggie Theus, a second-team all-American for us, loved to draw charging fouls. So did Glen Gondrezick. Reggie would take a charge from a Mack truck. He used to take charges with a smile on his face. He wanted the Coaches' "Rebel" Award that we give every year to the player who takes the most charging fouls. Our superstars take the charges.

In effect, then, we're giving the wing man the baseline, and after he starts toward the baseline we want to get to the cutoff point in time to stop him if we can. When the ball handler starts his drive to the baseline, the defender will pivot sharply, take two quick steps, and run beside him as closely as he can get so the dribbler can't switch hands, pivot inside, and take the ball to the middle. When the defender reaches the cut-off point ahead of the dribbler, he pivots, snaps into a wide, low defensive stance, and cuts the man off.

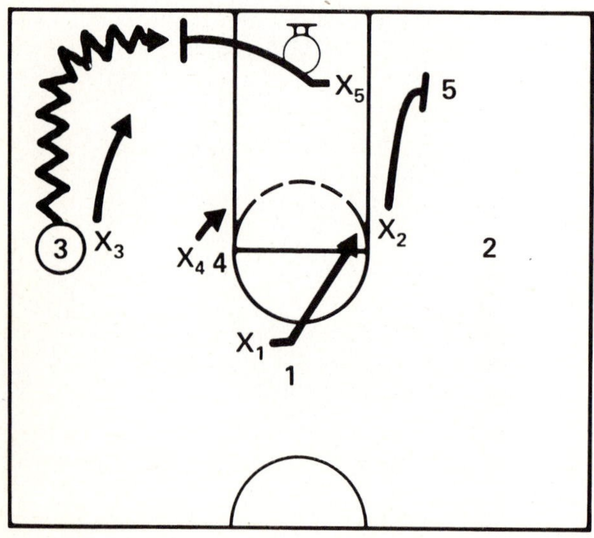

Figure 8–10 Defensive Rotation to Stop Baseline Drives: *Example #1*

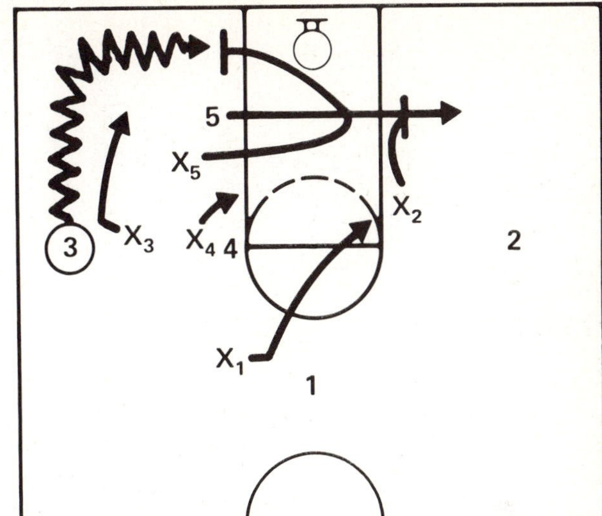

Figure 8–11 Defensive Rotation to Stop Baseline Drives: *Example #2*

Sometimes the defender simply will not be able to reach the cutoff point before the offensive player. In such cases, the inside defenders will have to rotate their coverage (Figures 8–10 and 8–11). Sometimes you have to switch; however, don't let your players think they can count on automatic switches—not if you want them to give you 100 percent effort on defense.

When the ball handler drives the baseline and turns the corner successfully, the defense will have to rotate its inside coverage to stop the drive. If the defensive center is at the high post, a weak-side forward will take the charge. In Figure 8–10, X_5 on the weak side will move across the lane to stop the penetration, with X_2 picking up 05 on the weak side. Figure 8–11 shows the same rotation, except with 05 starting out at the low post and emptying to the weak side when he sees 03 driving.

Actually, we use a variation of the coverage shown in Figures 8–10 and 8–11. When X_5 picks up 03, X_4 rotates to cover the weak side in our system of play, with X_1 dropping to cover the high post 04. (See Figures 8–12 and 8–13.)

Once the ball handler picks up his dribble, we'll overguard everything on the court that moves except the referees. We've taken away the dribble, and we intend to deny all passes as well. We expect the man guarding the ball to do his part by trying to deflect the pass. To do this, he must keep at least one hand near the ball at all times. Many players forget to do this, but we try to make getting a hand on the ball an automatic response by our players. The ball handler can throw up a shot if he wants to, but since he's stationary and closely guarded, the shot isn't likely to be the one he had in mind when he started dribbling. Sometimes

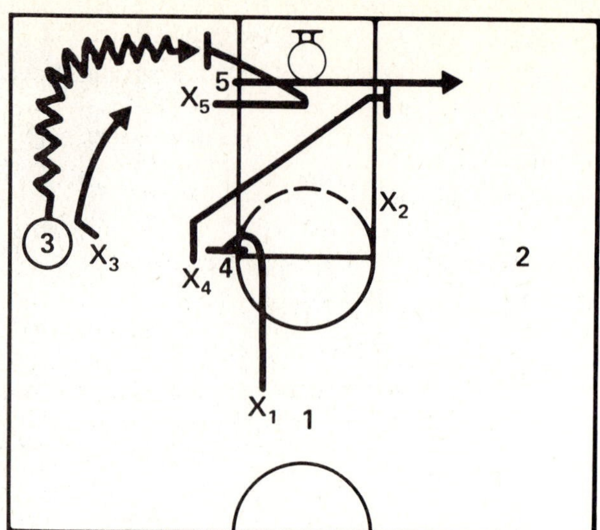

Figure 8–12 Variations of Defensive Control to Stop Baseline Drives:
Example #1

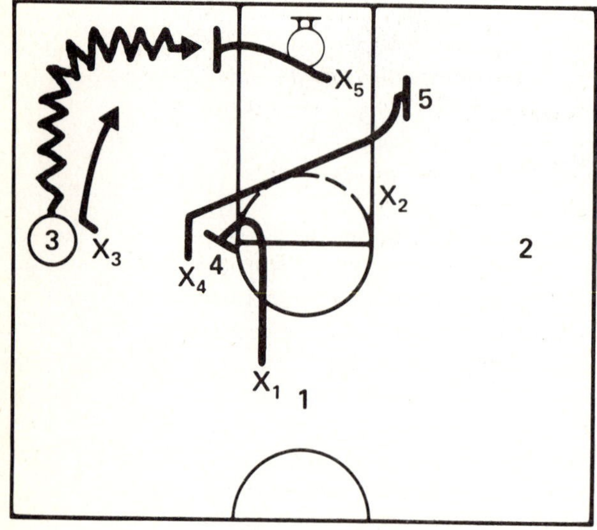

Figure 8–13 Variations of Defensive Control to Stop Baseline Drives:
Example #2

we get burned on backdoor passes, which has led a lot of people to think that we don't play good defense. A University of North Carolina player said after they played us that he was disappointed that, after all he'd heard about our tough defense, they were open all night for backdoor cuts and layups. What he failed to realize was that they also had 26 turnovers, which is more than double their ordinary amount, if memory serves me correctly.

It is true that we give up a lot of backdoor layups. We probably give up more backdoor layups in the course of a season than anybody, but it's not because we play poor defense. It's because *we place greater emphasis on cutting off the passing lanes than on stopping the backdoor cuts!* There's a very good reason for this. No team uses backdoor cuts as its primary offensive thrust. Every coach tells his players to go backdoor if opponents play the primary passing lanes, but whenever one or more players cutting backdoor fail to get the pass, they have to go back out and reset the offense before they can run the rest of the pattern. Backdoor cuts are automatics, not a regular part of the offensive pattern. *We want to take away our opponents' regular patterns,* first by *forcing* the ball to the sideline, and then by denying all passes that would allow them to continue the pattern. Because most teams are pattern oriented, they tend to lose their composure when they have to rely on automatics for any kind of offensive flow or continuity. This in turn makes them more likely to force passes to teammates who are overguarded.

We don't like to give up backdoor passes and layups. Our players are taught to cover the backdoor cuts the same way they cover baseline drives: by snapping their head and inside arm back, taking two quick steps and running alongside the cutter with arms raised to deflect the pass. However, we can't shut off all of the passing lanes and options all of the time. It's our objective, but we have to be realistic enough to grant that we cannot shut off all of the passing options 100 percent of the time. We expect our players to work hard on overplaying the passing lanes, fronting the high post, and denying the reversal to the middle.

Playing hard-nosed, aggressive pressure man-to-man defense is exhausting. We like to think that our defensive efforts force our opponents to work harder on offense than they're used to working, but these efforts also take a lot out of our kids. We've found that our players cannot play for more than six or seven minutes at a time with the kind of intensity our system requires, so we use a continuous shuttle system involving eight or nine players, sometimes substituting as many as three players at a time to keep our players fresh.

When an opponent is able to pass to a teammate, we want the defender to close on the pass receiver as quickly as possible and keep him from turning and looking inside. If he manages to turn, the defender will get so close that he'll have to bend over backward to protect the ball. However, we want to keep him turned away from the basket. We want to make him dribble rather than letting him pass the ball. Our whole defensive effort is in jeopardy if we let him turn and pass inside.

Concerning players two passes or more away from the ball, our rule is the same for both half-court and full-court defense: we want the defenders to play one step off the line of the ball as before, but they should sag away from their men about one-third of the distance to the ball. (See Figure 8–14.)

As before, X_3's position one step off the line of the ball allows him to

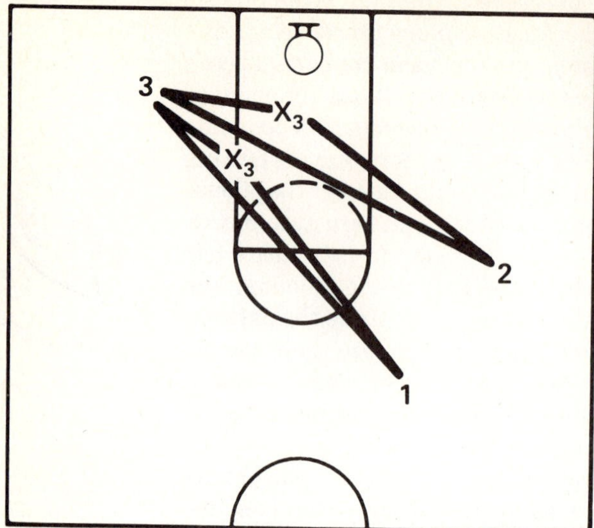

Figure 8–14 Covering Players Two or More Passes Away from the Ball

maintain vision of his man and the ball. Sagging away from his man permits him to move quickly into position to stop the drive if 02 gets by X_2, yet X_2's coverage will deny all but lob passes to 03. In other words, if an offensive player is not a threat to receive a pass, it is not necessary to cover him closely.

We want our players to point the ball; that is, to point one hand at the ball and the other at their man. We feel that pointing increases a defender's court awareness by requiring him to watch the ball and the man he is guarding at the same time. If he turns his head to watch the ball, a defender loses sight of his man and becomes vulnerable to backdoor cuts; if he watches his man but not the ball, he cannot play team defense effectively. Pointing reminds players of their dual responsibility regarding individual and team goals.

And that's our pressure man-to-man defense. I think it's the most effective theory of defense ever devised. It's not an easy defense to play—I couldn't imagine a more demanding style of defensive coverage—but the theory underlying its usage is incredibly simple. On paper it's the *ultimate* half-court defense: you're *forcing* the ball to the sideline, *forcing* the baseline drive, *taking away* the drive, and *denying* all passes away from the baseline. Regardless of what offensive patterns the opponents want to run, you're taking away *all* offensive movements, passes, cuts, and so on, except: (a) the dribble to the baseline, (b) the baseline drive, and possibly (c) the backdoor cut.

The next step is the hardest part, though: preparing your players to play defense that way.

Pressure Man-to-Man Defensive Drills

Everything we do at UNLV revolves around our full-court press and half-court pressing defense. We scored 100 points or more in 23 of our 31 games in 1975–76, and averaged 110.5 points per game in 1974–75 and 107 points per game in 1975–76, but it wasn't due to the offensive patterns we ran. We had good shooters, but we also played an extremely aggressive kind of pressure man-to-man defense that lent awesome proportions to our transition game. We demanded, and got, outstanding defensive efforts from our kids, and I think that *that* as much as anything else was the key to our success. Everything we did was geared toward high-speed, competitive drills and exercises that would train them to keep pressure on their opponents. We didn't let up on our players, because we wanted them to take charge of their men and not lose control even for a second. I don't think you can tell players to play hard and leave it at that. You have to show them exactly what you want, explain how they are to do it, and then drill them constantly under competitive conditions until they can do it. We'd take a simple one-on-one drill, with one coach cheering for the offensive player and another coach yelling for the defensive player, and run it up and down the court. I don't think you can expect any kid to play good pressure defense unless he can control his man. If he's thinking that his teammates are going to be there if he doesn't do it right, he may not be as highly motivated as he ought to be. We like to think of every one-on-one situation as a personal challenge to the player's pride.

Controlled Scrimmaging

Since *transitions* play such an important role in our team's style of play, it is necessary at this point to discuss our techniques for teaching our players to anticipate, and deal with, this phase of the game. Three factors contribute to the large number of turnovers that our team is able to force opponents into making: our aggressive pressure man-to-man defense, our overplaying of the passing lanes, and our opponents' natural tendency to initiate and maintain their offensive patterns by throwing passes into the same passing lanes we're overplaying. We get burned with backdoor passes from time to time, but when we don't we're likely to steal the ball.

We rarely scrimmage full-court during the season; instead we prefer to use a half-court scrimmage technique known as *controlled scrimmaging* (Figure 8–15). We feel that controlled scrimmaging provides more intensive work on specific skills than is possible in regular full-court play, yet it is broad enough in scope to include the various elements of the transition game.

Controlled scrimmaging is a defensive drill. The offensive players

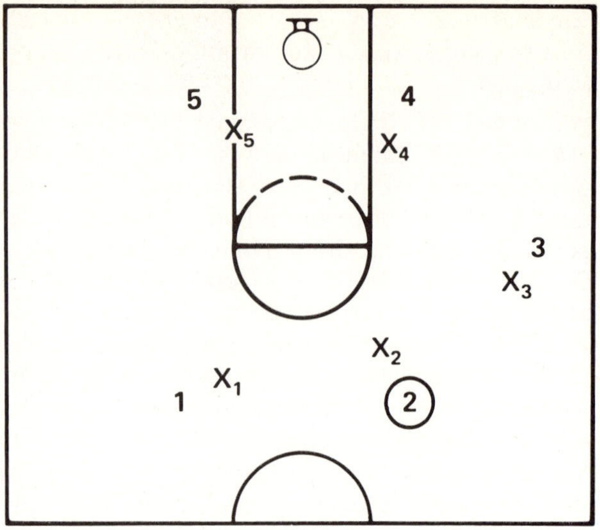

Figure 8–15 Controlled Scrimmaging, Basic Starting Positions

can do anything they want—drive, set screens, go backdoor, and so on—with the defenders playing pressure man-to-man defense. Each coach is responsible for watching certain defensive players, and he constantly reminds them to maintain their defensive stances and positioning, to concentrate, and to stay tense. We want them in an exaggerated stance with their feet wider apart than their shoulders. We do not want them to let their feet come any closer than shoulder width apart. We work extremely hard in keeping their feet wide apart. We also stress their positioning themselves in an over-guarded stance where they can still see, and point to, their man and the ball.

If the offensive team turns the ball over in any manner, the defensive team will fast break. If all of our players are positioned properly and are in their defensive stance, watching the ball as well as their man, we'll almost always have a numerical advantage in the fast break if transition occurs.

If the offensive team shoots and misses, the defensive team will fast break if it gets the rebound. If the offensive team gets the rebound, it will continue its half-court offense. If they score, the defensive team will try to fast break with the inbounds pass. If the defensive team scores, they'll go into their full-court press and play defense to the half-court line. If the defensive team fails to score, we give the ball back to the offensive team and play half-court pressure man-to-man defense.

This scrimmaging requires a great amount of concentration on the part of the defensive players. They have to (a) play tough, overguarding man-to-man defense without losing control of their men, (b) go to the boards and block out for rebounds after shots, (c) be ready to fill their lanes immediately whenever transition occurs, (d) fast break after rebounds or scores, and (e) set up to press full-court as soon as they score. Since none of those actions permits delays, each defensive player must concentrate on what he and everyone else on the court is doing. Admittedly, these segments place a great deal of pressure on the defensive players, but that's not necessarily bad. In our style of play, pressure is the rule rather than the exception.

We also use controlled scrimmaging to work on our press (Figure 8–16). As before, the offensive players can do anything they want to get open. Once they get the ball past the half-court line, we try to force the ball to the sideline. We work on overplaying to deny the reversal toward the middle of the court, but we don't intend to give up the baseline drive, either. When the ball handler starts to drive the baseline, his defender snaps around and tries to beat him to the cutoff point.

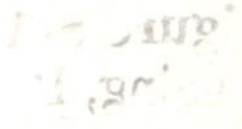

The defense will fast break after steals, defensive rebounds, and scores. If they score, they'll press full-court until the offensive team completes one pass. We do this drill for thirty to forty minutes at a time. It really wears down the players, but it teaches them to play defense the way we want it played.

Sometimes we practice fast breaking from defensive rebounds by setting the offense in a 2–1–2 alignment and assigning a good shooter to one of the outside positions. It's not really that good a defensive drill—there aren't many good, realistic rebounding drills—but it allows us to practice blocking out and fast breaking after rebounds.

It's also possible to practice rebounding and fast breaking after missed free throws. We practice our transition game from every kind of

Figure 8–16 Practicing Full-Court Pressing Defense

situation we're likely to encounter in games. We try to simulate game conditions as much as possible in our controlled scrimmaging.

The rest of our defensive drills are described in detail in Chapter 11.

RUN-AND-JUMP DEFENSE

Ever since I can remember, from the first time I learned that there were ways to stop ball handlers from driving besides jumping on their backs or slashing at them with karate chops, I have heard that players are not supposed to allow ball handlers to drive the baseline on them. Coaches have stressed that "there's always help in the middle, but when you let the dribbler go baseline, you're on your own." It was considered a cardinal sin to give up the baseline drive.

In recent years, however, a radically different defensive concept, popularly known as the *run-and-jump defense,* has arisen in which opponents are not only allowed but are actually *encouraged* to drive, particularly along the baseline. If you're not familiar with the tactic, you may find it hard to accept run-and-jump techniques, especially if your upbringing in basketball is diametrically opposed to using them. Still, too many teams have used run-and-jump defense successfully for it to be dismissed as a passing fad.

Actually, our pressure man-to-man defense at UNLV is similar in many respects to the run-and-jump defense. Both defenses attempt to cover the ball handler and primary pass receivers as closely and aggressively as possible; both deny the opponents the ball at the high and/or low post; both feature players two or three passes away from the ball who drop off their men to help out inside; and both systems will have those players switch off to cover the dribbler when he beats his man and goes baseline.

On the other hand, the players will rotate their coverage in pressure man-to-man defense after the switching occurs (Figure 8–17), but in run-and-jump defense the defender whose man is driving the baseline will not try to cut off his man at any point along the baseline, nor will he trap him with whomever is switching off to stop the drive. Instead, he will continue inside and pick up whoever is open as a result of the switching. (See Figure 8–18.)

In Figure 8–18, X_2 is overplaying 02, discouraging his drive to the middle if not actually encouraging the drive toward the baseline. If 02 takes the bait and begins driving in the direction of the baseline, X_2 will cover him closely as he drives, keeping defensive pressure on 02 so he will not be able to divert his attention to the player switching off to stop him. 02 will be driving to the basket at top speed, and if the run-and-jump movement is timed correctly, he should be unable to find his open teammate before the switch is completed. In many cases, 02's momentum to-

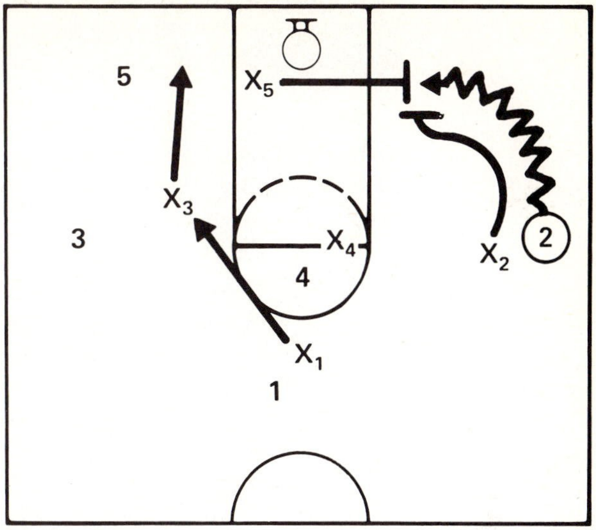

Figure 8–17 Comparing Man-to-Man Trapping (With Defensive Rotation) with Run-and-Jump Defense:
Man-to-Man Trapping (With Defensive Rotation)

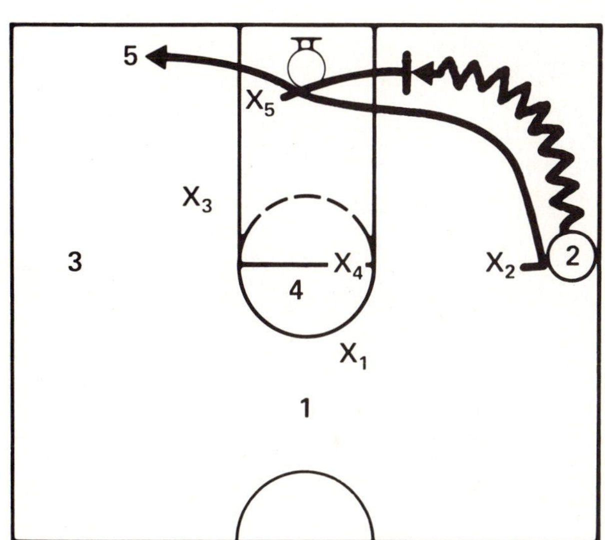

Figure 8–18 Comparing Man-to-Man Trapping (With Defensive Rotation) with Run-and-Jump Defense:
Run-and-Jump Defense

ward the basket will permit X_5 (or whoever is switching with X_2) to draw a charging foul.

It is obvious that timing is all-important in the run-and-jump defense, as is the location of the switch. If X_5 picks up 02 too far outside, 02 may be able to find the open man, or he may be able to dribble out of his predicament and take advantage of the resultant mismatch inside. It also should be obvious that this tactic by itself will not ensure success any more than the act of trapping in a zone defense will guarantee that a team will steal the ball or force a turnover. The element of surprise is all-important in the run-and-jump defense, since the ball handler is not likely to dribble into such unfriendly circumstances if he knows about them beforehand.

Still, the dribbler's alternatives are limited: the primary passing lanes are closed, and he is denied access to most areas of the court. He has to do something, but the only course of action not denied to him is dribbling to the baseline. The defense can further confuse the ball handler by varying the location of the run-and-jump movement and switch, or by using different players to effect the switches. (X_3, for example, could have dropped off to cover 02's drive instead of X_5 in Figure 8–18.) Of course, players must be alert and intelligent to learn the intricacies of such a complicated system, but when the players are both skilled and aggressive, the run-and-jump defense can be a potent defensive style.

Run-and-jump techniques are also used in certain forms of a man-to-man pressing defense. These techniques are described at length in Chapter 11.

SWITCHING MAN-TO-MAN DEFENSE

I don't believe in a switching defense, or at least in defenses in which switching is an automatic response to screens. (We may switch, especially *jump switch*, in response to screens on the ball, but we never switch on screens away from the ball.) If a kid knows in advance that he doesn't have to bust a gut to get through screens, he's not going to. I think little things, such as allowing a kid to take shortcuts, to go around screens

Figure 8–19 Fighting Through Screens vs. Automatic Switching: *Fighting Through Screens*

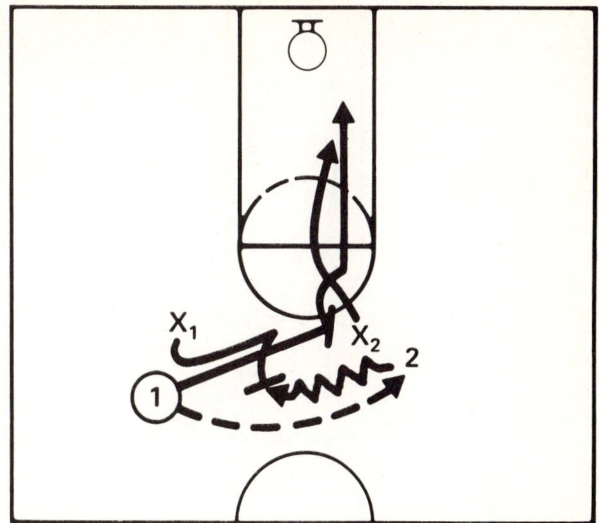

Figure 8–20 Fighting Through Screens vs. Automatic Switching: *Automatic Switching*

automatically instead of fighting through them, or to drop off his man just because he's not a primary pass receiver, chip away at a kid's dedication and determination. Switching is necessary sometimes, but I feel that, with the exception of *jump switching*, it should be used as a last resort, not as a planned part of a team's defensive strategy.

In Figure 8–19, X_2 goes on top of, or *through*, the screen set by 01, and continues to guard 02. X_1 continues to guard 01. Switching does not occur. In Figure 8–20, however, X_1 and X_2 switch defensive responsibilities, with X_1 picking up 02 as he dribbles around the screen, and X_2 covering 01 as he rolls away from the screen and cuts to the basket. Both techniques appear acceptable, and they are if the players do not grow lax in their anticipation of the screens and switches. The problem associated with anticipating the screens is illustrated in Figure 8–21.

When X_1 anticipates the switch and steps out to cover 02's dribble around the screen, his positioning is excellent to cover the dribbler's drive to his left; but when 01's roll to the basket draws X_2 away, 01 will be unable to stop 02's drive into the lane and to the basket.

The movements and coverages shown may occur anywhere on the court, of course; anywhere, that is, in which screens are set. The easiest way to resolve the resultant problems is to either avoid switching whenever possible, or to use jump-switching to combat the screen.

Jump Switching

In applying the jump-switch technique to the defensive coverage shown in Figure 8–21, X_1 will not only move quickly into position to overguard ball handler 02, but he likely will advance toward 02's ball side

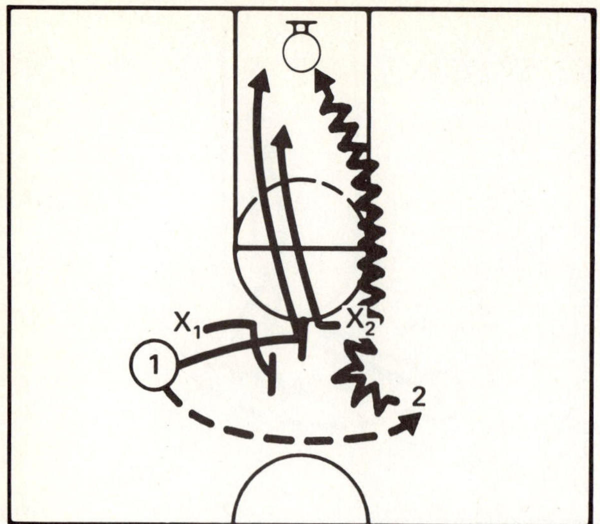

Figure 8–21 Foiling the Defensive Switch

from a low defensive stance and will attempt to steal the ball while it is unprotected. If 02 does not stop suddenly and spin-dribble away from X_1, he is likely to have the ball stolen from him.

Jump switching is risky, of course; its success will depend to a large extent upon two factors, the element of surprise and X_1's ability to jump into a close, low over-guarding position that will allow him to go after the ball before 02 can pivot away from him and move the ball to a protected position. The factor of surprise may arise because the screening movement itself is basically aggressive, and 02 may have trouble converting his attacking movement to a defensive posture in time to stop X_1 from taking the ball from him.

Of course, teams should jump switch only periodically, not every time a screen is set. Sometimes they will merely switch, as shown in Figure 8–20, and at other times X_2 will not follow 01 to the basket, but will trap the dribbler as X_1 forces him to reverse pivot.

Jump switching is also used in a full-court (man-to-man) pressing defense. We use it sometimes to vary our *bluff-and-run* and *trapping defense.*

Before leaving the subject completely, we repeat that there are times when switching simply cannot be avoided, such as when the offense features double screens or a series of repetitive inside screens. It is not improper for a team to use switching in such circumstances. The error lies in using switching as a shortcut to safe defensive coverage, or in expecting to control opponents defensively by switching automatically every time a screen is set.

Automatic switching is basically a negative approach to man-to-man coverage; it is, in my experience, as worthless as Edsel stock. If you're going to use a passive form of defense, play a basic zone defense. It's not worth your time to try to teach your players to play aggressively, except when the opponents decide to set a screen.

SINKING MAN-TO-MAN DEFENSE

Sinking, or sagging, defense refers to a technique in certain systems of man-to-man coverage whereby players two or more passes away from the ball drop back toward the basket, or away from their men to provide increased coverage elsewhere. The rationale for such movement is that whenever an offensive player is out of position to receive a pass, or is in a poor position to attack the defense if he does receive a pass, guarding him closely would be a waste of manpower that could be put to better use bolstering the defense elsewhere. Examples of such sinking or sagging coverage in a man-to-man defense are shown in Figures 8–22 through 8–24.

Figure 8–22 Sinking Defense, Ball at Intermediate Wing

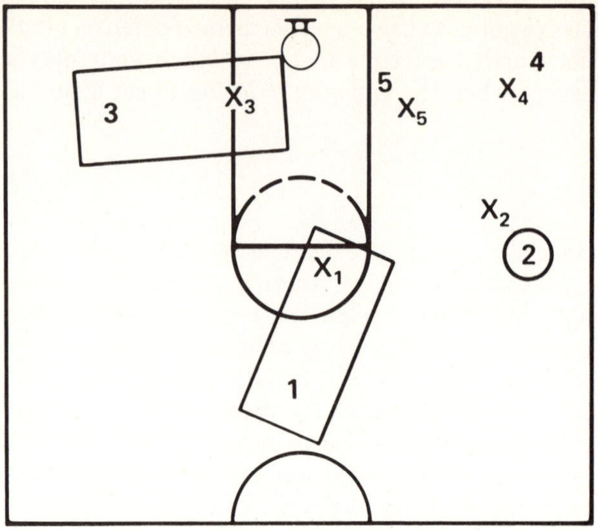

Figure 8–23 Sinking Defense, Ball at Wing

In Figure 8–23, the defense is overguarding at the post and is playing the passing lane along the baseline. The weak-side guard, however, has sagged away from his man to supplement the coverage of the post.

> **Note:** Since the weak-side forward has also sagged away from his man, the guard may stay outside to play the passing lane. Generally, though, he will sag as shown in Figure 8–23, particularly when the opponents have an outstanding offensive player at the high post.

Figure 8–23 shows the sinking procedure with the ball established on one side of the court. In Figure 8–24, with the ball in the corner, the defensive guard has dropped back to double-team the low post. (We used a variation of this kind of corner—low-post coverage in our 1–2–2 zone defense at Long Beach State.)

In each of the examples given, the sinking movements free at least one offensive player who would not be open in a tight pressure man-to-man coverage; still, passing to that player would not substantially weaken the defensive coverage or control. In Figure 8–24, for example, the ball may be returned to the wing, but the only shot that would be immediately available is the shot from the wing. The guard's sinking movement in no way increases the offensive team's chances of penetrating or working the ball inside.

In sinking defense, players tend to move back toward the basket, and slightly toward the ball handler. (See Figure 8–25.)

Figure 8–24 Sinking Defense, Ball in Corner

Figure 8–25 Weak-Side Sinking Movements

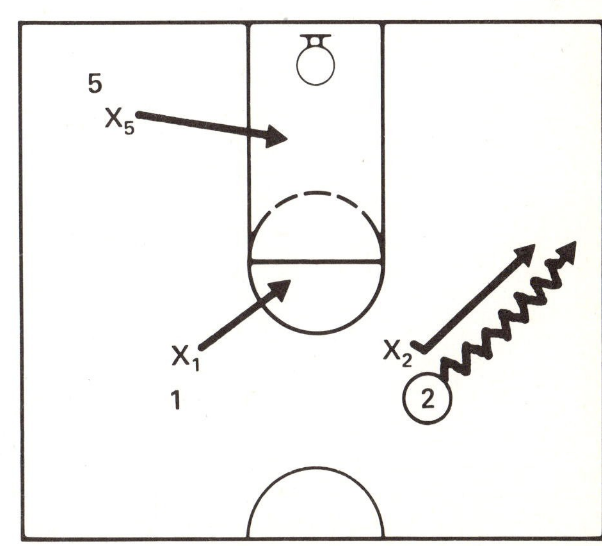

Many teams play an effective style of man-to-man defense that involves pressure on the ball and primary receivers, and sags away from players two or more passes away from the ball. This is probably the most popular form of man-to-man coverage in use today. It is extremely versatile: not only can a team use run-and-jump techniques (or our pressure man-to-man defense with inside rotation) from this style of play without modifying the rest of the coverage or having to teach the players a new or conflicting set of defensive rules, but within the coverage itself the amount of defensive pressure afforded each offensive player will vary with every pass. A player who was formerly receiving intense defensive pressure as a primary receiver may find himself open as the ball is passed away from his side of the court, yet he is no more likely to score than he was previously.

To add run-and-jump principles to the basic "pressure-on-the-ball-and-primary-passing-lanes, sagging-away-from-everybody-else" style, all the coach has to do is to teach his players how he wants them to execute the run-and-jump technique from various court positions and then tell them, "We'll play our regular man-to-man, but every time they drive we'll run-and-jump." I'm oversimplifying of course; neither the pressure-and-sinking man-to-man combination nor the run-and-jump technique is easy to teach or to learn. Both require constant drilling and practice to be successful. Still, the techniques fit together remarkably well for teams that are skilled enough to use them.

A sinking defense is seldom effective when it is extended to the ball handler. The most popular forms of sinking coverage involve pressure on the ball (always) and primary passing lanes (sometimes), with defenders two or more passes away from the ball sinking as described previously. In such situations, sinking does not transform the man-to-man coverage into passive defense. Man-to-man defense should be played aggressively; otherwise, a team is better off playing zone defense.

NLV
BASKETBALL

9

Basic Zone Defense

Of all kinds of zone coverage, *basic* zone defense offers perhaps the least opportunity for aggressively controlling opponents. In one sense, at least, basic zone defense does not provide control at all: its relatively passive coverage of pass receivers may permit opponents to control the tempo of the game. However, basic zone defense is not designed to force opponents into mistakes; rather, it represents the attempt to deny certain shots to the offensive team—usually shots from the posts or inside the lane—and to define and delimit the areas of the court from which shots eventually will be taken.

Basic zone defense is safe, conservative defense—safe, that is, because there is an absence of attacking movements by the defensive players which, if unsuccessful, would leave them vulnerable to penetration or attack by the offensive team. Teams use basic zone defense when their personnel limitations deny them more aggressive modes of coverage such as pressure man-to-man defense or trapping zone defense, or when the opponents' offensive strength is too great to attack them defensively. Zone defenses are effective if you have big, slow kids, or if you cannot match up with certain opponents individually.

BASIC ZONE DEFENSIVE PRIORITIES

1. Keep the ball away from the high and low post positions. Although defensive priorities change with alignments and team needs, this priority of basic zone defense never changes. While teams using other defenses may acknowledge the need to keep the ball outside and away from the opponents' big men inside, basic zone defensive coverage provides continuous coverage of inside players. While one or more ball-side or weak-side positions may go uncovered at times in order to ensure adequate coverage of the low post, the post positions will always be protected as thoroughly as necessary by double-teaming, fronting, or overguarding.

2. Force the ball wide of the point; that is, to one side of the court or the other. When the ball is at the top of the circle midway between the sidelines, the offensive team is able to establish its attack on either side of the court with equal facility. Forcing the ball wide of the point establishes the matchups or areas to be covered by each defensive player, and reduces the possibilities for effective inside penetration to one side of the court—the ball side.

The easiest way to force the ball to one side of the court or the other without losing defensive control of the high-post or wing positions in the process is to set, or move, a single defender out to the point, as will be explained in greater detail later in this chapter. When he is defended in this manner, the ball handler's best options are: (a) to shoot, an unlikely choice if the defensive point guard applies any kind of pressure; (b) to penetrate, a difficult task against a single defender backed by the rest of the zone defense; or (c) to pass or dribble the ball away from the top of the circle. The third option is the most likely choice because it entails the least risk.

3. Avoid unfavorable matchups or one-on-one confrontations inside. The defensive team may not be interested in matching up inside, but individual confrontations are inevitable. The coach whose team is using basic zone defense will want to ensure that, when the opponents are able to work the ball inside to the low post, momentum and control will not shift entirely to the offensive team. In order to combat unfavorable matchups inside, the defensive team may use such techniques as dropping back outside players to help cover the low-post position or realigning players to alter the matchups. By using basic zone coverage, the defenders have already sacrificed part of their ability to attack the offense in order to protect the area around the basket and lane; they can ill afford to lose this small advantage through unfavorable matchups or one-on-one situations that they cannot control.

4. Keep the ball away from the high post. After the low post, the high-post position gives zone defenses more trouble than any other position. When the offensive team is able to pass inside to the high post, the offensive player at the high post may have a distinct advantage over the defender covering him. First, neither of the inside defenders (X_4 or X_5) in Figures 9–1 through 9–3 will be able to help defend the high post. Thus, X_4 and X_5 are frozen in their positions, since moving up to help X_3 cover 03 would leave their own defensive positions unguarded. Second,

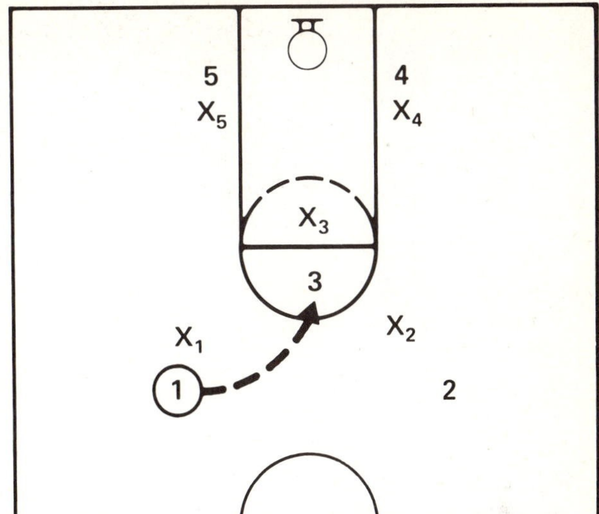

Figure 9–1 Passing to High Post Against Matchup Zone Coverage

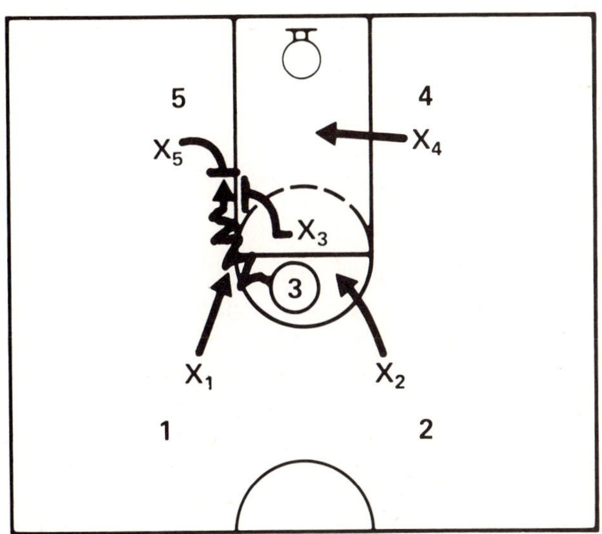

Figure 9–2 Forcing Inside Double-Teaming from High Post

the high-post player sometimes can force inside defenders to double-team him as shown in Figure 9–2, in which case the offensive team gains a distinct advantage in terms of attacking capability. Finally, the only defensive players capable of helping to cover the high-post position are the guards, but they too will have to leave their primary defensive responsibilities to assume high-post coverage. (See Figure 9–3.)

A fourth alternative for the ball handler at the high-post position arises when X_4 and X_5 stay low and guards X_1 and X_2 follow 01 and 02 in

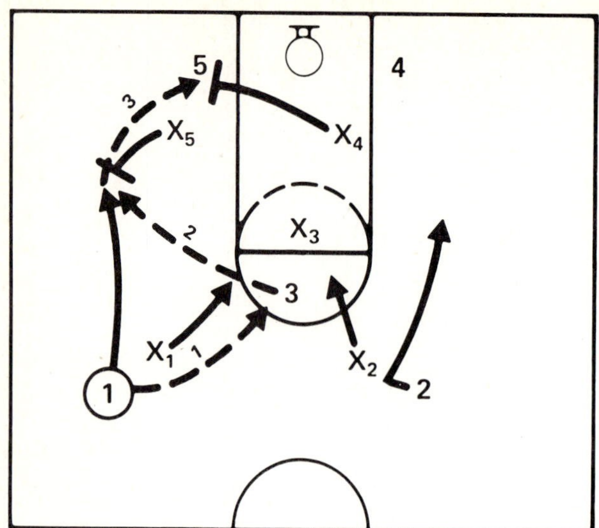

Figure 9–3 Guard Cut After Pass to High Post

their cuts: 03 may take advantage of the matchup alignment to work on X_3 one on one. A similar situation in the 1978 NCAA finals between Kentucky and Duke allowed Kentucky's Jack Givens to score 41 points, many of them from the high-post position against Duke's 6′10″ Mike Gminski, as Duke chose to match up with Kentucky's big men inside and their sharpshooting guards outside.

5. Decide which outside shot to give up. With the possible exception of matchup coverage, every zone defense tends to give up something in return for increased coverage of selected areas of the court. Although some teams are so aggressive in their zone defenses that neither inside nor outside shots are achieved without a great deal of effort, the defensive team still must know what it is trying to accomplish beyond merely keeping the ball outside. If personnel limitations dictate that a shot eventually must be given up somewhere, the coach must decide which areas of the court will yield the least advantageous shots for the opponents, or which shooters should be allowed to take the shots.

Figure 9–4 shows some of the difficulties associated with corner and/or high-post coverage when double-teaming the low post. 03 has the ball at the wing and is guarded by a single defender. 05, the offensive team's dominant big man, is double-teamed at the low post. A single defender is back to cover the weak side. The question is, with both the corner and high post unprotected, should the defense have a guard cover 04's possible cut to the high post, or a forward who is ready to drop low to help cover 05 when 04 cuts to the corner? Whichever mode of coverage the coach selects—probably a guard (usually the point guard X_1) covering the

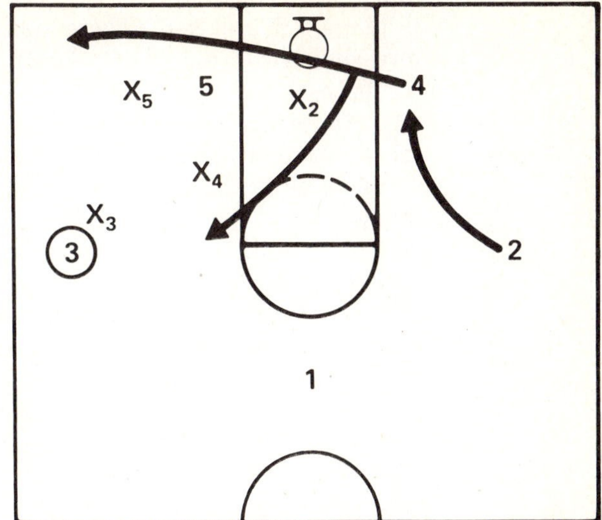

Figure 9–4 The Perils of Inside Double-Teaming in Basic Zone Defense

high post—it is obvious that the defensive coverage will have to give up a shot somewhere when they try to stop the opponents' inside game by double-teaming. (If you don't like the idea of double-teaming inside, envision yourself as the Memphis State coach in the 1972–73 NCAA championship game, with UCLA's Bill Walton playing the 05 low-post position against you, and your 6′9″ Larry Kenon, a superb player himself, trying to match up with him. Then picture your game plan after Walton hits 21 of 22 field goal attempts.) Therefore, if you have to give up a shot: (a) make sure you're giving up an outside shot and not surrendering your inside control, and (b) try to give up only the poorest percentage shots you can, especially to opponents who aren't particularly good outside shooters.

EVEN-FRONT VS. ODD-FRONT ZONE DEFENSES

Earlier we mentioned that man-to-man defenses have a greater potential than zone defenses for controlling opponents. However, it should be noted that the outside alignments of zone defenses exert considerable control over opponents in terms of ball position. Having one defensive player at or beyond the top of the circle tends to force the offensive guards, and thus the ball as well, to the sides of the court, as shown in Figure 9–5. On the other hand, having *two* defensive players occupy the outside positions along the free-throw circle tends to guide the offensive players toward the middle of the court and the wings (Figure 9–6). That this is so is due to the existence of a widely accepted offensive strategy known as *splitting* a zone defense. When the offensive team attempts to split a zone defense, it aligns its players in the gaps between the various defenders, as shown in Figures 9–5 and 9–6. (These and other splitting alignments and tactics are discussed in greater detail in Chapter 7, "Attacking the Zone Defenses."

In its basic alignment, a zone defense may position one, two, or three players outside, or have them near the top of the circle. If two players set up outside, as in the 2–1–2 zone defense shown in Figure 9–6, the zone is known as an *even front.* If one or three players set up outside, as in a 1–2–2, 1–3–1, 1–1–3, or 3–2 zone defense, the alignment is described as an *odd-front* zone defense.

The most important consideration regarding even-front and odd-front zone defenses is that *differences among the various alignments arise only when the ball is in the midcourt area;* for example, at the point (Figure 9–6) or intermediate wing position (Figure 9–5). A popular misconception exists that certain zone defenses are superior to others in all situations, but all zone defenses are alike in principle once the offensive team clearly establishes the ball on one side of the court. Different alignments may require different players to cover the various court positions after the initial pass, but the areas to be covered remain the same.

Although in isolated cases the reverse may hold true, it is generally accepted that *odd-front defenses are superior to even-front zone defenses.* With the exception of point trapping, zone defenses are most vulnerable when the ball is at the point: the defenders are in their basic positions, and the offense may be able to attack either side of the court before the defensive players can adjust their coverage. Additionally, a quick succession of

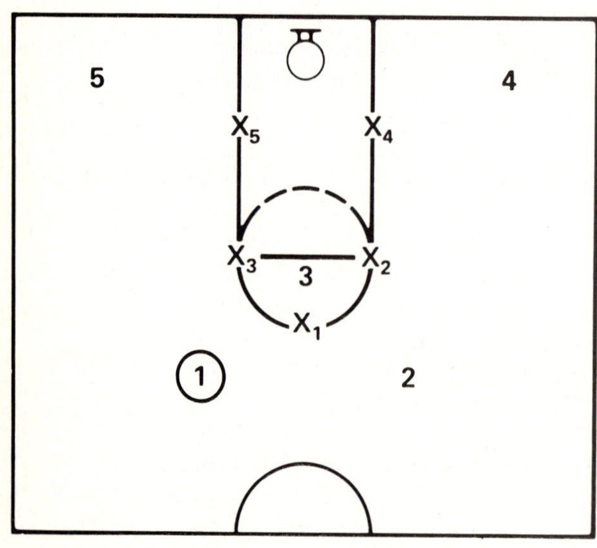

Figure 9–5 Splitting the 1–2–2 (Odd-Front) Zone Defense

Figure 9–6 2–1–2 Zone Defense, Basic Alignment

passes originating at the point can force the defense to match up one-on-one when they would prefer other modes of coverage.

The 1–3–1 zone, which is another even-front zone, is ideally suited for use as a half-court trapping defense: you can trap at the intermediate wing positions or corners on either side of the court, and you don't have to worry about the other team's attacking you from the high post, because it's covered naturally in the 1–3–1 alignment. However, you need three or four fine athletes who can really move in order for the trap to work the way it's supposed to. Trapping has to be aggressive, and by *aggressive* I mean really storming the beaches and going after them tooth and nail; otherwise, your opponents will wear you out with diagonal passes, layups, and short jumpers from 10 to 15 feet. Small guards will not be able to deny the diagonal passes against taller opponents except by standing up, and in standing up they give the ball handler the option of dribbling around (or through) the trap. We seldom trapped in our half-court zone defense except when the ball went inside to the high or low post.

As I said, you need three or four good athletes to make the 1–3–1 trap zone work: two to spring the trap, one to cover the corners before the trap is set, and one to deny the pass to the high post. I've always believed a team that plays effective half-court trapping defense can play *any* defense well.

We preferred to use the 1–2–2 zone defense instead of the 1–3–1. We weren't particularly interested in matching up, although matchups occur constantly in the course of playing zone defense. We wanted to force the ball wide of the point without surrendering any of our inside control in the process, and we felt that the 1–2–2 zone alignment was ideal for this purpose.

ZONE ALIGNMENTS

The term *alignment* refers to the basic positions assumed by the defensive players, not to their movements or responsibilities from those positions. The most widely used zone alignments are the 2–3 and 2–1–2 even-front zone defenses; the 1–3–1, 1–2–2, and 3–2 odd-front zone defenses; and the lesser known 2–2–1 zone defense. (The 1–1–3 alignment is a variation of the 2–3 zone defense.)

2–1–2 and 2–3 Zone Defenses

Although they are not as prevalent as they used to be, 2–1–2 and 2–3 zone defenses are still seen regularly in all areas of the country, and at all levels of play except the pros. The even-front defenses are probably overrated in their potential for controlling opponents, but the 2–1–2 and 2–3 zones are easy to teach and to learn. Also, the personnel requirements for operating a 2–1–2 or 2–3 zone are slightly more flexible than for other alignments. (See Figures 9–7 and 9–8.)

The 2–1–2 and 2–3 alignments may vary considerably from those shown in Figures 9–7 and 9–8; they may be used interchangeably, as when covering the high post. The two alignments differ in their coverage when the ball is passed to the wing: if a guard covers the wing, the defense is using 2–1–2 coverage; if a forward covers the wing pass, the defense is in 2–3 coverage.

Why should distinguishing between 2–1–2 and 2–3 zone coverage be important? Because the 2–1–2 alignment is susceptible to 01's penetrating dribble to free 02 or 03 for high-percentage shots. In other words, the alignment and coverage of a 2–1–2 zone defense tend to surrender control to offensive teams that have a good ball handler at the point guard position.

Both the 2–3 and 2–1–2 zone defenses can be used to match up or trap, but the 2–3 is probably superior for matching up because of the ease involved in covering the pass to the wing. (However, the 2–1–2 alignment may be more conducive to help-and-recover techniques.) Additionally, teams can use the even-front alignment for combination defense, with the two guards attempting to disrupt the flow of the offense by playing the opponents' guards man-to-man.

Basic 2–1–2 or 2–3 zone defensive coverage is weakest in the areas

Figure 9–7 2–1–2 Zone Defense, Covering the Wing Pass

Figure 9–8 2–3 Zone Defense, Covering the Wing Pass

indicated in Figure 9–9. However, these areas of weakness generally disappear when the defense matches up by rotating into a 1–2–2 alignment, or when X_4 and X_5 cover the wing and corner passes.

In one particular situation, the 2–3 zone alignment can prove extremely valuable to a team. When the opponents have two superior big men who are capable of dominating the inside positions, you can run a modified 2–3 zone, double-teaming at the ball-side low post and single-guarding the big man away from the ball as shown in Figures 9–10 through 9–12.

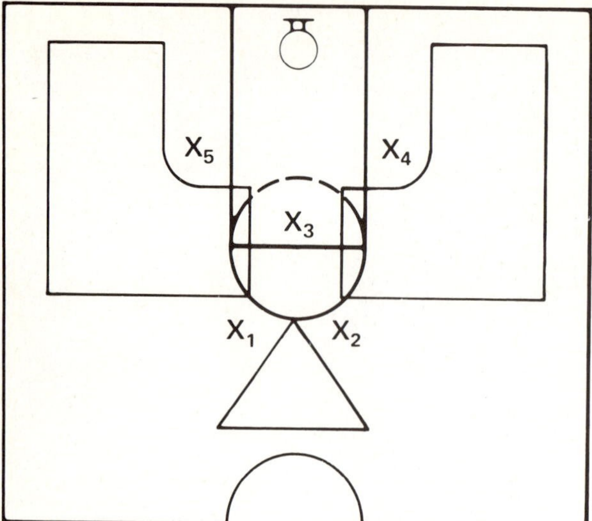

Figure 9–9 Weaknesses in Basic 2–1–2 (and 2–3) Zone Defense

Figure 9–10 Basic 2–1–2 Double-Teaming Alignment

Figure 9–11 Inside Double-Teaming from 2–1–2 Zone Defense, Ball at Wing

The big men front offensive players at the low post when the ball is at the point. If the ball handler tries to pass to either of his big men from the point, the middle inside defender will move into position to double-team the receiver. When the ball handler passes to the left wing, the ball-side low post will be double-teamed and the weak-side defender will cover the weak-side low post (Figure 9–12). However, we must acknowledge the likelihood that the guards will have to give up an outside shot sooner or later.

If one of the big men cuts to the high post, the weak-side defender will have to cover his cut until a guard can assume coverage. This cut will create a mismatch at the high-post position, of course, but if both big men are truly dominant offensive players, most coaches would rather have the mismatch occur at the free-throw line than at the weak-side low post. Similarly, if the weak-side low-post player cuts to the ball-side corner (or if the ball-side low-post player slides to the corner and the weak-side low post man cuts to the ball-side low post), the inside defender on the ball side will cover him one-on-one after he receives the pass, with teammates

Figure 9–12 Defensive Shift with Crosscourt Pass

double-teaming the other big man. The strategy, then, is to double-team the ball-side low post at all costs and to single-guard the big men whenever they go outside. If the opponents' big men are likely to beat you inside, your best bet is to play the percentages by: (a) harassing their other players as much as possible, but giving them the outside shot if you have to in order to maintain inside control and (b) influencing the big men to go outside by denying them the ball inside. They may beat you from the one-on-one matchups outside, but they're far more likely to beat you inside.

Other methods exist for combatting two outstanding big men, but not from zone defensive coverage. With the exception of the previous defensive tactic, zone coverage will result in unwanted matchups and inside confrontations. There are always gaps in zone coverage.

Player Characteristics for 2–1–2 and 2–3 Zone Defenses

1. X_1 and X_2 must be quick, and they must be able to cover the point and wing positions. (In a 2–3 zone defense, X_4 and X_5 must be able to cover the wings.)

2. X_3 is usually the tallest defensive player. He defends the high and low post positions, and rebounds from the middle of the lane. He must deny passes inside, and when defending the high post he should make it difficult for the high-post man to turn and face the basket. Obviously he must be a good rebounder.

3. X_4 and X_5 should be good rebounders. They must be able to deny the corner shots and help X_1 and X_2 cover the wings. They also must be able to rebound their side of the backboard.

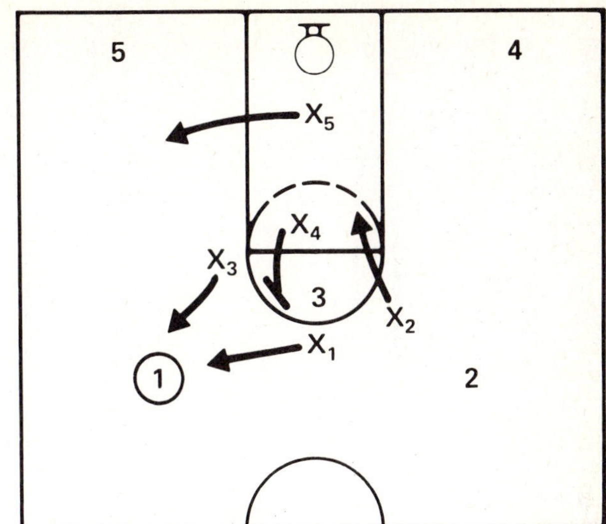

Figure 9–13 Basic 1–3–1 Zone Defense

1–3–1, 1–2–2, and 3–2 Zone Defenses

The 1–3–1 zone defense is probably the most versatile zone defensive alignment in basketball. Matching up and trapping are commonly seen from the 1–3–1 alignment; in fact, the basic form of the 1–3–1 probably is the zone's least effective usage.

While the basic 1–2–2 zone defense keeps a player on the ball constantly, basic 1–3–1 coverage spreads the offense without the benefit of covering the ball handler. Thus, rapid ball rotation and diagonal crosscourt passes are always a likelihood. In Figure 9–13, X_1 and X_3 may or may not advance on the ball handler. If they advance, X_2 may remain in position, or he may even advance slightly toward 02; however, if 01 is permitted to handle the ball freely, X_2 will have to retreat to cover the diagonal pass to 04 at the weak-side low post.

When the ball is passed to the corners, coverage is closer to normal than when at the intermediate wing position (Figure 9–14). X_3 will either move toward 05, in which case X_1 will cover the ball-side high post, or he will continue to cover the high post, with X_1 dropping back to the middle of the free-throw line. X_5 will approach the ball in the corner from the baseline side, attempting to deny both the shot and passes inside to the low post.

In its broadest sense, the 1–3–1 zone has no natural weaknesses except those resulting from personnel limitations. Matching up is easily achieved from the 1–3–1, and situations conducive to trapping can be found in any of five court positions: the corners, the intermediate wing positions, and the high post. In its basic form, however, the 1–3–1's weaknesses can be painfully obvious: in the corners if X_5 is not particularly

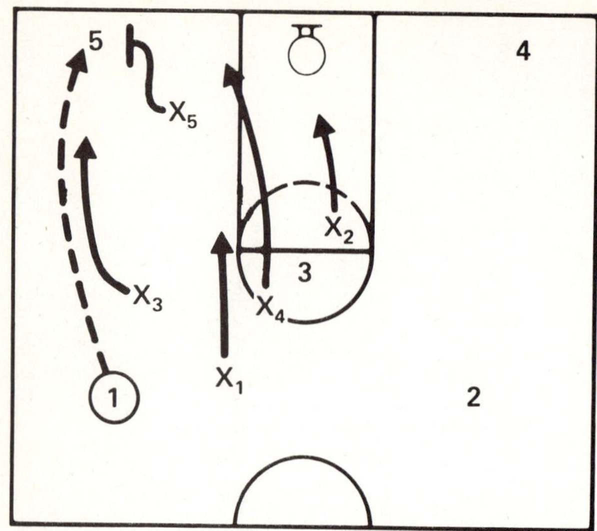

Figure 9–14 Basic 1–3–1 Zone Defense, Corner Coverage

quick; at the ball-side low post if the matchups do not favor the defense, since double-teaming inside is extremely difficult from basic 1–3–1 defense; and at the weak-side low post via diagonal crosscourt passes. (The basic 1–3–1 alignment is not conducive to rebounding effectiveness, either.)

The 1–2–2, or "Jug" defense, has many advocates because, beyond all other zone alignments, the 1–2–2 offers the greatest potential for basic coverage; that is, it gives up less in return for ensuring inside coverage

Figure 9–15 Basic 1–2–2 Zone Defensive Alignment

Figure 9–16 Weak-Side Rebounding Responsibilities, Basic Zone Defense

than other odd- or even-front zone defenses, regardless of the position of the ball or offensive players. (See Figure 9–15.)

The styles of basic defensive coverage available from the 1–2–2 and other zone alignments will be covered in the next section; however, we can mention at this point that the key to basic 1–2–2 zone defense is the coordinated movement of all five players on each pass.

The first of two weaknesses of the 1–2–2 zone defense involves coverage of the high post. This is best covered by making the opponents lob the ball into the high post, allowing the defense to swarm the high-post man as soon as he receives the ball. The other weakness is weak-side rebounding. If a shot is taken from the corner, the weak-side rebounder will be the small forward or big guard. (See Figure 9–16.)

Personnel Considerations

1. Player #14 (Figure 9–15) can be the smallest defensive player. He should be quick, and he should look for long rebounds. He must make

it difficult for offensive players to complete passes to the high post, and he must prevent passes from going through the top of the defense.

2. If possible, player #12 (Figure 9–15) should be a good rebounder. He must assist the point guard, defend the low post, and cover the corner on his side. He must be able to play the passing lanes.

3. Player #44 (Figure 9–15) should be a very good rebounder. He should be a better rebounder than player #12 because, according to existing statistical data as well as empirical evidence, most teams attack offensively from the right side of the court. (The majority of players, being right-handed, dribble better to their right than to their left.) Player #44 should have all the other qualifications required of player #12.

> **Note:** Players #12 and #44 are likely to steal or deflect more passes than their teammates, since the passing lanes in their zones of responsibility are more heavily traveled.

4. Player #32 (Figure 9–15) must be able to deny the corner shot, defend the low post, and rebound. He may be the slower of the two inside defenders.

5. Player #20 (Figure 9–15) must be able to alter his coverage from the low post to the corner on his side of the court as fast or faster than player #32, since most teams attack from the right side. Player #20 should have all the other qualifications required of player #32.

> **Note:** Players #20 and #32 provide much of the inside defense in 1–2–2 zone coverage. If possible, they should be excellent rebounders and shot blockers. They are extremely valuable when they are capable of containing the opponents' inside game.

The 3–2 zone defense is a variation of the 1–2–2 zone. The greatest difference between the two is that, in the 1–2–2, a guard drops back to front the high post, whereas in the 3–2 zone defense, a forward or the team's center usually covers the high post.

As might be suspected, the 3–2 zone defense is seen most frequently among teams with three-small, two-tall lineups. On the basis of the alignment shown in Figure 9–17, one might be tempted to conclude that the 3–2 zone is weak inside. Two factors negate this conclusion. First, teams will not use a 3–2 configuration unless it is advantageous for them to do so—which usually means that inside defenders X_4 and X_5 are good defensive players. Second, the defensive players may set up deeper (that is, nearer the basket) than usual to provide greater inside coverage. The latter technique is often seen at the junior high level or with high school teams that have unskilled personnel. (We should point out, however, that the 1–2–2 zone is more versatile in this respect than the 3–2 zone. It is

Figure 9–17 Basic 3–2 Zone Defense

always preferable to have your big men near the basket whenever possible.) Many coaches use the 3–2 with the wing men playing wide to force the offensive team to lob passes to the corner.

The 3–2 zone defense is almost always used in its basic form, primarily because its coverage offers less versatility than the 1–2–2 zone defense. (Basic defenses will be described fully in the next section.)

INSIDE AND WEAK-SIDE COVERAGE IN BASIC DEFENSE

While zone alignments and styles of coverage vary among zone defenses with the ball at the point, all zones are alike in terms of the positions to be covered when the ball is established on one side of the court. (See Figure 9–18.)

Basic zone defense is, paradoxically, both limited and versatile in its potential for exploiting offensive weaknesses. Three of the defensive positions remain constant in practically all forms of basic zone defense: ball coverage, the low post, and at least one player back to protect the weak side. Since at least three other positions—the corner, the ball-side high post, and the weak side away from the basket—may require coverage, it is obvious that defensive movements must be quick and be planned in advance. If every player does not understand beforehand which court positions he is responsible for, the defense is likely to surrender numerous shots from high-percentage scoring areas because the players are out of position.

After selecting a zone defensive alignment, a coach's first decision is to reduce the vulnerability of the high-post position when the ball is at the

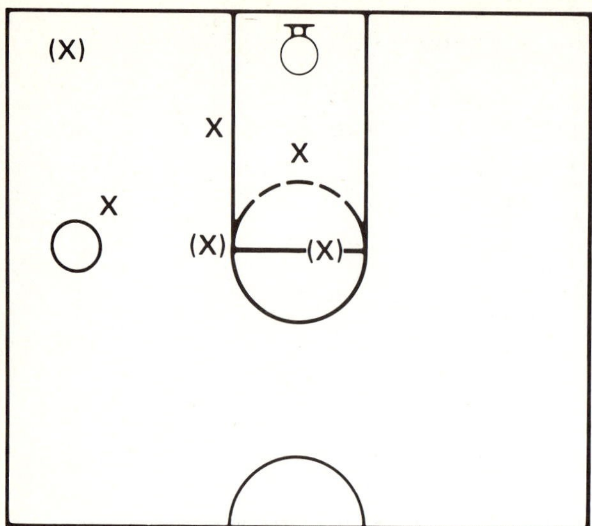

Figure 9–18 Basic Zone Defense, Ball at Wing

point. His next problem concerns the amount of coverage he will have to provide for the ball-side low post. If his inside defenders are small or unskilled, they may have to double-team the low post. (This technique is described in detail in Chapter 12.)

Assuming that inside double-teaming is unnecessary, the coach's next problem is to decide who covers the ball-side corner and/or the high post. At least part of his decision will be based on whether he has more than one inside defender who is capable of denying the inside pass to the low post.

In Figure 9–19, 04's cut to the corner to receive 03's pass will force X_4 to cover 05 as X_5 moves out to guard 04. The problem confronting the defense is obvious: X_4 cannot cover the ball-side corner and still remain in zone defense, and if X_5 is the only defender capable of matching up with 05 inside, sending X_5 to the corner to guard 04 will weaken the defense considerably. (Of course, X_3 could drop back to double-team 05 with X_4, but that's another mode of coverage entirely.) Incidentally, note that the defense shown in Figure 9–19 provides excellent coverage of the ball-side high-post position when the ball is at the wing, as long as X_4 covers 04's initial cut through the lane. X_2 can cover cuts or sliding by 01 or 02.

When the defense prefers not to switch responsibilities with the corner pass, the alignment shown in Figure 9–20 is preferable. As 01 passes to 03, X_5 slides out to a position approximately two steps beyond 05 at the low post, and X_4 moves into an overguarding stance on 05. (X_5 is *not* double-teaming 05 with X_4, although he will double-team if 03 passes in to the low post.) When 04 cuts to the corner and receives 03's pass, X_5 moves out to cover 05 and X_4 either fronts 05 or overguards him toward

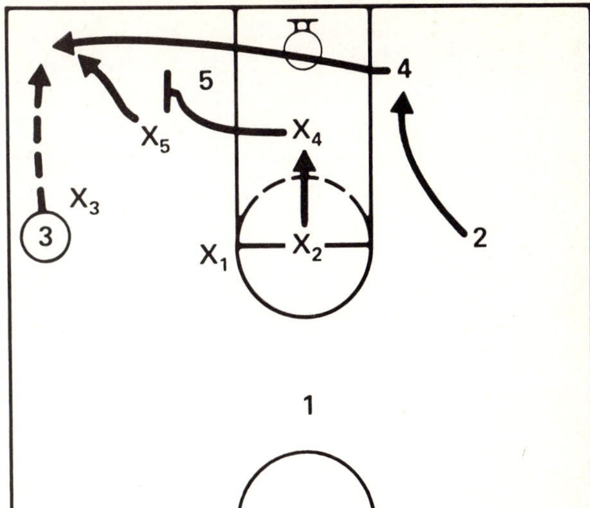

Figure 9–19 Switching the Inside Coverage to Cover the Cutter to the Corner

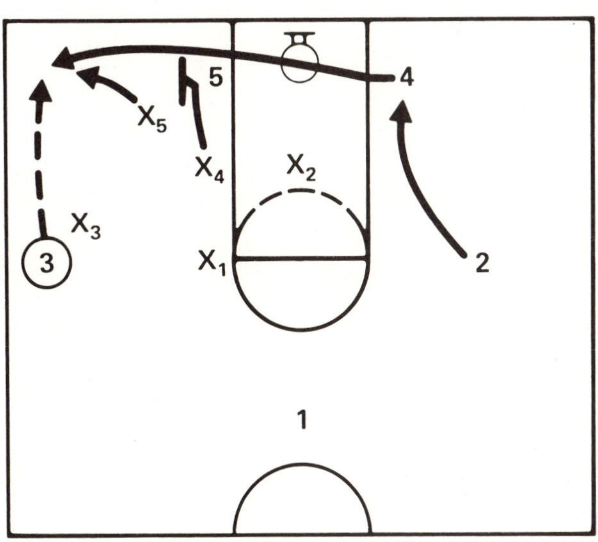

Figure 9–20 Covering the Corner Without Switching

the middle. (If 04 manages to pass to 05, you don't want 05 to go baseline!)

Basic zone defense primarily attempts to deny passes inside to the low post; however, it also attempts to deny the opponents access to the high post. Basic defense is, above all else, ball-side oriented; it represents the defensive team's attempt to control opponents through intensive coverage of the half of the court that the ball is on. Although corner coverage may or may not be aggressive, the high and low post positions will always be aggressively defended in basic zone defense.

Where, then, is basic zone defense weak? In the corners on the ball side, perhaps; or if the defense is double-teaming, the corner or high post. However, the area most vulnerable to attack is likely to be the weak side, as the result of the diagonal pass from the wing to the weak-side low post (Figure 9–21) or ball rotation (Figure 9–22).

Basic defense is not matchup defense. Matchups may arise in the course of ball and player movement, but the only matchups that really

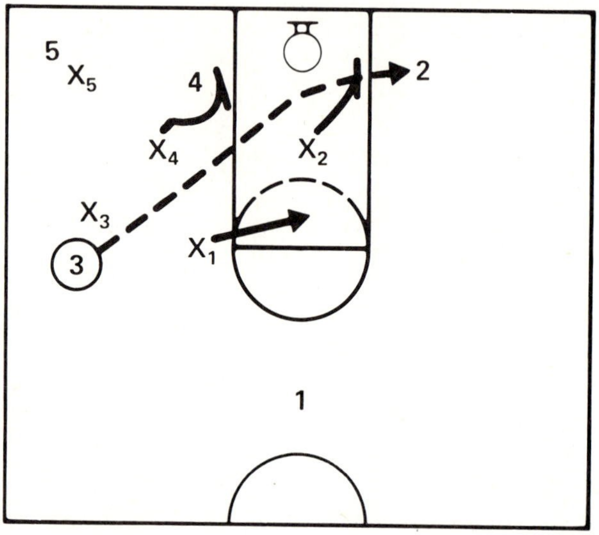

Figure 9–21 The Diagonal Pass Underneath Against Basic Zone Coverage

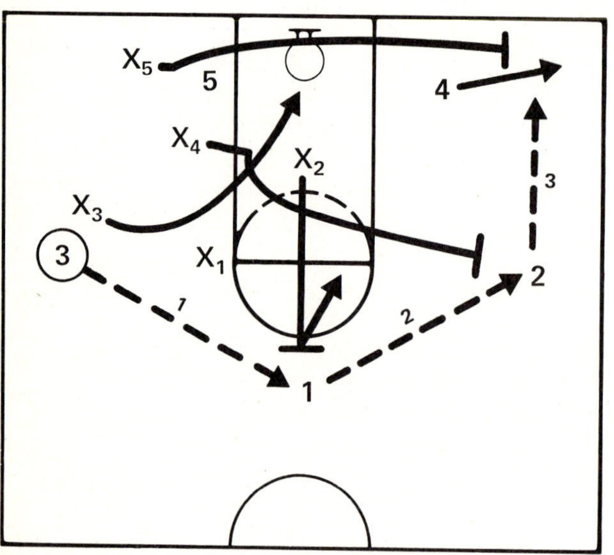

Figure 9–22 Ball Rotation Against Basic Zone Defense

matter are those that occur at the low post. Thus, the weaknesses in basic zone defense may arise on either side of the court, although the coach has no small part in determining where coverage is emphasized or neglected.

The diagonal pass from the wing to the weak-side low post (Figure 9–21) is always a possibility to be guarded against. Of course, the peril of the diagonal pass can be alleviated by keeping two players back on the weak side, as shown in Figure 9–24.

Ball rotation and its resultant problems are a different matter, though. Even when the defenders are able to match up, which, needless to say, is not always possible, the matchups may favor the offensive team. When X_2 has to move outside to cover 01 as in Figure 9–22 (or 02 in Figure 9–23), X_4 is likely to be slow in moving across the lane to guard players at the weak-side low post or baseline.* This situation exemplifies the kind of problem confronting teams using basic zone defense: knowing that you're likely to surrender defensive control somewhere, particularly on the weak side, do you alter your coverage, and thus run the risk of weakening your inside coverage, or do you maintain your inside control and hope for the best elsewhere?

The answer is, of course, *you play the percentages*. The percentages are what led you to use basic defense in the first place, or else you'd be in a man-to-man defense, trapping or matching up from zone defense. You may have to alter your inside coverage to a certain extent, but never to the extent of surrendering inside control to the opponents.

We are, of course, showing in Figures 9–23 and 9–24 the extremes of weak-side overloading favoring the offensive team. In an equal number of cases the defense will be able to match up without X_4's frantic scrambling to cover 02 in Figure 9–23, or X_5's mad rush to guard 04 in Figure 9–24.

In both cases, X_1's position at the high post will not permit him to cover 03's pass to 01 on the weak side, except when, as noted, the defense is in *help-and-recover* coverage. 01 will attempt to penetrate against X_2, leaving 02 free until X_4 picks him up. In Figure 9–24, X_4 will cover 02, but X_5 will have to move across the lane to cover 04, which is difficult but certainly not impossible since *three* passes along the perimeter are necessary to rotate the ball from 03 to 04 on the weak side. X_5 will have to move quickly, of course, but it can be done.

What *cannot* be done in the previous technique is to continue to provide the same level of intensive coverage of the ball-side low post while at the same time covering the weak-side passes. Assuming that X_4 and X_5 are the defensive team's two big men, both players will have to move across to cover rotation pass receivers, leaving a smaller player (X_1 or X_3) to cover 05.

* The need for this kind of coverage is eliminated if the defense is using help-and-recover techniques. In help-and-recover defense, X_2 will cover 01 until X_1 arrives, at which time X_2 will drop back or move to his left to cover 02 if 01 relays the ball to 02 in rotation.

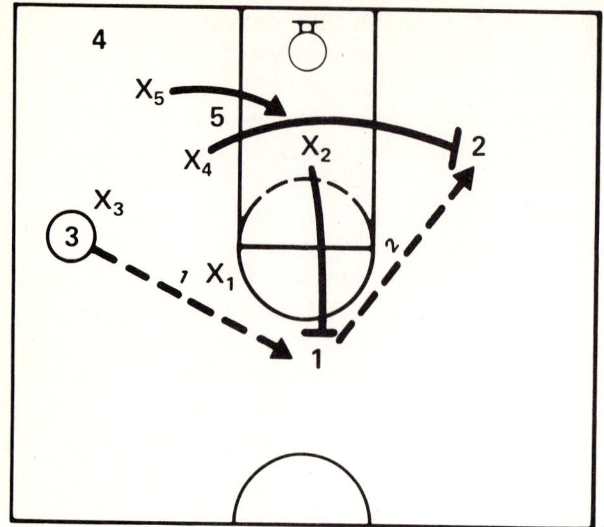

Figure 9–23 Covering Ball Rotation in Basic Zone Defense: *Example #1*

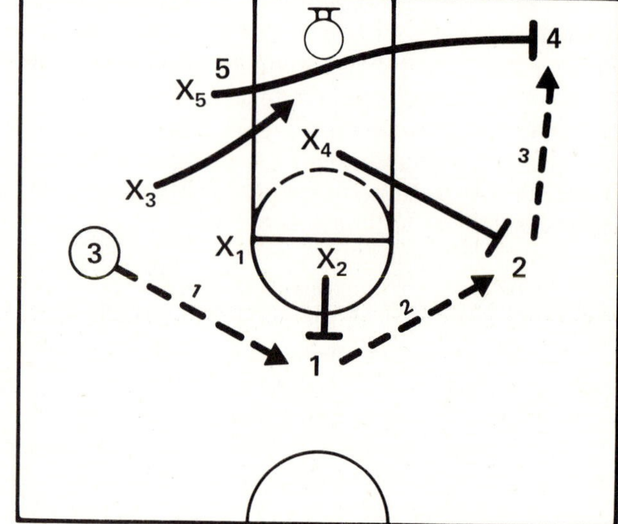

Figure 9–24 Covering Ball Rotation in Basic Zone Defense: *Example #2*

TWO STYLES OF BASIC ZONE DEFENSE

Either of the sequences of defensive movements from a 1–2–2 zone defensive alignment can be taught by simply setting five defensive players and five or more offensive players on the court. The offensive players, aligned along the perimeters of the defense, pass the ball from one player to another, with the defensive players shifting accordingly. As the defensive movements with ball rotation become automatic, more offensive players can be added—for example, at the high post and low post on either side of the court, both corners, or even in the middle of the lane to simulate cutting patterns.

Both styles of basic defense offer constant coverage of the ball, the ball-side low post, and the ball-side high post. If however, the defenders are capable of controlling their opponents with only three players on the ball side, they can keep two players back to cover rotation cuts and passes to the weak side.

Both kinds of coverage are basic. Both provide control of the crucial ball-side high and low post positions. The factors that determine which kind of basic coverage a coach will use are: (a) the amount of coverage necessary to deny passes to the low post, and (b) the extent of weak-side coverage required to counteract weak-side overload situations.

The only further point to be made in considering the previous coverage patterns is that, when the ball is in either corner and two players are back on the weak side, point guard X_1 will have to defend the low-post position.

It should be obvious by now that I favor putting a man on the ball constantly in basic zone defense. On the other hand, some coaches may prefer to use a trapping alignment without trapping, as it were, with no one directly guarding the ball handler, but with two players inviting the penetrating dribble as shown in Figure 9–25.

The object of such alignments is to spread the defensive coverage while at the same time avoiding the possibility of matchups that favor the offensive team. Technically, this is not basic defense at all, since the

Figure 9–25 Alternative to Single-Guarding the Ball Handler in Basic Zone Defense (From an Original 1–3–1 Zone Defense)

primary objective is to influence the ball handler and restrict perimeter passes rather than denying the inside passes. (Of course, the inside passes may be denied anyway, but that aspect of the defense is usually a lesser objective.)

The techniques used in deploying this defense are similar to those used in trapping zone defenses, except that the trap is not sprung. A 1–3–1 or 2–3 zone alignment is likely to be more conducive to running this defense. The reader is referred to Chapter 10 for a more involved analysis of techniques for setting up a trapping zone defense.

DECIDING WHICH SHOT TO GIVE UP IN BASIC ZONE DEFENSE

As has been explained, the concept of zone defense tends to limit the defensive team's ability to control opponents' offensive movements to a greater extent than some forms of man-to-man defense. At best, the zone defines and delimits the areas of the court from which the offense may attack the defense; however, it may also expand the offensive team's shooting possibilities from sideline to sideline. Using basic coverage can spread the defense to the extent that undesirable one-on-one confrontations arise as the offensive team runs its patterns. Teams using basic zone defense are understandably wary of matching up, since the use of basic defensive techniques is generally associated with offensive superiority or defensive weaknesses. (If the coach had no problems defensively, he would likely opt for a more aggressive form of defense.)

In deciding to use basic zone defense, a coach should attempt to identify areas of the court in which defensive coverage is likely to be weakest. (See Figures 9–26 and 9–27.)

On the ball side, the most vulnerable areas likely to be exploited by the offensive team are the corner and the high post. Of these, the less desirable alternative usually is to give up the pass to the high post, since the potential for penetrating against zone defenses is always great from high post.

In covering the high post and/or corner (or double-teaming the low post when the ball is in the corner), the wing position may be open. An effective wing shooter can make life miserable for teams using basic defense, but circumstances may dictate that the wing shot be given up rather than surrendering shots from the corner or high post. The wing shot is taken from farther outside than the other ball-side shooting positions, and thus may be a lower percentage shot. Admittedly, losing is the same whether it results from 25-foot shots or driving slam dunks, but of those alternatives, or others which the defense may have to consider, the

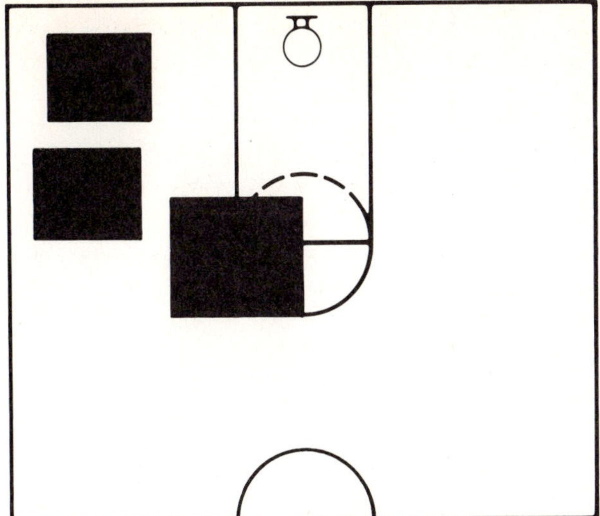

Figure 9–26 Ball-Side Areas of Penetration

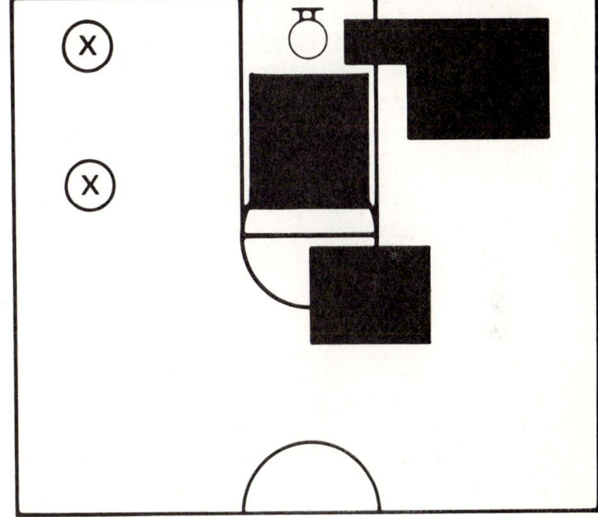

Figure 9–27 Weak-Side Areas of Penetration

wing shot will likely be the lowest percentage shot available on the ball side.

Three weak-side areas of penetration must be accounted for; they are, in order of their susceptibility to attack: the middle of the free-throw lane, the low post (and baseline area), and the high post.

The middle of the lane is usually attacked by the weak-side low post's cutting to the middle with the ball at the wing (Figure 9–28), or by

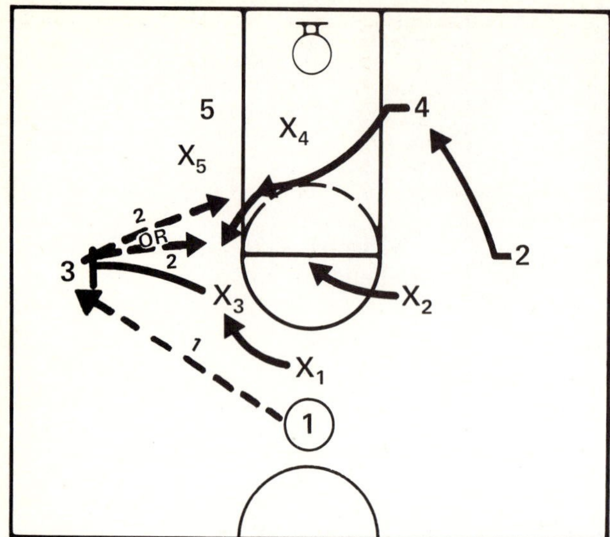

Figure 9–28 Passing into the Lane from the Wing

passing to cutters moving across the lane as the ball is rotated from one side of the court to the other (Figure 9–29). In both situations, X_4 will probably cover the cutter into, or across, the lane. Regardless of who covers the cutters, though, the coach should be aware that the area inside the lane is vitally important to the defense in terms of defensive control: in keeping the ball away from the low post and the free-throw lane, you automatically force the opponents to shift their attack to other areas of the court.

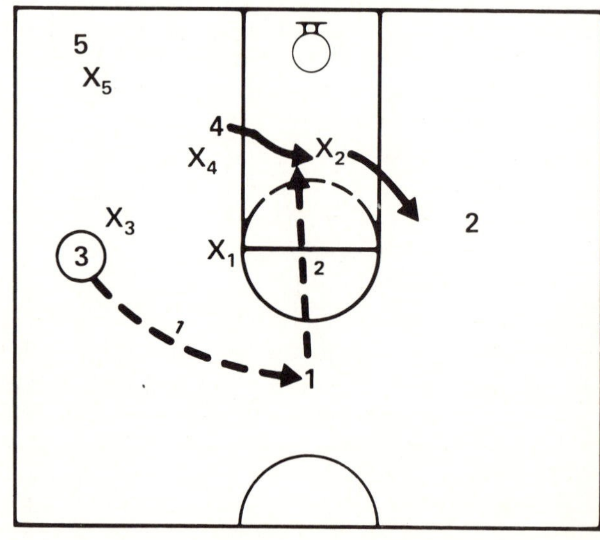

Figure 9–29 Passing into the Lane from the Point

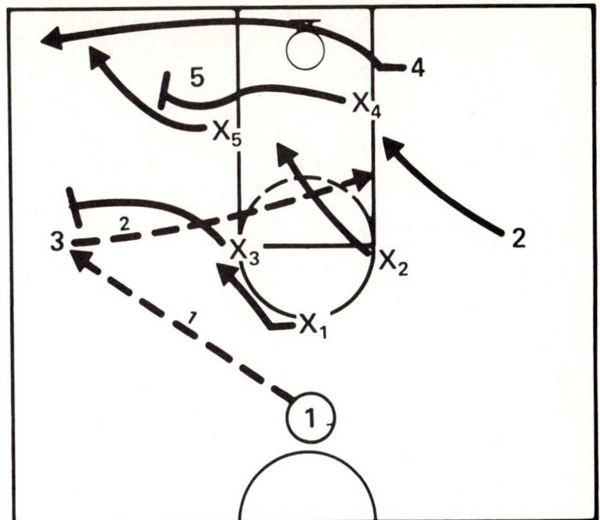

Figure 9–30 The "Alley Oop" Pass to Weak-Side Low Post

The weak-side low post is often the side for spectacular "Alley Oop" passes and resultant layups or slam dunk shots. 02 is the "Alley Oop" player in Figure 9–30. As 01 passes to wing 03, 04 cuts to the ball-side corner, X_3 covers the pass receiver, X_1 slides to the ball-side high post, X_5 slides two or three steps toward the corner, X_4 moves across to cover the ball-side low post, and X_2 drops back to the middle of the lane to cover the weak side. In most cases, he (X_2) can adequately cover both weak-side high and low post positions—at least until the ball is passed back to X_1. However, when 02 is an outstanding leaper, 03 may lob a high, arching pass over X_2 to 02 cutting to the basket, with spectacular results.

The high post is a third weak-side position that is capable of being exploited by the offense against a basic zone defense. (The area around the point, or top of the circle, is generally nonproductive, since it can be covered by X_1 as shown in Diagram 9–31. However, when point guard 01 moves toward the weak-side high post after passing to 03, X_1 can no longer cover 01 to the extent of stopping his penetration. X_2 will have to cover 01, which in turn means that X_4 must move across the lane to cover 02.)

Thus, either the weak-side high-post or baseline area may be exploited by the offensive team. In light of this, several considerations may occur to the coach who is attempting to defend against rapid ball rotation to the weak side. Can X_1 cover 01, or will X_2 have to move outside? If a shot must be given up: (a) which is the better shooter, 01 or 02? and (b) where would you prefer to give up the shot? Can you alter your coverage, if necessary, to provide adequate weak-side coverage?

Coaches who decide to use basic defense must avoid at all costs the

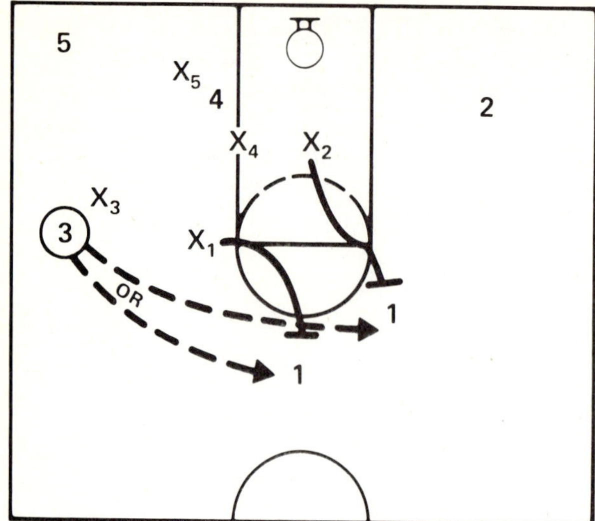

Figure 9–31 01's Positioning and Defensive Coverage of Rotation Passes

tendency to further weaken their defensive control by surrendering shots from areas of the court where the opponents are proficient offensively. Game plans should involve instructions that are more detailed than, for example, "We're going to use a 1–2–2 zone tonight." Players should be told precisely how the coach expects them to play their 1–2–2 zone defense. If basic techniques featuring intensified coverage of the low post are to be used, the coach should explain where and how the opponents are likely to attack that coverage, and he should provide instructions concerning how the defense should adjust to the various attempts to penetrate the areas made vulnerable by the use of basic defense.

ONE-MAN ZONE DEFENSE

Technically, the one-man zone defense is a combination zone defense, since it involves a big man playing zone defense inside while the other four players match up or assume man-to-man responsibilities. It has been included in this chapter because the basic principles underlying its usage closely parallel those of any basic zone defense; that is, outside coverage is more or less loose compared to the defensive coverage afforded by the presence of a big man inside.

For teams that have a lineup consisting of four small players and one dominating big man, a one-man zone defense provides versatility beyond that found in other basic zone defenses. Coverage consists of four players who match up while the big man covers any offensive player setting up inside or cutting to the middle. Alignments that are more conducive to running the one-man zone defense are those that feature a defensive player setting up at the middle of the lane—the 1–3–1, 2–1–2, or 2–3 zone. Any of the three alignments is acceptable, since the big man will stay inside constantly, and the other four players will match up with whatever formation the offense selects.

The other four players may be extremely aggressive in their man-to-man coverage of outside players, since the dominating big man tends to shut off the opponents' inside game as well as to cover mistakes made by defenders outside.

Matching Up in One-Man Zone Defense

Although matchup techniques are discussed at length in Chapter 10, perhaps some of the unique aspects of its usage should be considered at this point. The team using one-man zone principles will in most cases not merely match up with the offense but will also aggressively attempt to steal the ball, force turnovers, or otherwise regain possession of the ball. Matchup defense is considered safe only when the matchups favor the defensive team, but in the case of one-man zoning, the outside matchups are of only secondary importance, except in terms of stealing the ball. The defensive skills of the big man inside will deny the opponents ready access to the basket even when they get past their defenders outside.

Figures 9–32 through 9–34 depict some of the basics of one-man zone defense. In Figures 9–32 and 9–33 the defense is using matchup techniques from a 1–3–1 zone defensive alignment, with X_4 playing the "one-man" role. X_1, X_2, X_3, and X_5 will play as aggressively as directed

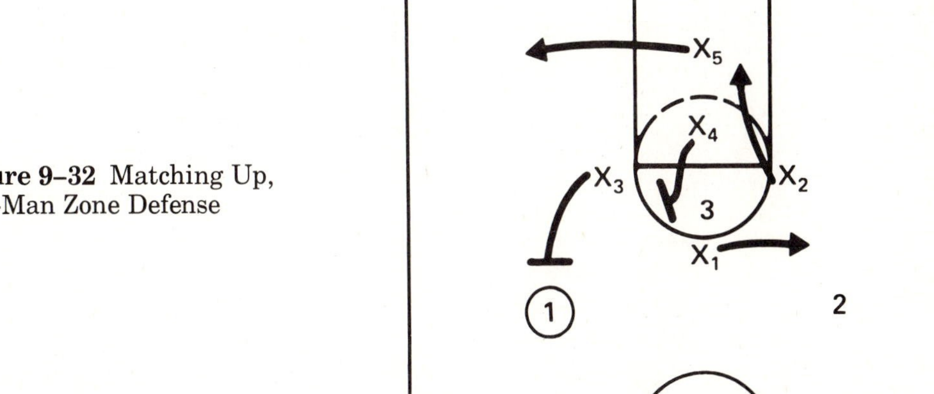

Figure 9–32 Matching Up, One-Man Zone Defense

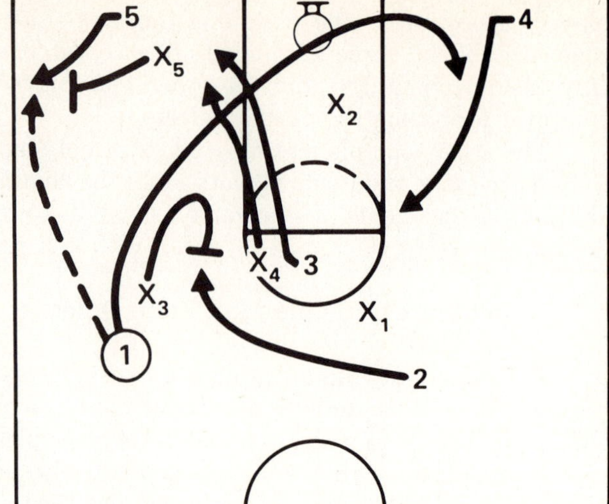

Figure 9–33 Maintaining the Matchups, One-Man Zone Defense

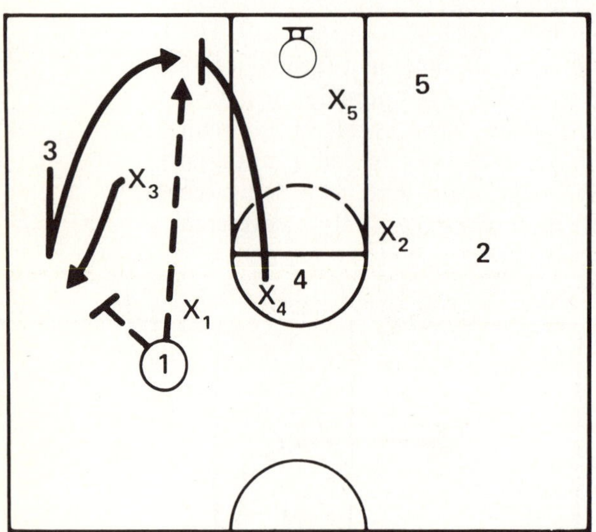

Figure 9–34 Covering the Backdoor Cutter, One-Man Zone Defense

within their matchups since, as shown in Figure 9–34, X_4 will cover his teammates' mistakes. 01 fakes a pass to 03 at the wing, and as X_3 moves out to intercept the pass, 03 cuts backdoor to the basket to receive 01's pass. X_4 drops low as the pass is made. X_4's coverage (of 03) will deny both the shot and the pass to 04 cutting to the basket or low post, but it will not deny 03's drive.

Note: If X_4 is a very outstanding defensive player, he will welcome 03's baseline drive so he can reject 03's shot. 03 is, after all, a guard or forward, not the opponents' big man.

X_4 will also cover cutters through the lane—at least, as long as they are primary pass receivers. If the tall player's defensive skills are sufficiently great, he can divide his coverage between two players without surrendering control of either, as shown in Figure 9–34.

The weakness inherent in this defense arises when the offensive center can score consistently from 15 to 18 feet from the basket. In such cases, the big man may be drawn away from the basket, opening up the middle for inside cuts and one-on-one confrontations at the low post.

The Boston Celtics used this kind of defense with great success during the Bill Russell years, and UCLA did likewise with Lew Alcindor (now Kareem Abdul-Jabbar) in the late 1960s. When the big man is capable of dominating opponents defensively by clogging up the middle, the one-man zone defense can be an exceedingly tough nut to crack.

Man-to-Man Defense with One-Man Zone Principles

Because the big man will not go outside in his coverage, switching defensive assignments will necessarily play a large role in the defensive coverage. Otherwise, the offense will set its own big man (or men) along the perimeters of the tall player's area of responsibility to draw him

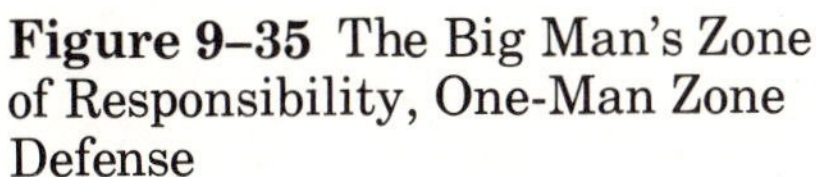
Figure 9–35 The Big Man's Zone of Responsibility, One-Man Zone Defense

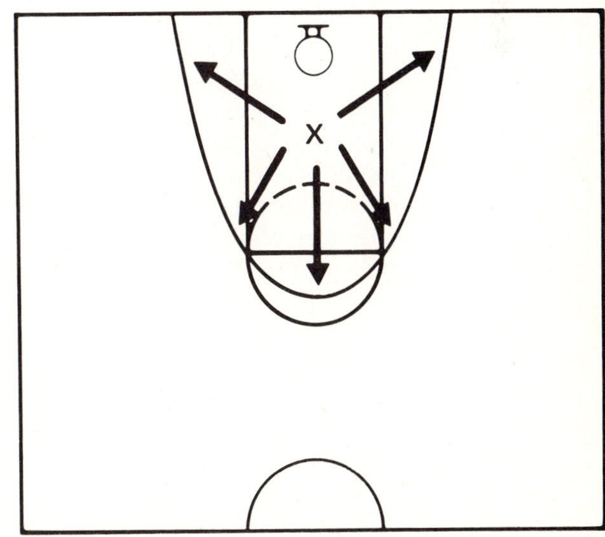

outside. If he goes out to cover opponents along the baseline or beyond the free-throw line, they can attack more favorable matchups inside. In cases where the opponents' big man moves out to the perimeter areas along the baseline or beyond the high post, the defensive team may prefer zone coverage.

As has been suggested, the big man must be a dominant figure defensively. He must be tall and strong enough to avoid being pushed around, but he must also be quick, mobile, and aggressive. If he lacks any of these attributes, he may be unable to dominate the inside game.

In patrolling the inside area, the big man will seldom leave the area shown in Figure 9–35. Thus, the relationship between the four small players and their taller teammate is reciprocal: he covers for them in their efforts to provide aggressive outside coverage, and they in turn will attempt to cover all players outside the area of his responsibility. Mismatches are of little consequence outside; if the opponents' big man is going outside to beat the one-man zone defense, it is more desirable to have a small forward try to rush his shot or force him away from his shooting areas than to bring the big man outside to try to cover him. As with any defense, man-to-man or zone, teamwork is imperative if the one-man zone tactic is to work.

CONCLUSION

There are no sure things in basketball, no absolutes or guarantees beyond the fact that the people in the stands won't understand or appreciate your use of offenses or defenses except in terms of points on the scoreboard. They want results; if you win, they'll love you forever, or until you lose four or five games in a row!

The better your material, the more options you'll be able to consider in your selection of defenses. With the exception of the one-man zone defense, basic zone defense is for coaches and teams with average or sub-par personnel, or for teams that are unable for any of several reasons to use a more aggressive half-court defense. Basic zone defense is *not* an easier way of playing defense, nor is it an excuse for relaxing on defense. It is a planned strategy for dealing with opponents when other forms of coverage are unlikely to provide a semblance of defensive control.

While basic zone defense does not yield the sideline-to-sideline coverage possible in other forms of defense, it is a *solid* defense. More than any other defensive strategy in basketball, basic zone defense is based on *priorities,* and therein lies its ultimate strength: regardless of the offensive patterns being used, teams using basic zone defense know what confrontations they want to avoid, where those confrontations are likely to occur, and how to prevent their occurrence.

The theory of basic defense is similar to that of preventive medicine:

an ounce of prevention is worth a pound of cure. In basic defense, above all else, *you don't beat yourself.* You don't surrender control of areas of the court where the opponents are most likely to beat you. If you stop your opponents' inside game, they'll have to create another point of attack. Deny them inside shots, and they'll have to beat you from the outside. Give them only the lowest-percentage outside shots available, and they'll have to make those shots to beat you.

24

10

Advanced Zone Defensive Techniques

INTRODUCTION

While basic zone defensive techniques are generally control oriented—that is, they apply pressure primarily to the ball handler and ball-side post positions—other concepts of zone defense can be used to satisfy different defensive goals. When a team has capable, skilled personnel, its coverage within the zone context can be broader throughout the half-court. The goal is, first of all, increased defensive control, not only of the ball handler and post men, but of all other offensive players as well.

Defensive control can be manifested in three ways: by reducing or delimiting the shooting areas, by forcing a team out of its basic patterns, or by forcing the offensive team into mistakes and turnovers. While the first tactic may or may not entail any great risk for the defense, the others may require far greater team and individual defensive skills in order to avoid surrendering control to the offensive team. Teams that indulge in such advanced forms of defense as pressure man-to-man, or trapping or help-and-recover zone defense, must be outstanding fundamentally, since the advantage swings to the offense when the coverage fails to contain the ball. In other words, teams are likely to use advanced forms of zone defensive coverage only when it is to their advantage to do so; at other times they will opt for more conventional (that is, basic) coverage.

When you see a team playing matchup zone defense, you should logically expect to find their players to be fundamentally sound on defense. Not only will they make fewer mistakes on defense than other teams or other players, but they will also recover more quickly from their mistakes, and they will confuse the offensive team considerably. If this were not the case, they would not be playing matchup zone defense. As we said earlier, you don't match up unless the matchups favor *your* team.

Aggressive coverage and defensive control go hand in glove. Where you find aggressive defensive coverage, you are also likely to find a team that is capable of controlling games defensively. Successful trapping from a zone defense requires considerable defensive skills, or else your team is in for the biggest struggle since the British troops evacuated Dunkirk in World War II. The opponents wouldn't be trapping in a half-court defense if they weren't good at it; after all, every time their traps fail to contain the ball, your offense gains both numerical superiority and attacking momentum toward the basket. The opponents probably know this even better than you, and that they still consider it to their advantage to trap you should tip you off (if you didn't know it before) that they're planning to do a job on you. Unless their coach is grossly incompetent, they're trapping because they're good at it, and because it pays off for them. You may still beat their traps, of course, but they won't call off the dogs until either you beat their traps consistently and decisively or they beat you.

MATCHUP ZONE DEFENSE

With the possible exception of defenses in which the low-post position is double-teamed, every defense eventually evolves into matchups or one-on-one confrontations. From the standpoint of zone defense, matching up is desirable only when the matchups favor the defensive team.

Matchup defense is difficult to operate, but once the defensive team matches up, the offense may be severely restricted in what it can do to attack the matchups. Offensive alignments no longer split the defense, and overloads and other patterns that served to flood certain zones against basic coverage merely make the matchups easier to maintain. By cutting off certain passing lanes and sagging away from others, the defense also may be able to dictate the direction of the offensive attack. Matchup defenses are used to confuse opponents, and they can be very effective in this regard when run properly.

Personnel Requirements for Matchup Zone Defense

Basically, matchup defense is a man-to-man defense played from a zone alignment. It can create one-on-one situations from the relative security of zone coverage. Having beaten a defender in the matchup situation, then, an offensive player still must contend with the rest of the zone defense. Obviously, players must be fundamentally sound and skilled in man-to-man defense if matchup techniques are to work as they are designed to.

Matchup defense also is unlikely to succeed without at least one or two players who are tall enough to deny the inside passes. The inside matchups are but one phase of the overall matchup technique, but they are an important part. Only in trapping defenses is protecting one's basket a secondary concern.

Rotating to Matchup

A matchup zone is not a kind of zone like, say, a 1–3–1 or 2–1–2; rather, it is a *style of play* that can be effected from practically any zone defensive alignment. (Matching up is seen most often from a 1–3–1 alignment.) Matching up is, simply, a defensive technique in which each player within a given zone defense assumes one-on-one responsibilities for a given offensive player. The matchups may change, of course, as offensive players cut through or across the lane, but the result will always be *new* matchups.

The difference between matchup and basic zone defense is shown in Figures 10–1 and 10–2. In Figure 10–1, all five defensive players are in man-to-man coverage within their zones of responsibility. In Figure 10–2, three players—X_3, X_4, and X_5—are matched up with their ball-side opponents. X_1, however, is not guarding 01, and he may not be responsible for 01 if 03 passes to him at the point. Why? Because X_1 is defending a *position*—in this case, the ball-side high post—rather than guarding a particular player. In basic zone defense, players guard positions and cover only those players who enter their zones of responsibility; in matchup zone defense, players may move out of, or expand beyond the normal limits of, their zones temporarily to provide coverage of the player they're responsible for.

Figure 10–1 Matching Up Against a Three-Man Overload Offense

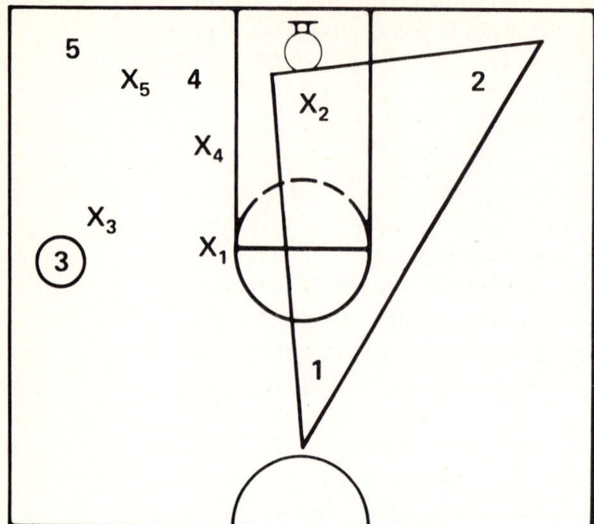

Figure 10–2 Basic Zone Defense Against a Three-Man Overload Offense

The first objective of matchup defense is to set up, or rotate into, a defensive alignment matching that of the offensive team. Two methods of rotating into matchup coverage are shown in Figures 10–3 and 10–4. That defensive rotation may be necessary is due to the existence of a basic offensive technique known as *splitting the defense.* In splitting the defense, the offensive team will, upon recognizing the defense's zone alignment (for example, the 1–3–1 or 2–1–2), set its players in the outside gaps between defensive players. Thus, 01 usually will set up between X_1 and

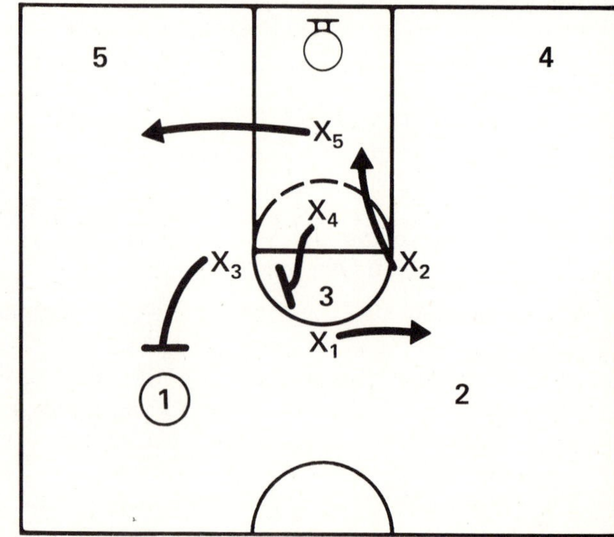

Figure 10–3 Counterclockwise Rotation into Matchup Zone Defense

Figure 10–4 Clockwise Rotation into Matchup Zone Defense

X_3, 02 between X_1 and X_2, 04 between X_2 and X_5, and so on. If the defense does not match up in a manner similar to those shown in Figures 10–3 or 10–4, the ball handler can set up scoring opportunities by penetrating between the outside defenders.

In Figure 10–3, the defensive team is in a 1–3–1 zone alignment, with the opponents in a 2–1–2 offensive alignment to split the defense. Using matchup techniques, the defense will rotate its coverage into the same 2–1–2 alignment used by the offensive team, and thereafter will continually rotate, or shift, its coverage to match whatever offensive alignments the offense assumes in ball and player movement.

Rotation to matchup may be either counterclockwise (Figure 10–3) or clockwise (Figure 10–4). Either method is acceptable, although the counterclockwise rotation more nearly duplicates the movements in basic zone defensive coverage. If the defense rotates clockwise as shown in Figure 10–4, the defensive wing will have to back up rather than move forward to assume his ball-side coverage, and the retreating movement will make him slightly more vulnerable to attack. (However, if the point guard is extremely unskilled, it may be easier to tell him to "guard the ball handler" initially.)

Methods of rotating to matchup defense from other alignments are shown in Figures 10–5 through 10–14. (In each case, the offense split the defense initially, but we are not particularly concerned at this point with showing all of the methods and alignments for splitting the defense.)

1–2–2 to Matchup Zone Defense. The 1–2–2 zone defense is outstanding in its basic form, offering possibly the most effective basic coverage of any zone alignment. As a matchup alignment, however, the 1–2–2

Figure 10–5 1–2–2 to Matchup Zone Defense, Ball at Point

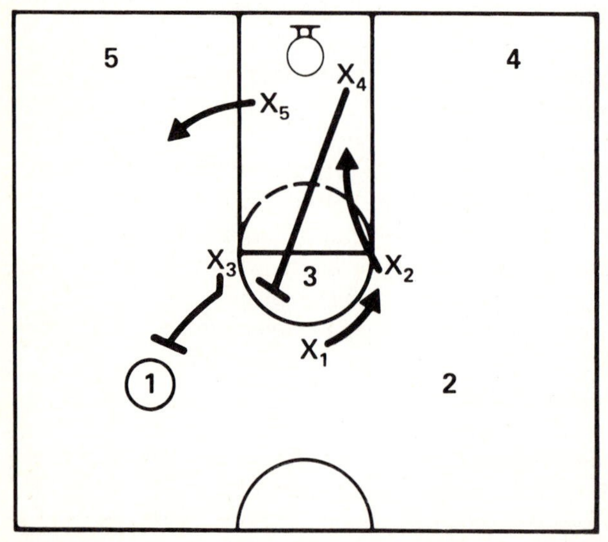

Figure 10–6 1–2–2 to Matchup, Ball at Intermediate Wing

loses much of its effectiveness. In Figure 10–5, for example, the weak-side inside defender must move up to cover the high post, which may leave the weak-side wing vulnerable to backdoor "Alley Oop" passes and layups or slam dunks. Matching up can be achieved from a 1–2–2 alignment, of course, but never as easily as, say, a 1–3–1 alignment.

2–3 to Matchup Zone Defense. The 2–3 zone does not adapt particularly well to matchup coverage—certainly no better than the 1–2–2 zone, and unquestionably less effectively than a 1–3–1 alignment. Even-front zones tend to invite penetration from the top of the circle, and matching up can help to alleviate this weakness of basic defense; still, X_1 and X_3's movements in Figure 10–7 may not yield the kind of defensive control that is necessary in matchup zone defense, since they are not really in position to control or contain 03 or 04 from a 1–3–1 offensive alignment. The 2–3 is generally sufficient in matching up against a 1–2–2 alignment (Figure 10–8), since only X_1 will have to move away from the ball to match up (or X_2 if the rotation to matchup coverage is counter-clockwise).

2–1–2 to Matchup Zone Defense. Since the characteristic that distinguishes the 2–1–2 from the 2–3 zone defense is whether the defensive guards (in 2–1–2) or the defensive forwards (in 2–3) cover the pass to the wing, the 2–1–2 zone cannot be used to match up. Another way of putting it is, if you match up from a 2–1–2 zone alignment, you're using 2–3 coverage, even when the alignment is 2–1–2.

In Figure 10–9, the logical movement to matchup defense is for the inside defender to cover the pass to the wing. However, this occurs only in

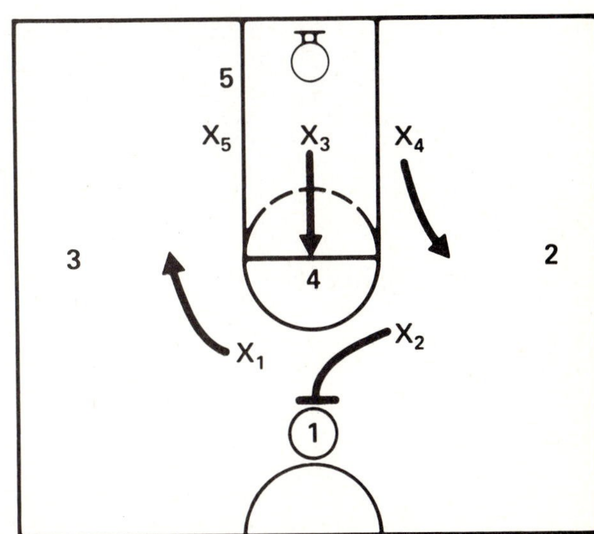

Figure 10–7 2–3 to Matchup, Clockwise Rotation Against 1–3–1 Offensive Alignment

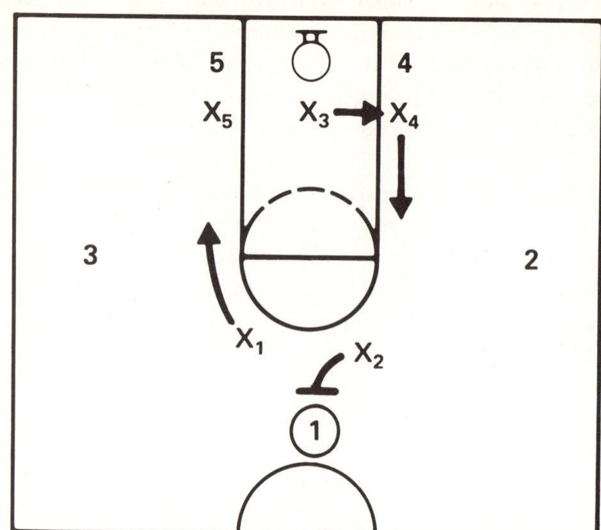

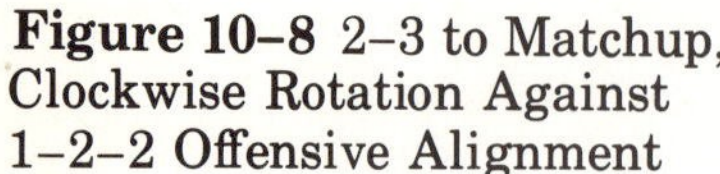

Figure 10–8 2–3 to Matchup, Clockwise Rotation Against 1–2–2 Offensive Alignment

Figure 10–9 Attempting to Match Up from 2–1–2 Zone Defense

a 2–3 defense, not in a 2–1–2. In 2–1–2 coverage, a guard will cover the wing pass and in order to complete the rotation, the other guard will cover the point guard. The question then arises as to how the inside defenders will match up with #30 and #40. The inside defenders can hardly leave the ball-side low-post position to move to the weak side, and if the inside defender stays at the low post, the team has not matched up.

1–1–3 to Matchup Zone Defense. The 1–1–3 zone defense is actually a 2–3 zone with the alignment altered to cover the high-post position. Most teams use this defense sparingly if at all, usually when they want to keep their big man inside rather than moving out to cover the high-post position. The 1–1–3 alignment generally tends to force the ball wide of the point; however, it is most effective in matchup form only when the offense assumes an even-front (for example, a 2–1–2) splitting alignment as shown in Diagram 10–10.

When the offensive team sets up 2–1–2, the defense can cover the high-post position without fear of surrendering defensive control inside, since the matchups can cut off the primary passing lanes (Figure 10–10).

The 1–1–3 alignment will match up with a 1–3–1 alignment (Figure 10–11), but only when the point guard passes to the left wing. When he passes to the right wing as shown in Diagram 10–12, the defender in the middle of the lane has to cover the ball-side low post regardless of whether any offensive player is occupying the position; thus, the 1–1–3 alignment will match up with a 1–3–1 offensive alignment only on one side of the court. When the ball is on the right side of the court (Figure 10–12), the defensive team will have to use basic defensive techniques, at least, until the offense sends someone across the lane to the low post or the ball-side baseline.

1–3–1 to Matchup. The 1–3–1 zone defensive alignment is the most versatile zone alignment in basketball. It forces the ball wide of the point, spreads the offensive alignment, permits matching up readily from practically any outside ball position, tends to keep a team's big man inside, and provides excellent opportunities for trapping. The 1–3–1

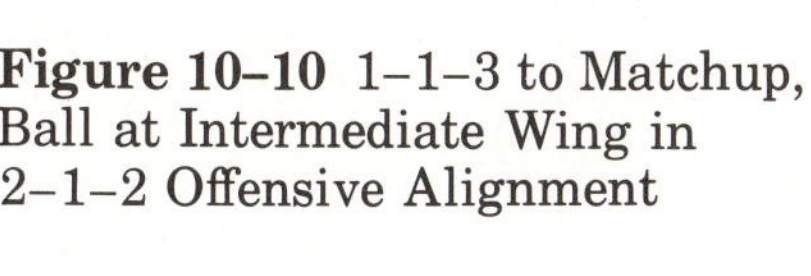

Figure 10–10 1–1–3 to Matchup, Ball at Intermediate Wing in 2–1–2 Offensive Alignment

Figure 10–11 1–1–3 Matches Up with 1–3–1 Offense When Point Guard Passes to Left Wing

Figure 10–12 1–1–3 Unable to Match Up with 1–3–1 when Point Guard Passes to Right Wing

alignment has only one shortcoming: it does not lend itself well to basic defensive techniques. Still, this is hardly a weakness of the alignment, since all three major styles of advanced defense—matching up, trapping, and help-and-recover—can be effected from the 1–3–1 alignment.

Most teams confronted with 1–3–1 zone defensive coverage will attempt to split the defense by setting up a 2–1–2 (Figure 10–13). However, the 1–3–1 matches up easily with the 2–1–2 offensive alignment, since the only defensive player who moves away from the ball to match up is the weak-side wing two passes away from the ball.

Against a 1–2–2 offensive alignment (Figure 10–14), the defenders will not match up until the ball is passed or dribbled wide of the point.

Before closing the discussion of rotation to matchups, we should note that sometimes the matchups occur before a pass is made, as in Figure 10–13, while at other times the defensive players wait until after the initial pass is made to match up (Figure 10–14). If the reason for this apparent delay in matching up has not been made clear, it is because the *defense cannot match up while the ball is at the top of the circle.* However, when the ball is wide of the point (even with, or beyond, the sides of the free-throw lane extended), defensive assignments become much clearer to the individual defenders. In Figure 10–14, for example, as long as the point guard has the ball at the top of the circle, the high-post defender will be unable to move away from the high post to cover 04 or 05.

When the pass is made to either wing position, the inside defenders will move quickly to their assigned positions and matchups. In this situation, either the high post will slide to the ball-side low post and the deep defender will drop back to cover the weak side, or the deep defender will

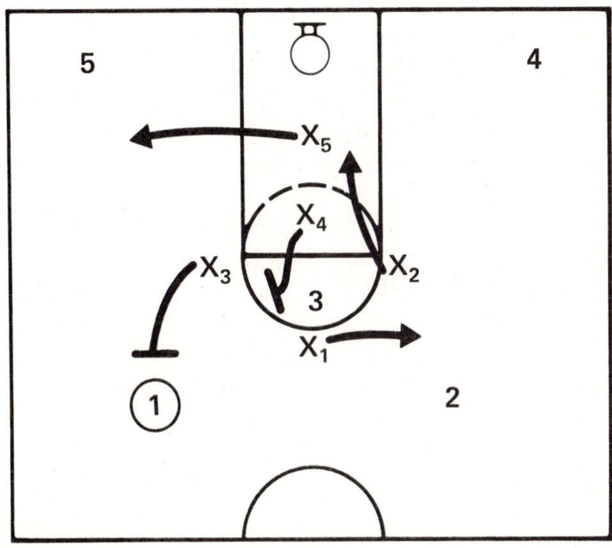

Figure 10–13 1–3–1 to Matchup vs. 2–1–2 Offensive Alignment

Figure 10–14 1–3–1 to Matchup vs. 1–2–2 Offensive Alignment

move to the ball-side low post and the high post will drop back to defend against the diagonal pass to the weak side low post.

The defenders may rotate their coverage from 1–3–1 to 1–2–2 before the point guard passes to the wing, but most coaches find it easier to wait until the ball is clearly established on one side of the court before matching up. Matchup techniques are already difficult to establish and maintain without adding nuances of coverage that may be unnecessary. The only primary receivers in the 1–2–2 offensive alignment when the ball is at the top of the circle as shown in Figure 10–14 are the wings, and premature rotation may be not only unnecessary but risky as well. If, for example, the high post man drops back to cover the weak side before the pass is made, an offensive player may flash to the high post in front of the defenders, or to the ball-side high post as the pass is made.

When matching up occurs *before* the ball handler's initial pass is made, the defense is said to be using "man-to-man to zone" matchup coverage. When the defenders remain in their 1–3–1 zone alignment until the ball handler passes the ball, the coverage is called "zone to man-to-man" matching up. In either case, though, defenders will attempt to maintain their matchup coverage regardless of ball and player movement after the initial matchups are established.

Maintaining the Matchups

Once matching up has been achieved, the defenders will attempt to maintain matchup coverage throughout the half-court. Offensive players cutting through the lane will be treated as if the defense were using switching man-to-man defensive techniques. This is perhaps one of the greatest advantages of matchup defense, that the coverage may be as loose or as tight as necessary to combat cutters, screens, and the like, without the subsequent loss of control sometimes encountered in man-to-man defense.

On the other hand, maintaining the matchups in the face of constantly changing offensive alignments and ball positions requires players who are capable of recognizing, and keeping up with, offensive movements and ball position. Whereas most teams can be taught to match up initially (although it may not always be to their advantage to do so), relatively few teams are capable of maintaining matchup coverage without eventually losing defensive control in high-percentage scoring areas.

One of the most frequently encountered problems associated with the use of matchup zone defense is the players' forgetting that they are in zone defense, and not man-to-man coverage. One example of the consequences of such momentary forgetfulness is shown in Figure 10–15.

In Figure 10–15, the defense has already matched up and the offensive team is temporarily in a 2–1–2 alignment. Player #30 cuts toward the sideline for #34's pass, and his defender follows him outside. The weak-side guard cuts backdoor behind the high post to the ball-side low post, and if neither the high post nor weak-side defender (probably the latter) switches defensive assignments to cover the cutter through the lane, he will be open under the basket for a pass and layup. (If the weak-side defender adjusts to cover the cut, the weak-side guard will have to remember to drop back to cover the diagonal pass to the weak-side low post.) The need for such switches is obvious when looking at the figure, but it may not be as readily apparent to youngsters who are worrying

Figure 10–15 The Necessity of Switching in Matchup Defense

about their own zones of responsibility, especially when a movement such as that shown in Figure 10–15 is but one of a series of cuts in a given pattern.

Covering the Single Cutter. In attacking not only matchup coverage but zone defenses in general, many coaches prefer to send one or more cutters through the lane to confuse the defenders or spread their zones of responsibility to limits beyond their effective coverage. The most ancient and basic of these cutter patterns is to send a single cutter through the lane, with other players rotating toward the ball to fill the vacated offensive positions. (Such movements may arise from any of several offensive alignments.)

In Figure 10–16, 01 has the ball in a 2–1–2 offensive alignment. 05 cuts outside to receive 01's pass. After passing to 05, 01 cuts to the basket and through the lane, with 03 sliding to the low post. 02 rotates toward the ball and 01's position, and 04 cuts outside to the vicinity of the weak-side high post. 05's passing options are, as shown in Figure 10–16, 03 at the low post, 01 cutting to the basket, 02 in the vicinity of the ball-side high post if the player guarding 01 follows him too far toward the basket, and 04 on the weak side if the defenders shift too much toward the ball side of the court in their coverage.

Effective matchup coverage will negate most, if not all, of 05's passing options (Figure 10–17). When 01 passes to 05, X_5 will move outside to cover 05. X_1 will drop back to a point slightly below the free-throw line in covering 01's cut through the lane, but he will not enter the lane to follow 01; instead, X_1 will move back outside, expecting to cover an offensive

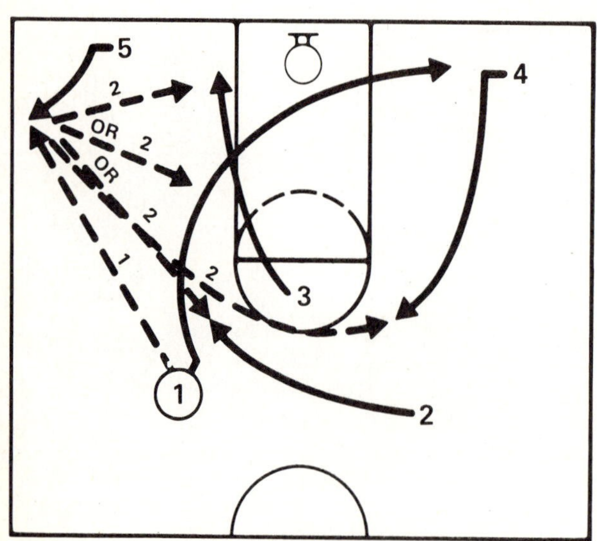

Figure 10–16 Single Cutter Through the Lane, with Outside Rotation

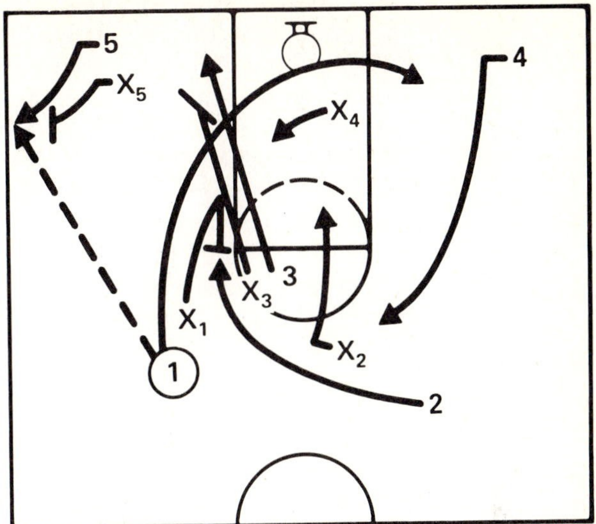

Figure 10–17 Defending Against the Single-Cutter Pattern, Matchup Zone Defense

player outside who is rotating toward the ball. X_3 will cover 03's cut to the low post. (If 03 doesn't cut to the low post, X_3 will stay at the high post, with X_4 covering any cutters to the ball-side low post.) X_4 will cover 01's cut as he enters and crosses the lane. X_2, who is dropping back to the free-throw line with 01's pass to 05, will cover 04's cut if it occurs. If X_4 has to move to the ball-side low post to cover a cutter from the weak side, X_2 will cover 01's cut. (This isn't as risky as it appears, since X_3 at the high post and X_4 at the low post will double-team any lob passes to 01.)

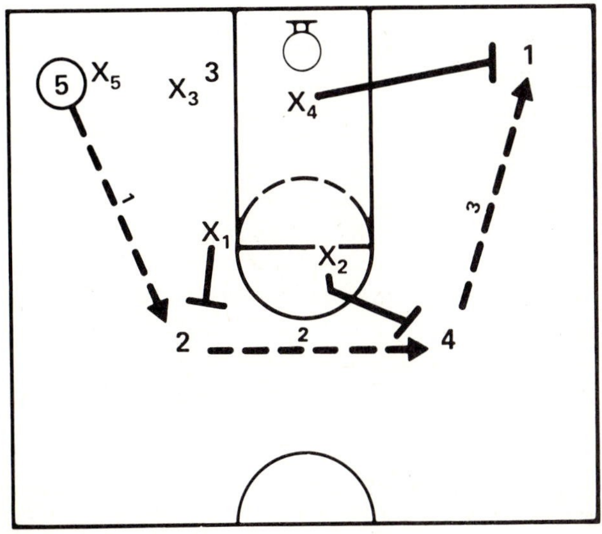

Figure 10–18 Covering the Rotation Passes, Matchup Defense

Covering the Rotation Passes. Once 01 cuts through the lane and 02 and 04 rotate outside, the offensive strategy usually involves rotating the ball quickly around the perimeters of the zone to the weak side, with the hope of taking advantage of any defensive players out of position (Figure 10–18).

Ball rotation may yield occasional scoring opportunities when the defensive team is using matchup coverage. However, the offensive players' penetration is limited when the defense is in *zone* coverage rather than man-to-man. The player who dribbles into the teeth of a zone defense does so at his own risk: coverage will always be intense, since zone defenses are designed specifically to stop such penetration.

TRAPPING ZONE DEFENSE

Two kinds of coaches use half-court trapping defenses: those whose squads are filled with blue-chip athletes and superior personnel, and those who have grossly overestimated their players' skills. Coaches who fall in the latter category should not take the trapping defense lightly. Trapping requires alert, aggressive, highly skilled players, and when it is used in its most aggressive form, the players must be at least as tall as their opponents; otherwise, the players springing the traps will not be able to contain the ball or force bad passes or turnovers.

There are several degrees of trapping, of course, but the only style I'd ever consider using is the most aggressive form in which, in addition to trapping the ball handler, the defenders play the passing lanes and deny passes to the primary receivers. However, if your players don't have the skills to control the ball handler and shut off the passes, you're making a big mistake to try it in the first place.

Of all the defenses in basketball, trapping unquestionably entails the most risk, especially when it is used as a half-court defense. When two players are guarding a single opponent, the offensive team holds a four-on-three advantage with attacking momentum toward the basket when it eludes the traps, since the defensive players' movements are, in almost every case, *away* from the basket. Unsuccessful trapping allows the offensive players to move to the basket aggressively when they might not have been able to otherwise.

Why, then, with so much working against the use of trapping techniques, would a team want to use them in its zone defense? If the defensive players are fundamentally sound, skilled, and aggressive, why might they prefer trapping to other defenses such as matching up, pressure man-to-man, or run-and-jump?

First, teams seldom announce their trapping intentions. They don't trap *every* offensive player every time the ball is passed; rather, they select their targets carefully, waiting until the offensive players aren't ready to deal with the traps or when they will be unlikely to escape them. Typically, a coach whose team uses a trapping defense will tell his players, "We want to steer the ball toward the right-hand corner and then trap the ball handler in the corner."* The positions from which traps may be sprung vary with the zone defensive alignment, the players' defensive skills, and the location of the offensive players to be trapped. Thus, the defensive team may play a form of basic or matchup zone defense when the ball is on one side of the court (setting their traps only when the ball moves to the other side of the court) or when a given offensive player has the ball. Teams also could choose to operate from a trapping alignment without trapping.

A second reason why teams might prefer trapping to other forms of zone coverage is its potential to spark a team's transition game. The possibility always exists that the offensive team will beat the traps and score easy baskets, but when the traps succeed, the defensive team gains an enormous advantage. Since trapping is always aggressive, defensive players who are prepared to fast break after steals will find transition baskets recurring with regularity whenever the defensive coverage forces bad passes and turnovers. Trapping defense is a *gambling* defense, not the conservative, wait-until-the-offense-makes-a-mistake type of defense found in basic zone coverage. Teams using the trapping defense aren't interested in keeping the ball away from the low post or in forcing opponents to take low-percentage shots; instead, they want to get the ball back without allowing the offense any kind of shot at all.

I've always liked the idea of the trapping defense because there are no shortcuts to success when you're trapping, and there are no easy ways of trapping the ball handler and covering the passing lanes without giving your all and busting your gut to attack the offensive team. However, if the offensive team has ball handlers who are capable of beating the traps despite the aggressive defense, and if other offensive players are able to take the ball to the basket while the defenders are at a disadvantage, your players may wind up guarding air a lot of the time.

Personnel Requirements

Specific player requirements for half-court trapping within a zone defense vary to a certain extent with the alignment used, but general requirements can be described as follows:

1. Regardless of where the traps are set, the trapping players must be tall enough to stop the passer from finding the open player and passing to him. Small players may be able to trap the dribbler or hinder his vision

*The trap can be achieved by overplaying and cutting off the passing lanes everywhere *except* the right-hand corner.

to a certain extent after he has picked up his dribble; however, if the ball handler hasn't started his dribble, the defenders cannot merely run up to him and stand tall, waving their hands around and leaping into the air. The ball handler will just dribble around them and continue unmolested on his merry way. However, small defenders cannot afford to assume their normal (low) defensive stance, either, since they will then be unable to hinder the ball handler's vision without faceguarding him. (In such cases, their best bet probably is to smother the ball handler and go after the ball. If they are sufficiently aggressive, they will force the ball handler to concentrate so heavily on protecting the ball and watching the trapping defenders that he will be unable to look for his teammates.)

Generally, then, trapping will work most often when the trappers are of the same size as the player they're trapping. The greater the height disparity favoring the ball handler, the less likely trapping will be successful—at least in terms of stealing the *pass*. If stealing the dribble is the goal, size may not be a factor at all.

2. One player must be capable of keeping the ball away from the high post. Whether the defenders front or overguard to keep the ball away, the ball must be kept away from the high-post position. Trapping at the high-post position is difficult (and usually undesirable) in any zone defense.

3. The corner positions must be covered whether trapping occurs there or not. If the defense is using a 1–3–1 alignment, the deep player will cover passes to either baseline; therefore, he must be among the fastest players in the lineup, although not necessarily one of the tallest. Many teams using a trapping defense from a 1–3–1 zone alignment put a guard at the deep position to provide adequate corner coverage, since the guard will not have to cover the ball-side low-post position.

Setting Up the Traps from Various Zone Alignments

The 3–2, 2–2–1, and 2–1–2 zone defenses are not often seen as trapping alignments. Among the remaining alignments shown in Figures 10–19 through 10–21, the advantages of the 1–3–1 alignment as a means of setting up trapping situations can be seen readily in Figure 10–19.

In Figure 10–20, trapping in the 1–2–2 zone occurs at the same positions as in the 1–3–1 zone: both corners and both intermediate wing positions. However, the 1–2–2 alignment is relatively weak in terms of covering the high post. Since X_2 and X_3 may have to trap at the high-post position, they cannot play as wide in their alignment as they would in a 1–3–1 alignment.

In Figure 10–21, only three areas are used for trapping: the point and the wing positions on either side of the court. Lacking a single defender at the point, the outside guards will be unable to force the ball wide without weakening their coverage.

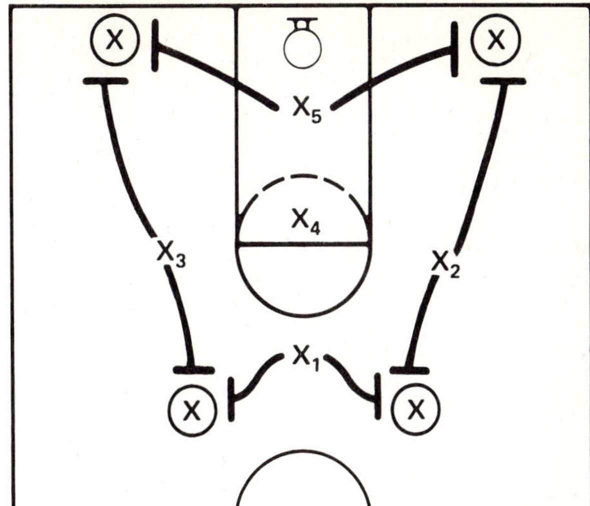

Figure 10–19 1–3–1 Zone Trapping Areas

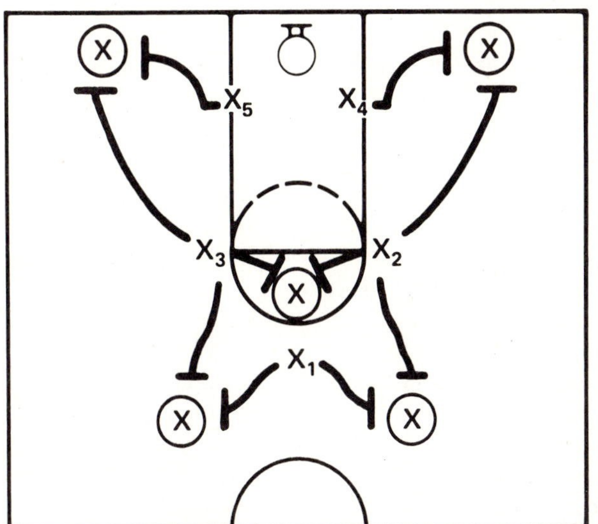

Figure 10–20 1–2–2 Zone Trapping Areas

The first step in setting up the trapping situations is to force the ball to one side of the court. Most teams will perform this service for you by splitting your defense—for example, by setting up a 2–1–2 against a 1–3–1 defensive alignment. From time to time, teams will set up in alignments that do *not* split the defense—for example, a 1–2–2 offense against a 1–3–1 defense—and in such cases the defense can force the ball toward the side of the court by sending its point guard out to cover the ball handler.

Once the ball is on one side of the court, the next step in setting up trapping situations is to force the ball handler to throw a lob pass to the

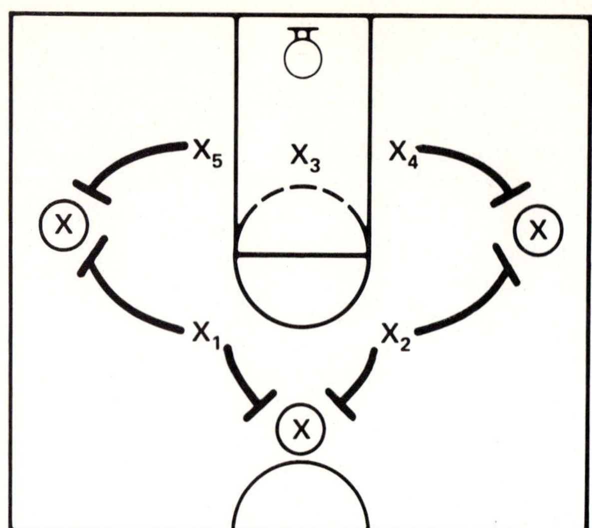

Figure 10–21 2–3 Zone Trapping Areas

intended receiver by moving into the passing lane between the ball and the primary receivers.

> **Note:** The ball can be kept away from any given pass receiver simply by moving out to guard him, as the inside defenders have done in Figure 10–22.

Point and Intermediate Wing Trapping

In Figure 10–22, the weak-side guard is the player to be trapped. The ball-side wing moves out to cover him, and the defensive guard moves into the passing lane between the guards. (At this point, he is guarding neither player. If, however, the ball handler attempts to penetrate, the defensive wing and point guard probably will trap him, with the weak-side guard moving into the passing lane to pick off the pass if it is made. The ball handler, being aware of this possibility, likely will not want to force the ball into a double-team. Thus, the outside defender probably will not have to guard the ball handler, and he can therefore direct his own efforts toward playing the passing lane and trapping the weak-side guard if and when the pass is made.)

Meanwhile, the high-post defender is overguarding (or fronting) his man, and the inside defender has moved outside to keep the ball-side corner player from getting the ball. The wing's coverage of the ball handler must be aggressive enough to stop him from passing diagonally crosscourt along the baseline, since the weak-side guard cannot drop back to cover the inside pass and still move out to trap the guard. The outside

Figure 10–22 Setting Up an Intermediate Wing Trap, 1–3–1 Zone Defense

defender will not double-team the ball, but he will remain in the passing lane between the guards.

When the ball handler passes to the other guard, the defenders will spring their trap. The outside defender and wing move quickly into close guarding positions on the ball, the high post will move his overguarding to the other side of his man, the weak-side wing will step into the passing lane to intercept the return pass to the guard if it is attempted, and the inside defender will move as rapidly as possible to the ball side and into the passing lane between the ball and the corner player, trying to steal *that* pass if it's made.

The weak-side low post is, of course, wide open for a lob pass, but the last time the ball handler looked, the inside defender was back on the weak side. Also, with two defenders harassing the ball handler by jumping around and reaching for the ball, he may forget to look for the weak-side low post or be unable to find him over the other players. His natural impulse will be to pass to one of the primary receivers (both of whom are now covered), since neither the high nor low post was open when the ball was on the other side of the court.

It is obvious that effective trapping depends to a great extent on the element of surprise as well as aggressive coverage, since the ball handler will simply toss a lob pass under the basket if he knows that the opponents are trapping (Figure 10–24). As a result, most teams don't trap the pass

Figure 10–23 Springing the Intermediate Wing Trap, 1–3–1 Zone Defense

receivers every time, but only in certain situations or at predetermined locations on the court.

Trapping at the intermediate wing positions from a 1–2–2 defense is slightly different than from a 1–3–1 defense. 1–2–2 trapping as shown in Figure 10–24 will not work if the wing cannot gain immediate defensive control of the ball handler: he will pass to the high post before the weak-side defender can move up to cover the position, and all hope of trapping will evaporate at that point. (The weak-side forward will likely get a backdoor layup behind the weak-side guard.) As a result, trapping cannot occur until the high post is covered. At the point when the high post is covered, however, the trap is set, and movements involved in springing the trap will occur exactly like those in 1–3–1 coverage.

Point trapping is overrated. I've seen a lot of teams trap at the point, but none that has ever been consistently good at it. Point trapping can steal the ball from a weak ball handler every now and then, but that's about the extent of the damage it can do. It will *not* succeed in cutting off the primary passing lanes or in stealing passes.

The problem associated with cutting off the outside passing lanes in point trapping can be seen in Figure 10–25: if the guards trap at the point and the forwards move outside to cut off both passing lanes (it would be senseless to cover only *one* wing and leave the other open), the high post defender will have to cover both offensive players inside, with specific

Figure 10–24 Intermediate Wing Trapping, 1–2–2 Coverage

Figure 10–25 Cutting Off the Primary (Wing) Passing Lanes in Point Trapping

responsibility for neither. If the ball were on one side of the court, the high post man's coverage would be more clearly defined: the pass inside from the top of the circle can be made with equal facility, but the crosscourt diagonal pass is far more difficult to find and execute.

Trapping at the Wings

The best I can say about wing trapping is to *forget it*. Trapping at the wings is as hopeless as expecting lower taxes or honest politicians. The wings usually set up too far outside to make wing trapping a practical

Figure 10–26 Wing Trapping, Offensive Overload Alignment

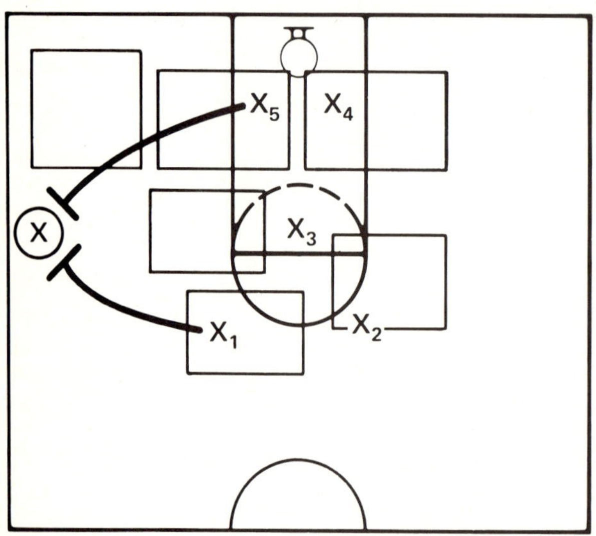

Figure 10–27 Areas to Be Covered in Wing Trapping

goal. When the ball is at the wing position, play the passing lanes and try to trap them somewhere else. Better still, run a 1–3–1 trapping zone defense and force the wings into a 2–1–2 offensive alignment that doesn't have a wing player. (One look at Figure 10–27 should suffice to exemplify the weakness of wing trapping.)

Although it is not impossible, it's extremely unlikely for trapping to occur with any high degree of success in an overload situation like the one shown in Figure 10–26. (The pass you're giving up—the crosscourt pass to the weak side—is the same one the offense looks for against regular zone coverage.)

Take my word for it, trapping a wing player is like being nice to your mother-in-law: it just doesn't matter; it doesn't change anything.

Corner Trapping

Many coaches feel that the corners provide the most effective trapping coverage anywhere on the court. There are several reasons for this. First, the player who dribbles into the corner before being trapped has nowhere to go to avoid the trap. Second, a player's passing lanes are limited and well defined in the corners to a greater extent than, say, the same player's being trapped at the point. When you trap a player in the corner, you *know* where he's going to try to pass the ball. Third, passing out of the corner usually means passing the ball *away from the basket,* indicating that defensive control is greater when the traps are sprung in the corners. Fourth, corner trapping is the only form of trapping that permits coverage of the ball-side low post in cutting off the primary passing lanes.

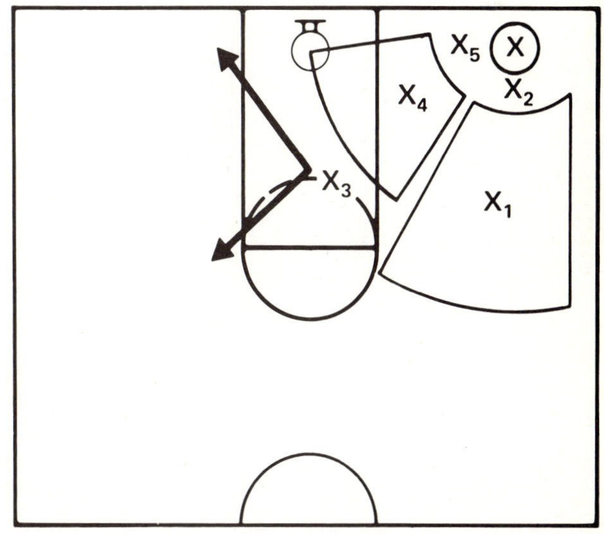

Figure 10–28 Cutting Off the Passing Lanes, Corner Trapping

Figure 10–28 shows the players in their basic positions before the trapping movement begins. When 02 passes to 04 as shown in Figure 10–29, the two primary passing lanes are between 04 and 02, and 04 and 03. With X_2 and X_5 trapping 04, X_4 must cover the opening between X_2 and X_5. 05 will be open on the weak side, but 04 probably will be unable to see him or make the pass over X_5, X_4, and possibly X_3. Even if the pass is made, it will have to be a lob pass over X_5, X_3, *and the rim,* which will allow X_3 to cover 05 after he receives the pass. Also, X_2 and X_5 will further hinder 04's passing effectiveness with their aggressive coverage in the corner. At the very least, X_2 and X_5 will not permit 04 to pass inside or to the weak-side low post without his being aware of their efforts to take the ball from him.

In Figure 10–28, X_2 and X_5 have trapped 04 in the corner. X_1 has moved across to cut off the primary outside passing lane along the sideline, and X_4 has moved from the high post to the area of the ball-side low post. X_4 will cover any offensive player (probably either 03 or 05 in Figure 10–29) who moves low on the ball side. X_3 then has the dual responsibility of covering both 05 and 01 on the weak side. Aggressive defense by X_2 and X_5 will deny the pass from 04 to 05, and X_3 will in most cases cheat outside toward 01 in his coverage, hoping to intercept the diagonal crosscourt pass.

All corner trapping situations, regardless of the zone defensive alignments from which they arise, will cover the positions and passing lanes as described, although the players used in trapping and cutting off the passing lanes will vary with the alignment.

If 04 makes the pass to 05 on the weak side consistently, despite X_5

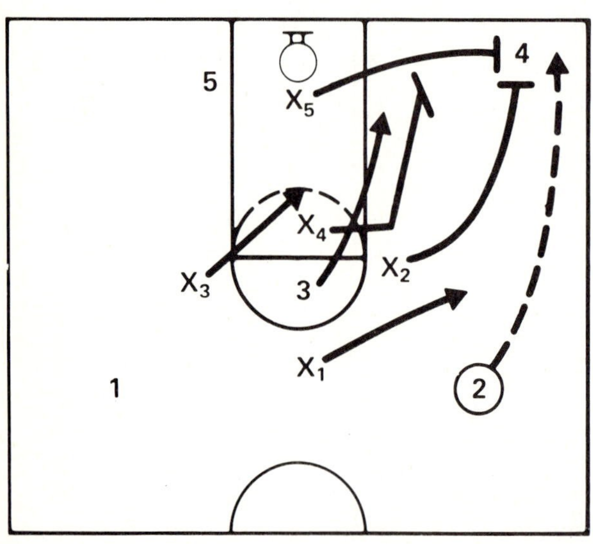

Figure 10–29 Movement to Corner Trapping, 1–3–1 Zone Defense

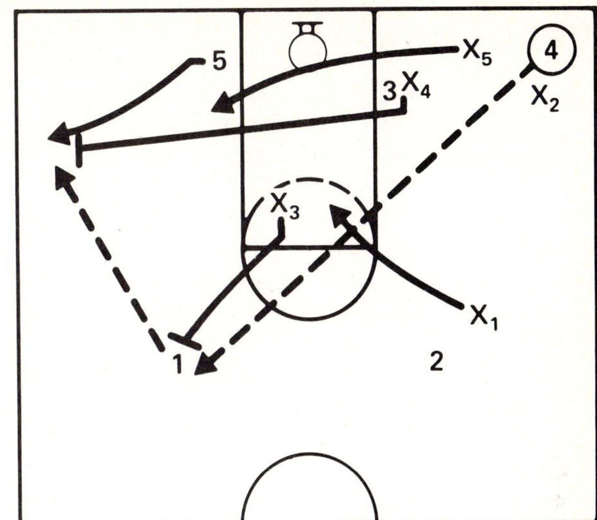

Figure 10–30 Making the Diagonal Pass Outside to Beat the Corner Trap

and X_3's best efforts to deny the pass, the defensive team is better advised to drop out of trapping coverage than to move X_3 nearer the basket. The defenders will then be trapping passively, and passive trapping provides far weaker coverage than basic zone defense. The traps *must* contain the ball; otherwise, the defenders should be in basic defense.

Covering the Diagonal Pass from the Corner

When the trap fails to contain the ball, the defenders will not be able to trap again until they re-establish defensive control in some other manner, such as matching up with each successive pass receiver in a manner similar to that shown in Figure 10–30. The new matchups will be as follows: X_1 and 02, X_3 and 01, X_4 and 05, X_5 and 03, and X_2 and 04. Once the matchups re-establish defensive control in terms of stopping penetration, the traps can be re-set to be sprung again.

Trapping at the High Post

As a rule, most teams prefer to deny the pass to any player who is set up at, or cuts into, the high-post position. It's easier to keep the ball away from the high post than it is to deal with players who get the ball there. A team may trap whenever the ball is passed in to the high post, but the difference between this and other trapping strategies is enormous: where the high post is concerned, you trap every time the opponents pass inside to that area; in regular trapping, you steer the ball toward a certain area of the court (for example, the right-hand corner as you face the basket from midcourt) and then trap the player with the ball and cut off all passing lanes away from that area. However, few teams using a trapping defense will try to steer the ball toward the high post. There are simply too many ways for the offense to penetrate the coverage from the high post. Teams may be prepared to deal with passes to the high post if they occur, but they will usually discourage such confrontations beforehand by overguarding or fronting at the high post.

Teams can trap at the high-post position either horizontally or vertically. In horizontal trapping (Figure 10–31), players trap the high post from the sides; in vertical trapping (Figure 10–32), the high-post player is trapped from front and back. In Figure 10–31, the wings are responsible for trapping at the high post whenever the ball is passed to that area. In Figure 10–32, the point guard and the high-post defender trap at the high post.

The difficulty in trapping at the high post is partly alleviated when the defense has an inside player who is directly responsible for the high-post player. Still, despite apparent weaknesses in horizontal trapping at the high post—the difficulty in covering the wings in Figure 10–31, for example—there is no solid evidence that vertical trapping offers any better prospects for covering the open players than horizontal trapping. If the defense is able to cover the inside positions while trapping at the high post, the best that the offensive team will achieve is an open shot along the perimeters of the defense.

Figure 10–31 Horizontal Trapping at High Post

Figure 10–32 Vertical Trapping at High Post

Still, the outside passing lanes cannot be cut off readily when the ball is trapped at the high post. In Figure 10–33, X_4 and X_5 move outside to deny the passes to 02 and 03, who have moved toward the open area near the baselines; Figure 10–34 shows X_2 and X_3 dropping back to cover 02 and 03. If in either case 01 cuts to the low post opposite 05, inside

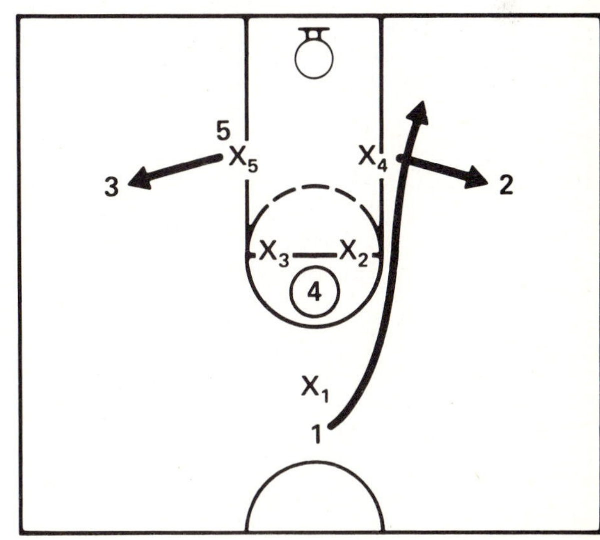

Figure 10–33 Cutting Off the Outside Passing Lanes

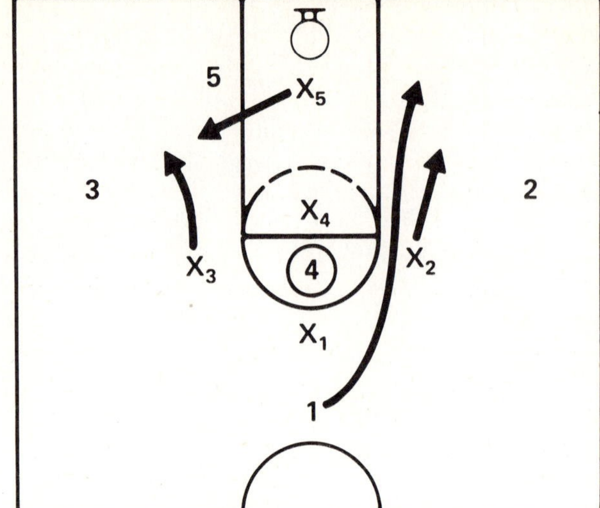

Figure 10–34 Cutting Off the Outside Passing Lanes

coverage will be weakened considerably, since X_1 cannot follow 01 to the low post and remain in zone coverage. One might be tempted to conclude that X_4 can prevent the pass inside from 04 to 01 in Figure 10–34, but the prospects are slim: if X_4 was capable of such effective coverage, the defense would probably be in matchup coverage, not trapping at the high post. You trap when you need help to stop someone, not when you can control him by yourself.

Trapping at the high post has relatively few advantages in attacking the offense. Basically, it is a response to an offensive attacking movement, and it becomes effective only when the offensive team is unable to press its advantage further, particularly when the high-post player is unable to fully exploit the deficiencies in coverage.

HELP-AND-RECOVER DEFENSE

I used a 1–2–2 zone defense at three different schools before switching to full-court pressure man-to-man defense at UNLV. The zone was always good to me. However, when I was originally considering how we were going to operate our zone coverage, I faced at least two problems that didn't particularly appeal to me: it seemed that, regardless of the alignment we used or how it was played, the opponents eventually were going to be able to create matchups that took our big men away from the basket, or else the opponents would pass the ball around until the shifting zone alignment gave them an open outside shot. I wanted to avoid both situations. I didn't want to concede the inside game or the outside shot.

Consider, for example, the previous analyses of the various basic zone defenses—double-teaming inside, setting four defenders on the ball side and one on the weak side, and keeping two players back to cover the weak side with only three ball-side defenders—or the advanced zone defenses described in this chapter, matching up and trapping. In every case except trapping, the lack of defensive pressure on the ball handler and/or receivers one pass away from the ball will eventually weaken the inside coverage or yield an open outside shot. A further problem is that, in covering the ball, the low post, the weak side, and cutters toward and away from the ball, the big men's rotation outside will inevitably take them out of position to do more than go after the long rebounds when shots are taken.

In considering possible alternate zone coverages, we decided early that we were going to have to use our big men—X_4 and X_5 in the 1–2–2 alignment—to cover the corners. However, we weren't going to give up the shot from the corners, and we were going to do everything possible to shut out the opponents' inside game at the same time. We did *not*, however, want to tie up our big men at the wing positions, nor were we interested in matching up or double-teaming inside constantly, except when the ball was in the corner.

We played our 1–2–2 similar to the way most teams play their basic zone defenses, except that when the opponents set two players outside in their offensive alignment (Figure 10–35), point guard X_1 was expected to cover both players, with help from X_2 and X_3. Then, when X_1 arrived, X_2 would slide away (Figure 10–36). This style of coverage is known as *help-and-recover* defense.

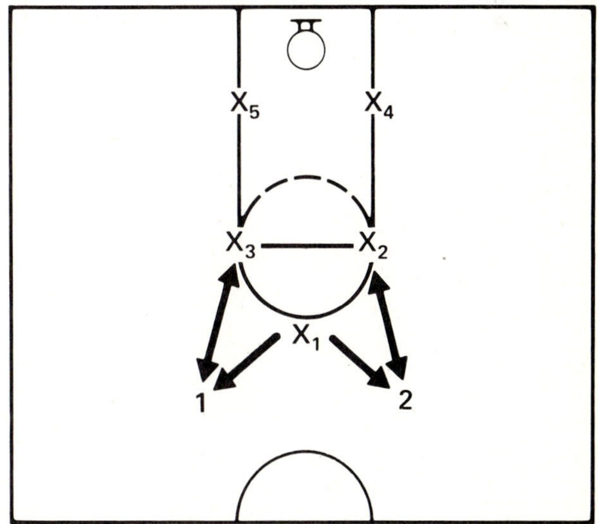

Figure 10–35 Point Coverage, Help-and-Recover Defense

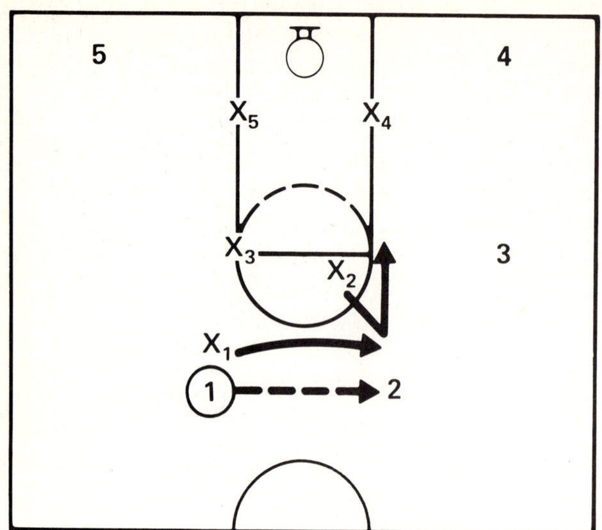

Figure 10–36 Starting the Help-and-Recover Sequence

In help-and-recover defense, X_1 will guard either 01 or 02 initially, whichever has the ball. X_1 will guard the ball handler closely, attempting to deny, or at least force, a slow (lob or bounce) pass to the high post, if the ball handler is determined to pass to the post. A slow pass can be stolen, or at worst it will give X_2 and X_3 time to trap the receiver at the high post. If 01 and 02 can shoot from these positions, X_2 or X_3 will move outside to cover the weak-side intermediate wing (Figure 10–35). If 01 and 02 are beyond the normal limits of their shooting range, X_1 will not need any help in covering both players. If 01 passes to 02, X_2 will cover him until X_1 arrives (Figure 10–36). X_2 will then drop back quickly.

If 02 relays the ball to 03, X_4 will move outside to cover 03 (if necessary) until X_2 arrives, as shown in Figure 10–37. (Of course, X_4 will stay inside if X_2 can recover and move into position to guard 03.) The wing man (X_2) approaches 02 with his inside foot forward, and drops that foot back when returning to his position.

When 02 passes to 03 at the wing position, X_1 will drop back to cover the high post. Whenever the ball is at the wing, the weak-side inside defender will move across the lane to deny the pass to the low post, and the weak-side wing will drop low inside the lane to protect the weak-side low post area (Figure 10–38).

Ideally, the guard will arrive in time to permit the forward to stay back (or to drop back) to cover the corner. When the wing passes to the corner, the guard will drop back quickly to double-team inside. If the corner player passes back outside, the defensive guard will move back out to guard him.

Figure 10–37 Continuing the Help-and-Recover Sequence

Figure 10–38 Corner and Low-Post Coverage, Help-and-Recover Defense

The advantage in using help-and-recover coverage is that the defense does not concede *any* outside shots, and at the same time it effectively shuts off the opponents' inside game. Players are constantly in motion in this defense—at least they had better be moving constantly, since their defensive responsibilities shift more quickly in this kind of coverage than in other zone defenses, and their reactions to ball and player movement must be exceedingly sharp.

As was discussed in Chapter 9, the major weakness of zone coverage involves the high-post position. The defenders *must* be able to discourage the opponents from attacking with passes from the high post. The methods used to hinder or discourage such passes are identical to those shown in Figures 10–31 and 10–32. Many point guards are small, and thus they may have difficulty in eliminating these passes. Often, the two wing defenders, X_2 and X_3, will have to pinch on the high post man, creating a natural double- or triple-team on the ball.

The observant reader will have noted that the help-and-recover technique is naturally conducive to trapping; in fact, some of the defense's success, particularly in the early stages of games, may be attributable to the opponents' confusing the coverage with trapping, with the attendant panic that trapping induces.

Generally, we didn't trap early in games; rather, we let our opponents establish their perimeter passing lanes, springing the traps only after we had sealed off their passing lanes into the inside seams of the zone and when we thought we had lulled our opponents into believing the passing lanes were safe. Corner trapping movements from the help-and-recover defense are shown in Figures 10–39 and 10–40.

The trapping movements from the help-and-recover defense are identical to those for the point, wing, and corner trapping described earlier in this chapter. For the sake of brevity, therefore, the reader is referred to that section for descriptions of trapping techniques, particularly in regard to cutting off the passing lanes. It's worth repeating, though, that to be most effective, trapping should be sporadic rather than regular if the element of surprise is to work its magic on the opponents.

Generally, the 1–2–2 defensive alignment will split the offense—that is, it will force the opponents to set two players at the intermediate wing positions as shown in Figure 10–35, rather than using a single (point) guard in their offensive set. In the latter instance, ball rotation may be severely hampered, or even eliminated entirely, if the outside guard stays out on the point guard. A wide 1–2–2 offensive alignment permits the defense to match up without difficulty; a 1–3–1 offensive alignment is not usually seen against a 1–2–2 zone, since the outside guard will tend to take 01 out of the offense entirely. Thus we are faced with the overwhelming likelihood of seeing an even-front offensive set used against the 1–2–2 defensive alignment. Further analysis reveals that, although we showed a rather strange offensive alignment in Figures

Figure 10–39 Intermediate Wing Trapping from Help-and-Recover Zone Defense

Figure 10–40 Corner Trapping from Help-and-Recover Zone Defense

10–36 through 10–38, most teams will operate from a 2–1–2 alignment. We used the intermediate wing/wing/corner formation to describe the limits of help-and-recover continuity on one side of the court. In practice, this kind of formation sometimes develops, but only after the 2–1–2 alignment fails to produce any kind of open outside shot or inside game.

The intermediate wing/wing/corner offensive alignment will arise when the low-post player—03 in Figure 10–41—cuts outside to the wing position, and high post 04 slides to the low post and, failing to get the ball

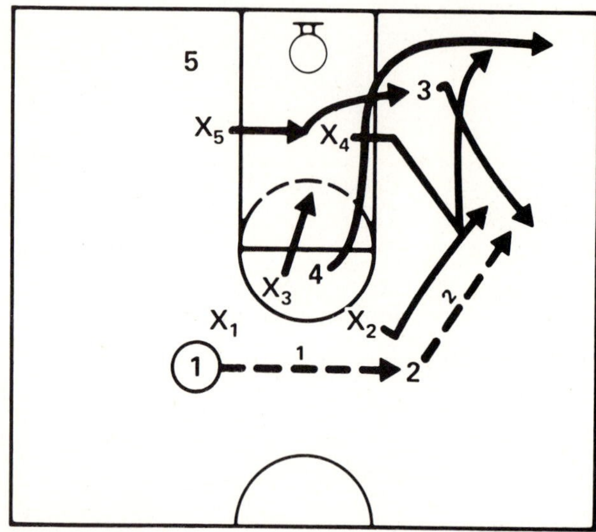

Figure 10–41 Wing and Corner Movements Against Help-and-Recover Defense

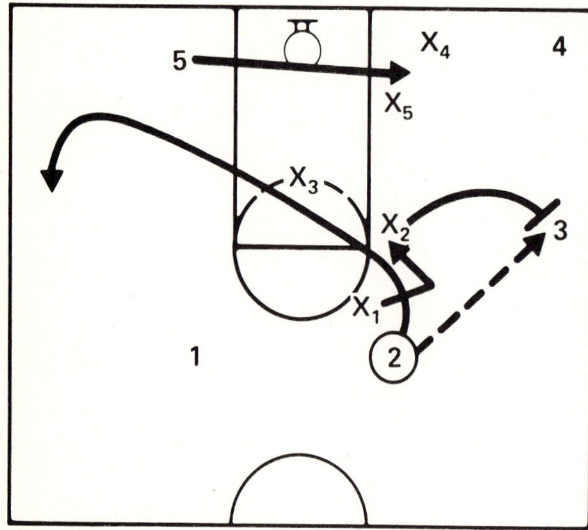

Figure 10–42 Establishing a Low-Post Overload and Weak-Side Attack Against Help-and-Recover Defense

there, cuts to the corner (Figure 10–41). (Of course, 01 could cut to the corner instead of 04.)

If 03 is not open at the low post, he may cut outside to the wing position to receive 02's pass. 04, filling 03's low-post position, is covered inside, so he cuts to the corner. Defensive coverage of these movements has already been shown.

Two additional offensive movements that may arise out of this attempt to confuse the defensive coverage are 05's cut to the ball-side low post and 02's cut through the lane to the weak side (Figure 10–42).

X_5 will cover 05's cut in Figure 10–42. X_3 will help and recover with X_2 if 03 reverses the ball to 01, and X_5 will help and recover with X_3 if 01 relays the ball to 02.

Help-and-Recover Defense with Ball Rotation

In help-and-recover defense, help is not offered if it is not needed. Thus, only once in the entire sequence of passes shown in Figures 10–43 through 10–47 will the players help and recover—in Figure 10–45, where X_1 cannot cover 01 and 02. In the other cases, the defense will not have to alter its original coverage to maintain pressure on the ball without changing the matchups even momentarily. For example, when 05 passes out of the corner to 01 in Figure 10–44, X_1 will move outside to cover the ball handler. Since X_1 was responsible for 01 at the time anyway, it is not necessary for any other defensive player, particularly X_2, to cover 01 until X_1 reaches him. If, however, X_1 had been responsible for someone else—say, the ball handler at the wing who is passing to the point, although this

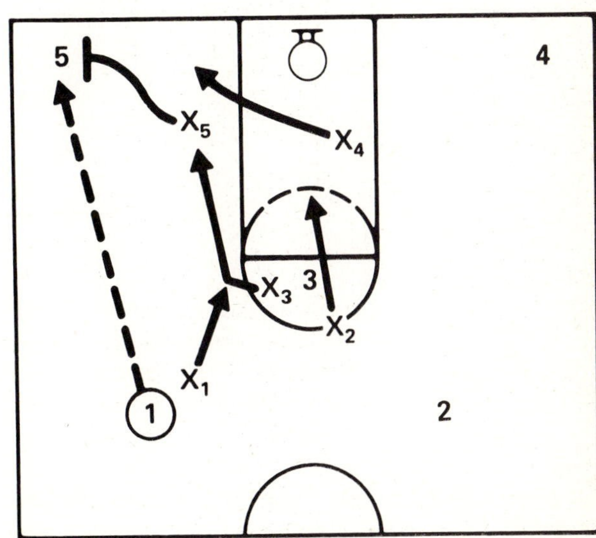

Figure 10–43 Help-and-Recover Defense with Ball Rotation (*a*)

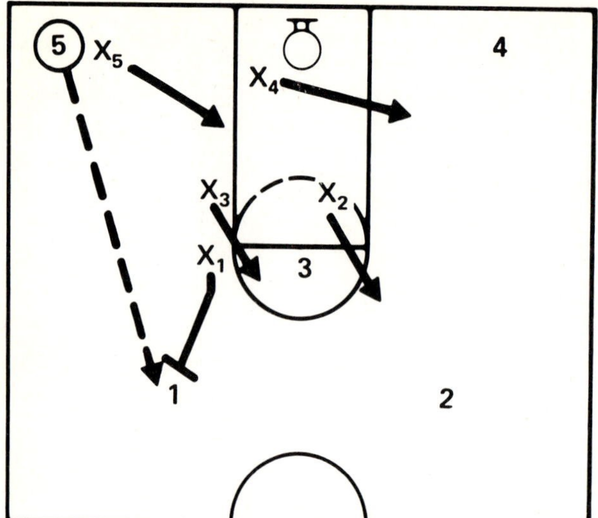

Figure 10–44 Help-and-Recover Defense with Ball Rotation (*b*)

Figure 10–45 Help-and-Recover Defense with Ball Rotation (*c*)

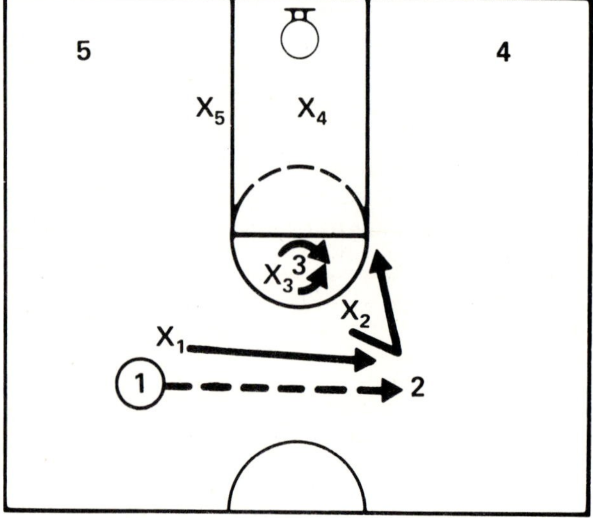

is an unlikely occurrence—X_2 would be expected to cover 01 until X_1 arrived or 01 passed to the next offensive player along the perimeter.

When the ball is in the corners (Figures 10–43 and 10–47), the defenders will usually double-team the ball-side low-post position, with one player back on the weak side. Coverage of the ball handler in the corner must be tight to prevent the crosscourt pass to the weak side and the resultant two-on-one offensive advantage. The defender on the ball will attempt to deny the pass, or at least force a slow lob pass that will give the rest of the defenders time to react to the pass.

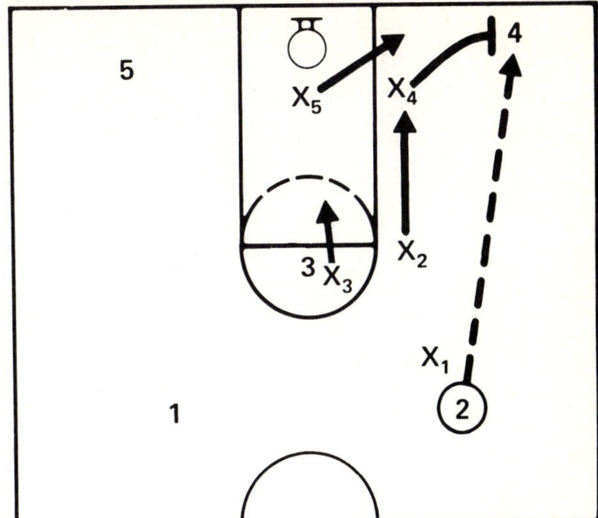

Figure 10–46 Help-and-Recover Defense with Ball Rotation (*d*)

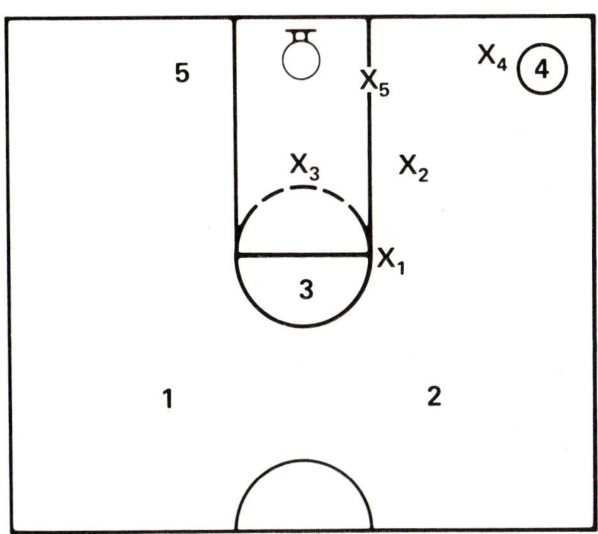

Figure 10–47 Help-and-Recover Defense with Ball Rotation (*e*)

Note: The defense could also trap the man in the corner, perhaps with X_3 and X_5, but trapping generally works better when the ball has been passed to the corner from the wing. Otherwise, the trapping player—X_3—usually will be unable to reach the corner before X_5 is able to dribble or pass the ball out of the corner.

Another problem associated with inside double-teaming when the ball is in the corner is that of weak-side rebounding. When 05 has the ball in the corner (Figure 10–44), X_2 is charged with weak-side rebounding responsibility, and X_2 is likely to be the team's fourth best rebounder on the floor. (Point guard X_1 is usually the smallest player, and is therefore the least effective rebounder.) Such coverage is necessary, though, and it underscores the importance of denying the corner shot. The defense is in far less tenuous circumstances when 05 passes the ball out of the corner and along the perimeter of the defense.

Many teams attempt to attack the 1–2–2 zone inside from the corners, since the other big man (X_4 in Figure 10–44) must move all the way across the lane to cover the low post. Other positions (the wings, point, and intermediate wings) are more easily covered by one man, and they generally do not require double-teaming. Also, only when the ball is in the corner is a situation likely to arise in which a guard or small forward has to cover the low post.

When the man in the corner is allowed to make the long crosscourt diagonal pass—a rather drastic move by the offense—help-and-recover defense can be used to keep the offense from gaining an advantage. (Figure 10–48).

When 05 passes to 02 on the weak side as shown in Figure 10–48, X_1 at the ball-side high post is out of position to cover the pass receiver. However, if X_2 moves out to cover 02 until X_1 arrives, X_4 will have time to move across the lane to cover 04. X_3 will cover the first half of 03's cut into the lane, and by then X_2 will be close enough to force a slow lob pass to 03 in the lane that X_3 and X_4 will double-team. If 02 passes to 04 along the baseline, X_2 may help and recover for X_4 (or cover the corner himself) if he can cover the distance between 02 and 04 in time; however, since the distance is so great, X_4 probably will have to cover the corner, in which case 02 will move inside quickly to defend the low-post position with X_5.

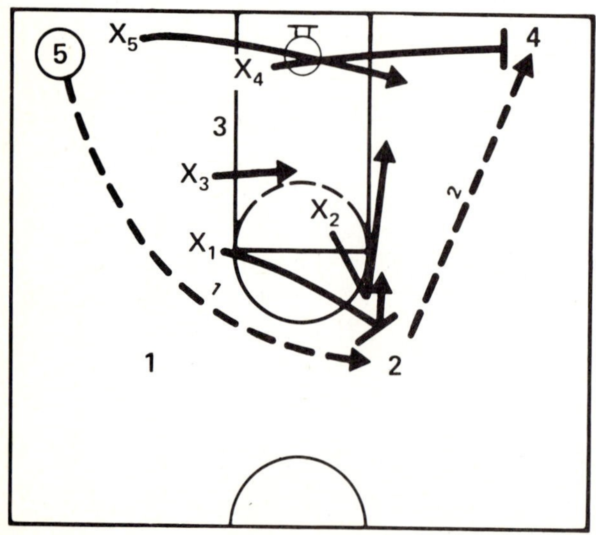

Figure 10–48 Help-and-Recover in Defending Against Diagonal Passes Out of the Corner

Before we leave the subject of help-and-recover techniques, we will answer a very basic question concerning its usage, and in answering the question provide some insight into the kinds of teams that can use help-and-recover techniques: *How do the players know whether to help and recover with any given pass?*

The answer is, of course, by looking around and being aware of what is going on elsewhere on the court. When a given pass is made, say, from guard to guard, wings X_2 and X_3 will know if X_1 is responsible for guarding the pass receiver and whether X_1 will be able to reach the receiver in time to prevent or hinder the shot. If X_1 is too far out of position to make the play, the wing will move out to cover the receiver, knowing at the same time that if the ball is reversed, he will drop back to his former position, and if the ball rotation continues beyond him, a teammate will help and recover until *he* reaches the ball.

The theory is basically simple, and it is surprisingly easy for players to understand for such an advanced form of defensive coverage: with every pass of the ball, if you're the nearest defensive player to the receiver, you assume coverage until the proper defender catches up. Then you drop back, either into your former coverage or to chase your man with a teammate helping and recovering until you get there. If, however, the defender responsible for guarding the pass receiver can move into position to deny the shot, his teammates will stay back in their regular coverage.

Players must move constantly in executing this defense. They should possess at least average quickness, and they should be fundamentally sound defensively. Also, they should be well drilled in the help-and-recover technique. One of the problems sometimes encountered in installing this defense is players' becoming so involved in the help-and-recover technique that they loosen their coverage of the high or low post, either of which can prove disastrous to any kind of zone coverage. Still, with proper instruction and drilling by the coach, players can learn the proper execution of the movements and skills associated with this type of coverage without too much difficulty, as long as the players are coachable, mobile, and at least moderately aggressive.

Thus we can see that, although help-and-recover defense shares with other types of zone coverage (except trapping) the fact that inside coverage is intense and the primary lanes are generally more or less open, it is unique in terms of its emphasis upon denying both inside and outside shots as well. While it is not the only kind of aggressive or advanced zone coverage, help-and-recover defense is the only "shutout" form of zone defense in use: other modes of zone defense may attempt to influence the ball toward certain areas of the court in order to more sharply delimit the opponents' shooting options, but in help-and-recover defense, the defensive goal is to deny *all* shooting options, on the ball side or the weak side.*

*Help-and-recover defense also may be used to influence the ball (or certain players) toward or away from certain areas of the court; however, the influencing should be considered a means to an end, not an end in itself.

CONCLUSION

Possibly the most important decision facing a coach beyond naming his starting lineup is his selection of the style of half-court defense his team will use. Such a decision should not be taken lightly, but should be made on the basis of a team's defensive capability.

Teams using matchup, trapping, or help-and-recover defense to control their opponents will never succeed when their coverage is lackadaisical or haphazard. The only way to use trapping effectively, for example, is to go after the opponents like sharks at mealtime and rely on superior defensive skills to avoid, or at least cover, mistakes. Thus, the meek and the peacemakers may be blessed,* but not with a great deal of success in the trapping defense. If your players aren't ready to go to war defensively, don't expect them to rip opponents apart with advanced defensive techniques. They won't do it.

Don't attack opponents unless the percentages swing in your favor by doing so. Basic zone defenses are designed to reduce unfavorable odds; advanced zone defenses are intended to increase odds already in your favor. The difference lies in reacting to the opponents' actions rather than initiating the actions yourself. Sometimes it's better to try to let them beat themselves.

*Matthew 5:5–9

11

Pressing Defenses

FULL-COURT MAN-TO-MAN PRESSING DEFENSE

I'm a firm believer in full-court pressing defense. I believe that full-court defense is, or should be, a vital part of any team's overall preparation. I know it is indispensable in our system of play. We have at least six important reasons for using the full-court pressing defense. Full-court presses:

(1) increase steals and forced turnovers;
(2) attack weak ball handling;
(3) fit into our philosophy of continuous pressure on the opponents offensively and defensively over forty minutes of play;
(4) hinder opponents from setting up offensively in their half-court attack, or from making the passes necessary to set their offensive patterns in motion;
(5) force opponents to start their patterns from farther out than they'd like; and
(6) slow down fast-breaking opponents.

We feel that the third point provides the most important reason for us to use the full-court pressure defense. Everything we do offensively or defensively is part of our planned strategy to keep continuous pressure on our opponents. Included in this scheme are all of our seemingly scatterbrained, helter-skelter movements: overplaying the passing lanes and sometimes giving up backdoor passes and layups as a result, fast-breaking after scores and going for the quick shot when other teams would bring the ball back outside and set up, and taking what some people consider to be low-percentage outside shots. We don't want our opponents to rest or relax for even a second—or, more specifically, for the ten seconds that it would take them to bring the ball down court and set up their offense if we *weren't* pressing them.

We run a man-to-man press, but we employ a lot of variations of it; we try to do anything we can to keep the opponents off guard. Usually we'll encounter offensive alignments that have three players in the backcourt and the other two positioned anywhere from midcourt to under the basket. (If they send three players down and keep only one man back to bring the ball down court, we'll double-team the receiver, and they won't be able to get the ball in at all.)

In guarding the inbounds passer in our pressing defense, the defender on the ball will guard the ball handler's passing arm—overplaying to his left, for example, if the passer is right-handed.

We like to mix up our coverage of the inbounds pass. Sometimes we'll go with straight pressure man-to-man, covering the inbounds passer as well as the cutters, and every now and then we'll leave the inbounds passer alone and use three players to guard the two cutters nearest the baseline (Figure 11–1), usually to force the ball to an inferior ball handler, or at least to keep it away from a superior one.

> **Note:** If no defender is guarding the inbounds passer, X_4 and X_5 will have to play closer than usual to their men until the ball is passed in. We'll overguard them toward certain areas of the court; for example, we'll front their primary receivers in their backcourt and dare them to throw the long, lead (lob) pass, or influence them toward one of the sidelines.

Another wrinkle in our coverage is to influence a receiver toward a given area, allow him to catch the ball, and then trap him. (See Figure 11–2.)

The success of our trapping in Figure 11–2 will depend to a great extent on three factors: X_3's hustling to make sure his man (03) doesn't break free to receive 02's inbounds pass, X_1's ability to influence 01's cut toward the ball-side corner, and X_2's ability to trap 01 before he can adjust to the trapping movement and dump the ball off to 02.

> **Note:** When we're trapping the inbounds pass receiver, X_2 will not attempt to deny the inbounds pass; instead, when the pass is made, he will pivot sharply and move into baseline trapping coverage as shown in Figure 11–2, trying to steal the ball or force a bad pass. X_2 will not be able to trap effectively if he is leaping and waving his arms around trying to deny the inbounds pass.

X_5 will be responsible for covering 01's return pass to 02 in the middle. (X_4 will cover 02's sideline cut.) X_5 must be ready to cut off the

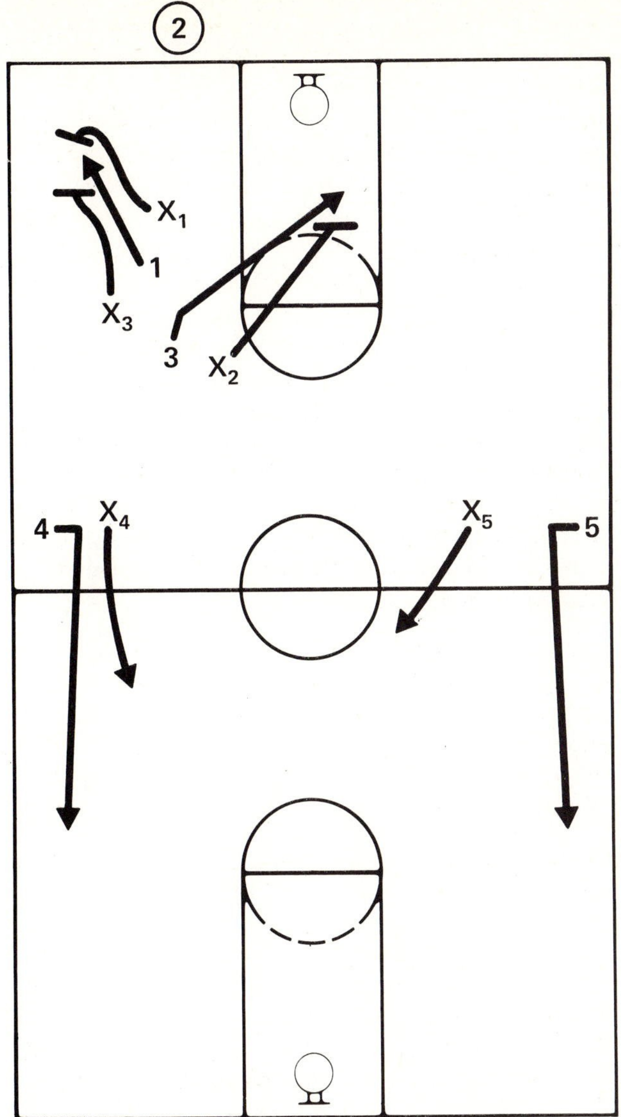

Figure 11–1 Full-Court Man-to-Man Pressure Defense, Covering the Inbounds Pass

passing lane as soon as the ball is inbounded, which means that he will be "cheating" forward even before the ball is passed inbounds in many cases.

> **Note:** Defensive rotation to the other side of the court once 01 successfully passes to 02 will consist of X_4 moving across to 05's side of the court and X_3 dropping back to cover 04's deep side.

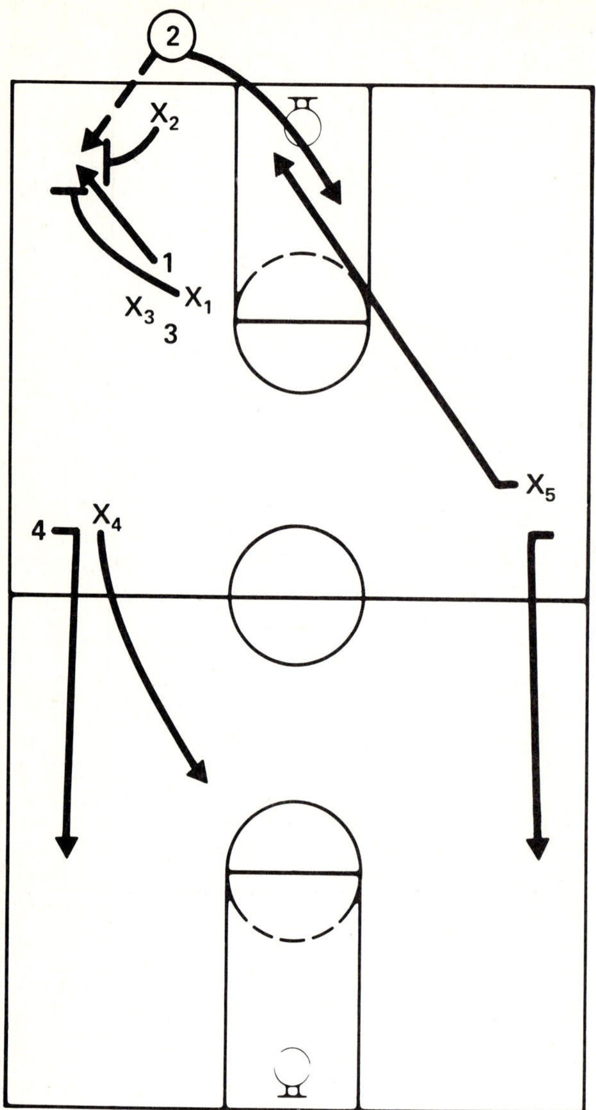

Figure 11–2 Trapping the Inbounds Pass Receiver

We try to mix up our coverage as much as possible. We'd like to keep our opponents confused and off balance, but even when we're unsuccessful, we still want to keep defensive pressure on them. We want to press them full-court every time, regardless of whom we're playing or what they are able to do against our press. We're going to keep the pressure on our opponents even if we make a mistake in our coverage and give up an occasional fast-break basket. Any team playing at the furious tempo that we're trying to force is going to make mistakes now and then, but we feel that in the long run the errors forced by our up-tempo full-court coverage will more than compensate for our own mistakes.

Once the inbounds pass is made successfully, we want the receiver to be covered immediately. We'll overguard all passing lanes until he dribbles. Our coverage may vary after he starts dribbling, but we want to make sure that he dribbles. We'd rather have him dribble before passing the ball.

One way our opponents try to combat our press is to clear 02 and

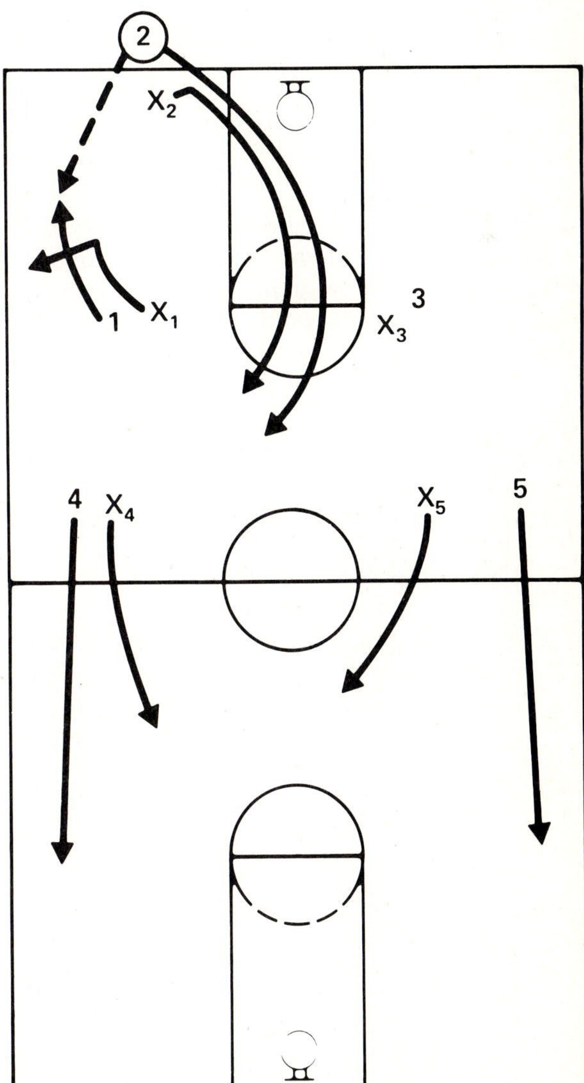

Figure 11–3 02 Clearing for One-on-One Against Full-Court Pressure Defense

spread the defense for one-on-one coverage (Figure 11–3). When this happens, we'll tell our players not to empty with the cutter every time as shown in the figure; instead, we tell them to double-team the pass receiver. Ball handlers are so good nowadays that you just aren't going to pick them apart in one-on-one press coverage. So we'll trap about every fourth inbounds pass, and the rest of the time we'll fake-step toward the receiver and retreat a bit, then bluff again and retreat, and every now and then we won't fake at all but will move quickly to trap the dribbler, hoping that he's not expecting it. Good bluffs will slow up a good dribbler.

When players are not double-teaming as their men clear away from the ball handler, we want them to maintain a one-third distance between their men and the ball, pointing one hand at the ball and the other at their men. We always want players away from the ball to point the ball and their man in our presses. Players should be drilled in this technique; anything that players don't do naturally, you'll have to drill them in.

Because we take so many chances in our press coverage, we sometimes get burned by good ball handlers or a series of quick passes. When this happens, it is extremely important to get your players to retreat as quickly as possible. You *don't* want them to give up and trot back down court watching the opponents fast break ahead of them. Our philosophy is that when the opponents beat our traps and get by us, they still are going to have to make two or three passes before they get to the basket. If we really work hard in getting back on defense, we have a reasonable chance of not only stopping the fast break but also deflecting or intercepting the pass. We don't do as good a job of getting back as we should–I don't think anybody ever does–but we drill our kids constantly in this phase of the game. We tell them, "If you're willing to trap the ball handler, steal the ball, and score an easy two points in our press, you're also going to have to be willing to high-tail it back on defense to stop them when they get past you!" You can't have one without the other. It's asking a lot to expect them to put out that kind of total effort, but if you have good kids and you've done a good job of selling them on the merits of hard-nosed defense, they'll usually work hard for you in this phase of the game.

We use a drill which I think is excellent for training kids to get back quickly on defense (Figure 11–4).

The defensive player starts one step away from the inbounds passer at one end of the court. An offensive second player stands along the backcourt free-throw line extended, a third player is at half-court, and a fourth player is waiting under the basket. A coach is at the free-throw line extended, ready to make the final pass.

When the first pass is made, the defensive player will turn and retreat down court at full speed, hoping to intercept the final pass. Meanwhile, the offensive players will be relaying the ball along the sideline. When the coach catches the ball, he may either pass under immediately or hold the ball or pretend to fumble the pass to give the defender extra time

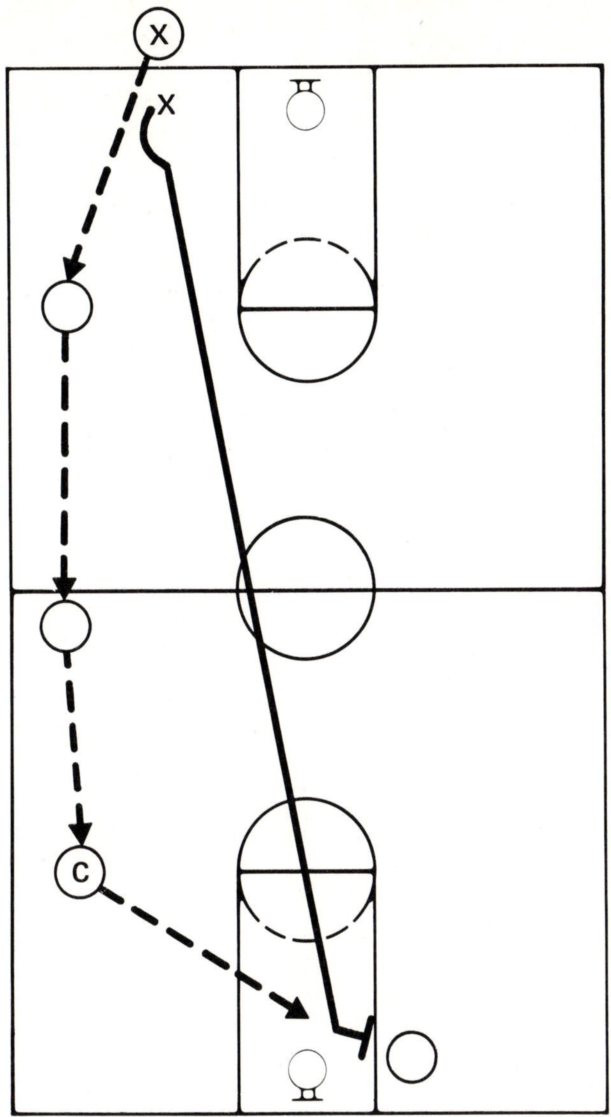

Figure 11–4 Recovery Drill

to get back, if necessary. Players should believe that if they go as hard as they can they'll be able to stop that last pass. They may *not* be able to, but they certainly *won't* be able to if they don't go all-out.

Finally, getting players used to converting from offense to defense after scores must be drilled into players through long hours of intensive practice. If the press is to be successful, the players' reaction must be instantaneous. A delay or hesitation of two seconds means that the opponents can take the ball out of bounds, pass to a cutter, and have the receiver turn to face the defense (and look for teammates to pass to). Pressing teams should devote part of their practice time not only to playing defense but also to *getting ready to play defense* as well.

In order to play good man-to-man pressing defense, it is imperative that players learn how to control the dribbler. We use the "Z-Drill" to teach players how to pick up their men in the press, influence them one way or another, and generally battle them all the way down court (Figure 11–5).

We put our guards and small forwards, paired up, on one side of the

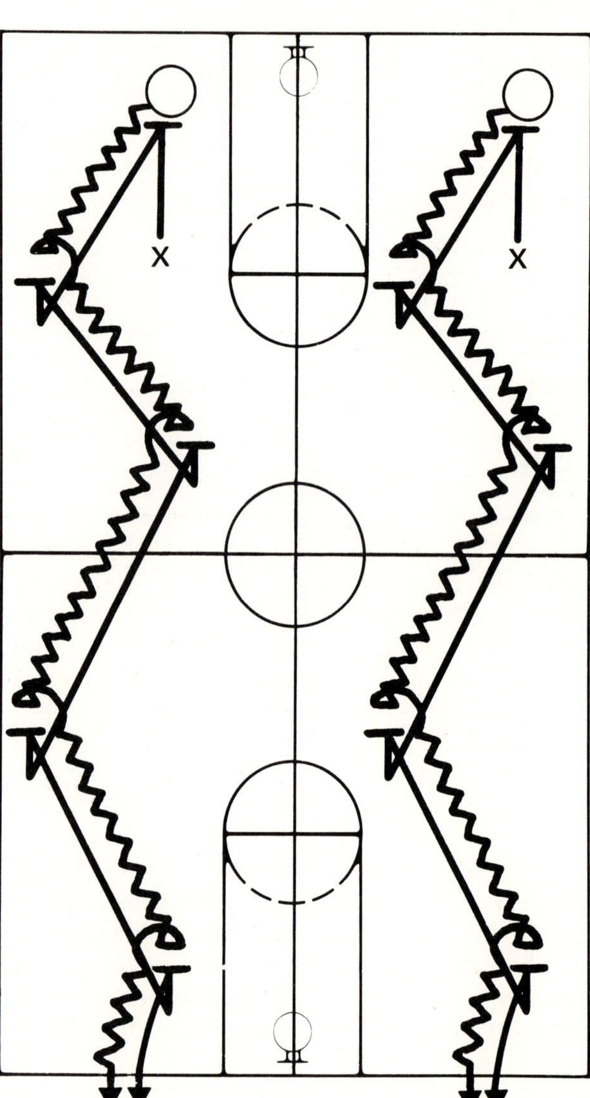

Figure 11–5 Z-Drill Used to Teach Pressure Defensive Control

court, with the big forwards and centers on the other side of the court. We put them nose to nose and make them battle all the way down court. (We use a split court to keep the players from standing around.) The only stipulation we put on the offensive player in early preseason practice is that he cannot change directions until the defensive man stops him and makes him reverse pivot. Later, we'll remove even this restriction.

We want the defensive player to move in close to his man in a good defensive stance, with his feet spread almost as wide as he can get them, his knees bent, his buttocks low, his back straight, and his head and shoulders up. We want him to keep his feet wide apart and near the floor when he's moving. We tell our players that we want them to keep their feet *on the floor* when they're moving. They won't be able to do it, of course, but we're working toward a close approximation. We don't want them taking big steps.

Whichever way the dribbler goes, we want the defensive man to pivot sharply, stay close to the dribbler, and outrun him until he reaches a point where he can turn around and face him, keeping his hands low to deny the crossover dribble, and force him to pivot away and dribble in the other direction. Then the defender repeats the process the other way. It's an extremely difficult skill to master, but we feel that it's vital to our press for our kids to master this technique.

We use the Z-Drill to teach our kids to draw a charging foul. We'll tell the offensive player not to stop when his man cuts him off; then we'll let them go. The defensive man will take a charge in the backcourt, bounce up and recover, catch his man, cut him off, and take another charge. We also use the Z-Drill to teach our players to steer the ball handler into a trap (Figure 11–6). Defenders X_2 and X_4 are not allowed to trap the dribblers unless X_1 and X_3 force them to reverse pivot into the trap in the area of the court shown. If the preliminary turning movement does not occur just beyond the half-court line, X_2 and X_4 will not trap the dribbler. Variations of coverage such as this emphasize the team aspects of individual coverage in ways the players will understand easily.

When the dribbler reaches a given point on the court (his own free-throw line extended, for example), we'll have him pick up the ball, and the defender will move into a close guarding position, moving his hands at the level of the ball and trying to keep the ball handler from making a pass for five seconds.

Our second full-court pressing drill is called "Stop The Dribbler." If it is possible, this drill is even more demanding than the Z-Drill. No matter how hard players try, situations are going to arise constantly in games in which their man receives a pass in the backcourt before they're in a position to cover him closely. We don't want a moving dribbler blowing by our stationary or advancing defender, but the art of stopping the dribbler is not easily acquired. So we'll divide the court again, giving the dribbler a head start on the dribble (Figure 11–7). The defensive man must get

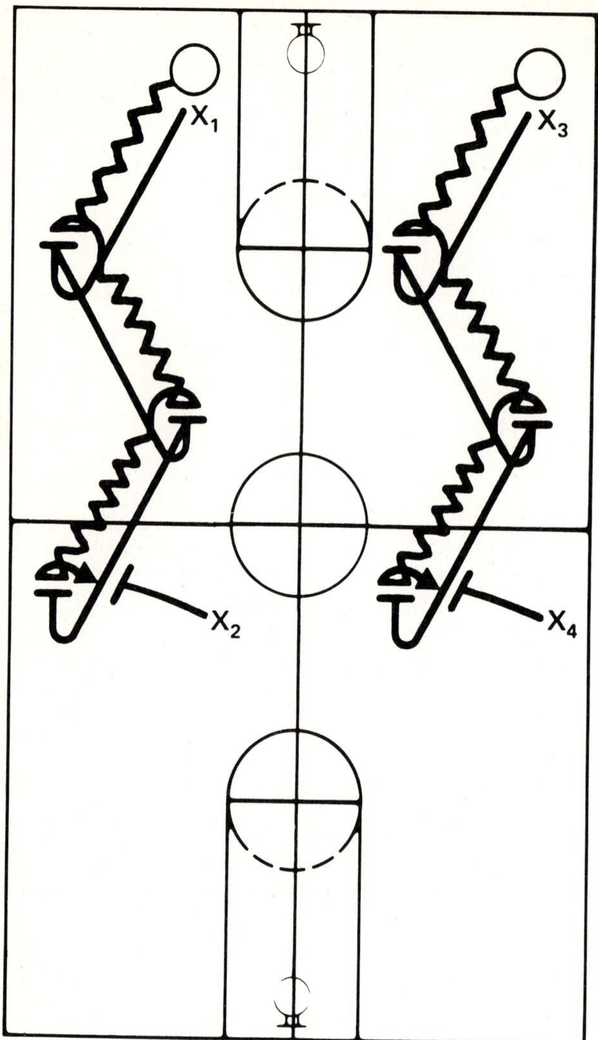

Figure 11–6 Z-Drill Used as a Trapping Drill

into rhythm with the dribbler, faking, bluffing, retreating, and trying to draw the charges, until he picks up his man and stays with him the rest of the way down court. We drill our players constantly throughout every season in stopping the dribbler.

Actually, our primary interest isn't to *stop* the dribbler; we're satisfied if the defensive player can *slow down* the dribbler's progress and gain a measure of defensive control over him. It's not an easy thing to do, especially when the dribbler is going full-speed. When he played for us at UNLV, Reggie Theus was uncanny in his ability to stop the dribbler. He went after charging fouls like a vampire in a blood bank. He'd bluff,

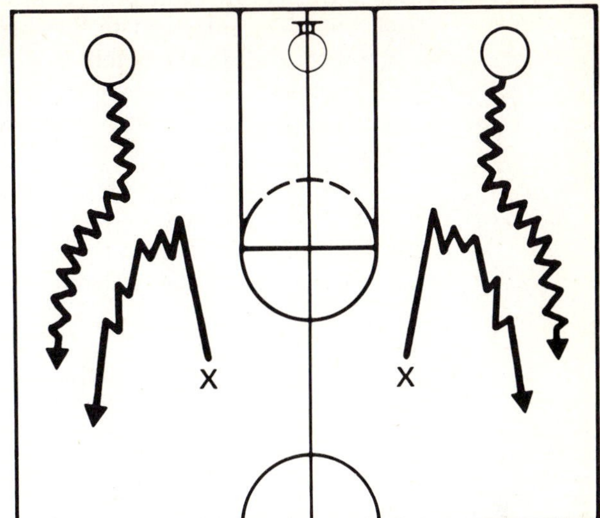

Figure 11–7 "Stop the Dribbler" Drill

retreat, bluff, and then suddenly leap toward an overguarded stance, forcing the ball handler to spin away. By the time the dribbler had completed his spin-dribble and started down court again, Reggie would be there in his path, having faked the steal in order to draw a charging foul.

In the early stages of practicing this drill, the dribbler will get by the defensive player consistently, but as the players get used to the bluff-and-retreat, they learn how to maneuver themselves into position to draw

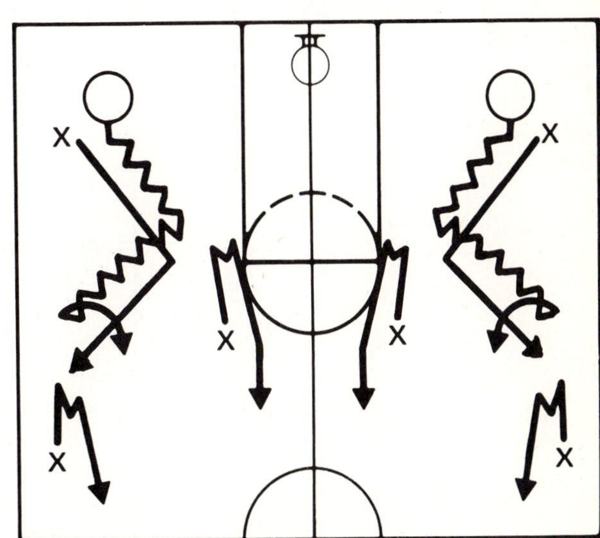

Figure 11–8 "Bluff" Drill

the charging foul. Our players get beat a lot in their initial press coverage, but we want them to be able to come back and recover defensive control to contain the dribbler.

Another pressing drill we use involves *teammates'* bluffing at, rather than double-teaming with, the man guarding the ball handler (Figure 11–8).

The ball handler and his defender start at the baseline. Two defensive players wait beyond the top of the circle. They don't guard anyone yet, but they are down in their defensive stance, turned to watch the ball and their man. As the offensive player and his man move down court in a

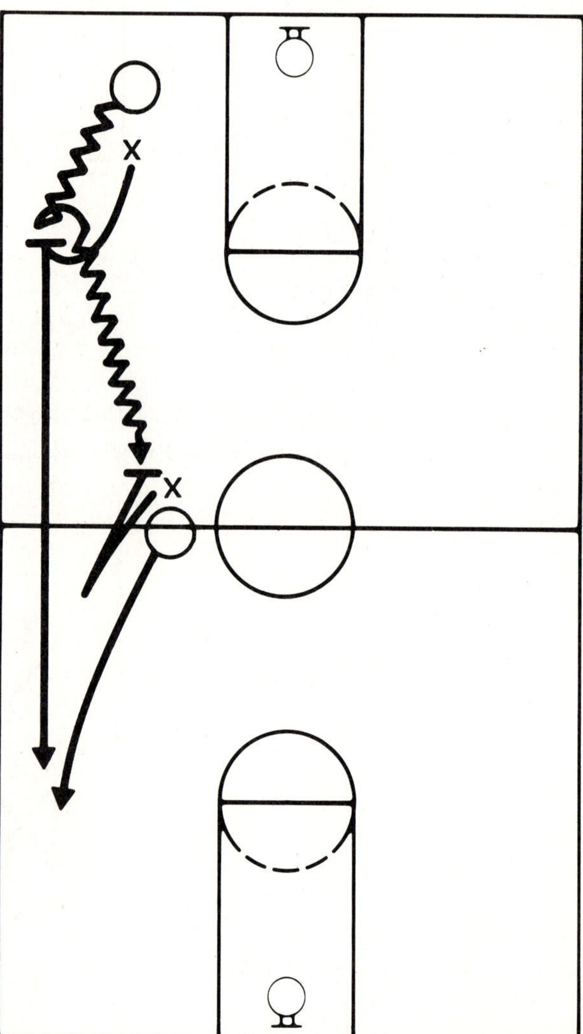

Figure 11–9 Switching to Stop the Dribbler—The "Jump" Drill

manner similar to that of the Z-Drill, the first defender at the top of the circle will bluff at the ball and retreat until the man on the ball turns the dribbler. Then the other dribbler will bluff and retreat until the man on the ball turns the dribbler again. It will definitely help the defense if players off the ball will bluff toward the dribbler every now and then.

To go along with this bluffing technique we run a switching drill for those occasions when the ball handler gets away from his man. We run it from the same side-by-side, split-court setup as the previous drills (Figure 11–9).

A ball handler and a defender start the drill at the baseline (Figure 11–9). A second offensive player and defender are between the top of the circle and the half-court line. The dribbler's task is, as he is advancing down court against his man, to spin and beat him the other way. The second defensive player will then come back and pick up the dribbler as the first defender hustles back to complete the switch and foil the pass to the open man. The second defender must contain the ball and stop the dribbler from getting by him.

The toughest drill we have is a full-court three-on-three drill in which we station two coaches along either sideline at the top of the circle beyond midcourt (Figure 11–10). When the ball crosses the half-court line, the offensive players must pass the ball, first to one coach and then to the other, before they're allowed to shoot. When the dribbler picks up the ball, the defender will move into a close-guarding position in his face, with his hands at the level of the ball. Then, when the pass is made, he will overplay his man to deny the return pass until the offensive player empties out of the area. The coach will eventually pass to one of the players, of course, but we want each defensive player to do all he can to deny the pass to the man he's guarding. When an offensive player receives the coach's pass, he and his teammates will work the ball to the other side of the court to pass to the other coach. We don't want to make it easy for him, though; if he becomes preoccupied with his crosscourt movement and pass to the other coach, one of the other two defenders will slip behind him and steal the ball. (I've seen teams lose games because their dribbler forgot about the other defenders in concentrating on getting where he was going.)

The movement down court and subsequent passes to the coaches and back generally take about forty-five seconds, which helps to prepare our kids to play hard-nosed defense for prolonged periods in games, and not just for the few seconds at a time when their man has the ball. A pro basketball player wrote a book a few years ago in which he said that he could steal the ball a lot more than he did, but he liked to lay back on defense and pick his spots, stealing the ball only when it was most advantageous to his team psychologically for him to do so. Well, maybe that's okay in the pros, but it would never work for me. I don't like to let the players make those kinds of decisions. The only decision I want them to

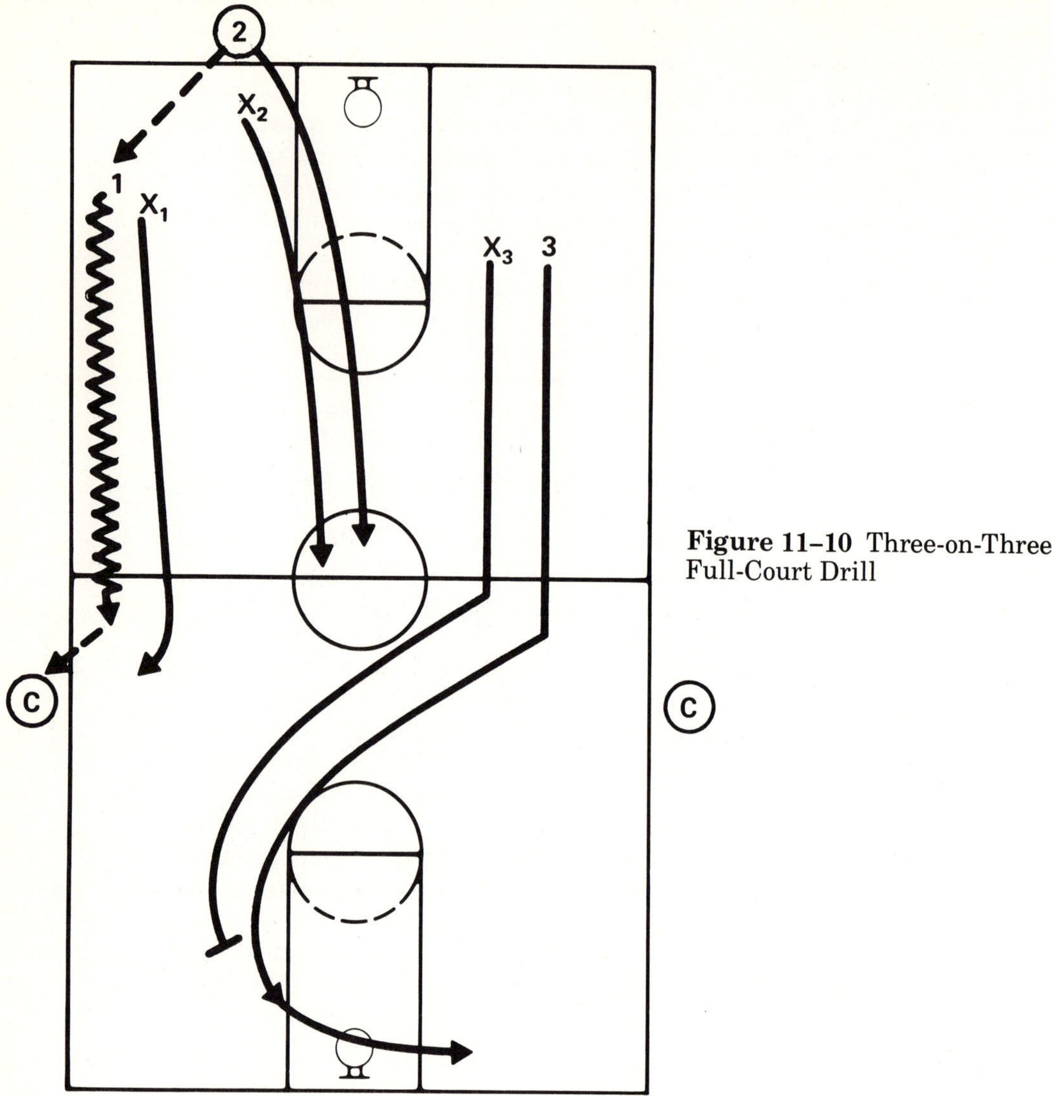

Figure 11–10 Three-on-Three Full-Court Drill

make is whether to pass or shoot the layup in the fast break following the steal. However, if you see one of our kids laying back on defense, you can believe that it *isn't* part of our planned defensive strategy, and the player in question is headed for some less enervating *pine time* (that is, riding the bench).

After both coaches have passed the ball back inbounds, the six players will go three-on-three until a shot is taken. Then we'll start over, or switch offensive and defensive teams and start over at that end of the court, pressing full-court as before.

RUN-AND-JUMP DEFENSE

Run-and-jump defense is a whole new ball game. Whereas other pressing techniques are used to contain the ball, to stop the ball handler's advance down court, to steal the ball, or to trap the dribbler, run-and-jump coverage may be used for entirely different purposes. Among the most often cited objectives of run-and-jump pressing coverage are: to provide a different look in the pressing defense to confuse the ball handler(s) and keep him unsure of the defense's intentions; to draw charging fouls; and to force turnovers by influencing, or steering, the ball handler toward

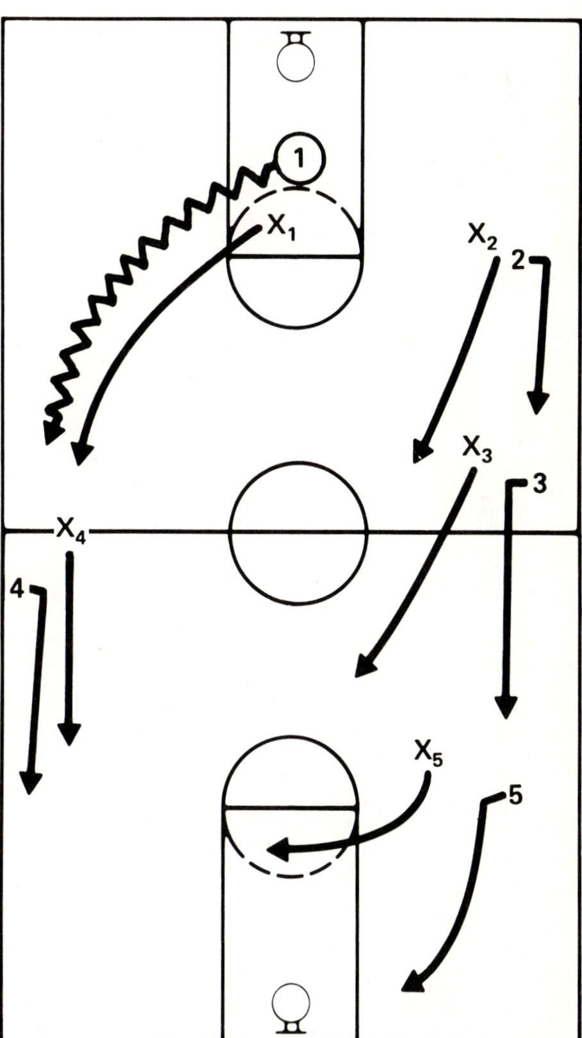

Figure 11–11 Setting Up the Run-and-Jump

predetermined areas of the court where the run-and-jump movement will occur. The run-and-jump pressing defense sometimes will cause ten-second backcourt violations and errant passes, but many coaches feel the main benefit of using it is that the ball handler faces the constant threat of committing charging fouls. When advancing the ball down court against teams that are prone to using run-and-jump coverage, players are advised to use controlled dribbling, as opposed to dribbling full-speed.

The run-and-jump defense contains elements of both trapping and switching man-to-man defense. Generally—but not necessarily—the run-and-jump movement will occur somewhere near the half-court line

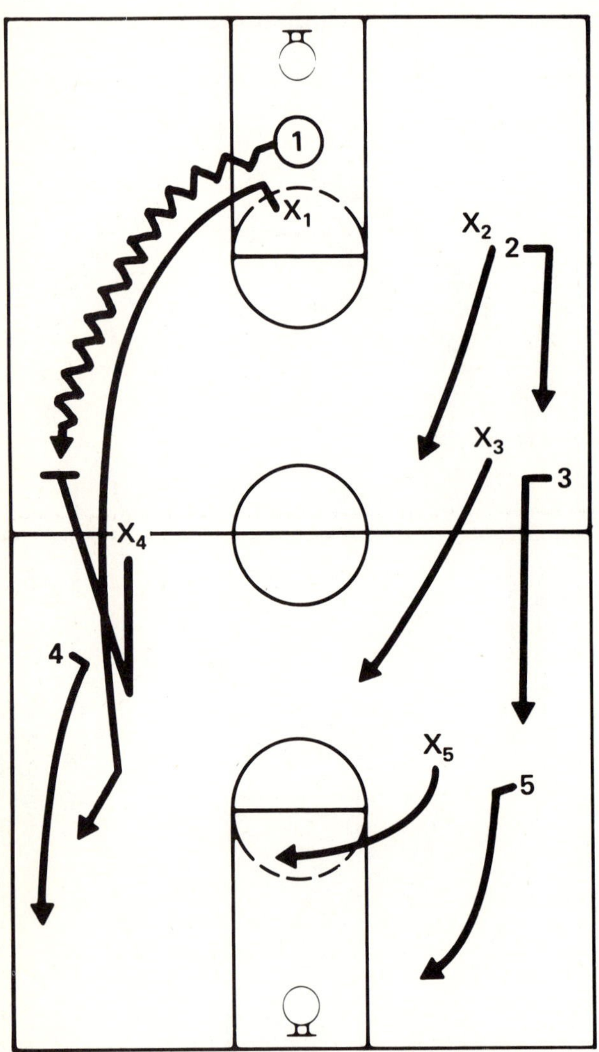

Figure 11–12 X_1 and X_4 Run and Jump

after the man guarding the ball handler has steered him toward one corner or the other (Figure 11–11).

The movements shown in Figure 11–11 are typical of those in other pressing offenses and defenses. With the rest of the defense in obvious one-on-one coverage, 01 dribbles down the open side of the court as 04 empties down court. The run-and-jump movement can be effected most easily in this situation by using X_4, X_5, or X_3 to stop the ball handler's advance (X_4 in Figure 11–12).

As 01 begins dribbling to his right, X_1 guards him closely but does not attempt to turn him or stop his progress. (In fact, X_1 may be more

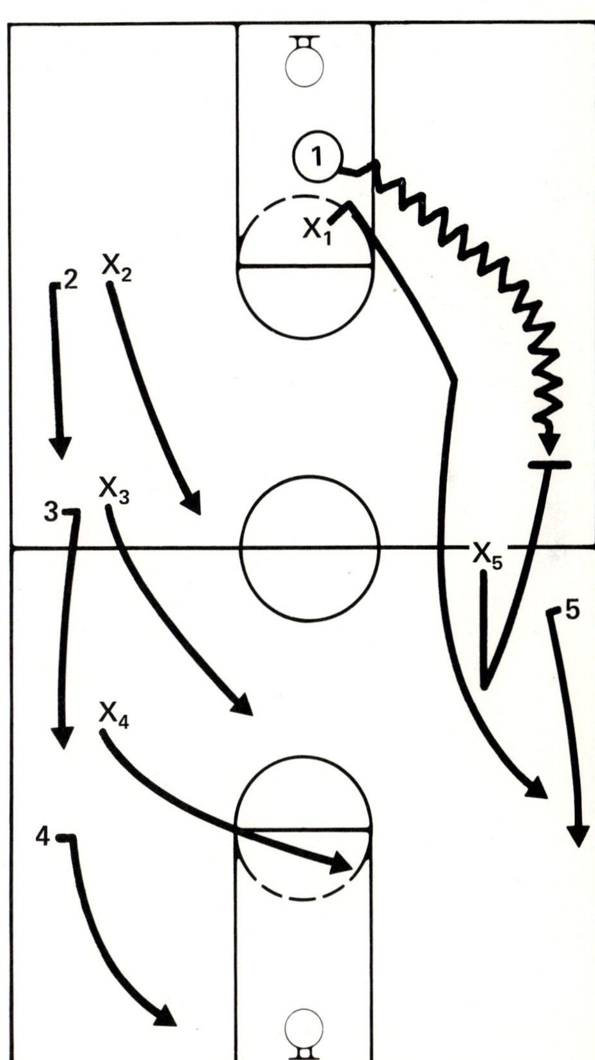

Figure 11–13 Run-and-Jump to the Other Side of the Court

interested in denying the reversal than in stopping the dribbler.) At the same time, X_4 is retreating with 04 down court, but at a given point X_4 will stop and move up quickly toward 01, who, if X_1's coverage is aggressive, may be preoccupied with X_1 and fail to see X_4's advance (Figure 11–12).

When 01 finally sees X_4 in his path, he may not be able to stop in time to avoid a charging foul. Even if he does stop, however, his natural tendency will be to pick up his dribble, reverse pivot away from X_4, and pass the ball away; after all, for all 01 knows, he is being double-teamed by X_4 and X_1.

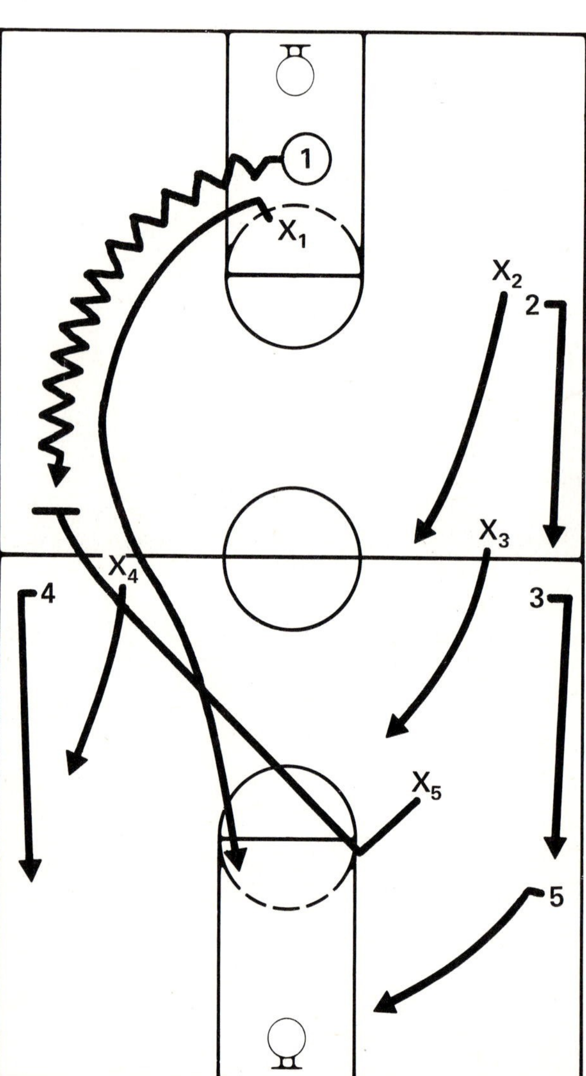

Figure 11–14 X_1 and X_5 Run and Jump

Instead of double-teaming, however, X_1 will continue down court to pick up 04 (X_4's man), and the rest of the defense will attempt to steal any passes to 01's teammates when 01 picks up his dribble.

When the run-and-jump occurs on the other side of the court, X_5 usually will be the player effecting the switch with 01 (Figure 11–13).

The run-and-jump can also be effected by having X_5 or X_3 perform the switch (Figures 11–14 and 11–15).

X_5's movement to the run-and-jump in Figure 11–14 is angled better than X_3's in Figure 11–15; however, the advantage may be offset by the added difficulty 01 will have in finding the open man before the switch is

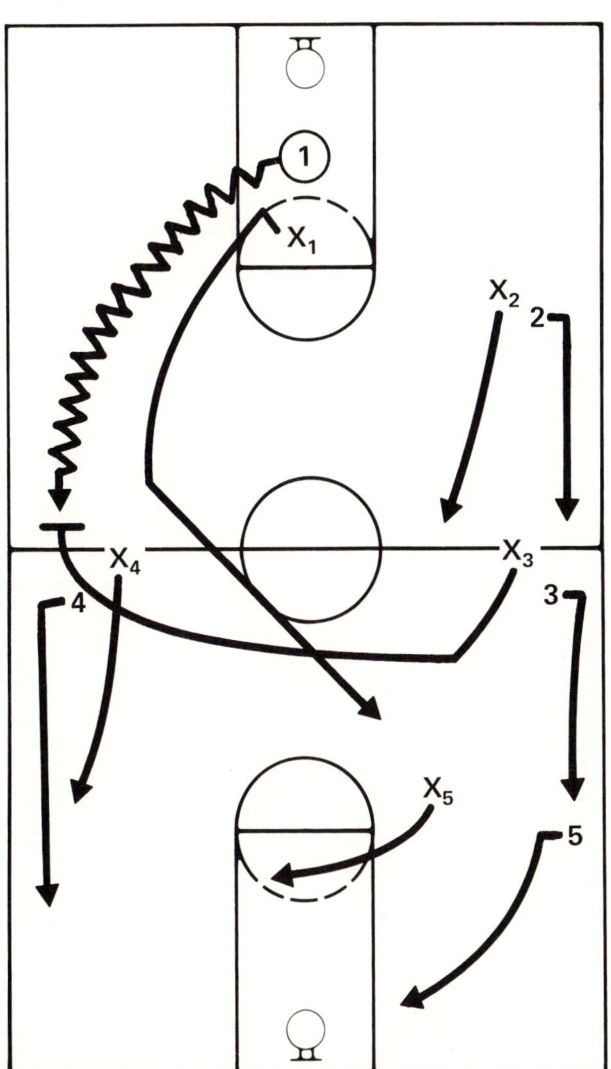

Figure 11–15 X_1 and X_3 Run and Jump

completed. (For the same reason, the run-and-jump with X_5 or X_3 may be superior to that with X_4, as shown in Figure 11–12.)

The difficulty usually encountered in using X_2 in the run-and-jump is that the other guard usually stays back as a safety valve in case the ball handler encounters such difficulties as those presented in the run-and-jump defense. Knowing this, the ball handler may be able to dump the ball off to safety valve 02 before another defender can reach that passing lane.

On the other hand, we always trap with our two guards in our full-court press. Even if we fail to contain the ball, the opponents will be in poor position to fast break against us.

Instead of designating a player in a given position (for example, the ball-side defender one pass away from the ball, X_4 in Figure 11–12, or the deep weak-side defender, X_5 in Figure 11–12) as the player effecting the run-and-jump, some teams prefer to use an extremely quick superior defensive player, regardless of his court position away from the ball. A team does not run and jump every time in its pressing defense, but a superior defender can be told, "Whenever you think you can get away with it, try to cut off the dribbler and draw a charging foul." While it is not always effective, this method works as well as any in ensuring that the best men are involved in the run-and-jump.

TRAPPING DEFENSE

Although it is always played aggressively, full-court or half-court zone trapping does not involve quite as much risk to the defense as when it is used as part of a team's zone defensive coverage at the other end of the court. In zone pressing, the opponents still have to move the ball a long way to enter high-percentage scoring areas after beating the initial double-team. Trapping as used in zone presses involves attempts to set up situations in which a single ball handler is double-teamed, preferably with no chance to dribble out of, or pass the ball away from, the trap. Although we trap the ball handler occasionally, maybe once in every four times, it should be understood that *trapping always involves zone defensive principles.* When we trap from our pressure man-to-man defense, we cover the return pass to the inbounds passer and other primary passing lanes by rotating our players like any trapping zone defense. We don't advertise that we're using zone coverage or principles, but it's practically impossible to trap from man-to-man coverage and cut off the passing lanes without resorting to zone coverage. The fakes, bluffs, and the like, that we use to keep the ball handler guessing about our intentions occur while we're in man-to-man coverage; however, when the trap is sprung, the only way to cut off the passing lanes is to revert to zone coverage.

Techniques for double-teaming players other than the inbounds passer before the ball is put in play are varied. Some coaches put their two best defensive players on the opponents' best ball handler, with the other defenders playing man-to-man; other coaches put their best defensive player on the opponents' second best ball handler, with two relatively weak defenders, or one weak and one strong defensive player, guarding the best offensive man. It's a matter of personal preference. It's helpful to know your personnel and find out what works best for them, of course, but in most cases the defenders will either make a concerted effort to deny the

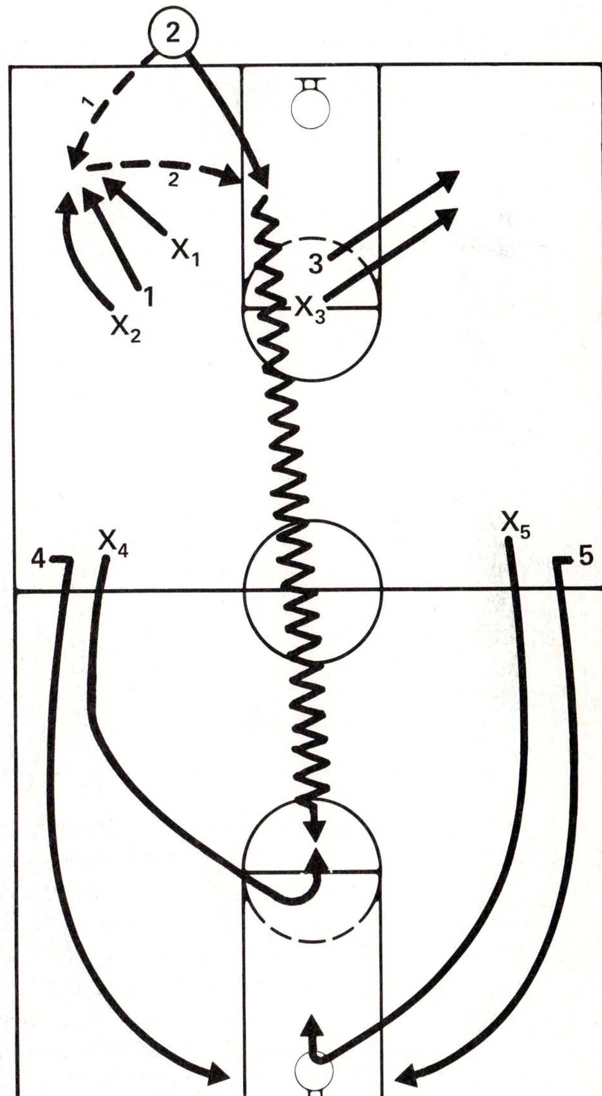

Figure 11–16 Fast Breaking Off Pass-and-Cut with Unguarded Inbounds Passer

inbounds pass to *any* offensive player, hoping to force the offense into a five-second violation, or they will double-team the best ball handler to keep the ball away from him and steer the secondary ball handler toward a certain area of the court.

The greatest problem of double-teaming before the inbounds pass is made is the danger of a successful pass and subsequent return pass to the inbounds passer cutting down court before the defense can recover (Figure 11–16).

If 02 successfully makes the inbounds pass to 01 or 03, the defense

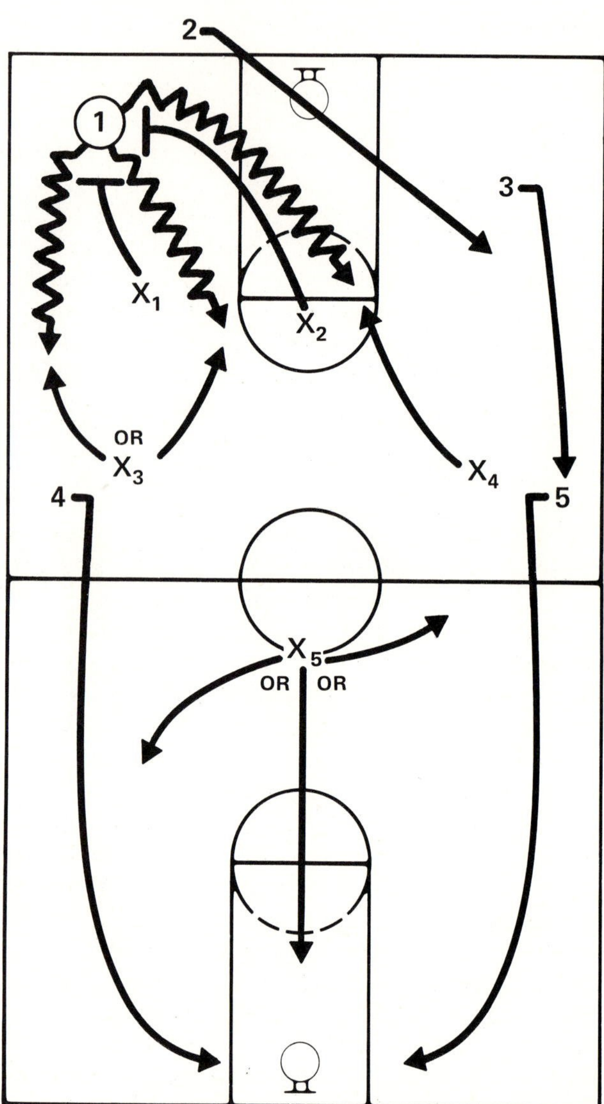

Figure 11–17 Dribbling Routes Through and Around the Double-Team

may not be able to adjust its coverage in time to stop the return pass to 02 cutting down court. The answer to this problem is that most teams don't double-team this way every time. Most of the time they'll be in their regular coverage, but every now and then they'll try the double-team to see if they can force a quick turnover.

The same difficulty is encountered in trapping *after* the inbounds pass is made but *before* the receiver has begun his dribble. Additionally, trapping as soon as the receiver catches the ball may result in his dribbling around, or through, the trap (Figure 11–17).

If the movements of defenders X_1 and X_2 to trap 01 are not synchronized properly, 01 may be able to dribble past the double-team and start a fast break. It will be difficult for X_1 and X_2 to maintain the kind of defensive stance necessary to stop 01's dribble and still deny the passes to 02, 03, or 04 if 01 decides to pass the ball away instead of dribbling. Trapping before the inbounds pass receiver's dribble can be effective, but the risks are considerable.

In order to give their teammates an idea of how the offense plans to attack the press, and to increase their own chances of stopping the dribbler, some teams will wait until the ball handler starts dribbling before they apply defensive pressure. However, this kind of coverage requires an excellent defender to control the inbounds pass receiver, and it also gives the offensive team time to set up its attack and direct it toward whichever defensive player or area of the court it chooses.

Combination (Delay) Trapping

Possibly the most effective form of trapping from full-court zone pressing defense is *combination*, or *delay*, trapping. Combination presses contain elements of both man-to-man and zone defense: in the initial stages before trapping occurs, the defense is in man-to-man coverage, although the matchups may arise from a zone alignment; however, when the trap is sprung, the action to cut off the passing lanes is unquestionably zone coverage (Figure 11–18).

Figure 11–18 depicts a familiar variety of delay trapping—that of using the guards to trap the dribbler as the forwards and center cut off the passing lanes. The first step in delay trapping is to set the matchups. A familiar style is to have X_1 (or X_2 if the ball is passed to his side of the court) cover the inbounds pass receiver, with the other defensive guard moving up to cover the inbounds passer if he cuts to the middle. (X_3 will cover the passer if he cuts along the sideline.) X_4 will cover 05 *until 03 dribbles,* and X_3 will hang back slightly, as if covering 04 beyond the half-court line. The key to this part of the press is X_1's closing in quickly on 01, turning him, and forcing him to dribble the ball. If 01 is able to pass the ball away, the press probably will not succeed.

At this point the perceptive reader will find several gaps in the

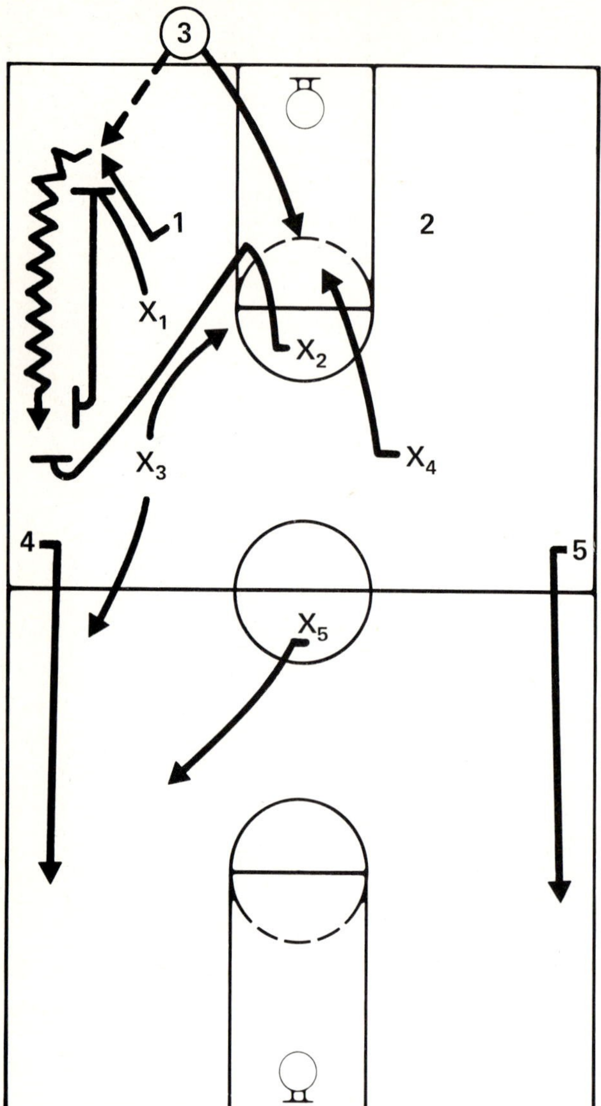

Figure 11–18 Delay Trapping with Guards X_1 and X_2

coverage—for example, X_3 having no one to guard while X_2 is responsible for both 02 and 03—but these problems will seem far less threatening to the defense if X_1 is able to turn 01, deny the pass, and force him to dribble. If this happens, X_4 will move up to cover 02, X_3 (who dropped back to cover 04 originally) will move up to guard 03, and X_5 will deny the deep pass to 04. (See Figure 11–19.)

At this point, 01 will either dribble, probably to the sideline, or pass crosscourt to 02. (A good ball-handling team will beat the press with the

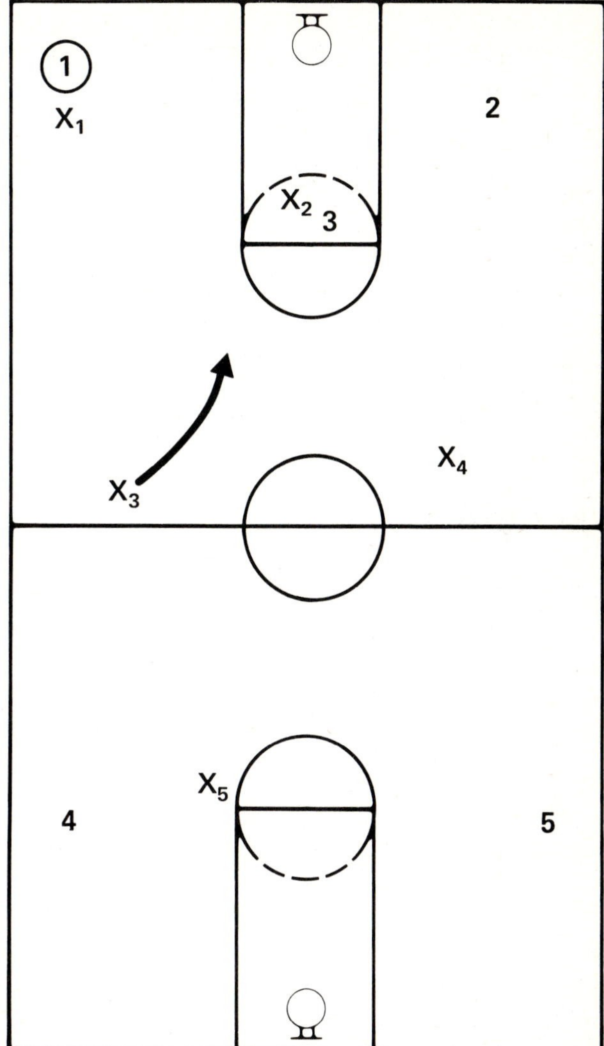

Figure 11–19 Delay Trapping, First Phase Completed

pass to 02 and the subsequent pass down court to 05, since X_5 is cheating toward 04.) If X_1 dribbles, X_2 will leave his man and hustle back to stop 01 along the sideline, X_4 will move up to cover 02, X_3 will move up to cover 03, and X_1 will trap the dribbler when X_2 stops and turns him. Deep defender X_5 will be responsible for both 04 and 05, but he will play toward 04, the more likely receiver.

When 01 passes crosscourt to 02, X_4 will be caught out of position (Figure 11–20). There are three different tactics a team can use: (a) drop X_4 back to cover 05 as shown, which simplifies the matchups but makes things extremely difficult for X_4; (b) keep X_4 where he is, but rotate X_5

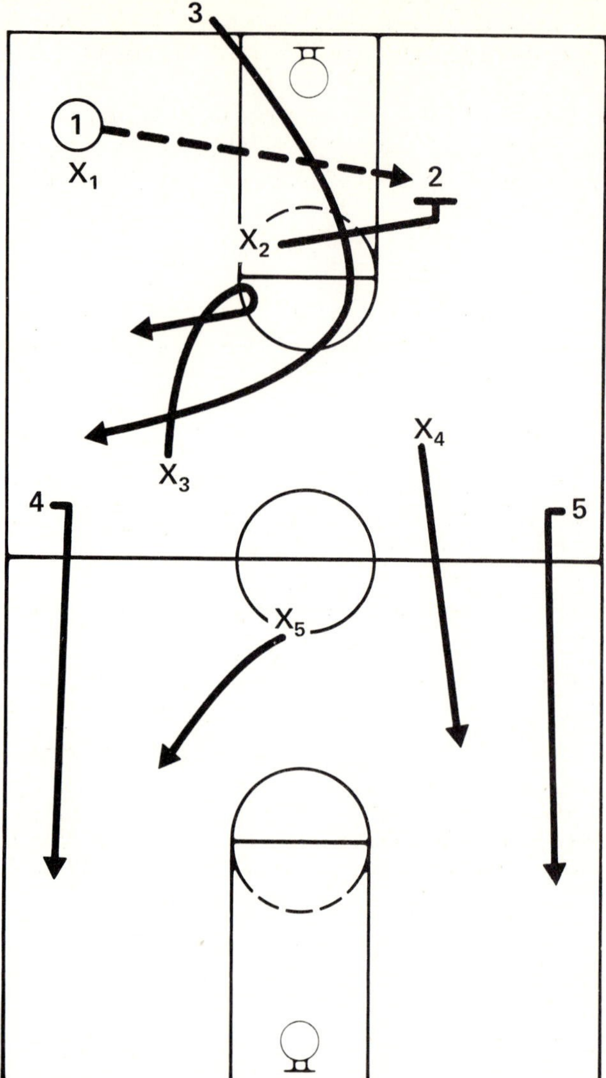

Figure 11–20 Maintaining the Matchups with Crosscourt Pass

over to cover 05 and X_3 back to cover 04, and drop X_1 back to cover 03's cut if it isn't toward X_4's half-court corner (X_1 can always move back to cover 01 again if 02 returns the ball to 01); or (c) move X_4 up to cover 02, and rotate X_1, X_3, and X_5 as before. (The third tactic may not be as desirable an alternative as it seems, since X_4's moving forward will slow down the coverage, and it may also prove more difficult to defend against 02's dribble.)

As with run-and-jump defense, *any* two defensive players may do the trapping. Generally, a guard will play X_1's position, but even that isn't mandatory. Regardless of who mans the positions, though, the players will cover them the same way, cutting off the passing lanes and forcing the ball handler to dribble toward and along the sideline where the trap will occur.

As may be seen by comparing Figures 11–18 and 11–26 with Figures 11–21 and 11–22, the trapping movements, positions, and areas to be covered are practically identical regardless of the zone alignment being

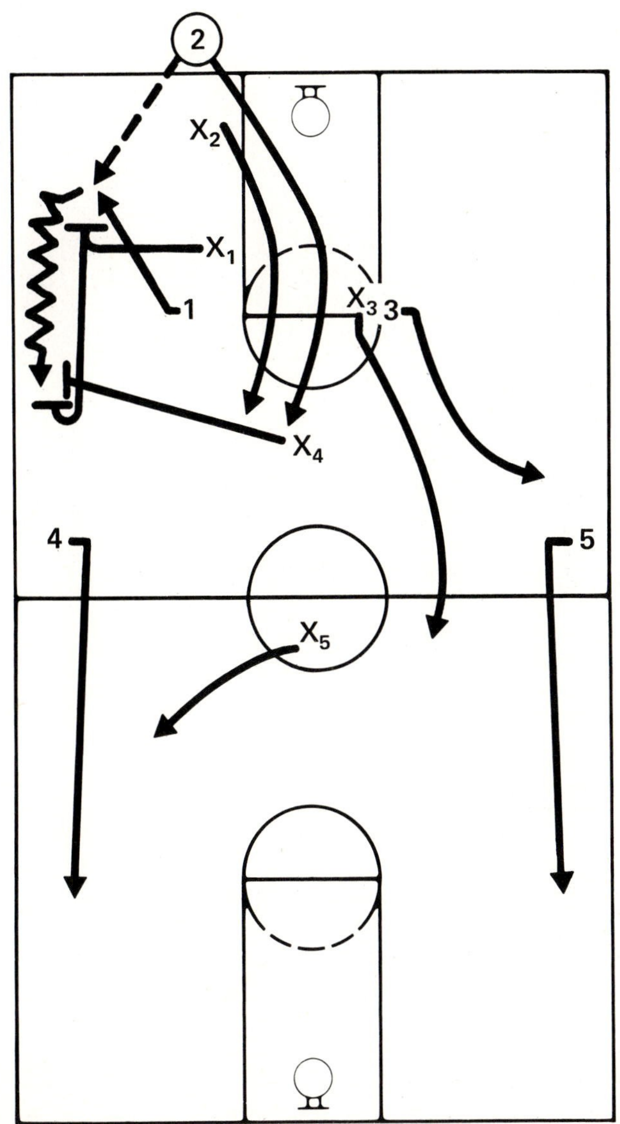

Figure 11–21 Trapping Variations with X_1 and X_4, Rather Than X_1 and X_2: *Example #1*

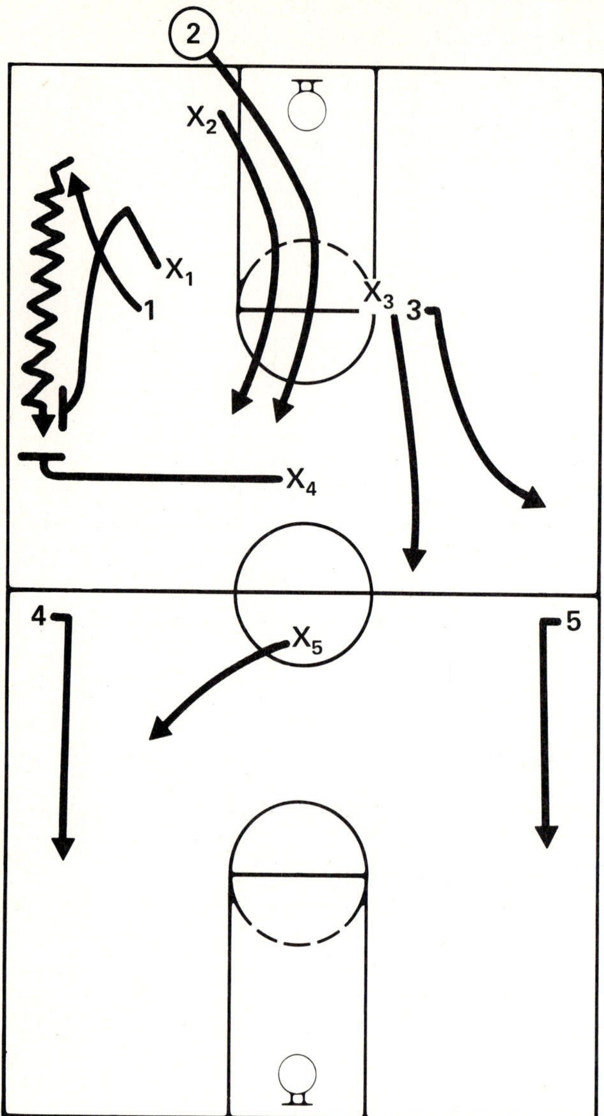

Figure 11–22 Trapping Variations with X_1 and X_4, Rather Than X_1 and X_2: *Example #2*

used. The only major difference is the choice of personnel to do the turning and/or trapping.

Most teams prefer to steer the ball toward, and then trap along, the sideline rather than the middle of the court because the effective passing angles are reduced by half at the sideline (Figures 11–23 and 11–24). It can be argued that the ball handler's passing angles increase to beyond 180° when the trapping occurs near the half-court corners, but the *effective* passing angle remains largely unaffected. A ball handler being trapped in

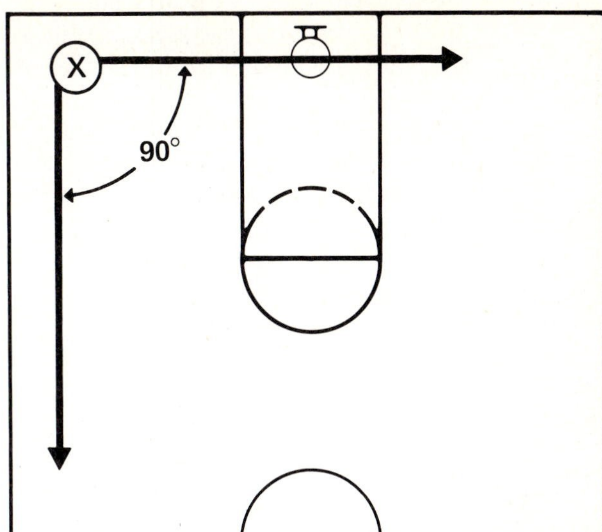

Figure 11–23 Passing Angles, Corner Trapping

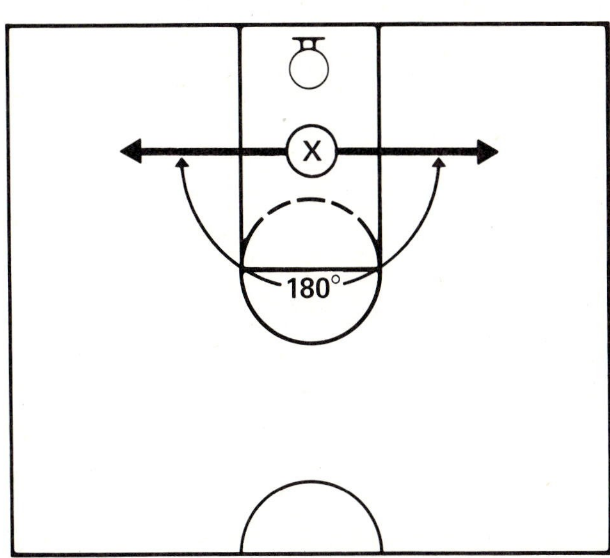

Figure 11–24 Passing Angles, Middle Trapping

his half-court corner could pass the ball to a teammate behind him, say, at his free-throw line, but two factors will negate most of the effectiveness of this theoretical advantage: first, the ball handler probably will have taken at least half of his allotted ten seconds to get the ball to midcourt, and passing back toward his own basket will run the clock closer to a ten-second backcourt violation without moving the ball nearer to his frontcourt; second, passing backwards usually will give the defenders time to match up, even if the trap fails to contain the ball, which means that the passing lanes will be denied and the player at the free-throw line will have to beat his man one-on-one and dribble across the half-court line in just two or three seconds (Figure 11–25). It can be done, but few teams want to take that kind of chance. After all, when 02 begins his dribble, the defense may trap him, too.

In the first example of guard trapping (refer back to Figure 11–18), X_1 turned the dribbler and X_2 cut him off. If X_1 is extremely fast, *he* can perform both tasks, with X_2 moving into the trapping position as shown in Figure 11–26.

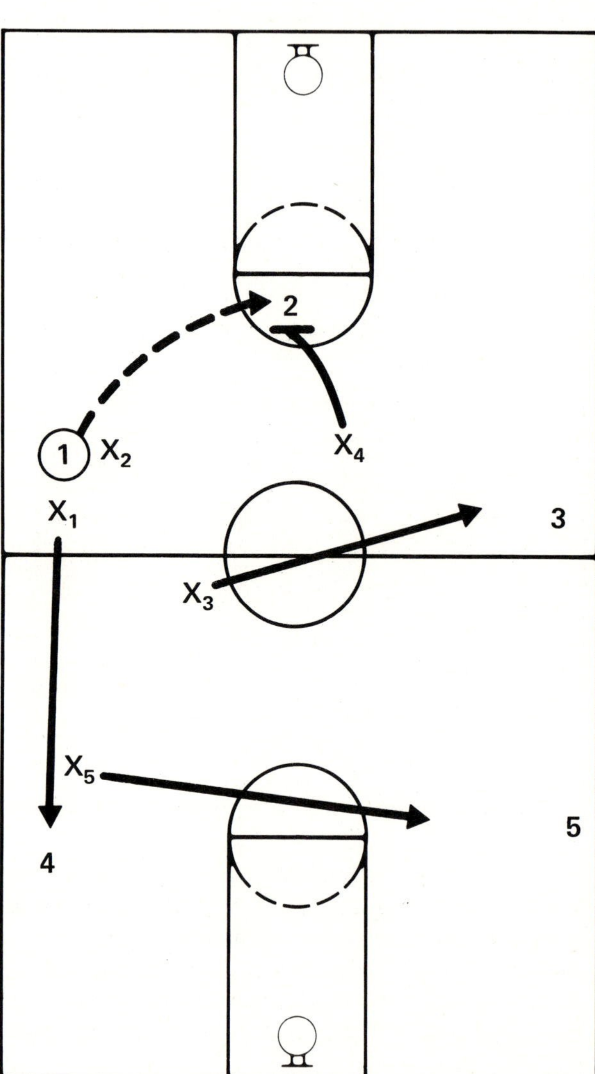

Figure 11–25 Matching Up from Pass to Safety Valve Playing Back

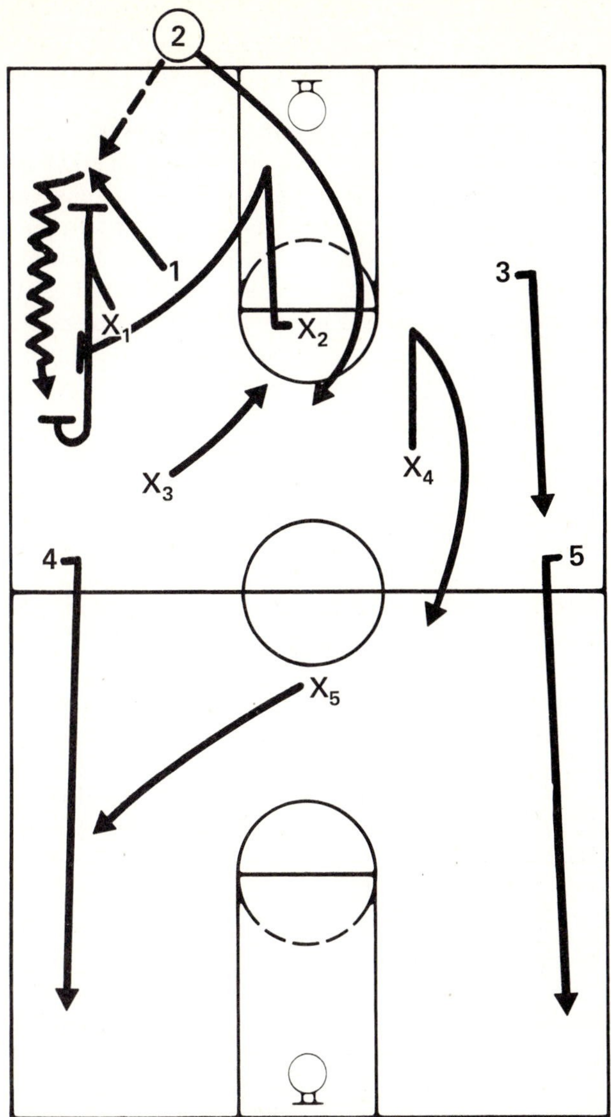

Figure 11–26 X_1 Turning and Then Cutting Off the Dribbler

As before, X_1's turning 01 away from a position facing his own basket is the first step in the delay trapping movement. In the present situation, however, X_1's task has just begun: after turning 01 toward the sideline, X_1 will pivot sharply and sprint down court alongside 01 as he dribbles along the sideline until he is in position to move in front of 01, cut him off, and turn him back toward the middle where X_2 is moving into trapping position (Figure 11–26).

HALF-COURT PRESSES

Zone Pressing

In theory, at least, teams generally will use half-court pressing defenses when they want to press but are too slow or immobile to press full-court. Bringing the press back to the half-court line shortens the court and thus compresses the area where the action occurs—the trapping area and primary passing lanes. This means that slower players don't have to run as far in dropping back to cover the area around the basket when their traps fail to contain the ball. This is basically a negative approach to the problem of pressing defenses, but a lot of teams use half-court zone presses effectively (especially in high school), and I'll concede that what they're doing may be right for them.

If you're intent on using a half-court zone pressing defense, you should be aware that a half-court press is just a full-court press shortened by 42 to 47 feet. The principles governing their execution should be the same:

1. **You will not consistently trap the ball handler at or near the middle of the floor and still cut off the primary passing lanes.** This is perhaps the greatest deterrent to success in half-court trapping, yet so many coaches will send their two guards out to trap the dribbler as he comes up the center of the court. He may panic and throw the ball away when he sees those two guards homing in on him, of course, but he's more likely to dump the ball off to a teammate along the sidelines (Figure 11–27). When that happens, you can expect to see another quick pass or two and then a race to the basket between four offensive players and the three remaining defensive players—and I'll take a four-on-three advantage heading for the bucket any time a team wants to give it to me!

Without going into a lengthy analysis I'll simply let Figure 11–27 speak for itself and ask: Regardless of your original defensive alignment, how would you cover the five areas shown with X_3, X_4, and X_5? Assuming that X_3 can (and will) cover the area behind X_1 and X_2, will you also have X_3 cover the passing lanes to 02 and 03? Or would you have 04 and 05 move up to split the difference in distance between 03 and 05 and 02 and 04? You could cover 02 or 03 one-on-one that way, but you aren't likely to steal the ball or force a turnover. (Also bear in mind that we're talking about using the middle of the court, as a trapping area; we're not describing the weakness of a given defensive alignment. If you trap at the middle the passing lanes *will* be the ones shown in Figure 11–27, regardless of your alignment.)

2. **Matching up defensively will not consistently beat a team with average to better-than-average ball handling.** All matching

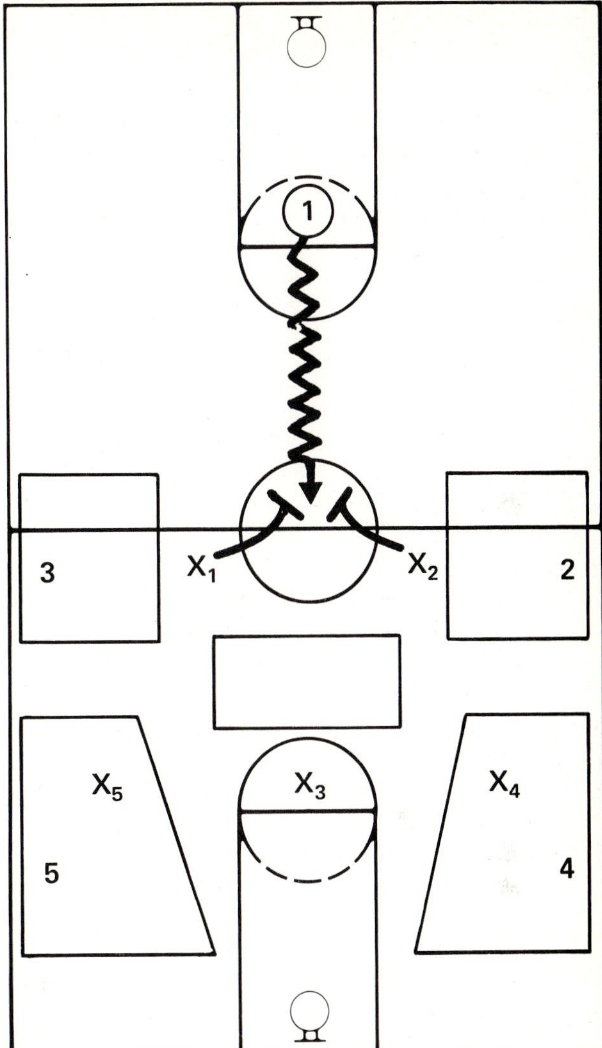

Figure 11–27 Trapping at the Middle, Half-Court Press

up will accomplish against decent ball handling is to allow the offensive team to attack the defense by forcing a double-team and attacking the area vacated by the trapping defender.

01, who is dribbling toward X_1 at the half-court line in a 1–3–1 half-court pressing alignment (Figure 11–28), suddenly veers to his right, dribbles toward X_2, and, as X_2 steps forward to trap him, dumps the ball off to 03 along the sideline. The only defender in position to cover 03 immediately is X_3, but in covering 03, X_3 is leaving the middle open for 01's cut into that area. If X_2 drops back to cover 01, the defense can match up, but they will have done nothing to take the ball away or force a

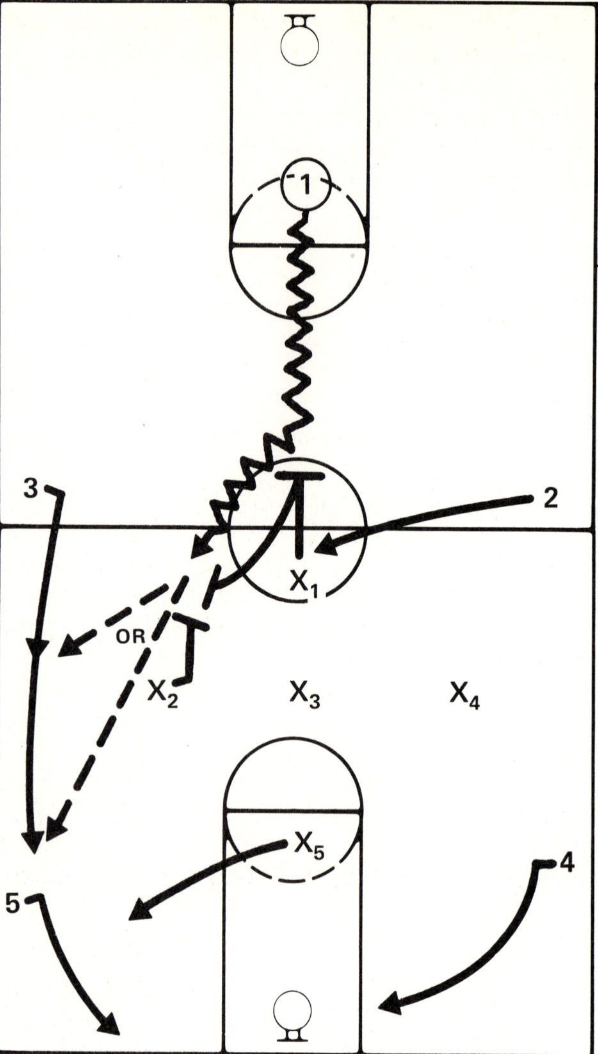

Figure 11–28 Forcing a Double-Team

turnover. If X_1 drops back, 02 will be open. If 02 is covered by X_1, the defense cannot trap 03 and still cover 01's pass and cut. If 02 is covered by X_4, 04 will be open underneath. The possibilities are limitless, but two key points arise from all of the preceding taken together: first, if the ball handler forces the defense to double-team from matchup coverage he will not be surprised by the trapping movement, and he will therefore be unlikely to throw the ball away blindly; second, once the ball handler has made his initial pass after forcing the double-team, the defense will be very unlikely to contain the ball or force a turnover by matching up or trapping.

No half-court defense, whether matching up, trapping, or run-and-jump, is likely to be successful when the passing lanes are not cut off and the pass receiver has not used his dribble.

3. From the two previous principles we can derive a workable half-court pressing technique. This technique is: cover the dribbler one-on-one, deny his pass to the sideline, turn him away from his basket to make him protect his dribble—but do *not* let him attack the defense by forcing a double team—and influence him toward one sideline or the other. Once the dribbler is slowed down, turned, and influenced toward a sideline, trapping or run-and-jump tactics will have a much greater chance of succeeding (Figure 11–29).

If the defense intends to run and jump from the court positions shown in Figure 11–29, a defender will double back to stop the dribbler as his man influences him toward the sideline, and the original defender will switch with whoever executed the run-and-jump. If the defense intends to trap—for example, with #30 and the defender on the ball, although other defenders could also be used to spring the trap—#30 will rush back to trap the dribbler, #20 will move up to cover #30's man, #32 will move across the lane to cover #20's man, and the weak-side guard will drop slightly away from his man, hinting at covering the weak-side low post, although he is really playing the crosscourt passing lane to his man.

The differences between the coverage in Figure 11–29 and the previous ones discussed are not as subtle as they might appear at first glance: first, the defense is in a tight *man-to-man* coverage, not zone defense; second, the defender on the ball must control the dribbler and turn him toward a sideline, and the wing defenders must cut off the passing lanes

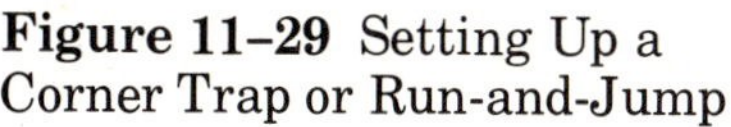
Figure 11–29 Setting Up a Corner Trap or Run-and-Jump

until the dribbler is turned one way or another; third, because the defense is dictating the offensive movements and options to a large extent, the defensive players are more likely to know where the primary passing lanes will be when the trap or run-and-jump is sprung. Concerning the third point, consider the trapping sequence in Figure 11–29. When #30 doubles back to cover the dribbler, #32 will always move up to cut off the passing lane, #30 will always be responsible for any player deep on the ball side, and the weak-side guard will cover any cut by his man toward the ball or any open area of the court.

Man-to-Man Pressing

Although we press full-court after scores and backcourt turnovers at UNLV, we drop back into half-court pressure man-to-man defense after missed shots. During our first year at UNLV, we half-court pressed the entire season, since our players, who were still learning our system of play and were not highly motivated to apply the kind of defensive pressure necessary in our full-court man-to-man pressure defense, were largely ineffective in full-court pressing. We went to full-court pressing in our second year at UNLV, but the half-court pressing concept has remained instrumental in our efforts to control taller opponents.

Generally, the more effective an opponent's post men are offensively,

Figure 11–30 Defending Against the Big Men, Ball at Wing vs. Half-Court Man-to-Man Press: *Example #1*

the farther out our style of sideline/baseline influence must be applied to deny passes inside to the high or low post. If the opponents have one or more dominating big men, we'd rather force the ball handler as far out toward the half-court line as we can without losing our ability to deny the reversal.

It should be obvious from Figures 11–30 and 11–31 that, when the opponents' inside players are outstanding offensively, the defense would prefer the ball handler to be as near to midcourt as possible—or, considered another way, as far from the wing position as possible. In Figure 11–30, the high and low post are over-guarded, with the weak-side guard standing ready to help out if necessary; however, even this may not be enough. When an opponent has a group of very effective offensive players, they may be able to pass inside even if your cheerleaders are fronting theirs. In such cases a coach may prefer to use a half-court pressing defense to force the ball to the sideline, farther away from the basket than usual.

In Figure 11–32, a defender picks up the ball handler as he crosses the half-court line, influencing him toward whichever sideline he turns to protect the ball. Once he turns the ball handler, the defender's primary responsibility is to deny the reversal back to the middle, and his secondary duty is to continue influencing the dribbler toward and along the sideline. Accomplishing the latter may be easier said than done, especially if the defender is expected to keep the ball handler at the sideline and out beyond the wing. Still, two factors are in the defensive team's favor in the sequence of movements shown in Figure 11–32: first, and most importantly, the low-post man has been eliminated as a pass receiver, at least until the wing vacates his position and empties to the weak side and

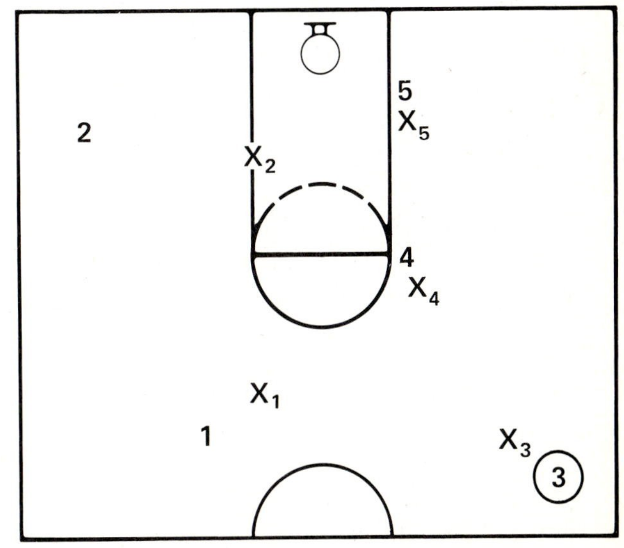

Figure 11–31 Defending Against the Big Men, Ball at Wing vs. Half-Court Man-to-Man Press: *Example #2*

Figure 11–32 Defending Against the Big Men, Ball at Wing vs. Half-Court Man-to-Man Press: *Example #3*

the dribbler reaches the wing area, and second, the ball handler will not be allowed to dribble interminably. (Depending upon whether he penetrates inside the hash marks along the sidelines, he can dribble for as long as thirteen seconds without having a held ball called; however, if he fails to penetrate beyond the hash marks within the first five seconds after crossing the half-court line, the referee will call a held ball.)

We don't always use a half-court pressing defense, of course. We'll use it after our missed shots are rebounded by the opponents, and we've gone to it occasionally when our players were unable to full-court press effectively.

We run our half-court press exactly as we run our regular pressing defense, except we pick up the opponents as they reach mid-court. Other than that, the defensive goals are identical: force the ball to the sideline (and then toward the baseline corner or the baseline), give up as little as possible in the process and deny the reverse dribble or ball rotation to the weak side; play the passing lanes to receivers one pass away from the ball; front at the high post; and bottom-front at the low post.

12

A Basic Winning System for Young or Unskilled Players

There are perhaps three classes of successful basketball coaches: those who have inherited a winning program and have continued the winning tradition; those who have developed their own comprehensive winning program where none existed previously; and those who are currently enjoying success but have not developed program continuity to ensure future success. In the third category, success is usually built around the skills of one or more players who are currently performing, but the success soon vanishes with the graduation of those players.

Of course, all of us would likely prefer to be in the first category, which involves the line of least resistance to success. Building a successful program from the ground up is a long, tiring, and often discouraging process. It's much more pleasant to consider the prospect of inheriting a winner and continuing to win; unfortunately, such opportunities are seldom encountered. The most desirable coaching vacancies are usually filled by ex-players or coaches who have stellar qualifications, connections, or experience. Coaching vacancies, it seems, operate under a principle similar to Murphy's Law*: *The best jobs go to someone else.* The 6′6″ boy you saw in the halls when you went for a job interview was a senior the past year, or else he plays third trombone in the band. If he plays basketball, either (a) the doctor told him that he couldn't run much because it triggers his asthma attacks, or (b) an aura of brown haze and the smell of burned rope surround him whenever you approach him unexpectedly in the dressing room. At any rate, you may as well expect the worst in a new coaching situation: the previous coach wasn't about to leave a flock of all-Americans behind.

Thus we are left with the unenviable prospect of days, months, and

*"If anything can go wrong, it will."

even years of hard work, disappointment, and frustration ahead. But that's as it should be. If building a successful basketball program were easy, everyone would be doing it. Dedication, hard work, willingness to put in long hours—these are the tools for building a quality program, and the coach who expects or demands those attributes from his players is advised to adopt them for himself.

You can build and maintain a winning basketball program at your school. If you don't believe you can win consistently either now or in the future in your present situation, you probably won't, so you might be better off seeking another coaching position. But the job of building a winner can be done. You may have to alter the level of your expectations as well as your definition of success—we're talking about winning *games,* not championships—but you can produce a successful team, even with unskilled players, if you know how to do it. That's what this chapter is all about.

In installing the thirteen-step system of control basketball that follows, one personnel requirement must be met: the coach must have players who are willing to make a sincere effort to hustle and follow instructions. Without this prerequisite, neither this nor any other system is likely to work.

It should be obvious that, all other things being equal, a team composed primarily of inexperienced or unskilled players will have greater difficulty in achieving offensive and/or defensive control of its opponents than a team of highly skilled players. While more experienced teams may or may not be able to run high-powered offenses or high-risk defenses, inexperienced squads are seldom able to master intricate patterns or systems of play. In coaching such players, then, *simplicity* is the first step toward building a basic system of winning basketball. (For that matter, it's not a bad first step for experienced teams, either.)

A THIRTEEN-STEP SYSTEM OF WINNING BASIC BASKETBALL FOR UNSKILLED SQUADS

1. Play within your limitations. *You* have a better idea than anyone else what your players can and cannot do. Don't try to make them do things they aren't capable of doing. They don't need failure to remind them of their shortcomings and lack of skill. You may want to run a 1–3–1 trap zone, but you're wasting your time if your players can't make it work. Find what they *can* do, and practice it until: (a) they can execute it properly without pausing to stop and think about what to do next, and (b) their reactions to unexpected situations flow naturally out of their understanding of how the system is supposed to work.

2. Don't let your players freelance on offense unless each of them knows exactly what he's doing. Contrary to popular notions, freelancing involves advanced offensive skills. Even when a player knows what he is doing, his teammates may not have the slightest idea what he intends to do with the ball. Thus, they may find themselves cutting away from the ball as he passes to them, moving out of rebounding position as he shoots, or standing around watching him as he dribbles. Unskilled players cannot afford to make mistakes, except when their teammates are capable of covering for them.

3. Teach your players the fundamentals of man-to-man defense. If you want your young players to learn basketball, teach them to play aggressive man-to-man defense. Be patient and take one step at a time. Keep rules simple and consistent.

You hear coaches say that pressure man-to-man defense is the best defense in basketball, and it's true—if you have the personnel to play it without surrendering defensive control. As we pointed out previously, though, you have to use what your players do best, not necessarily what looks best on paper.

4. Don't press. At least, don't press full- or half-court unless you stand a reasonable chance of forcing turnovers, stealing the ball, or at least controlling your opponents when the press fails to contain the ball. If your team isn't defensively sound or extremely quick, pressing can hurt you in two ways: by the layups scored against you and by the extra fouls your players will commit while pressing.

Pressing is likely to be effective only if you have kids who are highly motivated and are willing to put forth a strong effort defensively. A pressing team is defending 94 feet of floor space instead of 20 to 24 feet.

If you press, however, you can practice beating the presses at the same time. And if you can't beat the opponents' presses, you can't beat them. You won't score while the ball is at the opponents' end of the court.

5. Play 1–2–2 zone defense. For teams with limited personnel, the 1–2–2 zone defense may be the best in the game. In its basic form, the 1–2–2 zone defense keeps four players inside for rebounding and defensive purposes, and its odd-front aspect tends to force the ball wide of the point and to establish it on one side of the court or the other. The 1–2–2 should be played tight, double-teaming the ball-side low post when the ball is established on one side of the court, and giving up the shot from the top of the circle.

> **Note:** The 1–2–2 zone will be most effective when a team has at least one big guard in the lineup. He will be defending a wing position and will have weak-side rebounding responsibilities when shots are taken from the wings or corners away from him.

While even-front zone defenses—the 2–1–2, 2–3, and 2–2–1—tend to give up high-percentage wing shots as well as to confuse defensive coverage of the point, odd-front zone alignments—the 1–2–2, 1–3–1, 1–1–3, and 3–2—provide ample wing coverage while forcing the ball wide of the point. Of the odd-front zone defenses, the 1–3–1 zone is weak along the baselines and requires quick personnel to avoid being exploited by good ball handling, and the 1–1–3 zone is merely a variation of the 2–3 zone. The 1–3–1 is probably the best zone defensive alignment from which to match up or trap, but matching up and trapping are advanced maneuvers beyond the capabilities of beginners. The 3–2 zone defense is a variation of the 1–2–2 zone defense.

Personnel Requirements. The 1–2–2 zone defense with double coverage inside is designed primarily for teams with less than outstanding height or skilled players inside. (With adequate height or experience, a team probably would prefer to match up or use single coverage inside.) Obviously, then, teams using this defense must possess at least average overall speed in order to avoid getting beaten by 12- to 15-foot shots from the weak side via rapid ball rotation.

Surprisingly enough, however, the point-guard position does not require a quick or fast player. The only traits needed by the point guard are aggressiveness and mobility. More than any other player in the 1–2–2 zone defense, the point guard is capable of disrupting the outside passing sequences by constantly moving and keeping the ball handler unsure of his intentions. Sometimes he may cover the high post when the ball is at the wing position; at other times he may move outside (or fake such a movement) as if to intercept the pass to the point. A clever defensive point guard can help to slow down ball rotation considerably.

The inside defenders should be quick enough to cover the corners and move from the ball-side low post to the weak side without giving up the 6- to 10-foot shot in ball rotation, and they must be able to keep the ball away from low-post players by overguarding or siding. Thus, they likely (but not necessarily) will be the team's tallest players. They should be tall and/or aggressive defenders. Their task is vitally important: *keep the ball away from the low post.* When they fail to do their job, the entire defense falls apart.

The defenders at the wings should be the team's best defensive players, since they are likely to face one-on-one weak-side confrontations resulting from ball rotation. They should also be effective rebounders if it is at all possible. The inside players will always have help in blocking the low-post player away from the boards. (The inside defenders will be rebounding one-on-one with a weak-side player.) The wing players must be tall enough to discourage (and cover, if not deny) the diagonal pass from the wing or intermediate wing position to the weak-side low post.

Finally, someone—preferably one of the wings because of their favorable court position—must serve as the team's ball handler in transition and fast breaking. The point guard is the most likely prospect if the wings simply cannot fill the role.

Coverage from the 1–2–2 zone alignment is based on five outside court positions: the point, the wings on either side of the court, and the corners. All other court positions—for example, the intermediate wing positions between the point and the wings—are variations of these five basic court positions.

Ball at the Point. The greatest apparent weakness of the basic 1–2–2 zone defense is found in coverage of the high post. As can be seen in Figure 12–1, the high-post position at the center of the free-throw lane lies between the three outside defensive players. If the point guard drops back to provide additional coverage of the high post, the shot from the top of the circle will be open; if he moves outside to cover the ball handler as shown in Figure 12–2, the wing defenders may not be able to deny passes to the high post and still adequately defend against passes to offensive players at the wings.

Assuming that a shot will have to be given up somewhere eventually—and this is true of *all* zone defenses except the help-and-recover form—the coach will have to decide which shot to give up, the shot from the point, the wings, or the corners. (Of course, the defense could match up against a 2–1–2 offensive alignment merely by rotating the outside defenders, but matching up is dangerous when using unskilled players.)

If you don't think the opponents' point guard will beat you shooting from that position—and this is especially true at the junior high level—your point guard may drop back to cover the high post when the ball is at the point. Or if the point guard is a better outside shooter than the players

Figure 12–1 Point Coverage, 1–2–2 Zone Defense (*a*)

Figure 12–2 Point Coverage, 1–2–2 Zone Defense (*b*)

occupying the wing positions, you may have the point guard move outside to put pressure on the ball handler and force a lob pass to the wing while your wings pinch on the high-post player. (The lob pass to the wing will give the wing defenders time to cover the pass receiver.)

> **Note:** When the ball is at the point, it is seldom necessary to double-team at the low post. A possible exception to this rule occurs when the opponents have an unusually tall low-post player, but in such cases modes of coverage other than the 1–2–2 zone defense may prove more effective, such as the 2–3 zone defensive coverage described in Chapter 9.

Ball at the Wings. In both situations shown in Figures 12–3 and 12–4, the point guard will cover the ball-side high post after the pass to the wing. The inside defender on the ball side will move toward the corner slightly—no more than two or three steps—when the ball is at the wing position on their side of the court. The other inside defender will move to an inside (overguarding) position on the ball-side low post. The wings will move to the center of the free-throw lane to cover passes to the weak-side players. Their job is to stop the diagonal passes under the basket, but they will also cover outside positions on the weak side. For example, if the wing player in Figure 12–5 passes to the point, the weak-side guard will move outside to cover the ball and the forward will move quickly across the lane to cover the weak-side wing if the point guard relays the ball to him.

This alignment, with the inside defenders double-teaming passes inside, is especially strong on the ball side, particularly if the opponents' game plan is centered around a big man inside. The only way to effec-

Figure 12–3 Wing Coverage, 1–2–2 Zone Defense with Inside Double-Teaming: *Example #1*

Figure 12–4 Wing Coverage, 1–2–2 Zone Defense with Inside Double-Teaming: *Example #2*

tively attack it is to rotate the ball quickly to the weak side and hope that the weak-side guard will have to move outside to cover the point, and that as a result an inside defender will have to cover the weak-side wing. (Passing from the wing to the corner will not stop the double-teaming, as will be explained in the following section.)

Ball in the Corners. In covering the pass to the corners, the wings will not move from their weak-side positions at the center of the free-throw lane (Figures 12–6 and 12–7). The pass to the weak-side low post or the weak-side corner will have to be a lob pass over at least three players

Figure 12–5 Weak-Side Coverage in Ball Rotation, 1–2–2 Zone Defense with Inside Double-Teaming

Figure 12–6 Corner Coverage 1–2–2 Zone Defense with Inside Double-Teaming: *Example #1*

Figure 12–7 Corner Coverage, 1–2–2 Zone Defense with Inside Double-Teaming: *Example #2*

and the basket, and therefore will be extremely unlikely. Even if the pass is made, the wings will have time to cover the receiver. The point defender stays at the ball-side high post. The wing defender on the ball side covering the wing will drop low to double-team the low-post player with the inside defender who is not covering the corner.

The only open areas against this coverage are the ball-side wing and the weak-side high post. If the ball is passed back to the wing, a wing defender will move back out to cover him. If the corner player passes to the weak-side high post, coverage is identical to the one used when the ball is passed from the wing to the weak side. In Figure 12–6, the single weak-side defender will move out to cover the pass receiver, and the low-post defender will shift across the lane to cover any other weak-side offensive players.

As before, ball-side coverage is very strong. The philosophy behind this style of defensive coverage is obvious: if they're going to beat us, let's make them beat us from the outside, especially by long, crosscourt passes to the weak side. Deny all passes inside; make them pass the ball at least three or four times around the perimeter before they get a shot. (Note, too, that double-teaming the low post with the high post covered and a single defender on the weak side keeps four defenders inside.)

For the sake of simplicity, the point guard may cover the point until the ball is established on one side of the court or the other (Figure 12–8). *Established* means "beyond either side of the free-throw lane extended." When the ball crosses that imaginery line, the point guard will drop back to cover the ball-side high post at the free-throw line as a wing defender moves out to cover the ball (Figure 12–9). Thus, the 1–2–2 zone defense can be run as a 3–2 zone.

Figure 12–8 Point and High-Post Coverage, 1–2–2 Zone Defense (*a*)

Figure 12–9 Point and High-Post Coverage, 1–2–2 Zone Defense (*b*)

The 1–2–2 zone defense can be taught position by position. Most teams use the single-coverage of the low post with two players back on the weak side as described in Chapter 9. However, with single coverage it takes only one pass to beat you: the inside pass. With double-teaming denying the inside pass, it usually takes at least two passes to move the ball into scoring position.

The 1–2–2 double-teaming technique is far from foolproof, of course. The opponents may have the ball-handling and outside shooting skills to score almost at will from outside, and if they can attack you successfully from outside, they may not need an effective inside attack. However, we're talking now about playing the percentages, and with young or unskilled players, the percentages lie in giving up the outside shot rather than letting the opponents take the ball inside on you.

6. Work on fast breaking and high-speed ball handling. This is, I feel, imperative even if your team isn't particularly adept at fast breaking. We try to do every drill at top speed, no matter what it is. If a player can handle the ball at high speed, he can handle it as well or better when moving slow or standing still. But if he's not used to handling the ball at high speed (or playing defense at high speed, as in defending against a fast break), his play will be adversely affected if and when he has to play that kind of game.

Even if your fast break fails to produce points in terms of offensive mismatches and easy scores at the other end of the court, it will disrupt your opponents' pressing effectiveness. Even the best pressing teams need a few seconds to organize their defense; fast breaking will deny them the opportunity to set up their defensive attack.

7. If you're going to fast break, assign specific lanes and ball handlers.* Laning the fast break may slow it up slightly in some respects, but it will pay dividends in ball control. As was mentioned previously, your immediate goal in fast breaking with inexperienced players may be to beat the opponents' press rather than scoring. In such cases, you definitely want your best ball handler(s) to bring the ball down court, even if it slows down the fast break and reduces your chances of scoring.

In Figure 12–10, X_3 is the primary ball handler and X_2 is the secondary ball handler. X_3 should handle the ball every time down court in fast breaking, except when X_2 takes the ball down court. Under no circumstances should X_4 or X_5 dribble down court; their job is to get the ball by rebounding and then make the outlet pass and fill their lanes to the best of their ability after the fast break is started. X_1 does not handle the ball except after steals or when he is obviously ahead of everyone else. (Some coaches "hide" a particularly weak ball-handling guard at the X_1 position.)

You might also consider putting your best rebounding guard at the X_3 position, since it is a superior defensive rebounding position when shots are taken from the right wing. In like manner, X_2 is in position to rebound on the weak side when the left wing shoots. X_1 could be used as the primary ball handler, but many coaches prefer to use X_1 as a "streaker," taking off down court along his route *after the defense claims the rebound.* Such a strategy sometimes will pay off in shots, not for X_1, but for X_2:

*We note that, while we assign lanes in fast breaking, many other successful fast-breaking teams do not follow this practice.

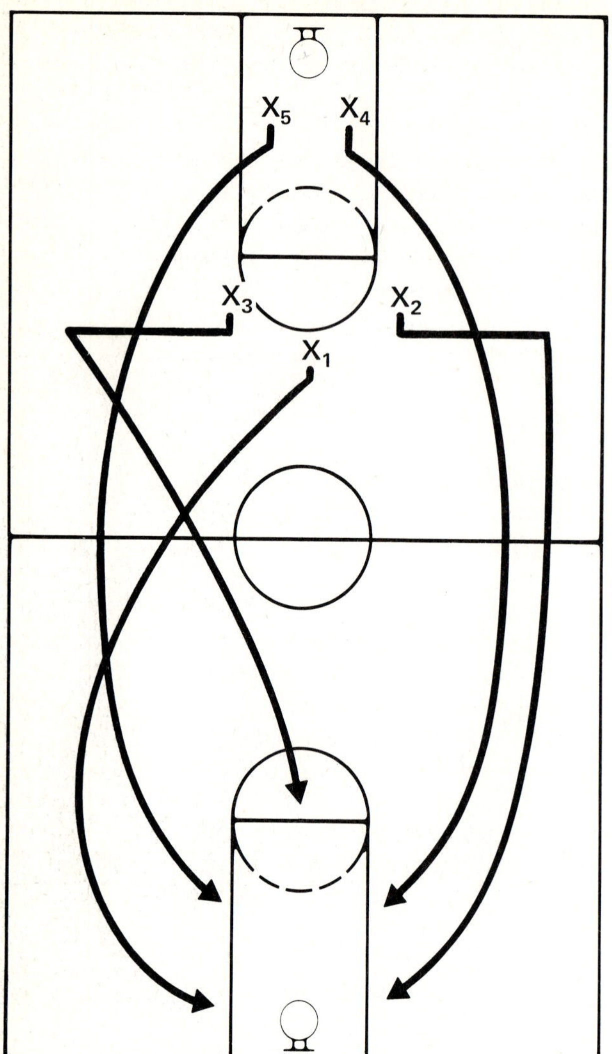

Figure 12–10 Laning the Fast Break from 1–2–2 Zone Defense

when X_4 or X_5 makes the outlet pass to X_3, X_1 is already streaking down court along the sideline. The opponents' first player back on defense often will cover X_1, with the second player picking up ball handler X_3 and leaving X_2 open for the pass and layup.

When following strict laning techniques, players are expected to fill the same lanes down court every time in fast breaking, no matter where they are when transition occurs. The fast break will be slowed down slightly as players find and fill their assigned lanes, but the time required for players to learn their roles in fast breaking will be reduced, and the team will gain increased control of the ball throughout the break.

8. Practice the transition game. Many teams may be able to get two people back to stop fast breaks, but relatively few will consistently get three players back in time to gain defensive control.

Any team can fast break at least occasionally, regardless of the players' speed, if they know how and when to do it. The main reason that most teams don't fast break well is players' failing to take advantage of the first critical seconds of ball possession after transition occurs.

In order to fast break well consistently, a team must have at least three players filling the passing lanes down court. Fast breaking begins while a team is on defense, with aggressive attitudes toward re-acquiring possession of the ball. If players are not actively working to get the ball back on defense, they will probably be unprepared to take advantage of the situation when their team finally gets the ball. All good fast-breaking teams play alert, aggressive defense.

9. Practice with your starters playing at a numerical disadvantage. Put seven players on defense, pressing full-court, and have your starters practice beating the press; or put seven players on offense with the five starters pressing full-court; or put your starters in a 1–2–2 zone with seven or eight players on offense, and practice transition by keeping score and permitting the starters to fast break after steals or defensive rebounds. (The starters are allowed only one shot at their end of the court, with the exception of follow shots after missed layups. If they make the layup or take the follow shot, play stops and the ball goes back to the other team to start the drill again.) This technique, known as *overloading* because of one team's numerical superiority, is extremely competitive and should provide your starters with at least as much opposition as they will face in games, with the quantity of players compensating for differences in quality.

10. Insist upon good shot selection in your zone and man-to-man offenses. If you're an insecure, inexperienced ninth grader, you may be well advised to take only the high-percentage shots your coach tells you to take. And if you're coaching a team of beginning players who consider a high-percentage shot to be any shot that might not be blocked, giving them total freedom of shot selection is tantamount to telling them it's okay to take hook shots from the top of the circle. When coaching young players, it is necessary—vital—to teach them to control their performance. Working for high-percentage shots from predetermined areas of the court is the key to this process where offense is concerned.

Although limitations in personnel may dictate otherwise, a team should try to present some kind of inside scoring threat, at least occasionally, for three important reasons. First, whether a legitimate inside threat exists, outside patterns will not work if the defenders know that the offensive team is not going to try to take the ball inside. Second, teams which rely solely upon outside shooting will seldom find their opponents getting into foul trouble. Finally, outside patterns and outside shooting may decrease the offensive team's rebounding potential.

11. Use ball and (limited) player movement in your offenses, especially against zone defenses. Neither ball nor player movement by itself will bother most zone defenses. As most players will testify, it is far more difficult to watch cutters and the ball simultaneously than it is to watch either the ball or the cutters. Without ball or player movement, offenses tend to become stagnant and predictable, and where predictability exists, you can wave goodbye to offensive effectiveness.

12. Stress defense rather than offense in your practice sessions. We spend at least 70 percent of our time working on defensive drills, free-throw shooting, and the transition game—which means that less than 30 percent of our time is spent actually working on half-court offense. (Five percent goes to special situations such as bring-in plays, practicing tipoffs, working for last-second shots, and so on.) With beginning players it is even more important to stress defense in your practices. Controlling opponents defensively is the first prerequisite for winning basketball games; with young players, it may be the *only* prerequisite.

In theory, at least, offensive control is more important than defensive control: a team may win by as low a score as 1–0, but it cannot win if it fails to score. In practice, offense is unpredictable, whereas solid defense doesn't have off nights. (One coach, defending his preference for defense, insisted that, "There's only one thing you can count on in basketball: sooner or later, your offense is going to let you down.") If you are undecided as to how to allocate your practice time, spend the bulk of it teaching your kids to play defense.

13. Take care not to overdo full-court, game-type scrimmages or working on nonessentials. All practicing should be purposeful and geared toward teaching as well as getting players into shape. In game-type scrimmages, mistakes go undetected and uncorrected, but even worse, the continuous action tends to blur the players' concepts of what they're trying to accomplish. Far better is the concept of *controlled scrimmaging*, in which selected skills are drilled repeatedly within stop-action full- or half-court scrimmage sequences. (All of our scrimmages at UNLV are controlled.) The five-on-seven drills described in Point #9 are examples of controlled scrimmaging. Thus, if emphasis is to be placed on continuous double-teaming of the low post in the 1–2–2 zone defense, the defenders will shift continually with ball and player movement until transition occurs via a steal, turnover, or defensive rebound, and then they will either fast break or return the ball to the offensive team. (The first alternative, stealing the ball, is clearly superior since every team should strive to take advantage of transitions at every opportunity.) Care must be taken, however, not to prolong the period following transition.

The purpose of controlled scrimmaging is to provide intensive drill on one or two aspects of a team's overall game plan, such as double-teaming inside and fast breaking after transition. Beginners are seldom able to absorb a complete game plan at one time—beating the press, setting up and running an offensive pattern, pressing or getting back on defense, setting up the defense, fast breaking, and so on, in rapid succession. Controlled scrimmaging allows players to learn the game one phase at a time and provides intensive, yet limited, sequences of game-type action.

SUMMARY

The coach who expects (or is expected) to win with unskilled players is practically impelled toward a system of high-percentage basketball. In such circumstances, a coach soon learns to avoid high-risk offenses and defenses in favor of simpler patterns and systems of play.

The thirteen points outlined in this chapter describe such a simplified system. As was pointed out, not all teams will benefit from such a basic system, but limitations in personnel could dictate a move in that direction in certain situations. At any rate, conservative styles of play have their place in basketball, and the coach who summarily rejects them out of hand could be depriving his team of its best chance of winning.

IV

Basketball Fundamentals

Practice is the best of all instructors.

Publilius Syrus

UNLV

UNLV

UNLV
BASKETBALL
BASKETBALL

13

Individual Fundamentals

It is an unfortunate truism that practically every movement in basketball except running is artificial and unnatural. From the apparently simple act of pivoting away from an opponent to the incredible awkwardness one feels the first time he attempts a jump shot, the player's movements must be learned with the same kind of diligent training that accompanies learning in ballet. However, if it were otherwise, everyone would be a superstar and there would be no need for coaching or instructional textbooks.

The fundamental skills of basketball—passing, shooting, rebounding, dribbling, stance, and footwork—provide the basis for individual development and improvement. Players may excel in certain aspects of the game by virtue of their natural abilities, such as using vertical jumping ability (or height) in rebounding rather than learning to block their opponents away from the boards; still, attention to fundamentals is never wasted. However talented a player may be by virtue of his speed, quickness, coordination, peripheral vision, and so on, he cannot help but improve through practicing fundamentals. To think otherwise is to ignore the role coaching plays in preparing athletes to play the game.

Ultimately, the game can be reduced to its fundamentals. The tall player must be mobile enough to free himself to receive the ball when facing defensive pressure inside, and he must be sound enough defensively not to commit fouls every time the opponents' big man gets the ball. Smaller men, no matter how quick they are, must be able to play position defense, or else they will surrender offensive numerical superiority to the opponents whenever opposing ball handlers penetrate beyond them. Natural ability is certainly a factor in a player's ability to master the skills involved in basketball—as Bobby Knight has said, you can teach a kid to shoot or play defense, but you can't teach him to be 7 feet tall—but

I think we as coaches sometimes forget our responsibility for helping players to reach their potential through working with fundamentals.

When left to their own devices, most players will either develop bad habits—such as erratic shooting form, ignoring weak-hand dribbling, and standing up on defense—or they'll fail to develop at all because of the most insidious, crippling agent of all—laziness. It is the coach's role to provide a planned program of drills and practice that will develop his players toward eventual mastery of the skills that are necessary for them to reach their full potential in basketball. Regardless of the amount of talented players he has, the coach owes it to himself and his team to attempt to improve his players' fundamental skills at every opportunity.

OFFENSIVE STANCE AND FOOTWORK

Offensive Stance

Before discussing the footwork patterns that are required of moving players, we should mention that proper footwork begins with a player's

Figure 13–1 Triple-Threat Stance

stance. Balance is a primary factor in controlling one's body, whether a player is stationary or in motion. Controlling one's body while moving is far more difficult than when one is stationary, of course, but a player's stance will help to determine the speed (and body control) with which he can begin moving from a stationary position or vice versa.

The basic offensive stance of a player with the ball is identical to that of the basic defensive stance, with the single exception that the player has the ball in his hands. This position, shown in Figure 13–1, is commonly known as the "triple-threat" position, since a player who has not used up his dribble may pass, shoot, or dribble from that stance. (If, for example, the player is standing erect and holding the ball overhead as shown in Figure 13–2, he is restricted to using an overhead pass or bringing the ball down low to begin dribbling. None of these alterations is necessary if he holds the ball in the low, balanced triple-threat position.

Circumstances may dictate that the player assume a stance such as the erect stance with the ball overhead, or with the ball held low and his body turned away from the defender in order to protect the ball (Figure 13–3). Still, players must learn to assume the triple-threat position if they

Figure 13–2 Erect Stance, Ball Overhead

Figure 13–3 Protected Stance

are to derive the benefits to be gained from its usage—and those benefits are considerable.

Post Positioning

When posting inside, a player should attempt to make his body as broad as possible in order to give the passer as big a target as possible, and at the same time he should force his defender to the side and away from him (Figure 13–4).

The most commonly encountered mistakes made by inexperienced players are: standing erect with hands at the side, which permits the defender to reach all the way across the post man's body to deny passes, and not fighting to maintain a positioning advantage when it arises. Concerning the latter case, it is unreasonable to expect the defender to surrender an offensive positioning advantage without fighting to retain defensive control of the post position. If the low-post defender is guarding "from the inside out" as shown in Figure 13–5, he will move toward the free-throw line in sliding around to overguard or front his man, and the offensive post man who wants to maintain or improve his advantage will not merely let the defender step up to overguard or front him, but he will move toward the free-throw line with the defender, making it harder for the defender to get around him into position to deny the pass. In maintaining an erect stance, the post player should keep his hands and arms extended upward and outward, even while moving, in order to keep the defender away from him. If the defender fails to adjust to this situation, he will find himself (and in all likelihood his team as well) vulnerable to a lob pass inside to the post man, who is cutting back toward the basket. (See Figures 13–5 through 13–7.)

Figure 13–4 Stance at Low Post

Figure 13–5 Combatting "Inside-Out" Defensive Coverage at Low Post (*a*)

Figure 13–6 Combatting "Inside-Out" Defensive Coverage at Low Post (*b*)

Figure 13–7 Combatting "Inside-Out" Defensive Coverage at Low Post (*c*)

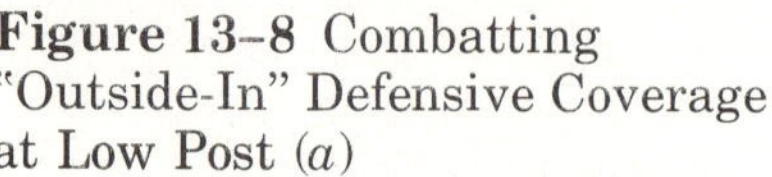

Figure 13–8 Combatting "Outside-In" Defensive Coverage at Low Post (*a*)

Figure 13–9 Combatting "Outside-In" Defensive Coverage at Low Post (*b*)

Of course, if the defender's post positioning is "from the outside in" as shown in Figures 13–8 through 13–10, the offensive post man will move toward the sideline with his man to keep him outside and away from him, with the same end result, the cut to the basket and lob pass for the layup.

It should be noted that this technique is far less common than the "inside-out" technique, particularly in zone defense; still, we use "outside-in" low-post coverage in our pressure man-to-man defense, relying on pressure on the ball to deny the pass to the post man reversing to the basket.

Footwork

One of the most neglected phases of basketball instruction, from both an offensive and a defensive standpoint, involves the proper use of footwork. Coaches often neglect this part of the game, and they consequently delay to a certain extent their players' individual improvement. A great deal of time early in the season should be spent teaching proper

Figure 13–10 Combatting "Outside-In" Defensive Coverage at Low Post (*c*)

footwork, turns, pivots, fakes, changes of direction, body balance, and running under control.

Proper body balance requires that the player's weight be distributed evenly. The knees must be flexed, with the center of gravity carried on an imaginary line through the hips. The feet should be spread, but only comfortably (except in the defensive stance). The arms are positioned away from the body, but the elbows should still be in close enough so that the player can move his hands quickly in either direction.

To be effective in basketball, players generally must establish a low base of operation. The flexed-knee position and low center of gravity assure rapid movement in all directions and improve the player's ability to jump quickly. Players should, at all times on the court and whether they are on offense or defense, maintain a flexed-knee stance. Every part of basketball, every phase of the game, is initiated from the flexed-knee position. Special drills should be used to help an individual develop proper body balance, with particular emphasis placed on the tall player in using these drills. It will appear that many of these large players had developed overnight once these footwork drills are mastered.

Changes of Direction. Every player eventually discovers the importance of being able to fake in one direction and then cut in a different direction. The move is easy to execute, but difficult to do effectively. Some players try to jump into the move rather than to stride into it. To be effective, the first step, or fake step, must mean something to the defensive man. If the step is too short, the defensive man will not react; if it is too long, it will be too hard to make the second step. If a player wants to fake left and go right, the first step with the left foot should be a strong step carrying most of the weight on the inside and on the ball of the foot. The left foot should point in slightly to help in the pushing out of the right foot in the other direction. To accentuate the fake, the head, eyes, and shoulders should be shifted to the left.

Figure 13–11 Fake and Cut (Without the Ball) *(a)*

Figure 13–12 Fake and Cut (Without the Ball) *(b)*

Figure 13–16 Stride Stop (*a*)

Figure 13–17 Stride Stop (*b*)

The mechanics for executing a stride stop require that the forward foot be slapped down hard on the court with an equal distribution of weight through the foot to prevent its sliding. The rear foot moves forward to maintain balance. The forward foot that has been slapped down hard is the pivot foot. Full body control is not necessary in the stride stop, and it can be executed at a higher rate of speed than the jump stop. The body position must be low and the knees must be flexed to execute either stop properly.

Pivots. For many years we have used four different pivots. We spend a great deal of time early in the year teaching our players to use these pivots, until their usage is natural and established as a habit. The player receiving the ball will use any of four pivots, and the way he is played defensively will dictate the pivot he uses. Proper pivoting technique is achieved through continuous repetition in practice and through drills performed throughout the season.

The first pivot to be considered is the *front turn* (Figures 13–18 through 13–20). When a guard passes the ball to a center, for example, the center will step toward the ball and catch it while at the same time executing a jump stop or stride stop. Upon making this stop, he will land

Figure 13–18 Front Turn (Pivot) (*a*)

Figure 13–19 Front Turn (Pivot) (*b*)

with his inside foot as his pivot foot and bring his outside foot around into a front turn. In making this turn, the player's body weight should be equally distributed. The ball should be protected by being kept outside, and away from, the defensive man. The front turn should be made from a wide, low stance with the ball close to the body and protected from the defender's reach.

The *rear turn* (Figures 13–21 and 13–22) is executed with the same pivot foot as the front turn. Just as the player will receive the ball with his front foot forward in the front turn, stop, and turn to the front, in the

Figure 13–20 Front Turn (Pivot) (*c*)

Figure 13–21 Rear Turn (Pivot) (*a*)

rear turn he turns in the opposite direction, pivoting off his front foot, but this time bringing his back foot to the inside and making a rear turn. This move is particularly effective if the defensive man is playing loose on a player when he receives the ball, since he can close the gap between himself and his defender by making a rear turn.

The same fundamental rules exist in the rear turn and the front turn; that is, the knees should be bent, the weight evenly distributed, and

Figure 13–22 Rear Turn (Pivot) (*b*)

Figure 13–23 Outside Pivot (*a*)

the ball protected throughout. These pivots should be made only when the player has complete control of his body. In developing these skills, particular effort should be made to master these pivoting movements at a low speed. Once the pivots and the footwork are mastered, the speed of the drill can be increased.

We also teach two other pivots that are executed by pivoting from the *outside* foot. Whereas in the front and rear turns the pivot is used off the front, or inside, foot, the outside and reverse pivots are used off the back, or outside, foot.

Figure 13–24 Outside Pivot (*b*)

Figure 13–25 Outside Pivot (*c*)

In executing the *outside pivot* (Figures 13–23 through 13–25), the player will receive the ball in the same manner as in the front and rear turns, only when he receives the ball he pivots on his back, or outside, foot, raises his front, or inside, foot, and turns it toward the baseline or sideline, using the back foot as his pivot foot. The outside pivot is used if the player is being guarded closely and wants to get a little more space between himself and the opposing player.

The *reverse pivot* (Figures 13–26 and 13–27) is used only when being overplayed. For example, if the defensive player overplays the forward in

Figure 13–26 Reverse Pivot (*a*)

Figure 13–27 Reverse Pivot (*b*)

such a manner that he cannot receive the ball from the guard because his man is playing the passing lane, the forward advances using the same footwork as on the three previous drills, only as he lands he pivots immediately off his outside foot, reverses his direction, and cuts to the basket.

Fakes and Feints

It is important that a basketball player be able to disguise his intent if he wishes to increase his potential as an all-around performer. This disguise of intent is termed *faking*, or *feinting*. The ability to feint direction of movement is as important to the player as is the faking of a shot or pass. Faking can be accomplished by using the ball, eyes, body, head, arm, or foot. It can also combine several of these media. The same moves may be accomplished with or without the ball.

As players increase their skills, their ability to fake well becomes more noticeable. Faking lends additional cleverness to their game with the employment of step-off moves, cross-over steps, change of pace movements, and other advanced moves that mark the outstanding performers in the game. These moves, done without conscious reflection, are developed only through continuous repetition.

INDIVIDUAL OFFENSIVE MANEUVERS

Various maneuvers can help an offensive player become a more effective offensive threat once he receives the ball. To free himself for a shot, a player must first evade the defense. Proper footwork and fakes enable a player to gain an offensive advantage and develop confidence in his ability to do so. There are three steps: the rocker step, the hesitation step, and the crossover step. If a player can master these three moves, he should prove to be an effective offensive threat, particularly when he utilizes his individual skills within the context of team skills.

In the *rocker step*, when the ball handler takes a step forward (faking), the defensive man usually retreats; when the player steps back to his original position, his defender normally moves back to *his* original position, too. In executing the rocker step fake, the offensive man makes the

Figure 13–28 Rocker Step (Fake and Drive) (*a*)

first step forward (Figure 13–28), but *fakes* the second step back with his head and shoulders. He then shifts his weight to his back foot (Figure 13–29) and drives around his man with his forward foot as the defender leans forward (Figures 13–30 and 13–31). This fake, with its back-and-forth movement resembling a *rocker* motion, may be effective in dealing with aggressive defenders who attempt to deny both the drive and the outside shot.

An even better maneuver to fake the defensive man out of position for a quick jump shot or drive to the basket involves the use of the *hesita-*

Figure 13–29 Rocker Step (Fake and Drive) (*b*)

Figure 13–30 Rocker Step (Fake and Drive) (*c*)

Figure 13–31 Rocker Step (Fake and Drive) (*d*)

Figure 13–32 Hesitation Step (Fake) (*a*)

tion step. The first step is a half-step, which is made with the heel contacting the floor first in a normal walking motion (Figure 13–32). The step is made at a slow pace and without any convincing attempt to move forward. The player's weight is kept on his pivot foot, allowing him to then pick up his forward foot and step off in full stride (Figure 13–33). The first step is a casual motion resulting in little reaction from the defender. The hesitation step is particularly effective when used in conjunction with the rocker step; the latter is used to set up the defensive man, who then is much more easily fooled by the hesitation step.

Of all the individual offensive maneuvers, the *cross-over step* is the most difficult to execute. It demands good body balance, footwork, and rhythm. It must be accomplished as one motion. The first step is actually a *jab* step, or half-step (Figure 13–34). It should be a slightly diagonal step to the side, with the player's weight on the inside ball of his foot, allowing his forward foot to push off and cross over in front of his body in the other direction (Figures 13–35 and 13–36).

Once a player has mastered these three moves—the rocker step, the hesitation step, and the cross-over step—he then can incorporate other

Figure 13–33 Hesitation Step (Fake) (*b*)

Figure 13–34 Crossover Step (Fake) (*a*)

Figure 13–35 Crossover Step (Fake) (*b*)

Figure 13–36 Crossover Step (Fake) (*c*)

moves from this position. He can fake right, go left, fake left and go right, or combine these movements in other ways to keep his defender off balance through the proper use of footwork and head and shoulder fakes.

Screening

Although the terms *screen* and *pick* once differed slightly in their meanings, those differences have disappeared in recent years, and the words are now used interchangeably to refer to any technique whereby one or more offensive players move into the path of a moving defensive player, or between a defender and the player he is guarding, for the purpose of blocking the defensive player out of the play.

The first rule to consider in discussing screening is that the player who sets the screen must not be moving when contact is made with the defender, nor may the screener lean toward the defender or otherwise extend one or more parts of his body (for example, an arm or leg) unnaturally in an attempt to impede the defender's movement to cover his man. Another rule is that, when setting a blind screen (one that the player being screened cannot see until he turns around), the defender must be given room to turn around completely before contact occurs. A violation of these rules is a personal foul. Therefore, a player who desires to set a screen must set his screen far enough from the defender to give him room to see the screen and avoid crashing into the screener. Also, the screener's task is merely to set the screen; it is the responsibility of the player receiving the screen to take his man into the screen by cutting or faking.

Countless opportunities for screening arise in the course of any given game. Among the most popular screening variations are: the screen-and-roll, splitting the post, double screens, and screening away from the ball.

In the *screen-and-roll*, the ball handler may be either dribbling or holding the ball when a teammate moves up to set a screen on his man (Figure 13–37); however, as the screen is set, the ball handler will dribble around the screen, brushing his man off on the screener (Figure 13–38).

Figure 13–37 Screen-and-Roll (*a*)

Figure 13–38 Screen-and-Roll (*b*)

Figure 13–39 Screen-and-Roll (*c*)

As the dribbler goes around the screen, the screener will pivot and roll to the basket, maintaining position on the player he screened in case the defenders switch and the screener's original defender picks up the dribbler (Figure 13–39).

Splitting the post has not been widely used in recent years, due largely to the emergence of defensive techniques such as collapsing toward the middle whenever the ball is passed inside. Still, the techniques involved in splitting the post are ideal for teaching players to brush their men off on the post man or another teammate.

In Figures 13–40 and 13–41, a guard passes inside to the high post and begins his cut around him. The other guard is maneuvering himself to cut immediately behind the ball handler in his cut around the high post, giving him *two* chances to brush his man off (Figure 13–42). In order to avoid having the cutters run into each other, teams usually have the player who passed inside make the first cut, with the other cutter scissoring immediately after him.

The offense can also split the post from the side of the court. The movements are the same as the first time, only the angles of the cuts are different.

Figure 13–40 Splitting the Post (*a*)

Figure 13–41 Splitting the Post (*b*)

Figure 13–42 Splitting the Post (*c*)

Figure 13–43 Double Screen (*a*)

Double screens, or screens in which two offensive players set screens on a single defender, sometimes confuse the defenders as to which of them will switch to cover the player with the ball behind the screen. Double screens may be effected from practically any offensive pattern; they occur regularly in many continuity patterns, such as the Wheel or Shuffle.

In Figures 13–43 and 13–44, #44 (in white) cuts behind an inside double screen along the baseline to receive the ball. If his defender tries to get around the screen, he will be too late to stop the shot. If the defender nearest the baseline switches to cover the ball, an offensive mismatch may occur inside along the baseline, and if the defender nearest the free-

Figure 13–44 Double Screen (*b*)

throw line makes the switch, the mismatch will arise inside the lane. In both cases, though, forcing the defenders to switch will alter the defense's timing as well as its matchups.

Screening away from the ball is representative of most of today's man-to-man offensive patterns. The so-called "passing game" offenses rely heavily on cuts and screens away from the ball under the premises that players tend to relax slightly when the player they're covering is on, or cutting to, the weak side; even when the defenders remain vigilant, their attention is divided between the opposite sides of the court, which reduces their ability to prepare to combat the screen.

INDIVIDUAL DEFENSE

The Basic Defensive Stance

One of the more popular descriptions of the defensive stance is the familiar litany, "Feet spread, knees bent, tail down, back straight, head and shoulders up." Some coaches teach their players to "keep your knees as wide apart as your shoulders," but we believe that doesn't go far enough. We believe that good defense is, like a solidly constructed house, built from the ground up; therefore, we want our players to have their knees bent, of course, but we want them to spread their *feet* almost as wide apart as they can get them. We want their knees wider apart than their shoulders in order to create a low center of gravity, which permits quick movement in any direction and enables the players to jump quickly—and the easiest way to do this is to keep the feet spread.

Figure 13–45 Defensive Stance

Basketball is played (correctly) almost exclusively from a bent-knee stance with the buttocks kept low (Figure 13–45). The lower the player's bottom, and the greater the bend in his knees, the quicker the player's reaction to offensive movements will be. Sometimes a coach will tell his players to stand tall with arms outstretched when they are defending the post positions, but players generally should be discouraged from standing up on defense. Anybody can stand up; if all we wanted was somebody to stand up, we could get a fifty-year-old fan out of the stands.

One of the easiest ways to simulate (read: *fake*) a low defensive stance is for a player to bend his back or lean forward at the waist, rather than bending his knees, spreading his feet, and lowering his buttocks (Figure 13–46). Leaning forward at the waist doesn't hurt a player's legs as much as the low, sitting-down stance shown in Figure 13–45, but it doesn't afford much balance, quickness, or mobility, either. Leaning forward has absolutely *nothing* to do with improved anticipation or reaction, and the perceptive coach will correct this posture whenever it arises. If the player's torso is tilted forward, his eyes will naturally be forced downward, and he will be forced to compensate by craning his neck backward to see the action around him. This can be avoided by making the players keep their backs straight in the first place.

The last part of the basic defensive stance, "head and shoulders up," follows naturally if the positioning of the feet, knees, buttocks, and back are given proper attention. Unless a player keeps his head up, he is un-

Figure 13–46 Incorrect Bending in the Defensive Stance

likely to be able to follow the action as it evolves in the court.

Thus, we can see the basics of the defensive stance in its entirety: low, spread, poised—in short, *coiled* like a giant spring. All of these elements are necessary if the defensive player is to anticipate, and then react swiftly to, offensive movements.

Some coaches feel that, since in most court positions (particularly in zone defenses) the defenders are between the offensive players and the basket, the defense holds the initial advantage in confrontations. Other coaches insist that, since the offensive player knows where he is going and the defender generally (but not always) must react to his man's movements, the edge lies initially with the offense. As might be expected, my sentiments lie with the former since our pressure man-to-man defense is unquestionably an attempt to reduce the options available to the offensive team. We don't play between the offensive men and the basket, we overplay the ball toward the sidelines, play the passing lanes, front at the high post, and V-front at the low post. However, because we are attempting to reduce the opponents' effective ball and player movement, we feel that at the same time we are reducing any natural advantages the offensive team might have.

Make no mistake about it: *assuming and maintaining an effective defensive stance is one of the most important fundamentals in basketball that a coach can teach his players.*

Defensive Movement

Once players are able to assume and maintain a stationary defensive stance, the coach's next step is to teach them to maintain a broad, low

Figure 13–47 "Step-Slide" Movement (*a*)

Figure 13–48 "Step-Slide" Movement (*b*)

base while moving. This is accomplished by drilling the players in the "step-slide" movement and by constantly stressing the need for *sliding* in the defensive coverage rather than running. Even when playing zone defense, players should run only as a last resort. Running is not conducive to sudden changes of direction, and it doesn't afford the good balance that sliding offers.

In sliding, the player should not allow his knees to come any closer together than when he was in his stationary stance (Figure 13–47). Sliding is done with the feet and lower legs (calves) rather than with the thighs (Figure 13–48). We also stress keeping the feet in constant motion and keeping them near the floor. It's called "quick feet," and we believe it's the key to such aspects of defensive play as drawing charging fouls, keeping pressure on the ball handler, and maintaining defensive pressure on men without the ball. A player cannot have quick feet without a good defensive stance, and he cannot take large steps if he keeps his knees wide apart.

Using the Hands on Defense

In attempting to deny passes, a defender will usually keep his hands wide if he is attempting to establish a wide defensive base, as in covering the low post or denying passes to the high post (Figure 13–49). If he is guarding the ball closely, his hands are held high to force a lob pass (Figure 13–50). Many coaches teach their players to keep their hands low with palms upraised when guarding the dribbler (Figure 13–51). This is probably as effective a technique as any, as long as the defensive player is taught to keep his hands away from the dribbler (except when going for the ball) in order to avoid needless defensive fouls. In our defense, for example, we want the man on the ball to be practically inside the dribbler's jersey. We want him all over the dribbler, harassing him constantly, and we set 6 inches as the maximum working distance from his man. There's just no way he can stay that close to his man without fouling him

Figure 13–49 Wide Hand Position on Defense

Figure 13–50 High Hand Position on Defense

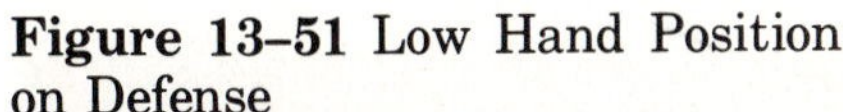

Figure 13–51 Low Hand Position on Defense

if his elbows are by his sides and his hands are out toward the dribbler. We may use hands outstretched to the sides in an overguarded stance on the ball to stop the dribbler or to discourage him from reversing to the middle or the other side of the court; however, we don't want the defender absent-mindedly or needlessly hand-checking the dribbler when he's not going after the ball or otherwise pursuing team goals. Hand-checking generally is a sign of lazy defense. Good defense is played first with the feet, and only secondarily with the hands.

When the dribbler picks up the ball, his defender should keep one or both hands at the level of the ball. If the ball handler holds the ball overhead, the defender will wave both hands overhead, perhaps when leaping up and down in an effort to force a lob pass that can be intercepted. If the ball is held to one side, the defender should keep one hand at the level of the ball and one hand held high to prevent or deflect a pass over the hand at the level of the ball (Figure 13–52).

When guarding a player at the high or low post, players generally should extend their hands to full length to discourage passes, particularly when fronting.

When guarding players one pass away from the ball, particularly in overplaying the passing lanes in pressure man-to-man or run-and-jump defense, players are often coached to "keep a hand in the passing lane." This means that, while keeping his ball-side foot forward and overplaying toward the ball, the defender will also thrust his ball-side hand into the passing lane, or an invisible line between the ball and the player he's guarding, to discourage or deflect passes (Figure 13–53).

When guarding players two or more passes away from the ball, defenders should "point their men and the ball"; that is, they should point

Figure 13–52 Covering the Ball Held to One Side

Figure 13–53 "A Hand in the Passing Lane"

Figure 13–54 Pointing Your Man and the Ball

one hand at the ball and the other hand at the players they are guarding (Figure 13–54). This "pointing" technique forces defenders to divide their attention between the ball and their men, and thus keeps them alert for changes in ball or court positions. Also, it stresses the "sinking" aspect of such coverage, since a defender guarding his man too closely would have no need to "point" his man.

Overplaying the Dribbler

When overguarding, overplaying, or influencing the dribbler toward or away from a given area of the court, the defender's foot positioning assumes great importance. In using sideline influence on the dribbler as shown in Figure 13–55, for example, the defender's right, or *inside,* foot is forward and his left, or *outside,* foot is dropped back. This stance facilitates quick movement to the defender's right if necessary to deny a reversal, and it keeps the stance open to cover the sideline movement and a possible drive along the baseline.

The "overplaying" principle is the same whether the defender is denying the dribbler access to a given area of the court or forcing him toward a certain area in order to reduce his options from that area: the foot on the vulnerable side is placed ahead of the other in a modified walking or running fashion (although the body is crouched in a low, spread, and balanced stance). Of course, the dribbler also can be overplayed

Figure 13–55 Sideline Influence

toward the middle of the court, which is the case in most variations of man-to-man and zone defenses. In such cases, the defender's outside foot (the one nearest the sideline or baseline) is placed ahead of the other foot to influence the dribbler away from the sideline or baseline.

Overplaying the Passing Lanes

When overplaying the passing lanes, a defender may be expected to either "front" his man (face him with hands upraised or spread-eagled) by playing between him and the ball, or, as is more often the case, partially front his man by overplaying him to one side with an arm and a foot in the passing lane to discourage passes. (See Figures 13–56 and 13–57.)

The distance the defender maintains from his man will vary with offensive movement, court position, the defensive player's skills, and coaching preferences, of course, but it is generally considered unwise to guard the offensive player too closely outside. First, it is unlikely that the pass can be made, and therefore no steal or deflection will occur; second, the offensive player is far more likely to use fakes to work himself open, particularly for backdoor passes.

In our pressure man-to-man defense, we teach our kids to play "one step off the ball"—that is, one step behind the imaginary line (or toward the basket) between the ball and the men they're guarding—and one-third of the distance toward the ball from their man. When facing a

Figure 13–56 Fronting at the Wing

Figure 13–57 Partially Fronting at the Wing

Figure 13–58 Playing "One Step Off the Ball" Defense

two-guard offensive alignment, for example, this usually means playing one step off the line of the ball and two steps toward the ball (Figure 13–58).

When a player away from the ball cuts behind his defender, as when a wing cuts through the lane to the weak side, the defender should move into a close guarding position facing his man and follow him with arms raised or outstretched to deflect possible passes. We prefer not to have to switch when we get "backdoored," so we insist that the defender whip his arm around and sprint to catch his man and cut him off if he gets the pass. (These and other pressure man-to-man techniques are covered in greater detail in Chapter 4.)

Covering the Posts

Our philosophy concerning low-post coverage at UNLV differs slightly from most other forms of man-to-man defense because of the unique nature of our needs. In considering a familiar example, take the case of a ball handler passing from the point to a wing, as shown in Figures 13–59 and 13–60.

Before the point guard passes to the wing, the inside defender fronts the low post to discourage the inside pass and, even more importantly, to *deny his man access to the high post.* We do not want our opponents to attack us from the high post, so we deny the pass by pressuring the ball handler and fronting the low post (Figure 13–59).

When the opponents are able to pass (or dribble) to the wing, our low-post coverage changes to what we call *V-fronting* or *siding* (Figure 13–60). Traditional coverage entails overplaying from the inside out (that

Figure 13–59 Low Post Fronting

Figure 13–60 Low-Post Siding (V-Fronting)

is, forcing the pass toward the baseline if it is to be made), or fronting, which in this case means playing between the ball and the low post. In our man-to-man coverage, however, we position our defender between his man *and the sideline.* We're fronting him from the sideline because, of all the offensive options available from the low-post position, the one we most want to deny with the ball at the wing is the low-post player's cut to the ball-side corner. If the low-post player cuts to the high post, we can continue to front him; if he clears to the weak side to give the ball handler at the wing room to drive, we can cover that, too. If the low-post player cuts to the corner, however, our coverage will be reduced because: (a) the ball handler may be able to force a double-team from the baseline, which will give the offensive team a high-percentage open shot or baseline drive, (b) a pass-and-cut through the lane from the wing may permit the offensive team to attack us one-on-one from the baseline, or (c) if the ball handler in the corner drives, his defender will never be able to reach the cutoff point in time to stop him, which means that another defender will have to switch off to stop him. We feel that the easiest way to reduce the likelihood of this kind of attack is to deny the offense access to the ball-side corner by *siding.*

Many coaches inadvertently neglect working on defensive footwork, but we feel that such practice is never wasted, and that it is of paramount importance in teaching any style of individual defense. It is incorrect to assume that players will use proper footwork techniques naturally. Players must be taught and drilled to translate sliding movements into running (and vice versa) with the least possible loss of defensive control.

A good example of the problem involved may be seen in covering the ball handler at the point in our pressure man-to-man defense. We want to play the ball handler so closely that he'll have to turn and dribble toward one side or the other. When he begins dribbling, we want the defender to slide along with him from a close, overguarded position, ready to deny the reverse dribble to the middle or a pass to the weak side as he forces the ball handler toward the sideline.

Sometimes, though, the ball handler will elude his defender and drive toward the basket. When this happens, we expect the defender to stop sliding, pivot sharply, and sprint full speed to a point where he can cut off the dribbler (Figure 13–61).

Figure 13–61 Cutting Off the Dribbler

Figure 13–62 Steering the Dribbler Toward the Ten-Second Mark Cutoff Point

Figure 13–63 Steering the Dribbler Toward the Corner Cutoff Point

Figure 13–64 The Low-Post Cutoff Point

The defender's first cutoff point is the ten-second mark along the sideline; that is, ideally the defender will drive his man to the sideline at or near the mark and force him to pick up the ball at that point (Figure 13–62). If the defender fails in this regard, a common occurrence since he is conscious of denying the dribbler's reversal to the middle of the court, his second cutoff point is the corner; that is, if he is unable to contain the dribbler at the ten-second mark, he will attempt to force him toward the corner (Figure 13–63). If this effort fails, his final cutoff point is 3 feet outside the free-throw line along the baseline (Figure 13–64). When he reaches his cutoff point, he pivots and slides into position facing the dribbler. These movements—sliding, running, sliding—must be drilled into players if transition between them is to be quick, smooth, and efficient.

Switching

Sometimes it is necessary for players to switch defensive responsibilities in order to retain (or recover) defensive control in a given situation. Defensive switching is usually associated with reacting to screens, but it also is used whenever an offensive player is either open with the ball or in scoring position without the ball but is likely to receive a pass. In the latter case, court awareness and anticipation are the keys to defensive success in switching; after all, a defender will not be likely to diagnose a need to switch defensive responsibilities if he is unaware of the court positions of the rest of the players.

We consider switching to be a last-ditch maneuver to be resorted to only when other measures prove ineffective. In reacting to screens involving the ball handler, for example, we prefer trapping the dribbler to the more passive act of switching. Also, concerning screens away from the ball, we simply do not switch. We always try to go over the top of screens, depending on our pressure on the ball handler to delay (or deny) the pass to the cutter while the defender catches him.

Still, many coaches teach switching techniques in reaction to screens, and while we consider automatic switching too passive for our needs, we cannot (and would not) say that the technique is inherently wrong. We don't spend much time working on zone defenses, either; however, that's not to say that zone defenses are unimportant. It's simply a matter of priorities, and in our particular system of play we'd rather fight (through screens) than switch.

Switches may be either automatic or called; that is, players may either switch every time a screening situation arises, or they may attempt to fight through screens, switching only when they cannot go over the top of the screen. In both cases it is important for the player switching onto the ball to assume control quickly and decisively. He cannot stand back and wait for the offensive player to make a move or pass the ball. In like manner, the defender who has been screened out must move quickly to a point between the screener and the basket (or trap the dribbler with his switching teammate), or else face the possibility of a roll to the basket and a subsequent layup by the player setting the screen.

Perhaps the most decisive way to effect the switch is for the player picking up the cutter to step directly into his path as he comes around the screen (Figures 13–65 and 13–66). Many times the switching defender can draw a charging foul by stepping into the cutter's path as he sprints around the screen. If the defender fails to draw the charging foul, his position will at least stop the cutter's progress around the screen, and the

Figure 13–65 A Simple Defensive Switch (*a*)

Figure 13–66 A Simple Defensive Switch (*b*)

switching defender will then move into a close guarding position between his new man and the basket to deny the inside pass. (If the cutter has *dribbled* around the screen, the switching defender may move into a low stance in the dribbler's path and go for the steal when the dribbler approaches him.)

Either player may call the switch if switching is not performed automatically in response to screens. It is preferable, though, to have the player who picks up the dribbler or cutter call the switch, rather than having the defender who receives the screen call out "Switch!" when he sees that he cannot get through the screen. The defender being screened may not even see the screen until it is too late to call it, and having his teammate call out "Screen right!" or "Screen left!" before calling the switch may help to avoid a defensive foul.

Going Over the Top of Screens

The term "going over the top of a screen" refers to the defensive technique of going around the screen on the same side of the player setting the screen as the offensive player who receives the screen (Figure 13–67). Switching is unnecessary when the defensive player is able to fight through the screen.

> **Note:** The most familiar alternative to switching other than going over the top—*going behind the screen*—is fraught with difficulty, since two players, the screener and the player guarding him, are between the defender and the cutter, and the cutter thus has *two* men screening for him whichever way he goes around the screen. (See Figure 13–68.)

In going over the top of a screen, the first step involves knowing that a screen is being set, or is going to be set. Players are sometimes coached to extend a hand behind them as they move, especially when guarding the dribbler, in situations where screens are likely to occur. (It would not be wise to have the players look away from their men to look for screens while following cuts, for reasons that should be obvious.)

The second, and most important, aspect of going over the top of a

Figure 13–67 Going Over the Top of the Screen

Figure 13–68 Going Behind the Screen

screen involves a quick step forward by the defender after the screen is set and just before the cutter goes around the screen. The rules provide that the player setting the screen must be stationary when the cutter goes around the screen; however, the defender's step forward into the cutter's path must occur *after* the screen is set and before the cutter is entirely past the screen. Timing is all-important—which means that the technique requires constant practice—but the defensive player also must be willing to accept the contact involved. He runs the risk of being "sandwiched" between the two offensive players, so it helps if he has an aggressive attitude about the screen. (That's also why some coaches prefer to call it "fighting through" screens.)

We feel that combatting screens is largely a matter of attitude. Passive or unobservant players seldom deal forcefully with screens. Our philosophy of intensity and aggressive play at all times lends itself naturally to going over the top of screens, but we really have to motivate our kids not to slack off and go behind the screen or switch. We look at our philosophy as a matter of pride. We ask the players, "Are you going to let your man go wherever he wants just because someone is in your way? If you let him do *that* to you, where will you draw the line at what you *won't* let him do to you?" We want our kids to believe that, through constant hustle and alertness, they can control their men in *any* situation, including screens. Sometimes it simply may not be possible to get through the screen despite a player's best efforts; however, we don't want to limit him beforehand by telling him to switch whenever he sees a screen. Even though it may be necessary in some situations, switching is always easier than going over the top of the screen. In our system, at least, we don't want our players looking for shortcuts. Other than being 7 feet tall and extremely mobile, there are no shortcuts to success. All teams that handle screens and picks well are likely to be outstanding defensively.

Blocking Out (Rebounding)

Height and vertical jumping ability are unquestionably important in basketball. A player whose standing vertical reach is 8′10″ has a decided natural advantage over one whose reach is only 7′9″. The smaller player will have to jump some 13 inches to match the *standing* reach of the taller player—and when the taller man's vertical jump reaches skyward to 36 inches, as was the case with Wilt Chamberlain and Kareem Abdul-Jabbar, to name two famous tall leapers, the problem grows accordingly. How can opponents hope to rebound against such awesome performers?

Perhaps the best way to answer the question is to consider a contemporary of both Chamberlain and Abdul-Jabbar, 6′7″, 240 lb. Wesley Unseld. Although he did not possess the skyscraping altitude of either man, the 300 lb. weight of Chamberlain, or the speed of Abdul-Jabbar, Unseld used his 240 lbs. and broad body structure to block bigger men away from the boards. No one who has ever played the game has depended more on blocking opponents away from the boards than Wes has. It is perhaps fitting, then, that we consider Wes's comments on rebounding from *The Basketball Skill Book,* written for young basketballers by Unseld and Earl "The Pearl" Monroe:

> It is possible to develop an instinct for anticipating where the ball is going to be after a shot. The first thing you do is treat every shot as though it were going to be missed. . . .
>
> It takes an average of three seconds for the ball to leave the shooter's hand, form its arc to the basket, hit the rim, bounce to its highest point, and start its descent to the point where you can reach it. . . .
>
> If a shot is made from the right-hand side of the goal, about seventy percent of the time it will rebound long and come off the left side. Naturally the reverse is true. A good rebounder makes a mental note of every shot and how it comes off the rim. Before long, you develop the ability to make an automatic mental calculation that can point you to the right spot. . . .
>
> When you move into the area where the ball should be coming down, you have to establish yourself there. A lot of bodies will be pushing around, so you've got to be prepared to hold your position. It's like defending territory. Once you get it, it's yours, and you don't want anyone else coming in. You have to make yourself as strong and as wide as you can. Use your

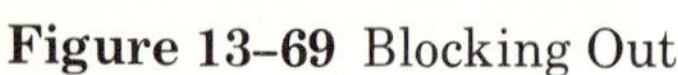

Figure 13–69 Blocking Out

Figure 13–70 Going Up for the Rebound

> bulk; keep your elbows out, prepare to spring with both legs under you, then go up aggressively to meet the ball.*

Blocking out is a way of equalizing rebounding disadvantages as well as of improving one's own superiority under the boards. Wes Unseld, an unchallenged authority on the subject, stresses "getting there first" and then maintaining inside position by spreading your body over as wide a base as possible and fighting the contact as it arises (Figures 13–69 through 13–71). Unseld considered offensive rebounding not necessarily easy, but at least feasible, since familiarity with teammates' shooting habits can help an aggressive rebounder to position himself to grab errant shots or tip in shots as they come off the rim (Figure 13–72).

* From THE BASKETBALL SKILL BOOK by Earl Monroe & Wes Unseld, edited by Ray Siegener. Copyright © 1973 by Earl Monroe, Wes Unseld, and Ray Siegener. Reprinted by permission of Atheneum Publishers.

Figure 13–71 Protecting the Ball

Figure 13–72 Tipping the Ball

PASSING

Passing certainly ranks among the most important skills in basketball. While most coaches and players understand and appreciate the value of the more obvious aspects of the game—shooting, dribbling, and defensive skills—passing often is overlooked in terms of practice. Passing requires alertness, concentration, finesse, and a great deal of practice to become a potent part of a team's (or player's) offensive arsenal.

A team should appreciate, and take pride in, ball possession. Teams that pass the ball well generally are able to retain possession of the ball long enough to work for at least one good shot, and as a result they are also usually able to dictate the tempo of the game to a certain extent. Thus, they are seldom blown out of games, since the opponents cannot run up the score when they don't have the ball.

General Considerations

1. A player should be able to make crisp, accurate passes most of the time. All he needs to practice and improve his passing is a ball and a wall. He doesn't even need a partner. No single offensive skill is more often overlooked, unless it is setting screens, yet no skill is more basic to the game than passing.

A player can make up for a lack of shooting skills with skillful defense, but no amount of shooting skill can compensate for the inability to pass the ball. The player who cannot pass the ball is helpless against pressing defenses, and he is always a threat to lose the ball in pressure situations, especially if he is equally unskilled as a dribbler.

2. Keep the passes simple. A better way to state the proposition is, "Use the pass that is most likely to get to your receiver." The most intricate, difficult pass is worthless if it can't be controlled, and it is meaningless if it doesn't increase a team's chances of scoring.

We're not saying, of course, that there is no place in basketball for fancy passes. There are many cases in which simple chest passes just won't work, and in such situations the passer is justified in throwing whatever pass he thinks will reach the receiver. However, we've all seen cases where players tried behind-the-back or between-the-legs passes in such situations as three-on-none fast breaks, only to lose the ball out of bounds and fail to score at all. In most cases, the primary purpose of passing is to advance the ball into scoring areas, and passes that cannot be controlled should not be used. The truly outstanding passer may or may not be flashy or throw behind-the-back or between-the-legs passes, but he seldom has passes stolen or deflected, and he can get the ball to his teammates when they're open.

3. Throw passes the receiver can catch. What can be more frustrating for a player than to work himself free and have a teammate's pass hit him on the knee or foot, or to have an inexperienced teammate dribble up to him and release a hard chest pass directly at his face at point-blank range?

An experienced ball handler will throw either hard or soft passes as the occasion warrants, and he can recognize the limitations of his teammates and the situation in deciding the speed, direction, and type of pass to be thrown.

A player is unlikely to catch a pass if he isn't expecting it. Part of the responsibility is the receiver's, of course, since he should have his hands up and constantly be prepared to receive passes; however, the passer should also be aware that his goal is to deceive the opposition, not his teammates. If the receiver isn't expecting a pass, it should not be made.

In passing to a stationary teammate, or to one who is coming straight at you, passes should be made to a point in the region of the receiver's hips. If passed to his head, or even as high as his shoulders, the ball may be fumbled because it must be adjusted before it can be passed again. Hard passes can be handled best if they are passed to the area of the receiver's waist.

In passing to a player moving diagonally across the floor, the pass may be thrown higher, but never above the shoulders. It takes skill gained only by practice to be able to pass accurately to running players at different distances and speeds so that the ball will reach the player at the proper point for easy and quick handling. Timing is an essential element in accurate passing. It is therefore necessary to be able to judge the speed of the players and to determine how hard the passes should be thrown to them.

4. Beginning players should watch where they're passing the ball, but as their skills increase, they should consciously avoid watching the receiver. The reason for this apparent contradiction is that a player's first consideration is always to *control* the pass, and until he can throw his passes with accuracy regardless of the kind of pass required, he should attempt to insure the accuracy of his passes by watching his intended receiver. The art of deceptive passing involves advanced skills, and only when he is confident in his basic skills in passing should a player pursue advanced skills.

5. Players should resist the temptation to make low-percentage passes. When a teammate is closely guarded, he is usually a poor risk as a pass receiver, and the ball handler should avoid attempting to force passes to him in such cases. (This is a prime reason why he should not leave his feet when he has no shot, since he will often be forced into desperation passes in order to avoid coming down with the ball.) If you can't make the pass, don't throw the ball. And don't throw crosscourt passes when other alternatives are present.

6. Passing (and dribbling) skills equalize the small players with the taller players. Although height can provide an advantage for a player, it is not necessary for ball handling skill. Small players who have trouble passing over taller opponents can use speed and deception to maneuver opponents out of position and then pass over, under, or around their outstretched arms. Skill in passing may be an added advantage for tall players, but it is a necessity for small players.

7. A pivot player who is also a good passer can control the tempo of the game. The center can take his own best shots and pass to teammates when they are open. In professional basketball, centers often lead the league in assists, or passes that lead directly to baskets.

8. Teammates always appreciate a player who will pass to them, especially when the passes lead to scores. If you dribble endlessly to set up your own shot, or if you shoot practically every time you get your hands on the ball, your teammates will likely resent it. On the other hand, they will never complain that you "hog the ball" when your maneuvers and fakes set *them* up for easy baskets. When you pass the ball to a teammate in the clear, you have, at least momentarily, sacrificed your own chances of scoring and increased *his* chances of scoring, which leads to appreciation of your own unselfish role of team playmaker.

9. After passing the ball, don't just stand there—do something! You can set screens for the receiver or other teammates, break to the basket for a return pass, or simply move away from the ball in order to permit the ball handler to work one-on-one. Practically the only thing you can do to hurt your team's efforts is to stand still and watch the game.

The Chest Pass

The chest pass is to basketball what the dive play handoff is to football: it's the game's basic pass. It is versatile, easily controlled within a range of about 20 feet, and it can be executed with accuracy at any speed. It is called a chest pass because the passer brings the ball with two hands to the vicinity of his chest, with his fingers covering the sides of the ball and his thumbs behind the ball, pointing inward. (Actually, the ball should be held close to the stomach, not the chest. Holding the ball high tends to eliminate the effective use of bounce passes.) The elbows should be in close to the body, and the ball should be released with a push and snap of the wrists and fingers (Figure 13–73). Follow-through with both

Figure 13–73 Chest Pass

arms completes the pass. A slight backspin is imparted by having the fingers and wrists flip the ball as it leaves the passer's hand.

The chest pass may be made with one or two hands. In the two-hand form, the passer's thumbs will point toward the floor, with his palms facing the receiver after he releases the ball. Beginners are advised to step toward the person to whom they are passing, although there are many situations in which taking a step is inadvisable or impossible. In a one-hand pass, the foot opposite the passer's throwing arm should go forward with the throw.

The Bounce Pass

A bounce pass is a chest pass thrown so that it strikes the floor before it reaches the receiver (Figure 13–74). It is a soft, relatively safe pass, since the usual means of deflecting it is to kick at it. Bounce passes are used primarily in two situations: passing inside against zone defenses, and at the end of fast breaks. A bounce pass is likely to be successful any time the defender has his hands up; for example, when a defender is waving his arms overhead to prevent a long pass down court or a lob pass inside to the low-post area.

Every effort should be made to reduce the spin imparted to bounce passes. A little backspin won't seriously impair the pass, but too much

Figure 13–74 Bounce Pass

backspin will cause the ball to bounce high. The passer's body should be in a balanced, crouched stance, and he should release the ball with a wrist and finger snap so that the palms of the hands will be facing the floor with thumbs in.

The Lob Pass

A lob pass is a high, arching pass that is usually used for passing over a defensive player. It may be thrown from a regular chest pass position if the ball handler is not guarded closely, but it occurs more often as a two-hand overhead pass. Due to its high arc and the amount of time the ball is free (not in the possession of either team), lob passes are considered risky in most situations.

General Considerations Concerning Lob Passes:

1. Use passes other than lob passes when the ball must be passed quickly.
2. When passing inside, pass to the side of the forward away from his defender.
3. Avoid crosscourt lob passes.

Lob passes are always dangerous, since the possibility always exists that a defender might step between the passer and receiver to intercept or deflect the pass, especially in situations such as stalling or advancing the ball down court against presses. When the passer intends to lob inside to a player posted low, his task is usually made more difficult by the inside defender's overplaying the low post, which means that the passer must not only lob over his own defender but also direct the pass to the side of his teammate away from the inside guard.

Most players, lacking the necessary strength to make full-court, two-hand, overhead lob passes, prefer the baseball pass for long passes down court, although the two-hand overhead pass is faster and more accurate as an outlet pass to start a fast break. The player does not have to bring the ball down after rebounding; he merely pivots and passes the ball. In such cases the ball is thrown directly to a teammate rather than lobbed, but the strength required to make such passes negates its use in many cases.

The Two-Hand Overhead Pass

The two-hand overhead pass is a highly specialized kind of pass whose usage belies its difficulty. It is often used by tall players or by a receiver who has caught a high pass and wishes to make a quick return pass. This pass–return pass sequence has become popular in recent years. We used it with a high degree of success at Long Beach State, with 6′6″ guard Ed Ratleff passing to a forward, then cutting into the pivot for a return pass. We loved to see Ed take small guards inside via the pass–return pass.

The two-hand overhead pass is very difficult to defend against. The ball should be held high overhead with both hands, and the pass is made by flicking the wrists. The elbows remain locked in a straight-arm position throughout. The pass is best executed by stepping forward with either foot and throwing the ball with a slight downward motion of the arms. The advantages of the two-hand overhead pass are: (1) the defensive player must stand up straighter to block overhead passes, (2) the ball can be protected rather easily, and (3) it provides a natural way of making lob passes. Its disadvantages include: (1) beginners experience difficulty in controlling the pass, (2) only a lob pass can be made effectively from a position above the passer's head, although beginners often try to make straight or bounce passes while moving, and (3) most players are unable to make long two-hand overhead passes.

The Baseball Pass

The baseball pass, so named because the throwing motion resembles that involved in throwing a baseball, is a more specialized kind of pass than the two-hand overhead pass. Its chief value is as a means of throwing long down court passes, although it is difficult to throw without put-

Figure 13–75 Baseball Pass (*a*)

Figure 13–76 Baseball Pass (*b*)

ting sidespin on the ball. (Sidespin not only causes the ball to curve, but it tends to make it slide through the receiver's hands.)

Thrown properly, the baseball pass can be a formidable offensive weapon. A simple checkpoint to determine whether it is being thrown correctly is the position of the palm and fingers of the passer's throwing hand after releasing the ball: if the fingers point toward the intended receiver, with the palm toward the floor, the pass will have backspin—and in passing and shooting, *backspin* means *control* of the ball. (See Figures 13–75 and 13–76.) On the other hand, if sidespin is evident, the passer's fingers and palm will point perpendicular to the intended line of flight.

The Shovel Pass

The shovel pass is an underhand pass thrown or handed with one or both hands. Such passes can be useful in situations in which: (a) the ball is caught low and passed from that position, (b) the defender's hands are high, (c) the ball is transferred as teammates cross (as in splitting the post or weave patterns), or (d) extremely cautious ball handling is indicated.

When two hands are used, the shovel pass may be thrown with backspin or no spin at all. When the ball is handed to a teammate, the passer extends the ball waist to shoulder high, then holds it until the teammate takes it out of his hands. In weave patterns the ball should not be passed at close range, but should be handed to the intended teammate.

In the three-on-two fast break, the shovel pass is often used as follows: the player bringing the ball down the middle catches the ball low, strides and fakes upward with his head and shoulders as if he was going to bring the ball up for the layup, and when the defender raises his hands to stop the shot, the ball handler shovels the ball underhand to whichever receiver he chooses.

The Hook Pass

Although the hook pass can be used in a variety of ways, it occurs most often after rebounds as a means of clearing the ball to the sideline to start the fast break. Passing the ball in heavy traffic, particularly around the basket after shots are taken, always entails a certain amount of risk, which explains why hook passes aren't seen more often. However, it is undeniably true that using a hook pass as an outlet pass to start the fast break is faster than having the rebounder dribble out of traffic before making the pass.

In making a hook pass, the ball is held in the throwing hand, waist high, with fingers spread and the ball against the wrist. The free hand and arm are turned toward the defensive man. The passer takes one step away from his man, jumps, turns in the air, makes a modified hook shot pass to a teammate, and lands with knees bent, perhaps to swing into a sideline lane in the fast break.

Fancy Passes

Any pass that is more difficult than necessary to get the ball to the receiver may be termed "fancy." The fancy passes—behind the back, between the legs, behind the neck, and trailer pass—are not necessarily harder to throw than other types of passes, although they may require a greater degree of ball control to be executed successfully. They are "crowd pleasers," and therein lies their danger: that players might get so caught up in entertaining the fans with clever passes that they lose sight of their primary offensive goal, which is scoring points.

1. Behind-the-Back Pass. The behind-the-back pass is usually thrown off the dribble; that is, the ball handler never actually catches the ball with both hands, but catches it one-handed and flips it behind his back to a teammate. The dribbler catches the ball with his hand on top of the ball, gaining control as it rises, then quickly turns the ball to a point where his hand is slightly under and to the side of the ball. Without interrupting the movement, he swings his hand (and the ball) across his

Figure 13–77 Behind-the-Back Pass

back, then flips the ball with his wrist and fingers toward the intended receiver (Figure 13–77).

The passer's wrist and fingers guide the ball, and speed is supplied by his hand swinging across his back. Behind-the-back passes may be thrown as either straight or bounce passes, but in both cases they usually have topspin or sidespin.

2. Between-the-Legs Pass. Unless you have long legs and extremely good coordination and ball control, you aren't likely to make a between-the-legs pass while running. There are a few people who can do it, but it is such an extremely advanced skill that it is not really worth discussing. Most players who pass between their legs make such passes while sliding, not running, which tends to further lessen its effectiveness because the defender is permitted to slow down, too.

Perhaps the best situation for passing between your legs—if you're determined to do it, since a chest, bounce, or shovel pass would get the job done more safely and easily—is when leading a three-on-two fast break. As you reach the top of the circle, you begin to slow down slightly and slide toward the outside guard, moving the ball to a position almost behind your body. If you're dribbling right-handed, the ball will be back in a protected position on your right side and your left foot will be sliding forward. As your foot slides forward, your right hand swings the ball down and between your legs. If aimed properly, the ball will strike the floor somewhere beneath your body, which should give it enough rebounding height to reach the area of the receiver's waist.

You'll have to be in a semi-crouched position as you advance your dribble, however, because you must be prepared to make the pass as soon as the outside defender moves to guard you. If he's too far away when you make the pass he might hinder you from making the pass at all. The ideal situation is when he overguards you to your right, trying to stop your drive, because the passing lane will then be wide open. (Of course, if he isn't in an overguarding position you can still make the pass, but you might also drive on him.)

Between-the-legs passes are not particularly effective in many cases—they're simply too risky, and there are too many other, easier passes available—but there is no reason why a good ball handler couldn't learn to use them judiciously.

3. Behind-the-Neck Pass. There are limited opportunities for using the behind-the-neck pass; however, players are always interested in advanced or hazardous techniques, so here's an example of how to use this pass:

As you're coming down the middle leading a three-on-one fast break, the defender, staying back to protect the basket, gives you the outside shot if you want it. (You don't, of course, so you drive on toward the basket.) As you near the guard, you catch the ball, take a step with your left foot, and leap into the air, turning toward your teammate on the right and extending the ball outward with both hands as if you were passing to him.

Of course, the defender thinks you're going to make the pass, so he moves over to his left, whereupon you bring the ball back to your body and then flip it behind your head with both hands. Your teammate on the left scores an unmolested layup, and the crowd goes berserk!

You have just completed a behind-the-neck pass, which qualifies you for using the fanciest pass of them all—the pass to a trailer, if you ever get the chance to use it!

4. Trailer Pass. Passing to a trailer is a unique situation; its requirements are: (a) that only one guard be back to stop the fast break, and (b) that the ball handler dribble well enough to turn his head and check to see that a teammate is trailing him. The maneuver itself is simple; it is *setting it up* that is difficult.

As you're dribbling toward the defender in a one-on-one fast break, you glance around quickly for teammates and discover one behind you, trailing the play. Sensing an ideal situation for using a trailer pass, you drive hard toward the basket. The defender, who picked you up at the free-throw line, goes with you, of course, and when you go up to shoot the layup, extending your arms and the ball upward toward the basket, he goes up with you to block the shot and perhaps rearrange your face in the process. You knew he'd do this, of course—if he hadn't you'd have taken the shot yourself—so when he leaves his feet, you simply flip the ball without looking behind your back to your trailing teammate, who lays the ball in for two points.

You then bask in the adoration and approval of the crowd, most of whom have never seen anything like this. The pass has to appear to be an expression of your natural ability, of course, and not of something you've practiced thousands of times. Therefore, don't show any emotion about the play, even though you'd like the officials to stop the game and give you the game ball right then and there.

Remember, it takes a special kind of person to throw fancy passes—someone who'll be willing to take a chance when he doesn't really have to, and maybe will lose the game in the process! If you make the pass and your team scores, you're the crowd's darling (for the moment at least); however, if you throw the ball away or otherwise fail to score, you're a bum. You wasted two easy points on the chance of "looking good" for the crowd, and you further contributed to your coach's developing ulcer and need for a new employer.

If you're going to try the fancy passes, try them in practice until you have a reasonable chance of succeeding with them in games. Behind-the-back passers are made, not born.

Common Mistakes in Passing

1. Telegraphing the pass. The easiest way to have a pass stolen is to "telegraph" it, or show the defender where (or how) you're going to pass the ball. Although a good defensive player doesn't rely upon the passer's eyes as a reliable indicator of where the ball is likely to be passed, that information, when combined with other visual cues such as turning toward the intended receiver, can prematurely tip off the direction of the pass and result in a steal or deflection.

The ball handler must resist the urge to watch the receiver, although the temptation will be great to do otherwise. Numerous drills exist that provide practice in using peripheral vision in passing, but the determining factor is the player's ability to discipline himself not to betray his movements. Much of the success of individual techniques in basketball depends on deception, and the player who telegraphs his passes isn't likely to surprise his opponents. Passers should release potential receivers with a deceptive move before passing to them.

2. Putting too much spin on passes. If any kind of spin is to be imparted to a pass, it should be *backspin,* since the downward flip of the wrists and fingers in the two-hand chest pass produces backspin. However, the spin should not be too severe, since a spinning ball is harder to catch than a spinless, "dead ball" pass. A bounce pass thrown with spin may veer away from the receiver's hands after it bounces.

3. Throwing jump passes. A jump pass is one in which the passer leaps into the air before passing. It can be a formidable pass when used properly, but it is among the most difficult and risky of passes to master. In order to successfully execute a jump pass, the passer must force the defender to commit himself, then pass over or around him before landing. If, however, the defender does *not* commit himself, or another defender moves between the passer and receiver, the passer is likely to throw the ball away or commit a traveling violation by landing without having thrown the ball.

The jump pass is almost exclusively a two-hand pass, although it is sometimes thrown baseball style in making long passes. (The hook pass is a variation of the jump pass.)

Jump passes are sometimes effective when performed at high speed, as in beating presses, when the defender is unable to set himself to jump and block the pass. The only situation in which jump passes are consistently effective is when taller players, who can use their height and jumping ability to get the ball above their opponents, flip the ball quickly to a teammate. The player leaps into the air, extending his arms and the ball above his head, and then directs a hard pass to his waiting teammate. The force generated in the pass must come from the passer's wrists and fingers; if he throws with his arms, it is likely that his follow-through will cause him to foul his defender. Jump passes are seldom used as lob passes, since the primary purpose of jump passes is to get the ball to the receiver as quickly as possible.

Jump passes should be avoided by all but the most experienced of passers, and even then their use should be dictated by necessity rather than whimsy. In the long run, constant use of jump passes will beat you in situations where other passes would suffice.

4. Bringing the ball high (or extending it outward from the body) before making a chest pass. Possibly the most inopportune passing situation in which to bring the ball high is when occupying the middle position in a three-on-two fast break. At such times the ball handler wants as many passing options as possible, and when he holds the ball at waist level in a low, balanced stance after catching it, he may either shoot or make a chest pass or bounce pass. Holding the ball high tends to reduce the available passing options (except when used in faking situations).

The moral is: *don't bring the ball high* (in the vicinity of your head) *in passing unless you know exactly what you're going to do with it.* The same holds true for leaving your feet.

One situation in which you can leave your feet, bring the ball high, and still have an excellent chance of completing your pass most of the time (assuming, of course, that you have control of your body and the ball), is the two-on-one fast break. There are two ways of making the pass in two-on-one fast breaks, and both depend for their success on good ball control, alertness, and, to a lesser extent, on faking ability. The ball handler can pass directly off the dribble using head, eye, and ball movements to convince the defender that he intends to shoot and not pass the ball. As another tactic, he can go up with the ball off the dribble intending to shoot, but he'll be ready to pass to his teammate if the guard moves to block his shot. In the latter case, the defender must extend his arms upward to block the shot, and if the ball handler is prepared to pass off if the need arises, he should have little trouble in bringing the ball down slightly and passing it under the defender's extended arms to his waiting teammate. The key to the pass's success lies in the ball handler's ability to make shooting his first priority, with passing used as a last resort.

The ball should be held close to the body in order to generate greater force when needed in passing, to protect the ball, and to help disguise passes (both straight chest passes and bounce passes can be thrown from the extended elbows position without leaving the ball vulnerable to stealing or deflection).

5. Passing Without Faking. While faking is neither desirable nor necessary in all situations, it is essential in certain situations. For example, when guarding a player closely, one or both of the defender's hands is usually at ball level, and in such a position he is likely to deflect passes or steal the ball unless the ball handler can force him into a situation in which his hands are no longer in the vicinity of the ball.

In order to be effective, a fake should look exactly like a regular pass up to the point where the ball would normally be released. It is here that the need for discipline arises, since there is a temptation to abbreviate the fake and get rid of the ball as quickly as possible. However, if the passer fails to convince his defender that he is going to make a certain pass from a given angle, the defender is far more likely to be able to block the pass than he would if he were unsure how the pass was to be made.

The most common faking sequences are: (a) fake high and pass low, and (b) fake low and pass high.

In the *fake high–pass low* sequence, the ball handler swings the ball forward from an overhead position as if he were making a two-hand overhead pass, and as the defender raises his hands to block the pass, he brings the ball down quickly and passes the ball under the defender's upraised arms—usually (but not always) with a bounce pass.

The *fake low–pass high* technique is, as might be expected, the opposite of the fake high–pass low movement. The passer fakes the low bounce pass, and when the defender drops his hand(s) to block the pass, he brings the ball up quickly and flips it by the defender's head.

Since some players "take" certain fakes more than others, a player should be able to execute both faking techniques.*

6. Failing to stop on both feet before passing. Although it is not essential in all situations, the ability to stop quickly and catch the ball with feet and torso squared to the basket is a skill that every basketball player should possess.

The technique is easily learned, even by beginners; however, only constant practice will ensure its success in games. The most important aspect of the movement is its timing: if you catch the ball and then attempt to get your feet together, you may commit a traveling violation; therefore you must attempt to catch the ball and land with feet squared to the basket at approximately the same time.

7. Carelessly aiming or timing passes. The beginning to average player seldom aims his passes; he merely throws them in the general direction of the receiver and hopes for the best.

When the receiver is stationary, he should not have to reach to catch a pass; that is, if the pass is thrown accurately, it will strike his body at some point between the waist and shoulders if he fails to catch it. Such passes are easier to handle than passes to the receiver's knees or over his head. No matter how fast the passer is traveling, or how many contortions he has to go through before releasing the ball, his goal should always be to make his passes as easy to catch as possible. You should never be in too big a hurry to make a good pass.

Ball handlers should avoid making wild or blind passes. Don't make passes when you don't know who is going to catch the ball. You should know exactly where your receiver and the nearest defenders are before you pass the ball. A familiar example is the player who leaps to catch a ball going out of bounds, and then throws it wildly over his head back into play only to find that he's thrown the ball to the opponents and started their fast break for them. *If you don't know where you're passing the ball or whom you're throwing it to, don't make the pass!*

Catching the Ball

You can wheel around opponents with the most breathless set of moves and fakes ever seen, or you can make passes over, around, and through opponents, but it all will have been done in vain if your teammates cannot catch your passes. Catching the ball is a vital aspect of any player's total game. Catching passes is easy, but several points should be explored:

*To "take" a fake means to react to it.

1. The receiver's fingers should be spread, and they should not point toward the ball, in order to avoid jammed fingers.

2. The receiver should reach out for the ball, rather than catch it near his body. This cushions the impact and helps to protect the ball. (He also should step toward the ball.)

3. The receiver should watch the ball all the way into his hands. A player should know where his teammates (and the opponents) are, and he should determine their whereabouts before the pass is attempted.

4. A good player goes to the pass rather than waiting for it to come to him. He should not go all the way to the passer, of course, but he should move up a step or two to help avoid stolen or deflected passes.

5. Probably the most common mistake associated with catching passes on all levels of play is failing to gain control of the ball before beginning other movements. This does not mean that the player should stand still until he catches the ball; it merely points out that, regardless of what he intends to do with the ball after he catches it, he must first catch the ball and *control it.*

6. Players should practice catching the ball and moving it quickly into shooting position. Some of the best basketball players in the world have been at their best offensively when playing *without the ball,* working their way around screens for passes and then going up for the shot without dribbling. It's a good skill to develop. Players also should learn to receive the ball and pass in one motion.

7. When you can't catch the ball with two hands (for example, in rebounding), bring the ball to your body and place both hands on the ball as quickly as possible. Even when a player with large hands can control the ball one-handed, he can seldom control it as well with one hand as with two hands, and the threat always exists of his having the ball batted away when he holds it with one hand.

8. If a player is having trouble getting passes (or dropping them), chances are that he is: (a) not moving toward the ball to meet the pass, (b) taking his eyes off the ball, (c) not expecting the pass, or (d) not positioned properly to receive a pass. Ball handlers are understandably reluctant to pass to a teammate who is moving away from them. The player who wants the ball will position himself in such a manner that passes can be made to him, and he will watch the ball constantly, expecting the passes to be attempted. No harm will be done if the pass is not made; however, anticipating the pass will make him a better receiver when the ball is passed to him.

After catching the ball off the dribble, young players sometimes will stand with their elbows at their sides and the ball extended in front of them. Such a stance forces the ball either outward (toward their defender), where it can be stolen more easily, or upward (toward their neck or head area), where their passing options may be diminished. The ball should be held near the body at stomach level, with the player's elbows extended to his sides only as far as necessary to protect the ball from defenders on either side.

Two for the Road

Before concluding our discussion of passing, there are two passing patterns that can make beginning-to-average players look good beyond their experience: the pass-and-cut and quick return pass.

The Pass-and-Cut. The pass-and-cut maneuver is basic to offensive basketball; however, many players fail to use it as effectively as they should. The player with the ball simply passes to a teammate and then breaks toward the basket for a return pass. It is a surprisingly successful maneuver, since many defensive players have the bad habit of watching the ball rather than the player they're guarding. When the defender turns his head to watch the ball, the passer cuts behind him to the basket; even if the defender recovers, he will be out of position to defend his man.

The Quick Return Pass. The pass-and-cut actually involves a form of quick return pass. However, there are other situations in which catching the pass and returning it immediately to the original passer can catch the defense unaware. In three-on-two or two-on-one fast breaks, for example, the passer can become the shooter by using the quick return technique. It is successful in such instances because, although the defensive guard can change his intentions after he has committed himself to a particular strategy, he will have difficulty changing his intentions in the middle of his movement.

DRIBBLING

Dribbling, an art that used to be reserved for the "little man" in basketball, has now become a requirement for all players. Even the big men have acquired this skill of being able to bounce the ball more than once without catching it. Few would question the dribbling ability of 6′7″ Rick Barry, 6′8″ Julius Erving, or 6′8″ Earvin Johnson—especially Johnson, who played *guard* at Michigan State.

There was a time when a team might have only one man on the squad who was an outstanding dribbler, and all the dribbling was left to him. Today, every player on the team is expected to dribble in various parts of the game, and it is therefore a very important skill for them to learn. However, the danger also exists that a team can dribble too much. It is the responsibility of the coach and players to arrive at an understanding concerning the relative values of dribbling and passing the ball. It is easier (and faster) to pass a ball up the floor to a teammate than to dribble it; still, there are times when passes are not available and dribbling is necessary.

With all the improvements in dribbling techniques over the years, one would expect a corresponding increase in its use in team offenses. Now, as the game is played at ever-increasing tempos with more fast-breaking and pressing defenses than ever before, dribbling has become much more important and popular.

Dribbling is used to advance the ball to the offensive end of the court. It can be used to initiate offensive motion and to set up teammates for shots or play opportunities. As an offensive threat, it puts pressure on the defense. It can be used to clear the ball away from the defensive boards after rebounds, and to start the fast break by using a long first bounce in turning directly upcourt. Defenses are forced to adjust to the motion of the ball, and it is sometimes advantageous for the offense to use dribbling for this purpose. Fast-breaking opportunities depend on the use of dribbling to a great extent. Dribbling can be used as a weapon in delay games or stalling situations. Most stalling situations are based on spreading the five players out in the court and forcing the defense into one-on-one confrontations, and in such cases the dribbler holds a tremendous advantage. Man-to-man pressing defenses force the offense to dribble, and a good dribbler can usually beat a pressing defense.

Dribbling is merely one way of moving the ball in basketball; the others are passing and shooting. However, many players use dribbling as if it were their moral obligation to dribble whenever they have the ball. All dribbling should be purposeful and not haphazard; that is, you should dribble only when you intend to use it to score or otherwise contribute to team objectives—and, once begun, you should continue to dribble until you have either accomplished your original purpose or changed it to something else that does not involve dribbling. Dribbling is a means to an end, not an end in itself.

General Considerations Concerning Dribbling

1. Dribble right-handed when going to your right, and left-handed when going to your left.
2. Always protect the ball with your body when you are guarded closely while dribbling. Don't invite the defender to steal the ball unless you're sure he can't get it, or you can drive around or away from him if he tries to get it.
3. Pass the ball away when opponents try to double-team you as you dribble. If two opponents are guarding you, someone else on your team must be open.
4. Never dribble into a corner and stop unless you have a specific

purpose in mind. You can be trapped in the corners more easily than anywhere else on the court—even if you keep dribbling—but when you pick up your dribble in the corner, you have eliminated one way of getting out of the corner.

5. Don't waste fakes. Use them to maintain your original advantage over your defender—after all, *you* know where you're going before the defender does. If you watch your guard's movements closely, you may find that you don't need to fake at all.
6. Don't try to dribble through zone defenses. You may make it every now and then, but you'll fail more often than you'll succeed. Zone defenses are designed to keep you from driving, and if you try it you'll probably be double-teamed.
7. Don't try movements in games that you can't do in practice. You'll probably have a hard enough time performing the skills you *can* do, without experimenting at your team's expense. (Of course, if you're an outstanding ball handler you can do as you like, but if you're learning to play the game you'd be best advised to rehearse your movements in practice before trying them in games.
8. Practice weak-hand dribbling until you can dribble confidently with either hand. If a right-handed player, for example, cannot dribble at all with his left hand, the defense may force him to his left and take the ball away from him while he's dribbling left-handed. Many players never learn to dribble with both hands because they haven't taken the time to master dribbling with their weak hand.

Basic Dribbling Techniques

In its simplest form, dribbling is merely bouncing the ball. You push it down, it comes back up. Nothing could be simpler, right?

Not exactly. In order to control the ball and make it do what you want it to, you need all five fingers touching the ball on every dribble, and you have to push the ball straight down toward the floor; otherwise it won't bounce straight back up to your hand. This problem is compounded by such facts as you *can't* push straight down and maintain ball control while you're moving (you'll leave the ball behind you), the position of your body is constantly changing in relation to the ball, sudden changes of speed or direction require equivalent changes in dribbling technique, and if you watch the ball while you're dribbling, you can't watch the person guarding you. It therefore becomes obvious that the subtle changes required in dribbling techniques are as many and varied as the dribbling situations in basketball.

The beginning player should devote much of his practice time to the art and science of dribbling. You will never become a complete basketball player without learning to dribble.

In his stance for dribbling, the dribbler should bend his knees, carry his body weight low, keep his head up, and look straight ahead. He should *never* watch the ball as he dribbles. (He can see the ball at the lower edges of his peripheral vision without looking directly at it.) The ball is held in front, and slightly to the side, of his body. The dribbler should keep his elbow close to his body so he can have better control of the ball and be able to change hands rapidly while dribbling.

In dribbling, you spread your fingers (and thumb) and push the ball downward by flipping your wrist and fingers. Some elbow action occurs, but the majority of push comes from your fingers and wrist. If you are dribbling correctly, your fingers will point toward the floor after you release the ball downward, but your forearm will point downward only slightly. As soon as the ball leaves your hand, you should cock your wrist again and spread your fingers to prepare to catch the ball as it rebounds from the floor.

The old teaching axiom, "Don't let the ball touch the palms of your hands while dribbling," is not exactly true; however, it is true that the control you exert over the height and direction of the bounce is determined primarily by your fingers. "Fingertip control" also includes the pads of the hands (to cushion the impact between ball and fingers), although your fingers should do the actual work involved in catching the ball and guiding it on each dribble.

Notice the word *catching* associated with the dribbling motion. After pushing the ball downward, your wrist, which was fully bent after releasing the ball, immediately straightens and returns to its original position to prepare for the next dribble. You should not pat or slap the ball, but *catch* it low with your wrist flexed and arm bent to soften the impact, allowing the force of its bounce to continue the ball's upward flight. (Actually, you are not "catching" the ball at all, since: (a) your hand is on *top* of the ball, where you would need extra large hands to catch the ball one-handed, and (b) catching the ball while dribbling, called *palming* the ball, is a violation of the rules.) Controlling the dribble consists of using the time that your hand is on top of the ball to gain control of the upward bounce and guide the ball downward accurately in the next dribble.

You should practice until you have mastered this and other dribbling techniques with either hand. (You should not, of course, use both hands at the same time, since it is a violation.) You can stand still and dribble, walk or run while dribbling, and even talk to people while dribbling; it is important to practice as much as possible to overcome such natural limitations as the inability to dribble well with the weak hand. Players should spend part of their practice time changing hands while dribbling, turning (pivoting), and changing direction and speed.

You should not watch the ball while you're dribbling. An occasional glance at the ball cannot be avoided, especially in pressure situations; however, your goal as a ball handler should be to have such control of the ball that you can see *all* of what is going on around you in order to react as quickly as possible to situations as they arise. Watching the ball while you're dribbling will take your attention away from everything else on the court, including the man guarding you. The best way to learn not to watch the ball while dribbling is to practice not watching it. You'll have to force your gaze away from it at first, but if you start by selecting a spot or object near the ball, then a spot that is slightly farther away, then distant objects, then objects at eye level, and then objects higher than your head, you should be able to gain control of the ball rather easily with either hand without losing awareness of court situations.

The height of your dribble also affects the amount of control you exert over the ball. A low dribble is easier to control, but it forces you to move more slowly. A high dribble permits faster movement, but it decreases the dribbler's control of the ball. As a result, although practice or natural ability sometimes makes up the difference, a tall player who dribbles well is usually superior to small players who dribble well.

When learning to dribble, players should not practice dribbling high. Their first concern is to *control* the ball and, as previously stated, dribbling low allows more control. Therefore, beginners are not likely to show rapid improvement in their dribbling if they permit the ball to rise above their waists. (Another way of putting it is, "Dribble low and slow, high and fly." However, low comes first.)

When the dribbler is challenged, he should protect the ball with his body; when he is unchallenged and wants to move quickly, he should dribble high, with the ball rising to a point between his waist and shoulders in front of him. A good ball handler can dribble at nearly top speed without losing control of the ball—almost as fast as he can run without the ball. As he runs, his longer strides will force him to push the ball out in front of him rather than straight down, and the faster he moves, the farther he will have to push the ball to keep it in front of him.

Problems arise when the ball is not dribbled straight down. The ball doesn't bounce as usual, and the dribbler's hand is often slightly ahead, or to either side, of the top of the ball as he dribbles. Acquiring skill in controlling the ball regardless of the angle of the bounce is imperative for all players. Many dribbling drills exist that can help to improve dribbling skills.

The Crossover Dribble. The crossover dribble, or changing from one hand to the other, is an essential dribbling skill. As the player dribbles with his right hand, for example, his right foot is planted hard, allowing him to step off with the left foot in a slightly opposite direction. On his next dribble he angles the ball to his left, allowing his left hand to catch the dribble. The left hand should contact the ball near the floor. The right hand is then extended to give protection from the defensive player who may be reaching for the ball.

The Drag Dribble. The drag dribble, sometimes referred to as "protective" or "crab" dribbling, is used primarily by players who take their defender into the center position. The drag dribble is used to gain a more advantageous shooting position after a player receives the ball with his back to the basket. (It is also used occasionally by players receiving close defensive pressure outside when they have no intention of driving or otherwise taking the ball to the basket, as in freezing the ball.) A player operating at a normal post position along the side of the lane may use drag dribbling to maneuver himself directly in front of the basket for a close-in shot. When drag dribbling, he will slide, not run with the ball, and his body will be between the defender and the ball. He will keep the ball near his rear foot in a low, spread stance, with the ball dribbled as low as possible for added control (Figure 13–78).

Protecting the Dribble. All players should be taught the importance of protecting the ball. This is especially true when a dribbler is moving laterally across the court and the defensive man is close to him. In such cases dribbling should be performed with the outside hand, or the hand away from the defender, with his free arm extended to protect the ball. If the dribbler is moving from the left side of the court to the right side, he should dribble with his right hand; if going from right to left, he should use his left hand. If he is dribbling down the right side of the court under defensive pressure, he should use his right hand; on the other side of the court, the left. Players should, therefore, be able to dribble with either hand.

Figure 13–78 Drag Dribble

Pivoting and Dribbling

Although pivoting can refer to any movement of the feet that establishes a pivot foot, we are using it here to mean "changing the direction of your intended dribbling path by partially or wholly turning your back on your opponent at least momentarily"; for example, dribbling to your right, then turning to your left and away from your guard to dribble in a new direction.

The pivoting movement in dribbling is exactly like that involved in pivoting without the ball, except that ball control must be maintained throughout the movement. In the course of a game a player might be required to pivot any number of times while dribbling, and every mistake can produce a turnover and/or score for the opponents.

A backward, yet effective, way of describing the pivoting-while-dribbling technique is through analysis of the common mistakes associated with the maneuver. They are: (1) Pivoting on the wrong foot, (2) not pivoting fully enough, and (3) keeping the ball forward.

1. Pivoting on the wrong foot. The proper pivoting foot is always the foot nearest the defender. In going to your right, your pivot foot should be your *left* foot. You should stop on your left foot, then step backward and away from the guard, turning on your left foot until you have established a new dribbling path. If you pivot to your left on your *right* foot, you probably will lose your balance, and you definitely will leave the ball unprotected. In pivoting on your inside foot you protect the ball with your body as you turn, especially when you also bring the ball back to a point near your outside foot before pivoting.

2. Not pivoting fully enough. Pivoting is used to get a player out of danger, to move the ball away from an unprotected position while dribbling, or to change direction of the dribble. Failing to pivot fully may allow the defender to recover his defensive position and cut off your newly established dribbling route.

3. Keeping the ball forward. This refers to keeping the ball in front of you or slightly outside your body as you start to pivot. If you commit this error, it tends to be compounded by your either having the ball stolen while it is in an unprotected position, or palming the ball. (As you pivot away from the defender, you will also pivot away from the ball.)

You should keep the ball slightly outside and in advance of your body when dribbling, except when guarded closely; however, as you begin to pivot, you should bring the ball back to a point near your back (outside) foot. The ball will then be close to your other hand as you turn, and you will not have to reach back for it or carry it around your body.

Players should practice pivoting at angles up to 135° (or 1½ right angles) away from their original dribbling routes.

SHOOTING

Shooting is unquestionably the most important fundamental offensive skill in basketball. A team that shoots well will always be in ball games. In this regard, knowing when not to shoot is just as important as knowing when to shoot. Under normal conditions, players should shoot only when they can reasonably expect to make their shots. Some teams are more disciplined than others in their shooting preferences, but shooting when little hope exists for making the shot is merely inviting the opponents to take the ball. Such strategy should be saved for occasions late in games when a team is behind and has to catch up quickly.

Many years ago, a team that had a field goal percentage of .333 or thereabouts had an excellent chance of winning its games. However, with the advent of fast-break basket-basketball, slam dunking, and the emergence of the jump shot, shooting has improved to the extent that team field goal accuracy percentages of 45 to 50 percent are not only common but are *expected* of winning teams. National leaders in shooting accuracy now hit about 55 percent of their shots, with individual shooters hitting as high as 65 to 70 percent of their shots for the season.

Shooting a basketball is both an art and a science. It is considered an art form because it involves finely tuned hand-eye coordinations and individualistic skills rather than gross motor skills—for example, while such skills as the defensive stance and pivoting are relatively invariable, shooting form is highly individualistic. There is no one *correct* way of shooting a basketball, although certain elements of shooting form common to all good shooters may be identified.

Basketball shooting also is a science, because it deals with such mechanical processes as depth perception, velocity, angle of release, and trajectory of the ball in flight. A popular syndicated comic strip once featured an episode about a mathematically inclined student who became an outstanding shooter on his basketball team by virtue of his mechanical analysis of the scientific principles involved in shooting a basketball. While the episode was rather far-fetched, it points out that awareness of the scientific bases for good shooting can help to improve a player's shot within the limitations of his ability and time spent practicing his shooting.

The Mechanics of Shooting

All the fundamentals of offensive basketball are interrelated. Shooting depends on good balance in executing the various shots, and on the footwork that enables a player to get open for a shot. The actual release of all shots depends on the proper finger and wrist control of the ball. The arc given to the flight of the ball depends on individual preferences; however, most players are comfortable with a medium arch. Other players use a flat shot that looks like it could hardly clear the rim and enter the basket. Lowering the arch enables players to extend their range without increasing the force applied to the shot.

Elements of Shooting Accuracy

It is probably true that everyone in basketball would like to be a good shooter and high scorer. That not everyone turns out to be a good shooter or high scorer is perhaps indicative of a lack of understanding of the elements involved in shooting proficiency as much as anything else (with the possible exception of time spent practicing shooting.) While individual skills may limit a player's ultimate shooting ability, in far too many cases the player limits himself by inattention to the details involved in shooting. We have identified nine elements of shooting accuracy, arranged sequentially according to importance and the order in which they occur as the player shoots.

1. Practice. Even without possessing what coaches consider to be "good" shooting form, a player can, through long hours of practice, become a good shooter and effective scorer, if he possesses at least minimal hand-eye coordination. In most cases, good shooters are the product of long hours alone on the basketball court practicing their shooting. Like practically everything else in life, shooting a ball well is a habitual thing; that is, it involves endless repetition of a given set of movements until those movements are learned to the extent that they become an unconscious part of a player's court behavior.

A member of the traveling Redheads women's professional basketball team used to shoot, and make, free throws while lying on her back at the free-throw line. Pete Maravich has said that he could make eight of ten shots under the basket by spinning the ball on his finger and then bouncing it off his head. It's all a matter of practice. A person could probably *kick* the ball into the basket a fair percentage of the time if he practiced long and hard enough.

A player may somehow be a decent shooter without practicing, if he is highly coordinated in the first place. However, *he will never be as good a shooter without practicing as he will be if he practices shooting regularly.* In this regard, we like to use the example of former Purdue great Rick Mount, who as a high schooler followed a schedule whereby he took at least 200 jump shots at home every morning before going to school, and kept detailed records of where and how many shots he made and missed. Not everyone has to follow this kind of schedule to become a better shooter, of course, but without a willingness to put in those kinds of hours practicing, a person is far less likely to become a good shooter.

In order to become a good defensive player, a person must be willing to work harder than his opponents, to adopt and maintain a low defensive stance, and generally to play with the kind of leg discomfort associated with defensive hustle. However, no amount of hustle is going to make an errant shot go in. We recently saw a player who was working very hard on defense miss *thirteen* consecutive free throws in a single game. Poor shooting is perhaps indicative of many things, but it does *not* show whether a player is hustling on the court. The "hustle" required to become a good shooter is manifested in the long hours spent on the court outside of practice.

2. Stance. Since shots can be taken from practically any body position, there is no one identifiable "correct" stance beyond the need for balance when setting oneself to take the shot. The "triple-threat" position offers the greatest balance and versatility, so when we talk about shooter's stance we should begin at that point.

The triple-threat position is just that—a stance from which the ball handler may attack the defense in any of three ways. It refers to a low, spread stance from which the ball handler may shoot, drive, or pass the ball. It may seem incongruous to have the shooter lower his center of gravity before taking the shot since he has to get the ball *over* his defender, but two factors make this move almost mandatory. First, he needs the lowered stance to gather upward momentum for his jump shot; second, he is more limited in what he can do with the ball when he is standing upright than when he is in a crouched position.

Integral to any positioning before taking a shot is the concept of *squaring yourself to the basket,* or turning your body so that your shoulders and torso are facing the basket. In their haste to get a shot away before it is blocked, players sometimes will receive a pass or catch the ball off the dribble while facing perpendicular to the basket, and they'll shoot without ever having squared themselves to the basket. This often occurs with young players at the wing positions on zone offenses, and coaches should at every opportunity urge players to turn to the basket when they catch a pass or pick up their dribble. They may have to keep the ball in a protected position as they turn to face the basket, but they still need to turn.

3. Grip. Shooting a basketball is not as natural a skill as we sometimes think. Many of the fundamentals of shooting must be learned through endless repetition. Good shooting begins with a balanced stance and hours of practice, but a proper grip is also fundamental to shooting success.

The two-hand shot is a thing of the past. While studies made in the early 1950s indicated that the two-hand, underhand free throw is superior to all other forms of shooting, few players or coaches put much stock in two-hand shooting nowadays. The emergence of the jump shot as the premier shot in basketball is largely responsible for this, but whatever the reason, the one-hand jump or set shot is preferred by the vast majority of players and coaches.

The basic grip varies slightly from player to player, but certain common traits are preferable: the hands close together on the ball, fingers (and thumb) of the shooting hand spread, the shooting hand under (not behind) the ball, and the ball resting on the pads of the fingers and hand, not in the palm of the hand (Figure 13–79).

A one-hand shot is just that—a shot taken with one hand providing most of the force and direction. The other hand is applied to the ball mainly to stabilize the grip; that is, to keep the ball from falling out of the shooting hand and to make it more difficult for a defender to knock the ball out of the shooter's hand. The two hands should be fairly close together, with the thumbs 2 to 3 inches apart on the ball. The shooting hand should be under the ball, with the other hand on the side of the ball.

The fingers of the shooting hand should be spread almost to maximum. A good way of telling if the spread is adequate is to check the amount of daylight that can be seen between the ball and the shooting thumb and index finger: if more than a half-inch of daylight is showing, the shooter is placing the ball on a pedestal formed by his thumb and fingers. (At the same time, no part of the palm of the shooting hand should

Figure 13–79 Shooting Grip (One Hand)

be touching the ball except the pads nearest the fingers—and the fingertips, of course.)

When a player consistently overshoots the basket, he is using too much arm (particularly forearm) action and too little wrist action. The player should attempt to get his shooting hand farther *under* the ball in his basic grip, and then use his wrists more and his arms less in releasing the ball. When a player gets his hand under the ball, the shot may be made more softly and with less force than when he catapults the ball toward the basket with his arms alone. Good shooting requires finesse, not brute force. (There are some limited exceptions to this rule, as in slam dunks and shots coming off power moves to the basket, but we're talking about general rules applied to shooting, not to specialized shots.) A player is unlikely to be able to apply the kind of finesse needed in shooting a basketball through arm action alone.

The ball should rest on the pads of the fingers, thumb, and callused parts of the palm of the shooting hand. Good shooters don't necessarily hold the ball in their fingertips, but they *use* their fingertips in guiding the shot. If the ball rests in the shooter's palm, fingertip control will be reduced accordingly.

Finally, the shooter's elbows should be close to the body as the ball is held in front. Throughout the shot, the shooter's elbows should be kept fairly close together, as opposed to being extended to the sides. (This holds true for both one- and two-hand set and jump shots.) If the shooting elbow is extended to the side, the shooting hand will not be under the ball, and the shooter will thus shoot with either side spin or no spin at all, both of which provide less control than backspin.

4. Timing. Since timing for the jump shot will be discussed in the appropriate section, we will confine our discussion of timing at this point to the release of the ball *as the arms reach full extension.* Whether shooting a set or jump shot (or, for that matter, a layup), the ball should remain in the shooter's hand(s) until the arms are extended fully. Whereas a premature release means a jerky shot (in addition to making the shot easier to block), full extension of the arms before releasing the shot permits wrist action to impart backspin and "soften" the shot.

5. Release. In addition to fully extending the arms before the ball leaves the shooter's hand, two other aspects of proper release of the ball should be noted: the shooter's hands should be held high after the ball leaves his hands, and his wrists, or at least the wrist of the shooting hand, should be bent fully (Figure 13–80). A high release not only makes a shot more difficult to block, but it also facilitates the wrist flex that imparts backspin to the ball. (Using a high release does not necessarily mean that the shot will follow a high arching path to the basket. It is possible to shoot

Figure 13–80 Release (Free Throw)

with relatively low trajectory while using a high release, since "high release" refers to keeping the ball in the shooting hand until the arms are fully extended.)

6. Concentration. Shooting a basketball involves more than physical skill. The player who hopes to "groove" his shot—that is, to establish proper shooting habits through repetition—must be willing to put in long hours of practice on his own. Also, whether practicing shooting in games or in practice, he must be able to concentrate on his shot if he is to be a consistently good shooter. We've seen junior high school players actually watch the man guarding them as they shot, rather than looking up at the rim where they were supposed to be aiming. We've also seen players blow easy layups when they heard the footsteps of defensive players closing in on them from behind. And we've seen players get open under the basket only to fumble passes out of bounds in their haste to shoot before they catch the ball.

In each case, the culprit is easily identifiable: it is inattentiveness, or loss of concentration. Although it is probably impossible to concentrate

100 percent over an entire forty-minute ball game, that should be the goal each player sets for himself. Shooters in particular need to concentrate as fully as possible at the end of whatever movement frees them for a shot, since all the moves in the world that can break them free from their defender for an open shot are useless if they cannot make the shot.

It's difficult, but certainly not impossible, to concentrate on your shot and the target you're aiming at when an opponent is applying defensive pressure. First, the truly outstanding offensive player will develop moves to free him from tight defensive pressure. Second, through practice under competitive conditions he knows which shots to take and which to pass up. Third, when he decides to shoot, he is able to concentrate on the rim and his shot regardless of whether defensive pressure is applied. The prudent coach will, at every opportunity, provide competitive drills, including shooting drills that are designed to improve his players' concentration. Lapses in concentration lose games. In many cases it is not the spectacular play that wins the game, but the normal play, or open shot taken and made, under circumstances in which other players are panicking and losing their cool.

7. Confidence. Successful quarterbacks in football and high scorers in basketball share at least one common trait: confidence in their ability to generate offense. Without confidence, neither would be likely to achieve success. Good shooters expect to make every shot. Jerry West, for example, wanted the ball in pressure situations because he *knew* he could make the shot. He had total confidence in his ability to score, and as a result the pressure didn't bother him. Jerry's nickname, "Mr. Clutch," reflects his success in making the key baskets. He was proud of his ability to perform at his best in clutch situations, which in turn made him even more successful.

West was never a cocky player or person; he just knew what he could do, and his confidence helped to ensure that he performed at high levels regardless of the situation. He knew he had ample moves to work himself free for shots, he knew he could make the shots once the opportunities arose, and as a result he seldom worried about the consequences of possible failure. He didn't expect to fail. Thus, all good shooters should be "confidence" men.

8. Relaxation. A relaxed shooting style is the result of a combination of everything we've talked about thus far. No matter how hard a player works for his shot, he should be relaxed enough in his release to shoot softly, applying as much finesse as necessary to make the shot. If a player has "grooved" his shot to the extent that he can make it consistently in practice with little or no variation in stance, grip, or release, he must be able to duplicate that style under the pressure of game situations to be effective. Confidence and concentration will help a player to relax as he shoots the ball.

9. Shot Selection. Ours is rapidly becoming the era of the shooter in basketball. The kids are getting better every year at putting the ball through the hoop, as evidenced by the present widespread occurrence of team shooting percentages above .500. Fifteen or twenty years ago, a team shooting percentage of .450 was considered exceptional; nowadays, a shooting percentage *under* .450 is considered poor.

Shot selection plays an important role in contributing to players' shooting percentages. Questions that naturally arise in discussing shot selection are: Who decides which shots are "good" shots to take, the coach or his players? To what extent should the coach dictate which players should shoot, or where they should shoot from? Should the players themselves be responsible for shot selection?

The logical answer to the first question is that both the coach and his players should know what constitutes a good shot for them, and their game plan should involve taking as many of those high-percentage shots from prime scoring areas as possible. If a team has a Bill Walton or Kareem Abdul-Jabbar who is capable of hitting at a 65 percent clip inside, it would be unwise to adopt an offense based primarily on outside shooting. If, as was the case with our Long Beach State teams with 6′6″ guard Ed Ratleff, the team has a superlative player who can dominate one-on-one matchups, it would naturally want to create opportunities for such confrontations as often as possible. A team with small, quick players might run a continuity pattern (for example, the Shuffle or Wheel) with constant motion and screens to free players for layups or short jumpers. Shot selection for this kind of team would involve looking for layups or short jumpers off the pattern, while at the same time ignoring outside shooting opportunities that arise.

Every coach has his own notions about what constitutes a "good" shot. Before I adopted a fast-breaking style of play, I considered a "good" shot to be our best offensive players shooting from 15 feet or closer. I did not want *any* player shooting from farther out than the free-throw line. Logic dictated to me that a shot taken from 30 feet out was harder to make than one from 10 feet. My players wanted to take the open outside shots, but they knew I had little faith in their ability to make the shots. I gave them relatively little leeway in choosing their shots—or at least I restricted within narrow limits their responsibility to choose the shots *they* thought they could make. The worse I grumbled, griped, and groaned about their outside shooting, the worse they shot, not only outside but inside as well. They began to share my doubts about their shooting ability, and as a result I finally realized I was messing up the minds of some fine shooters by severely restricting their shot selection.

In installing an up-tempo style at UNLV, I probably went overboard at first in giving the responsibility for shot selection back to the players, and as a result we took a lot of shots most coaches (including me) would prefer that their players not take. Still, while we redefined our shot-selection process to eliminate some of the shots that landed in the bleachers, I'm firmly convinced that our relatively unrestricted shooting style reinforced our players' confidence in their ability to make the shots they select. Our shooters gained confidence that they could make their shots, and as a result our shooting percentages at UNLV are comparable to the old days at Riverside, Pasadena, and Long Beach. We're scoring a lot more, and the kids love it!

What is a "good" shot? I now define a "good" shot as "any shot taken within the shooter's effective shooting range that (a) he thinks he can make, and (b) doesn't force him to alter his shooting style or the arch of the ball to get the shot away." It just isn't true any more that kids can't shoot effectively with a defender in their face. If a player thinks he can make a given shot without altering his style to compensate for defensive coverage, we let him take it. It frees his mind to concentrate on the shot if he doesn't have to look over at the bench to see if the coaches think it's okay for him to take the shot. Our kids still put up some pretty outlandish shots from time to time, but every year we can see improvement in their shot selection as well as in their confidence and ability to make the shots. We expect our players to work for good shots, but we've allowed them considerable leeway in interpreting in their own minds what constitutes a good shot to take.

The Layup

In preparing to shoot a layup, the player must first work out his stride pattern toward the basket. The right-handed shooter should plant his left foot and bring his right leg up high to allow maximum extension of his right arm in releasing the ball. To do this, the next to last step with his right foot is a long step, and his last step, the *takeout* step, must be short to ensure a *high* rather than *broad* jump. (The short takeout step also eliminates the hard bounce of the ball off the backboard that a broad jumper sometimes gets.)

If the player is allowed to dribble to the basket, he will develop his stride pattern more easily. He should be instructed to dribble in from a 45° angle to the basket, which allows him optimal use of the backboard in his shot. The ball is carried up with both hands from the right side of the body. (The dribbler should not swing the ball to his left during his last two steps after catching the ball.) The ball should be aimed approximately 1 foot above the basket. It is not necessary to put spin on the ball; the natural spin resulting from finger release will give the ball sufficient spin.

There are two kinds of hand positions when the ball is released, with the use of each dictated by the kind of shot taken. When traffic is heavy around the basket or when the shooter must protect the ball as he takes off toward the basket, he may elect to shoot a power layup, which is actually a high-speed jump shot taken at point-blank range (1 to 4 feet) from the basket. In a *power layup,* the player's shooting hand is behind the ball and his palm faces the backboard as he jumps, usually from both feet simultaneously. Power layups feature increased protection and control of the ball when defensive pressure is anticipated.

The other kind of layup commonly encountered is the *underhand layup*. The underhand layup is more of a finesse shot, and it leaves the shooter's hand more quickly, than the power layup. Whereas a power layup might be used when a player cuts backdoor around a double screen to receive a pass under the basket in a Wheel or Shuffle cut, a player probably would prefer the quicker underhand layup if he stole the ball and dribbled the length of the court for a layup.

In shooting an underhand layup, the player catches the ball off his last dribble as usual, but he turns the ball so that his shooting hand is directly *under* the ball, allowing it to roll off his fingers toward a point about 1 foot above the basket. His arms should be extended full length either outward or upward (preferably the latter) as he begins his jump (Figure 13–81). If the ball is released with the shooting hand beneath the ball, the shot will be placed on the backboard softly, and it will stand a much greater chance of going in than if shots were taken with a power layup grip (knuckles facing the shooter) (Figure 13–82).

Figure 13–81 Underhand Layup

Figure 13–82 Power Layup

The Jump Shot

No offensive weapon is more important to the game than the jump shot. The jump shot has done more to change basketball than any single phase of the game. Jump shooters give defenses nightmares. Also, the jump shot is one of the main reasons for the higher scores in basketball today. On the professional level, for example, even the best defenders cannot consistently hold opposing teams under 100 points per game. They simply cannot stop the versatile, ever-present jump shot.

In a typical game, more baskets are scored by jump shots than by all other shots together. The jump shot might be termed today's all-purpose shot because it can be taken from practically any angle by any player. For example, the *turnaround* jump shot is effective when the offensive player's back is to the basket. Jump shots can be taken while standing still or on the move in practically any direction. (In *fallaway* jumpers the shooter is moving *away* from the basket.) The defender has no idea when the ball handler is going up to shoot, which makes it impossible to shut off his shot completely. The flexibility of the shot makes it difficult to defend against.

Usually the jump shot is preceded by some form of movement, whether it's a dribble or some form of foot or body motion. The jump shooter's first move is to position his feet close together in readiness for the jump. If the player is standing still, he may take a fake step, preferably forward, and then bring his foot back close to his other, pivot foot. This will give his body momentum for the jump. If he is dribbling laterally, he should pivot on the balls of his feet as he starts his jump. His knees must be bent, of course, and he should hold the ball with both hands close to his body (Figure 13–83). He should jump as high as possible, although the height of the jump is not as important as the timing involved and will vary with the shooter's distance from the basket.

As the shooter leaves the floor and rises into the air, he brings the ball up, keeping it close to his body until the ball is above his head at the top of the jump, or possibly even on the way down (Figures 13–84 and 13–85). (This eliminates having too much body action in the shot.) Some jump shooters—Jerry Lucas was one—have been proficient in executing the jump shot from shoulder level, sighting over the top of the ball. However, the above-the-head position makes the shot more difficult for the defense to deflect if the shooter isn't 6′10″ like Lucas. In either position, the shooting elbow must be bent.

Two of the most important points to remember in executing the jump

Figure 13–83 Jump Shot in Sequence (*a*)

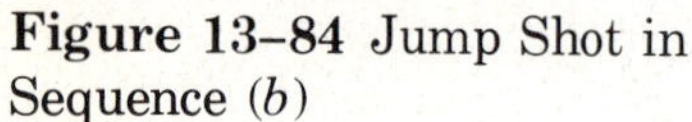
Figure 13–84 Jump Shot in Sequence (*b*)

Figure 13–85 Jump Shot in Sequence (*c*)

shot are to make a proper stop before shooting and to jump *up* rather than *forward.* Stopping before shooting will allow the jump shooter to go straight up in his jump, and thus it will afford him better body balance. Jumping forward in going up for the shot gives an alert defender the opportunity to draw an offensive foul on the shooter. It may be better to lean backward slightly (and away from the defender) than to jump into the defender, although the former makes following one's shot to the boards more difficult.

The turnaround jump shot requires good footwork, since the shot is initiated with the shooter's back to the basket. For a right-handed shooter, the left foot is his pivot foot in executing a turnaround jump shot. He takes a crossover step in front of his body with his right foot, pivoting on the ball of his left foot. His body is now facing the basket. His right foot is then brought close to the left foot for the jump. (This motion can be accomplished in one step if the shooter's right foot can be placed close to his left foot without losing balance.) A left-handed shooter uses his right foot as his pivot foot, stepping across his body to his right with his left foot in order to keep the ball protected by his body as he turns.

The Hook Shot

Many big men have earned their reputation at least partly through effective use of the hook shot. (Kareem Abdul-Jabbar, for example, created the concept of the "sky hook.") The step away from the defender and the actual release of the ball render the hook shot virtually impossible to stop. The ability to hook with either hand gives the offensive man that much greater advantage.

In order to use hook shots effectively, a player must first develop his footwork and then his body positioning for the execution of the shot. When receiving the ball, the player should have both feet in contact with the floor. A little jump toward the ball will help make this possible. Jumping toward the ball allows either foot to be used as the pivot foot in initiating

Figure 13–86 Hook Shot

fakes with the head and shoulders, and it permits the receiver to go in either direction.

The right-handed hook shooter makes his first step with his left foot at an angle that maintains his distance from the basket. In other words, he steps away from his defender, but not from the basket. His left toe faces in the direction of this step to allow the right side of his body to move naturally. He should turn his eyes toward the basket as he takes the first step.

As his body swings around, the hook shooter's right knee is raised high to allow a good follow-through. (He would raise his left knee if he were left-handed.) The ball is held in both hands, with the left hand supporting the ball. As the ball is released to the right hand before shooting the hook shot, the left hand is raised to shoulder height and extended to protect the shot. The shooter's right hand moves under and behind the ball as his right arm begins a full arc upward. The movement of his body and arm will give a natural spin to the ball (Figure 13–86).

The ball should be banked off the backboard when the shooter pivots to one side or the other from the middle of the lane, and it should be shot directly at the basket when turning into the middle of the lane from the side. The distance the ball will have to travel in the air will determine the angle used on the backboard. When the shot is completed, the shooter's body should be completely turned around, and his arm should be in a follow-through position indicating practically the same position as a set shot would have been.

Set Shots and Free Throws

The two-hand set shot, once the most favored shot in basketball, is largely a relic. Pros Dolph Schayes and Clyde Lovellette were probably the last of the truly great two-hand set shooters. Many coaches today have contributed to this decline by cutting down the distances from which they allow their players to shoot. Also, the universalization of the one-hand jump shot, with players being able to get a shot off much closer to the basket, has contributed to the decline, as have the players' increased mobility and up-tempo play in recent years. The best that can be said for two-hand set shots is that they increase a player's effective shooting range.

In shooting a two-hand set shot, the feet should be parallel rather than staggered, and they should be perpendicular to the basket. The ball is held in front of the body in both hands. The elbows are down at the shooter's side rather than extended. Both hands guide the ball toward the basket. In releasing the ball, backspin is imparted by an outward flipping motion of the hands as they rotate toward a position in which the palms of the hands face the basket. The arms should be extended fully toward a straight-arm position with the hands held high in follow-through.

Another of basketball's dinosaurs is the two-hand underhand free throw. Beyond pro Rick Barry, one of the finest free-throw shooters in the history of basketball by anybody's standards, nobody in recent years has made his mark using underhand free throws. It's an extremely accurate but also extremely specialized form of shooting, and most players nowadays prefer to use a one-handed set shot when practicing free throws. The two-hand underhand free throw is a very soft shot that often results in the ball's rolling in even when the shot is slightly off-line. Also, muscular fatigue is not as detrimental as in other shots in which the ball must be supported from beneath before releasing the shot.

In preparing for this shot, the shooter places his feet in a position that is comfortable to him. His arms should be relaxed and his elbows should be bent but resting at his sides. The fingers of both hands are pointed down as the ball is held in front below his hips. His hands should be slightly below the center of the ball with fingers spread. The shooter bends his knees as he lowers the ball, and the fingers of both hands move down and back toward his body. As the upward shooting motion begins, the shooter's elbows should start forward before his hands. He guides the ball with his arms, and his hands follow the ball toward the basket as his wrists flip the ball.

The one-hand free throw is nothing more than a modified one-hand set shot taken from the free-throw line. The shooter's feet can be parallel or staggered, depending on which is the most comfortable for the player. There should be relatively little knee action—just enough to gain a sense of rhythm. The shooting arm should be held chest high with the elbow bent, and there should be little arm action from this position. The less arm and leg action occurring, the less chance there will be for mistakes to arise.

Follow-through should be full and complete. As the ball is released, the shooting hand, which initially was under the ball (wrist cocked) rather than behind it or on the side of the ball, should continue through until the wrists are extended fully and the palm of the shooting hand is facing the floor.

No other shot in basketball allows a player the time or freedom of choice concerning style of delivery that he has in shooting a free throw. The distance is always the same and there is no defensive man to worry about. Once the player has selected a style, he should *not* experiment with other styles. (This is more true of college players than high school or junior high school players.)

Even teams with poor field-goal percentages can be good free-throw shooting teams. Free throws often spell the difference between being in a game or out of it. When as many as one-quarter of the total points scored in games come as a result of free throws, it becomes a major factor in victories.

The most important factor in building a good free-throw shooting team is the team's ability to practice and concentrate on their free throws. Too often this is a part of practice in which the players have little interest; consequently they do not concentrate on their free throws and gain little or no benefit from their practice. It is the responsibility of both the coach and his players to understand the importance of free throws, and to concentrate on them at practice. To use a rough parallel, free throws are to basketball what putting is to golf. Recall the old golfing adage, "You drive for show, but you putt for dough." Free-throw shooting is an important part of basketball, and concentration often determines the amount (or lack) of improvement a player can make.

CONCLUSION

If players are instructed in individual offensive or defensive maneuvers, it is much easier to have a successful team offense or defense, since team skills are nothing more than a composite of individual skills. These individual skills and the use of proper footwork develop confidence and poise in the player throughout the other phases of his game.

Basketball is a game of habits. I cannot emphasize strongly enough the importance of spending a great deal of time creating sound fundamental habits. To create sound habits of play, a basketball player must have a thorough working knowledge of the fundamentals of the game—not just a general understanding of them, but a mastery of their detail. Some individual fundamentals are synonymous with sound habits of team play. Only one way exists to develop them—through rigorous repetitive work and daily practice sessions. Mastery of fundamental skills is the first principle in winning basketball.

Players should be encouraged to work individually on their own maneuvers in the off-season. Many players develop their skills after basketball season, and by the time the next season starts, they are much better players because of the sound fundamental habits they have developed. It is very important to be exact in teaching fundamental skills. Often, some minor, seemingly insignificant factor determines whether the skill is learned properly or not—and, once learned incorrectly, a skill must be "unlearned" before it can be replaced by proper techniques.

Index

EXPLANATION OF DIAGRAMS

3	Offensive Player
(3)	Offensive Player with Ball
X_1	Defensive Player
←- - - -(2)	Pass
⊢- - - -(4)	Fake Pass
←- -2- -(3)	Second Pass in a Series
←〰〰(2)	Path of Dribbler
←——— 5	Offensive Movement Without Ball
4	Fake in One Direction, Cut in Another
⊢———(1)	Offensive Screen or Defensive Overguarding
3	Screen and Continued Movement
2	Reverse Pivot
	Sequential Movement
OR	Alternative Movement*
(X)	One of Two or More Possible Defensive Positions

*Dotted lines indicate alternative passes.